VOLUME FORTY NINE

ADVANCES IN CHILD DEVELOPMENT AND BEHAVIOR

Children Learn by Observing and Contributing to Family and Community Endeavors: A Cultural Paradigm

ADVANCES IN CHILD DEVELOPMENT AND BEHAVIOR

Series Editor

JANETTE B. BENSON
Morgridge College of Education,
Department of Psychology,
University of Denver,
Denver, Colorado, USA

VOLUME FORTY NINE

ADVANCES IN CHILD DEVELOPMENT AND BEHAVIOR

Children Learn by Observing and Contributing to Family and Community Endeavors: A Cultural Paradigm

Edited by

MARICELA CORREA-CHÁVEZ

California State University, Long Beach

REBECA MEJÍA-ARAUZ

ITESO University, Guadalajara, Mexico

BARBARA ROGOFF

University of California, Santa Cruz, California, USA

ELSEVIER

AMSTERDAM • BOSTON • HEIDELBERG • LONDON
NEW YORK • OXFORD • PARIS • SAN DIEGO
SAN FRANCISCO • SINGAPORE • SYDNEY • TOKYO
Academic Press is an imprint of Elsevier

Academic Press is an imprint of Elsevier
225 Wyman Street, Waltham, MA 02451, USA
525 B Street, Suite 1800, San Diego, CA 92101-4495, USA
The Boulevard, Langford Lane, Kidlington, Oxford OX5 1GB, UK
125 London Wall, London, EC2Y 5AS, UK

First edition 2015

ISBN: 978-0-12-803121-6
ISSN: 0065-2407 (Series)

For information on all Academic Press publications
visit our website at http://store.elsevier.com/

CONTENTS

Section II
Learning by Observing and Pitching in (LOPI) Fits with Cultural Cosmovisions

CONTRIBUTORS

Itzel Aceves-Azuara
ITESO University, Guadalajara, Mexico

Jennifer Keys Adair
The University of Texas at Austin, Austin, Texas, USA

Lucía Alcalá
Departamento de Cultura y Educación, Universidad Intercultural Maya, de Quintana Roo, Mexico

Megan Bang
University of Washington, Seattle, Washington, USA

Marie-Noëlle Chamoux
Centre National de la Recherche Scientifique and CERMA-Mondes américains (UMR 8168), École des Hautes Études en Sciences Sociales, 190 Avenue de France, 75013 Paris, France

Andrew D. Coppens
Department of Education, University of New Hampshire, Durham, New Hampshire, USA

Yolanda Corona
Autonomous Metropolitan University, Mexico City, Mexico

Maricela Correa-Chávez
California State University, Long Beach and Clark University; University of California, Los Angeles

Lourdes de León
CIESAS, Mexico City, Mexico

David Lorente Fernández
National Institute of Anthropology and History of Mexico

Rubén Flores
Department of American Studies, The University of Kansas, Lawrence, Kansas

Fernando A. García
Program for the Formation of Bilingual Teachers in the Peruvian Amazonia (FORMABIAP) and the Ministry of Education of Peru, Lima, Peru

Isabel T. Gutiérrez
Raritan Valley Community College, Branchburg, New Jersey, USA

Kris Gutiérrez*
University of California, Los Angeles, California, USA

Rafael Cardoso Jiménez

Ulrike Keyser Ohrt
Universidad Pedagógica Nacional, Unidad 162, Zamora, Mich., Mexico

*Now at University of California Berkeley.

Angélica López
Psychology Department, University of California, Santa Cruz and Marymount California University

Ananda Marin
Department of Psychology, Northwestern University, Evanston, Illinois, USA

Margarita Martínez-Pérez
Centro de Investigación y Estudios Superiores en Antropología Social (CIESAS) and Universidad de Ciencias y Artes de Chiapas (UNICACH)

Douglas Medin
Department of Psychology, Northwestern University, Evanston, Illinois, USA

Rebeca Mejía-Arauz
ITESO University, Guadalajara, Mexico

Peggy J. Miller
University of Illinois, Urbana-Champaign, Illinois, USA

Dewa Ayu Eka Putri
Udayana University, Denpasar, Bali, Indonesia

Graciela Quinteros
Autonomous Metropolitan University, Mexico City, Mexico

Carolina Remorini
Consejo Nacional de Investigaciones Científicas y Técnicas, Universidad Nacional de La Plata, La Plata, Argentina

Barbara Rogoff
University of California, Santa Cruz, California, USA

Karl S. Rosengren
University of Wisconsin, Madison, Wisconsin, USA

Omar Ruvalcaba[†]
University of California, Santa Cruz, California, USA

Priya M. Shimpi
University of California, Santa Cruz, and Mills College, Oakland, California, USA

Katie G. Silva
University of California, Santa Cruz, California, USA

Luis Urrieta Jr.
Department of Curriculum & Instruction, Cultural Studies in Education Program, University of Texas at Austin, Austin, Texas, USA

Karen Washinawatok
Menominee Nation, Menominee, Wisconsin, USA

[†]Now at California State University Northridge, Sierra Hall 305, 18111 Nordhoff St, Northridge CA 91330.

CHAPTER ONE

A Cultural Paradigm—Learning by Observing and Pitching In

Barbara Rogoff*[,1], Rebeca Mejía-Arauz†, Maricela Correa-Chávez‡[,2]
*University of California, Santa Cruz, California, USA
†ITESO University, Guadalajara, Mexico
‡California State University, Long Beach
[1]Corresponding author: e-mail address: brogoff@ucsc.edu

Contents

Abstract

We discuss *Learning by Observing and Pitching In* (LOPI) as a cultural paradigm that provides an interesting alternative to *Assembly-Line Instruction* for supporting children's learning. Although LOPI may occur in all communities, it appears to be especially prevalent in many Indigenous and Indigenous-heritage communities of the Americas. We explain key features of this paradigm, previewing the chapters of this volume, which examine LOPI as it occurs in the lives of families and communities. In this introductory chapter, we focus especially on one feature of the paradigm that plays an important role in its uptake and maintenance in families, institutions, and communities—the nature of assessment. We consider the power of the dominant paradigm and the challenges in making paradigm shifts.

[2] Current affiliation: California State University, Long Beach, California, USA

Advances in Child Development and Behavior, Volume 49
ISSN 0065-2407
http://dx.doi.org/10.1016/bs.acdb.2015.10.008

1. INTRODUCTION

We and the other authors in this volume hope to deepen understanding of children's approaches to learning and the often-implicit organization of their communities' distinct approaches to providing learning opportunities. We especially hope to increase awareness and respect for a way of learning that we regard as a resource for all, by articulating and describing how *Learning by Observing and Pitching In* works, conceptually as well as in life. This is an approach that appears to be especially common among Indigenous communities of the Americas and among families that have history in or contact with such communities. The volume provides definition to *Learning by Observing and Pitching In* and descriptions of how this approach occurs in communities in Mexico, Guatemala, Perú, Argentina, and the United States. (However, this approach probably is used everywhere, such as when children learn their first language.)

To deepen understanding of this approach, we contrast it with an approach that is common in Western schooling and among people with extensive experience with that institution and related practices: *Assembly-Line Instruction*. Underlying our contrasts are our assumptions that people everywhere can benefit from learning to learn in more than one way, and that *Learning by Observing and Pitching In* deserves particular attention as a valuable but overlooked resource for all.

In this introductory chapter, we make the case that *Learning by Observing and Pitching In* (LOPI) and *Assembly-Line Instruction* (ALI) are identifiable paradigms with multifaceted characteristics. Their contrasting features are not just conglomerations of variables. Rather, we argue, the features of each paradigm show coherence in the repertoires of practices that are commonly associated with each other in distinct communities (Gutiérrez & Rogoff, 2003; Rogoff & Angelillo, 2002). LOPI and ALI differ in systematic ways in their societal and interpersonal organization, and their theories of the goals as well as the means of learning, the basis of motivation, forms of communication, and how learning is to be assessed.

LOPI and ALI paradigms connect with distinct worldviews (Dewey & Bentley, 1949; Pepper, 1942). For example, within Indigenous communities of the Americas, LOPI is embedded in Indigenous Knowledge Systems (see Urrieta, 2015). In such communities, LOPI connects with related views about time, economic systems, and deep cultural values regarding the importance of tasks versus relationships with the human and the natural world.

We have a double purpose in focusing especially on Indigenous and Indigenous-heritage people of the Americas. Our focus on Indigenous American approaches provides a tool for understanding LOPI in families and communities where this approach appears to be central, and to have been central for centuries, unlike in the currently dominant way of life in the Americas. We and the authors of this volume also share a goal of bringing understanding and respect to the ways of learning of Indigenous American peoples, from whom the dominant society has a great deal to learn.

All of the chapters in this volume have been authored by scholars who have worked extensively in Indigenous or Indigenous-heritage communities of North, Central, or South America. Many of the authors themselves grew up in Indigenous American communities and most also have extensive experience with ALI in their schooling and associated institutions and practices of the dominant society.

We and an international, interdisciplinary group of colleagues (and ancestor colleagues) have been working to understand *Learning by Observing and Pitching In* over some decades. This introduction discusses the latest version of a conceptual model of the LOPI approach (Rogoff, 2014), which this volume contributes to developing further. Major research and theoretical predecessors of the present volume include Rogoff, Mistry, Göncü, and Mosier (1993), Rogoff, Paradise, Mejía-Arauz, Correa-Chávez, and Angelillo (2003), Rogoff et al. (2007), Paradise and Rogoff (2009), and Rogoff, Alcalá et al. (2014). Some of the previous versions of this model were referred to as learning by "intent participation" and "intent community participation"; the newer label *Learning by Observing and Pitching In* is a simpler way to describe this paradigm.

To illustrate the first six of the seven interrelated facets of LOPI, we provide an introduction to key points from the chapters of this volume that help to deepen understanding of the processes involved in LOPI. After going over the first six facets, our introductory chapter gives some greater focus on the 7th facet—dealing with processes of assessment.

Although processes of assessment have received relatively little focus in research on LOPI, they are extraordinarily influential in the other six features of both LOPI and ALI. Assessment processes support the rest of each paradigm and have tremendous power in determining children's opportunities for learning as well as communities' opportunities to support children's learning. In particular, the power of the ALI form of assessment is key to understanding why good ideas for the transformation of instruction in schools have been very difficult to accomplish and have had a short shelf-life in many efforts to change away from ALI over the past century. The power of the ALI form of assessment also contributes to the difficulties of museums and other informal learning institutions in the United States in using alternatives to ALI, such as inquiry learning. And the power of the ALI form of assessment may contribute to the reduction of LOPI learning opportunities over the past century in families from Native heritages across the Americas. Following our focus on Facet 7 (assessment in LOPI and ALI), we conclude with a brief discussion of how difficult it is for people and institutions that are familiar with only one of these paradigms to adapt to another paradigm when they first encounter it.

2. WHAT ARE KEY FEATURES OF *LEARNING BY OBSERVING AND PITCHING IN*?

Seven facets define LOPI's key features (see Figure 1 and Rogoff, 2014). Of course, the seven facets are not separable; they are aspects on which we can focus, with the others kept in mind in the background. In the words of David Lorente Fernández, "There are connecting threads among all the facets; aspects that are central in some and secondary in others link them like a kind of continuation. The combination is like a textile in

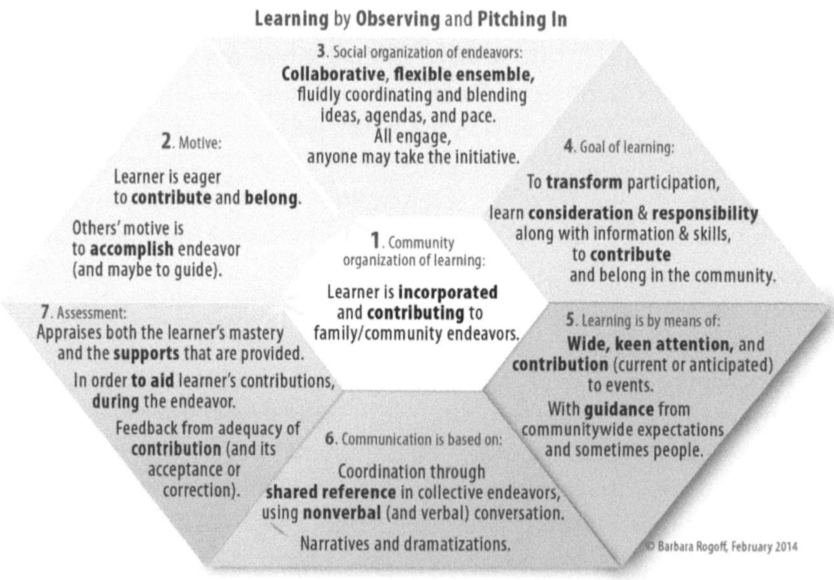

Figure 1 *The facets comprising the model of* Learning by Observing and Pitching In *(LOPI)*. (See also our website on *Learning by Observing and Pitching In* www.learningbyobservingandpitchingin.com.)

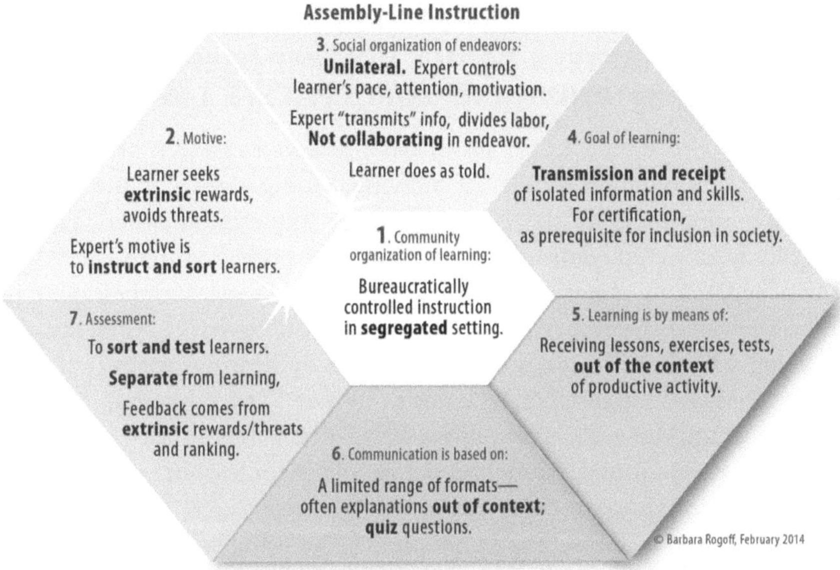

Figure 2 *The facets comprising the model of* Assembly-Line Instruction (ALI).

which each figure receives or contains echoes of the rest" (October 2015, Personal communication).

We illustrate each facet of LOPI by citing some past research that focuses on that facet, and briefly describing the relevant chapters presented in this volume. Some chapters, especially those using ethnographic analyses, address the whole LOPI prism. Other chapters, including those using more controlled procedures, focus on one or two facets while keeping the holistic nature of the prism in the background. All of the chapters contribute to more than one facet of LOPI, but we preview each chapter within the description of one facet that represents a central theme of that chapter. Together, the ethnographic and the more controlled approaches help to understand the holistic LOPI phenomenon and test the conceptual model.

The key features of *Learning by Observing and Pitching In* contrast with the key features of *Assembly-Line Instruction* in important ways (see Figure 2 and Rogoff, 2014). In particular, LOPI's central feature (Facet 1)—inclusion of children in the endeavors of their families and communities—contrasts with the central feature of ALI: segregation of children from community life, creating child-worlds separate from adult-worlds (Morelli, Rogoff, & Angelillo, 2003; Rogoff, Morelli, & Chavajay, 2010). The other six facets of ALI likewise contrast with the relevant six features of LOPI, forming a coherent ALI paradigm.

3. THE CHAPTERS OF THIS VOLUME DEEPEN UNDERSTANDING OF LOPI'S FACETS 1–6

Facets 1–6 of the LOPI prism have received research attention for decades in ethnographic studies of individual Indigenous and Indigenous-heritage communities of the Americas. Often the ethnographers, coming from highly schooled communities, note with surprise the interest and capability of very young children to help out with family work and their involvement in community endeavors. They sometimes note that children learn by observing what is going on around them and by hearing stories, and they indicate that didactic instruction tends to be rare. The ethnographers' surprise in making these observations is likely to be based, at least in part, on their own expectations derived from the paradigm for learning that has dominated Western schooling for generations—*Assembly-Line Instruction.*

Our goal in developing the LOPI model is to bring greater clarity to the aspects of LOPI that the ethnographers document, and to enhance understanding of the integration among them that provide the coherence of a paradigm. In doing so, we integrate ethnographic observations with research that employs systematic comparisons of communities to test expectations of LOPI-like or ALI-like ways of learning and supporting learning. In this section, we summarize Facets 1–6 of the LOPI model, and in the process we preview how each chapter of this volume contributes to greater understanding of this paradigm.

Facet 1. Community organization incorporates children as ordinary contributors in the wide range of endeavors of their families and communities. Children and adults are in the same "world," working for common goals, not segregated into child- and adult-worlds (Morelli et al., 2003; Rogoff et al., 2010; Velásquez Morales, 2015).

In this volume, Cardoso's chapter focuses on how children learn through work in an Indigenous Mexican (Mixe) community, where cultural values emphasize that human dignity is derived from collaborative work among people as well as natural phenomena.

Remorini's chapter emphasizes the key roles of reciprocity, respect, autonomy, and interdependence of lives in children's learning of skills to inhabit the forest, using an ecological perspective that recognizes humans' relationship with other living beings, among Mbya Indigenous people of Argentina.

According to the chapter by Bang, Marin, Medin, and Washinawatok, such inclusive and reciprocal relations are central to Indigenous American epistemologies in which this kind of relational thinking regarding humans' relations with the natural world are parallel with relational thinking regarding the relations among children and adults.

Urrieta's chapter places this way of thinking in broader context, indicating that *Learning by Observing and Pitching In* is a description of Indigenous pedagogy in millennial systems of Native and Indigenous Knowledge Systems.

Flores, Urrieta, Chamoux, Lorente Fernández, and López's chapter examines how *Learning by Observing and Pitching In* to family and community endeavors, in contemporary Latin American communities in the United States and Mexico, reveals continuities with historical Mesoamerican cultural practices that may reach as far back as the sixteenth century, emphasizing communal norms of mutual respect, exchange, and personal initiative in pitching in.

Corona, Putri, and Quinteros' chapter extends the research about LOPI, which has focused on Indigenous communities of the Americas, to another region of the world, finding that the emphasis on observation, collaboration, and children's motivation to participate can be seen in the ways in which Balinese children participate and learn in ceremonial life.

Facet 2. Children's motivation derives from their interest to contribute and belong as valued members of their families and communities, together with other people who are trying to accomplish an activity and may guide or support children's contributions in that context. For example, children in a Mexican community with Indigenous history contributed to a wide range of complex household work, with their own initiative, and they reported that children do so simply as members of the family and everyone pitches in (Alcalá, Rogoff, Mejía-Arauz, Coppens, & Dexter, 2014; Coppens, Alcalá, Mejía-Arauz, & Rogoff, 2014; Rogoff, Moore, Correa-Chávez, & Dexter et al., 2014).

In the present volume, Mejía-Arauz, Correa-Chávez, Keyser Ohrt, and Aceves-Azuara's chapter proposes that such helpfulness at home is engendered in children as families organize work as a coparticipative and voluntary endeavor. They examine this in an Indigenous Mexican (P'urhépecha) community and contrast it with solo and assigned chores in a middle-class Mexican community.

Coppens and Alcalá speculate that Mexican-heritage children's collaborative initiative in family work is unencumbered by contingent rewards or contracts that may discourage voluntary involvement. US Mexican-heritage university students reported that when they received pocket money from their families, this was as a gift, noncontingent on their behavior, whereas European American university students reported that their parents used allowances as a contractual enticement to participate in household work.

Facet 3. The social organization in small groups involves collaborative engagement as an ensemble. Leadership is flexible as people coordinate fluidly with each other, with anyone taking initiative as they see a way to contribute (Chavajay & Rogoff, 2002; Mejía-Arauz, Rogoff, Dexter, & Najafi, 2007; Paradise, Mejía-Arauz, Silva, Dexter, & Rogoff, 2014).

Chamoux's chapter indicates that since the sixteenth century, there have been few modifications in central beliefs about learning among Nahua (Mexican) families. Nahua documents from four centuries ago and current Nahua adults indicate that across centuries, Nahua educational practices consist in facilitating observation by copresence, hiding nothing, and not preventing children from trying, as well as persuading children to be responsible, to work, and to adopt a calm attitude for paying close attention.

Gutiérrez, Rosengren, and Miller's chapter examines young children's learning about death in Puebla, Mexico, by hanging out, observing, pitching in, and listening as active participants in all aspects of the annual celebration for "día de muertos."

Martínez-Pérez' chapter finds that 2-year-old children's agency in attempting to actively participate in adult work in a Mayan community in Chiapas, Mexico, generates teaching from expert to novice as adults orient and reorient the activity to direct the children in coparticipatory interactions.

de León's chapter describes the interactional emergence of learning ecologies as a result of Mexican Mayan children's initiatives to engage in culturally relevant endeavors of family and community life. Children's initiative is shown in their requests for guidance to collaborate in a task and working on their own initiative with occasional monitoring and sometimes correction from others.

Facet 4. The goal of learning is transforming participation in order to contribute and belong in the community. This includes learning to collaborate with consideration and responsibility, as well as gaining information and skills (López, Najafi, Rogoff, & Mejía-Arauz, 2012; López, Ruvalcaba, & Rogoff, 2015).

Lorente Fernández examines how children learn the concept of "cuidado" (caring, or assuming responsibility) as they are integrated in everyday family activity such as tending domestic animals, in a Central Mexican Nahua community in which Indigenous language and dress have disappeared but Indigenous identity and cosmovision have been retained. Children learn to foster other beings, whether humans or animals, to reach those beings' potential and fulfill their responsible roles, continuing Indigenous practices across generations.

Adair describes Mexican-heritage children's use of agency in a US first grade classroom organized as a set of learning experiences that resemble *Learning by Observing and Pitching In.*

Facet 5. Learning involves wide, keen attention, and contribution to the endeavor, whether ongoing or anticipated. Guidance comes from community expectations and sometimes also from other people. A series of studies have found that Indigenous-heritage and Indigenous children from Mexico, Guatemala, and the United States are especially likely to observe and listen to what is going on around them even when they are not directly addressed, especially if their families are involved in traditional cultural practices (Chavajay & Rogoff, 1999; Correa-Chávez & Rogoff, 2009; Correa-Chávez, Rogoff, & Mejía-Arauz, 2005; López, Correa-Chávez, Rogoff, & Gutiérrez, 2010; Mejía-Arauz, Rogoff, & Paradise, 2005; Rogoff et al., 1993; Silva, Correa-Chávez, & Rogoff, 2010; Tsethlikai & Rogoff, 2013).

García's chapter shows that Peruvian Quechua children concentrate attentively on the activities of adults and exercise initiative as well as measured behaviors and respectful silence in the presence of their elders.

Silva, Shimpi, and Rogoff's chapter demonstrates especially wide, keen attention in a naturalistic situation among young Mayan children when their mother and toddler sibling operate interesting objects in their presence, compared with middle-class European-American children.

Facet 6. Communication is based on coordination that builds on shared reference that is available in participants' mutual endeavors. This includes nonverbal conversation as well as verbal means of coordination, in addition to narratives and dramatization (Mejía-Arauz, Roberts, & Rogoff, 2012; Roberts & Rogoff, 2012; Tsethlikai & Rogoff, 2013).

The chapter by Ruvalcaba, Rogoff, López, Correa-Chávez, and Gutiérrez describes collaborative communication, especially using nonverbal means that gives evidence of avoiding interruption of other people's work. Mexican-heritage US children's requests for help from an instructor in building a toy more often evidenced avoidance of interrupting, often using subtle nonverbal means, compared with requests for help by European-American middle-class children.

4. FACET 7. ASSESSMENT

In the LOPI model, assessment includes appraisal of how and how well a learner is supported in efforts to contribute, as well as appraisal of how and how well the learner is progressing in making a contribution to the endeavor.

This is done to aid learners' contributions while the endeavor is ongoing. Feedback to the learner is available from the outcome of their efforts—did it work?—and the response of other people to the outcome as a productive contribution—was it accepted as part of the endeavor or corrected or discarded? Some examples of this approach appear in this volume in the chapters by Martínez-Pérez and by Lorente Fernández, as adults provide correction and support while children try to wash clothes and care for poultry.

Here is an example of feedback that is directly available to the learner by observing the results of their efforts and by observing whether others accept their contributions as-is or fix them, for the sake of accomplishing the endeavor. "Daniela," a 5-year-old Indigenous-heritage Mexican child, regularly pitched in to make tortillas, but they were small and irregularly shaped. Her mother occasionally drew Daniela's attention to an aspect of her own shaping of a tortilla she was making, and Daniela would attempt to imitate the skilled movement.

> *Every attempt Daniela made at shaping a tortilla ended up cooked on the comal [clay griddle], and Isaura would quickly offer Daniela more dough.... Even when Daniela's dough ended up on the dirt floor, Isaura cooked it and fed it to the dog and advised Daniela by saying "cuidado Dani" (careful Dani). Daniela's better tortillas were always placed at the top of the pile, and were the first to be eaten as Daniela watched smiling silently, thus rewarding Daniela for her effort and contribution and encouraging her to continue to pitch in to tortilla making. (Urrieta, 2013, p. 325)*

Another example is a 9- or 10-year-old apprentice tailor in Liberia:

> *When Little M. sold his second hat to a tailor for ten cents, both he and the tailor were aware that the customary selling price for hats was a dollar fifty. There was a clear message to the apprentice in this transaction concerning the quality of what he produced. (Lave, 2011, p. 78)*

Feedback in LOPI can also come from being given responsibility for more difficult aspects of a task with less supervision (Mejía-Arauz, Keyser-Ohrt, & Correa-Chávez, 2013; Paoli, 2003; Urrieta, 2013; Whiting & Edwards, 1988). An example with apprentice tailors is provided by Jean Lave, at the key step of making trousers,

> *Every tailor who described his apprenticeship to me included an account of the day his master left the shop in the middle of sewing a pair of trousers for a customer and told him to finish it. The "test" indicated the master's willingness to have the apprentice's work treated as though it were produced by the master, for sale by the master in the shop. (2011, p. 79)*

Graduate students may experience similar transitions in writing manuscripts with their advisors.

In LOPI, evaluation also includes assessment of learners' interest and initiative as important aspects of learning (Nagai, 2001; Paoli, 2003; Rogoff, Goodman Turkanis, & Bartlett, 2001). Adults expect children to watch and to take initiative; if they do not develop interest in pitching in spontaneously, this may be seen as problematic (Chavajay, 1993). For example, a Mazahua (Mexican) father evaluated his 7-year-old as lacking interest and the strength to decide for himself to do what needs to be done (de Haan, 1999), unlike the 3-year-old son, who watches what the parents do and pitches in without needing explanation.

This form of assessment contrasts with the form of assessment that characterizes *Assembly-Line Instruction* and is common in Western schooling: In ALI, assessment tests students in contexts separate from the learning process and separate from contexts in which the learner is supposed to put the knowledge or skill to productive use. It compares learners with each other and sorts them by some measure of quality. Feedback to learners comes from rewards or threats that are not a part of the productive activity itself (e.g., grades) and from comparative ranking against other learners.

In this section, we consider how toddlers are often socialized into the forms of assessment that fit with *Assembly-Line Instruction* in many European-American families with extensive involvement in Western schooling. In particular, known-answer quizzing, where an adult asks a toddler a question that the adult already knows the answer to, fits with ALI, and resembles a form of assessment common in Western schooling.

This practice contrasts with adults asking questions to seek needed information. In *Learning by Observing and Pitching In* to family and community endeavors, questions from adults to children are asked to obtain new information that is needed to accomplish an activity at hand, such as "Where is the basket?" when preparing to shuck corn, or to seek otherwise relevant information, such as "What's going on up in town?" or "Where is your sister?" when a child returns home. Differential familiarity with known-answer quizzing in toddlerhood in distinct cultural communities problematizes the interpretation of test performance among people varying in experience with this specialized discourse format.

4.1 Known-Answer Quizzing in School Lessons and Evaluation

Quizzing with known-answer questions is a common format in school lessons and evaluations (Edwards & Mercer, 1987; Mehan, 1979; Wells, 1993). (However, it is not a necessary or obligatory format in schools—numerous innovative schools use alternative forms of assessment that are designed to assist students' learning and their contributions rather than to test receipt of information or to sort students; Campione & Brown, 1987; Chen & McNamee, 2007; Edwards, Gandini, & Forman, 1998; Erickson, 2007; Rogoff et al., 2001.)

Rather than requesting new information, known-answer questions frame a display of knowledge. Here is an example adapted from Mehan's (1979) classic analysis of classroom discourse, where he characterized such exchanges as "Initiation-Reply-Evaluation" sequences:

Initiation *Teacher: Ok, what's the name of this story?*
  Response Class: (no response)
Initiation *Teacher: Who remembers, what's the name, what's the story about?*
  Response Class: (no response)
Initiation *Teacher: Is it about taking a bath?*
  Response Many: No.
Initiation *Teacher: Is it about the sunshine?*
  Response Many: No.
Initiation *Teacher: Edward, what's it about?*
  Response Edward: The map.
    Evaluation *Teacher: The map. That's right, this says "the map."*

Known-answer questions are a specialized discourse format that is strange outside of classroom settings and certain language games. Consider the reaction if you sat at tea with your neighbor and asked, "Where is your nose?" or "What color is your shirt?" when you are looking right at it. Rather than simply answering these questions, the neighbor might wonder about your sanity or think you were asking a riddle.

4.2 Known-Answer Quizzing or Supportive Guidance with Toddlers

The use of known-answer quizzing in schools is prepped in infancy and toddler years among many middle-class European American families who play language games such as "Where is your belly button?" The questioners do not need the information about where the child's belly button is; presumably they already know. They also often ask other known-answer questions such as "What's that?" while pointing to a picture in a book or an object outside the window. These questions are not requests for new information; they may test the child's knowledge, show it off playfully, or comprise vocabulary lessons.

Cultural differences in the use of known-answer quizzing were reported in a study of mothers helping toddlers operate five novel objects during a home visit (Rogoff et al., 1993). The 14 middle-class European-American mothers often used known-answer quizzing questions with their 12- to 24-month-old toddlers, but this was rare in the 14 Guatemalan Mayan families, where communication was more focused on sharing information relevant to the ongoing activity. For example, a middle-class European family engaged in these known-answer questions (notice the Initiation-Response-Evaluation format):

While Sarah is handling a clown puppet, mother asks: What **is** that, Sarah?
Sarah responds pointing to the hat, labeling: Haa'.
Mother corrects Sarah's pronunciation: It is a **hattt**...

Mother points to the puppet's eye: What is **that**? *Sarah:* Haa'
Mother points more clearly to the eye: Wha'**dat**? *Sarah:* Aih.
Mother asks Sarah to clarify: **What** is it? *Sarah:* Aih. *Father clarifies:* **Eye**.
Mother questions: Eye? *Barbara confirms:* Uh huh. *Sarah:* Aih.
Father evaluates: She can do a little better.

The middle-class European-American mothers often asked known-answer questions like "What's that?" to request labels (during an average of 31% of the five novel object episodes) and "Where's the doll's eyes?" as a language game to be answered by a point at the correct location (in 20% of the episodes). In contrast, the Mayan mothers used these formats in an average of only 6% and 4% of the novel object episodes. The middle-class European-American mothers also often used other lesson formats: They labeled objects in 50% of the episodes (vs. 16% for Mayan mothers) and provided running commentary, narrating ongoing events that were visible to everyone (like teachers observed in Paradise et al., 2014), in 70% of the novel object episodes versus 21% among Mayan mothers. The middle-class European-American toddlers participated in such vocabulary lessons and tests three times as often as the Mayan toddlers, primarily by labeling objects but also by requesting labels and playing language games.

The idea that the middle-class European-American mothers' known-answer quizzing was part of a lesson-and-test approach resembling ALI was supported by other features of their interactions. These mothers usually attempted to motivate children's involvement by using mock excitement when introducing each object (for 74% of the five novel object episodes, e.g., "Oh, Sweetie, *look* at *that*!") and often praised the toddlers' performance (in 44% of episodes; Rogoff et al., 1993). They also insisted on their own agenda, trying to control the interaction in 52% of the episodes in which the toddlers refused or insisted on another agenda with a novel object.

Mayan mothers did not follow a lesson-and-test approach. They seldom used mock excitement to motivate the toddlers' involvement (13% of episodes) and almost never evaluated the toddlers' performance with praise (in only 4% of episodes). They rarely tried to overrule the toddler (in only 14% of episodes in which the toddler refused or insisted on another agenda).

Instead of organizing and controlling lessons, the Mayan mothers supported their toddlers' initiative with mutual coordination of attention, pace, and agendas, in line with the cultural tradition of *Learning by Observing and Pitching In* to family and community endeavors. The Mayan mothers were attentive and poised ready to help the toddlers in an average of 81% of the novel object episodes, assisting the toddlers smoothly even when engaged in other activities (vs. 23% for the middle-class European-American mothers). The Mayan mothers guided in alignment with the toddlers' direction, rather than trying to control the toddlers' motivation and behavior. Interestingly, the Mayan toddlers were more likely to refuse or insist on an agenda (in 63% vs. 33% of the novel object episodes), perhaps showing an expectation of being allowed to take initiative with their mothers' support.

The great increases in Western schooling in the Mayan community since the 1993 observations by Rogoff et al. (Rogoff, 2011; Rogoff, Correa-Chávez, & Navichoc Cotuc, 2005) may encourage current Mayan parents to more often use discourse formats they experienced in their own schooling when they speak with their toddlers. Tellingly, the only Mayan mothers who engaged consistently in mock excitement and vocabulary lessons in the 1993 data were a few with experience in Western schooling (6–9 grades; the other mothers had 3 or fewer grades). In another study, Mayan mothers with 12 or more grades of schooling asked known-answer questions in almost half of the minutes of a discussion with three children, whereas Mayan mothers with fewer than 2 grades almost never asked known-answer questions (Chavajay, 2006).

Experience of Western school is often related to lesser use of many aspects of *Learning by Observing and Pitching In* and greater use of practices associated with *Assembly-Line Instruction*, as seen in several chapters in this volume. In addition, the overlap of specific discourse formats such as known-answer quizzing between school and home contexts makes some connection between children's experience in these two settings compelling.

The middle-class European-American parents' use of discourse formats common in schools may also have changed in these two decades. The increased emphasis on multiple-choice testing in US public schools means that schools are using more known-answer questions, which may further increase the use of this discourse format by US parents.

4.3 Meeting Up with Tests

When middle-class European-American children attend school, they are likely to already be familiar with the rather strange format of known-answer quizzing (although success playing it is not simple to achieve; Hammersley, 1977). When people in communities where Western schooling has not been prevalent meet up with this discourse format, it is likely to be especially confusing (see also Heath, 1984; Luria, 1976; Rogoff, 2003). In the Mayan community, where schooling has only recently become prevalent, questions generally request new information; hence, quizzing could signal a riddle or joke. Known-answer questions seemingly confused Wolof (North African) research participants; when Piagetian questions were asked in a language consultation context that made sense, the Wolof interviewees no longer responded as if the questions were riddles with trick answers (Irvine, 1978).

In a Canadian Inuit community, it was rare to ask children known-answer questions (Crago, Annahatak, & Ningiuruvik, 1993). When a visiting audiologist requested her Inuit colleague to test language comprehension with questions such as "Where is your nose?" the children often just looked at her, not answering. The Inuit colleague commented that she had started teaching her child to answer such questions because she noticed that they were used in school; she reported that younger mothers had begun to talk like that with their children.

Art director and producer Joe Aubel recounted that after his first day of school in the US Southwest, he told his mother that he did not want to return to school because "*La maestra no sabe nada.* [The teacher doesn't know nuthin'.]" His mother probed, "*Pero cómo es eso? Es profesora.* [How can that be? She's a teacher.]" Joe told her that the teacher kept asking him the stupidest questions, ones that anyone would know the answer to. How could he learn anything from her if she had to turn to him to find out the answers to the simplest questions? (Joseph Aparicio Aubel, personal communication, July 2008).

The consequences can be serious when replies to unfamiliar formats are interpreted as a deficit. Pearl Yablonski, a young woman who tried to immigrate to the United States from Europe in 1922, did not make it through the Ellis Island entry test of mental functioning: "When it came her turn to be questioned, they asked her 'How many feet does a horse have?' And she thought he was making a *fool* of her, that that was a stupid question! And then she was detained on Ellis Island..." (Leah Shain, quoted in Conway,

2008). Pearl Yablonski was held in the Ellis Island Psychopathic Hospital and deported; she later died in the Holocaust.

Efforts to create culture-free tests often attend to familiarity of items but they usually overlook the format of testing itself, which is familiar to young children who have experienced informal prepping at home for years through parental quizzing. This means that 'standardized' assessments based on known-answer questions are inherently biased—they are not standard!—when used with populations that differ in their familiarity with this cultural format. The interpretation of individuals' test (and school) performance requires consideration of cultural practices and familiarity with the cultural formats used to attempt to assess knowledge and skills (cf Heath, 1983; Irvine, 1978; Levy, 1976; Michaels & Cazden, 1986; Nelson-Barber & Trumbull, 2007; Scribner & Cole, 1981; Scollon & Scollon, 1981; Serpell & Simatende, 2015).

5. THE POWER OF PARADIGMS

5.1 Paradigm Shifts by Individuals

It is difficult for individuals to shift paradigms, especially if they have functioned in only one paradigm for years, as is the case for many highly schooled adults. The adults in charge of schools and other institutions that now organize many children's lives often have experience in only the dominant ALI paradigm. For these adults, recognizing and understanding the repertoires of practices of children who are familiar with another paradigm may be a challenge.

Even for well-meaning adults, it is often difficult to avoid value judgments based on one's familiar paradigm and to be aware of the basis of one's own cultural experience as well as the paradigms of unfamiliar ways of life. Several studies reveal challenges for teachers and parents who are trying to expand their practices to be able to engage effectively with institutions and children whose cultural background likely involves a distinct paradigm for learning. They have difficulty observing and attempting to fit with a collaborative guidance model rather than a controlling model of instruction (Adair, 2015; Matusov & Rogoff, 2002; Paradise et al., 2014; Rogoff et al., 2001).

5.2 Paradigm Shifts by Institutions

It is especially difficult for *institutions* to shift paradigms, in the face of how powerful and "common sense" *Assembly-Line Instruction* has become in the practices of the dominant middle-class life over the past century. Many efforts to move beyond ALI have foundered on the use of assessment methods that remain aligned with ALI—such as known-answer quizzing—thereby pulling efforts to transform education back into the ALI approach. The dominant ALI paradigm gets in the way of evaluating innovations in ways that fit with the learning paradigm being implemented.

How could school assessment be transformed to fit more with *Learning by Observing and Pitching In* to family and community endeavors? Several ways are promising. Assessment could involve work samples and take into account the social context of individuals' performance. If we are interested in examining children's literacy, we can read with them, noting both how they proceed and the extent and type of support provided by the examiner and the setting (Rogoff, 1997).

Evaluating learning by observing involvement in the activity of interest occurs in dynamic assessment (Campione & Brown, 1987) and in what Erickson (2007) called *proximal formative assessment.* These forms of assessment are used in some schools that organize instruction and evaluation in a collaborative, ongoing manner that includes adults paying attention to children's ongoing efforts as well as to the contributions made by other people and the task set-up, in order to evaluate the process of children's growing understanding and skills (Chen & McNamee, 2007; Edwards et al., 1998; Erickson, 2007; Rogoff et al., 2001). Formative assessment has the additional advantage of supporting adjustments in instruction to better serve student learning (Black & Wiliam, 1998), because it includes ongoing assessment not only of the students but also of instruction.

To fit with the LOPI paradigm (and many other paradigms), assessment in schools would also examine children's *initiative* in learning and using new information and skills. Do they read when no one makes them do it? Do they puzzle over scientific phenomena even when no curriculum or high stakes test controls their efforts? Examining children's initiative would also encourage institutional support for its development, thus improving learning environments overall, especially in conceptual understanding, critical thinking, planning, and decision making. Assessment of children's initiative would examine learning in action.[1]

[1] It may be objected that these forms of assessment would be more costly than ALI forms of testing. (Unless, we consider the societal and individual costs of systematic mistaken assessments.) If our aim is to support children's learning, then it is counterproductive to use tests that have the effect of constraining learning, for bureaucratic convenience. We are ending up teaching children how to take tests rather than teaching them to read and use number systems, understand nature and human phenomena, think critically about scientific and social issues, express and examine ideas in words and images, and know how to work together for the common good. Testing spaceships undoubtedly involves expense, but that is necessary if we want them to fly safely. Appropriate evaluation equally applies to the learning of the next generation.

5.3 Learning to Navigate Several Paradigms

Many children in the United States and worldwide navigate between contrasting paradigms on a daily basis, as they move between differing paradigms of home and school or between the cultural heritages of different branches of their families (Vossoughi & Gutiérrez, 2014). They need to know how to function in the paradigms that are employed in the varied contexts of their lives. In the process, they may develop repertoires of practices that allow them to function skillfully in several paradigms. Indeed, everyone can learn more than one way—in today's world it is important for adults as well as children to know how to work within several paradigms.

Cultural and historical analyses indicate that it is a challenge for Indigenous and Indigenous-heritage families and communities of the Americas to sustain many aspects of their way of life that connect with *Learning by Observing and Pitching In*, in the face of the power of practices of the dominant society such as use of *Assembly-Line Instruction* (Flores et al. 2015; Adair, 2015; García, 2015; Lorente Fernández, 2015; Mejía-Arauz et al., 2015). Cultural and historical analyses are an important source of information regarding the resilience and adaptation of particular practices that make up each of these paradigms, as well as the deep and broad cosmologies that these learning approaches embody.

This volume is organized first with chapters focusing closely on observing and pitching in within Indigenous and Indigenous-heritage communities of the Americas. It progresses to chapters that help to place LOPI within the encompassing philosophies and cosmovisions of these communities, including Indigenous Knowledge Systems and ways of social interaction that extend beyond the Americas.

ACKNOWLEDGMENTS

Our work benefits deeply from the wisdom and generosity of Indigenous and Indigenous-heritage families and communities of the Americas, who provide the world with a valuable model for supporting children's learning and have helped us to understand it. We express heartfelt appreciation to our colleagues whose work also contributes to understanding *Learning by Observing and Pitching In*, and for joining together to share their knowledge. We are grateful to funding from the National Science Foundation (0837898), the UCSC Foundation Chair, and the UC Presidential Chair for funding our opportunities to discuss ideas and fostering the work we present in this volume.

REFERENCES

Adair, J. K. (2015). "My teacher is going to think they're crazy": Responses to LOPI practices in U.S. first grade classrooms. *Advances in Child Development and Behavior, 49*, 341–356.

Alcalá, L., Rogoff, B., Mejía-Arauz, R., Coppens, A. D., & Dexter, A. L. (2014). Children's initiative in contributions to family work in Indigenous-heritage and cosmopolitan communities in Mexico. *Human Development, 57*, 96–115.

Black, P., & Wiliam, D. (1998). Assessment and classroom learning. *Assessment in Education, 5*, 7–74.
Campione, J. C., & Brown, A. L. (1987). Linking dynamic assessment with school achievement. In C. S. Lidz (Ed.), *Dynamic assessment* (pp. 82–115). New York: Guilford.
Chavajay, P. (1993). Afterword: Independent analysis of cultural variations and similarities in San Pedro and Salt Lake. *Monographs of the Society for Research in Child Development, 58*(8, Serial no. 236), 162–165.
Chavajay, P. (2006). How Mayan mothers with different amounts of schooling organize a problem-solving discussion with children. *International Journal of Behavioral Development, 30*, 371–382.
Chavajay, P., & Rogoff, B. (1999). Cultural variation in management of attention by children and their caregivers. *Developmental Psychology, 35*, 1079–1090.
Chavajay, P., & Rogoff, B. (2002). Schooling and traditional collaborative social organization of problem solving by Mayan mothers and children. *Developmental Psychology, 38*, 55–66.
Chen, J.-Q., & McNamee, J. D. (2007). *Bridging: Assessment for teaching and learning in early childhood classrooms, PreK-3*. Thousand Oaks, CA: Corwin.
Conway, L. (2008). *Forgotten Ellis Island*. Film broadcast on PBS.
Coppens, A. D., Alcalá, L., Mejía-Arauz, R., & Rogoff, B. (2014). Children's initiative in family household work in Mexico. *Human Development, 57*, 116–130.
Correa-Chávez, M., & Rogoff, B. (2009). Children's attention to interactions directed to others: Guatemalan Mayan and European American patterns. *Developmental Psychology, 45*, 630–641.
Correa-Chávez, M., Rogoff, B., & Mejía-Arauz, R. (2005). Cultural patterns in attending to two events at once. *Child Development, 76*, 664–678.
Crago, M. B., Annahatak, B., & Ningiuruvik, L. (1993). Changing patterns of language socialization in Inuit homes. *Anthropology & Education Quarterly, 24*, 205–223.
de Haan, M. (1999). *Learning as cultural practice*. Amsterdam: Thela Thesis.
Dewey, J., & Bentley, A. F. (1949). *Knowing and the known*. Boston: Beacon.
Edwards, C., Gandini, L., & Forman, G. (1998). *The hundred languages of children*. Westport, CT: Ablex.
Edwards, D., & Mercer, N. (1987). *Common knowledge*. London: Methuen.
Erickson, F. (2007). Some thoughts on 'proximal' formative assessment of student learning. In P. Moss (Ed.), *Evidence and decision-making in education* (pp. 186–216). Chicago: National Society for the Study of Education.
Flores, R., Urrieta, L., Jr., Chamoux, M.-N., Fernández, D. L., & López, A. (2015). Using history to analyze the learning by observing and pitching in practices of contemporary mesoamerican societies. *Advances in Child Development and Behavior, 49*, 315–340.
García, F. A. (2015). Respect and autonomy in children's observation and participation in adults' activities. *Advances in Child Development and Behavior, 49*, 137–151.
Gutiérrez, K., & Rogoff, B. (2003). Cultural ways of learning: Individual traits or repertoires of practice. *Educational Researcher, 32*, 19–25.
Hammersley, M. (1977). School learning. In P. Woods & M. Hammersley (Eds.), *School experiences* (pp. 57–86). London: Croom Helm.
Heath, S. B. (1983). *Ways with words*. Cambridge, UK: Cambridge University Press.
Heath, S. B. (1984). Linguistics and education. *Annual Review of Anthropology, 13*, 251–274.
Irvine, J. T. (1978). Wolof "magical thinking". *Journal of Cross-Cultural Psychology, 9*, 300–310.
Lave, J. (2011). *Apprenticeship in critical ethnographic practice*. Chicago: University of Chicago Press.
Levy, R. I. (1976). A conjunctive pattern in middle class informal and formal education. In T. Schwartz (Ed.), *Socialization as cultural communication* (pp. 177–187). Berkeley: UC Press.

López, A., Correa-Chávez, M., Rogoff, B., & Gutiérrez, K. (2010). Attention to instruction directed to another by U.S. Mexican-heritage children of varying cultural backgrounds. *Developmental Psychology, 46*, 593–601.
López, A., Najafi, B., Rogoff, B., & Mejía-Arauz, R. (2012). Collaboration and helping as cultural practices. In J. Valsiner (Ed.), *The Oxford handbook of culture and psychology* (pp. 869–884). NY: Oxford University Press.
López, A., Ruvalcaba, O., & Rogoff, B. (2015). Attentive helping without being asked as a cultural practice of Mexican-heritage families. In Y. M. Caldera & E. Lindsey (Eds.), *Mexican American children and families*, NY: Routledge.
Lorente Fernández, D. (2015). Children's everyday learning by assuming responsibility for others: Indigenous practices as a cultural heritage across generations. *Advances in Child Development and Behavior, 49*, 53–89.
Luria, A. R. (1976). *Cognitive development.* Cambridge, MA: Harvard University Press.
Matusov, E., & Rogoff, B. (2002). Newcomers and oldtimers: Educational philosophies-in-action of parent volunteers in a community of learners school. *Anthropology & Education Quarterly, 33*, 415–440.
Mehan, H. (1979). *Learning lessons.* Cambridge, MA: Harvard University Press.
Mejía-Arauz, R., Rogoff, B., Dexter, A., & Najafi, B. (2007). Cultural variation in children's social organization. *Child Development, 78*, 1001–1014.
Mejía-Arauz, R., Rogoff, B., & Paradise, R. (2005). Cultural variation in children's observation during a demonstration. *International Journal of Behavioral Development, 29*, 282–291.
Mejía-Arauz, R., Keyser-Ohrt, U., & Correa-Chávez, M. (2013). Transformaciones culturales y generacionales en la participación colaborativa de niñas y niños de una comunidad púrhépecha. *Revista Mexicana de Investigación Educativa, 18*(59), 1019–1045.
Mejía-Arauz, R., Roberts, A. D., & Rogoff, B. (2012). Cultural variation in balance of *nonverbal conversation* and talk. *International Perspectives in Psychology, 1*, 207–220.
Mejía-Arauz, R., Correa-Chávez, M., Ohrt, U. K., & Aceves-Azuara, I. (2015). Collaborative work or individual chores: The role of family social organization in children's learning to collaborate and develop initiative. *Advances in Child Development and Behavior, 49*, 25–51.
Michaels, S., & Cazden, C. B. (1986). Teacher/child collaboration as oral preparation for literacy. In B. B. Schieffelin & P. Gilmore (Eds.), *The acquisition of literacy* (pp. 132–154). Norwood, NJ: Ablex.
Morelli, G., Rogoff, B., & Angelillo, C. (2003). Cultural variation in young children's access to work or involvement in specialized child-focused activities. *International Journal of Behavioral Development, 27*, 264–274.
Nagai, Y. (2001). Developing assessment and evaluation strategies for vernacular elementary school classrooms. *Anthropology & Education Quarterly, 32*, 80–103.
Nelson-Barber, S., & Trumbull, E. (2007). Making assessment practices valid for Native American students. *Journal of American Indian Education, 46*, 132–147.
Paoli, A. (2003). *Educación, autonomía, y lekil kuxlejal: Aproximaciones sociolingüísticas a la sabiduría de los tseltales.* Mexico City: Universidad Autónoma Metropolitana.
Paradise, R., Mejía-Arauz, R., Silva, K. G., Dexter, A. L., & Rogoff, B. (2014). One, two, three, Eyes on me! Adults attempting control versus guiding in support of initiative. *Human Development, 57*, 131–149.
Paradise, R., & Rogoff, B. (2009). Side by side: Learning through observing and pitching in. *Ethos, 37*, 102–138.
Pepper, S. C. (1942). *World hypotheses: A study in evidence.* Berkeley: University of California Press.
Roberts, A. L. D., & Rogoff, B. (2012). Children's reflections on two cultural ways of working together: "Talking with hands and eyes" or requiring words. *International Journal of Educational Psychology, 1*, 73–99.

Rogoff, B. (1997). Evaluating development in the process of participation: Theory, methods, and practice building on each other. In E. Amsel & A. Renninger (Eds.), *Change and development: Issues of theory, application, and method* (pp. 265–285). Hillsdale, NJ: Erlbaum.
Rogoff, B. (2003). *The cultural nature of human development*. New York: Oxford University Press.
Rogoff, B. (2011). *Developing destinies: A Mayan midwife and town*. NY: Oxford.
Rogoff, B. (2014). Learning by Observing and Pitching In to family and community endeavors: An orientation. *Human Development, 57*, 69–81.
Rogoff, B., Alcalá, L., Coppens, A. D., López, A., Ruvalcaba, O., & Silva, K. G. (2014). Learning by Observing and Pitching In to family and community endeavors. *Human Development, 57*, 65–171. Special Issue.
Rogoff, B., & Angelillo, C. (2002). Investigating the coordinated functioning of multifaceted cultural practices in human development. *Human Development, 45*, 211–225.
Rogoff, B., Correa-Chávez, M., & Navichoc Cotuc, M. (2005). A cultural-historical view of schooling in human development. In D. Pillemer & S. H. White (Eds.), *Developmental psychology and social change* (pp. 225–263). NY: Cambridge University Press.
Rogoff, B., Goodman Turkanis, C., & Bartlett, L. (2001). *Learning together: Children and adults in a school community*. New York: Oxford University Press.
Rogoff, B., Mistry, J. J., Göncü, A., & Mosier, C. (1993). Guided participation in cultural activity by toddlers and caregivers. *Monographs of the Society for Research in Child Development, 58*(7, Serial No. 236), i, iii, v, vi, 1–179.
Rogoff, B., Moore, L., Correa-Chávez, M., & Dexter, A. (2014). Children develop cultural repertoires through engaging in everyday routines and practices. In J. E. Grusec & P. D. Hastings (Eds.), *Handbook of socialization* (2nd ed., pp. 472–498). NY: Guilford.
Rogoff, B., Moore, L., Najafi, B., Dexter, A., Correa-Chávez, M., & Solís, J. (2007). Children's development of cultural repertoires through participation in everyday routines and practices. In J. E. Grusec & P. D. Hastings (Eds.), *Handbook of socialization* (pp. 490–515). NY: Guilford.
Rogoff, B., Morelli, G. A., & Chavajay, P. (2010). Children's integration in communities and segregation from people of differing ages. *Perspectives on Psychological Science, 5*, 431–440.
Rogoff, B., Paradise, R., Mejía-Arauz, R., Correa-Chávez, M., & Angelillo, C. (2003). Firsthand learning through intent participation. *Annual Review of Psychology, 54*, 175–203.
Scollon, R., & Scollon, S. (1981). *Narrative, literacy, and face in interethnic communication*. Norwood, NJ: Ablex.
Scribner, S., & Cole, M. (1981). *The psychology of literacy*. Cambridge, MA: Harvard University Press.
Serpell, R., & Simatende, B. (2015). Contextual responsiveness: An enduring challenge for educational assessment in Africa. *Journal of Intelligence, 3*, 1–22. www.mdpi.com/journal/jintelligence.
Silva, K., Correa-Chávez, M., & Rogoff, B. (2010). Mexican heritage children's attention and learning from interactions directed to others. *Child Development, 81*, 898–912.
Tsethlikai, M., & Rogoff, B. (2013). Involvement in traditional cultural practices and American Indian children's incidental recall of a folktale. *Developmental Psychology, 49*, 568–578.
Urrieta, L., Jr. (2013). Familia and comunidad-based saberes: Learning in an Indigenous heritage community. *Anthropology & Education Quarterly, 44*, 320–335.
Urrieta, L., Jr. (2015). Learning by Observing and Pitching In and the connections to native and indigenous knowledge systems. *Advances in Child Development and Behavior, 49*, 357–379.
Velásquez Morales, J.J. (2015, May). Niñas y niños en Cherán K'eri defendiendo el territorio. Subversiones. http://subversiones.org/archivos/115400.

Vossoughi, S., & Gutiérrez, K. (2014). Toward a multi-sited ethnographic sensibility. In J. Vadeboncoeur (Ed.), *NSEE yearbook: Vol. 113(2). Learning in and across contexts: Reimagining education* (pp. 603–632). New York: Teachers College Press.
Wells, G. (1993). Reevaluating the IRF sequence. *Linguistics and Education*, *5*, 1–38.
Whiting, B. B., & Edwards, C. P. (1988). *Children of different worlds*. Cambridge, MA: Harvard.

SECTION I

Children Observing And Pitching In

CHAPTER TWO

Collaborative Work or Individual Chores: The Role of Family Social Organization in Children's Learning to Collaborate and Develop Initiative

Rebeca Mejía-Arauz[1,*], Maricela Correa-Chávez[†], Ulrike Keyser Ohrt[‡], Itzel Aceves-Azuara[§]
*ITESO University, Guadalajara, Mexico
[†]California State University, Long Beach and Clark University
[‡]Universidad Pedagógica Nacional, Unidad 162, Zamora, Mich., Mexico
[§]Universidad ITESO, Guadalajara, Mexico
[1]Corresponding author: e-mail address: rebmejia@iteso.mx

Contents

Abstract

In many communities, children learn about family and community endeavors as they collaborate and become involved in community activities. This chapter analyzes how parents promote collaboration and learning to collaborate at home in an Indigenous and in a non-Indigenous Mexican community. We examine variation among parents

Advances in Child Development and Behavior, Volume 49
ISSN 0065-2407
http://dx.doi.org/10.1016/bs.acdb.2015.10.001

with different extent of experience with schooling and concepts regarding child development and relate these to patterns of child collaboration at home among Mexican Indigenous and urban families. Drawing on interviews with 34 mothers in the P'urhépecha community of Cherán, Michoacán, and 18 interviews in the cosmopolitan city of Guadalajara, Mexico, we argue that the social nature of participation may be a key feature of learning to collaborate and pitch in in families and communities where school has not been a central institution of childhood over generations.

1. INTRODUCTION

In this chapter, we examine the differing patterns of child collaboration at home in two Mexican cultural communities: one Indigenous and one non-Indigenous. Building on research we have conducted in the P'urhépecha town of Cherán in Michoacán, Mexico as well as in a middle-class community in the city of Guadalajara, we use data from maternal interviews to propose the idea that children's initiative in collaborating in Indigenous communities may be related to being included in "social helping" from a very early age. We explore this idea by contrasting mothers' reports of their children's helping in these two communities, as well as exploring how the helping itself is framed as either a child's desire to participate in ongoing interaction or as a child's responsibility.

We build extensively on our work with Rogoff and other colleagues who have suggested that in Indigenous communities of the Americas, a key feature of childhood involves collaboration and initiative in "Learning by Observing and Pitching In" to family and community endeavors (also called by its initials, LOPI; Paradise & Rogoff, 2009; Rogoff, 2014; Rogoff, Moore, Correa-Chávez, & Dexter, 2015). Here, we present research reporting children's collaboration and initiative in family and community activities and expand on it by analyzing the varied ways in which parents promote collaboration in their children, that is, *how the family in interaction* generates opportunities for learning to collaborate as well as child initiative for participating and helping. We contrast this with the ways cosmopolitan families in an urban setting orient their children to participate in household activities, not as part of a joint family endeavor, but as assigned and often solitary chores.

In the following section, we review some relevant literature on children's collaboration in family and community activity before turning to our research in Cherán and Guadalajara. We describe the sociocultural context of the communities as well as the methods used in our research. We briefly contrast the differing reports of helpfulness across the P'urhépecha and cosmopolitan families in our study, including differing patterns of initiative in collaboration. We then focus on elaborating the contrasting ways in which the mothers from each community frame children's helping: some as part of a larger family (or community) endeavor, and others as part of a child's assigned responsibilities. Based on the maternal reports, we propose that the differing patterns in children's collaboration and initiative in helping may be inexorably tied to the way work is framed as an important social activity in family and community in the Indigenous community, but framed as solo responsibility and obligation in the cosmopolitan one.

2. CULTURAL VARIATIONS IN CHILD COLLABORATION AT HOME AND IN COMMUNITY ENDEAVORS

The ethnographic record is full of reports that child collaboration in household and parental work activities is more common in many Indigenous and rural communities than in urban or cosmopolitan settings (Lancy, 2008; Ochs & Izquierdo, 2009; Rogoff, 2003). In many areas of the world where school has historically not been central to childhood development, ethnographic and cultural comparative research points to the idea that a fundamental way in which children learn is by integrating children from a young age in family and community activity (Cancian, 1964; Chamoux, 1992; Rogoff, 2003).

Through this integration, children have wide access to community activity with the expectation shared by community, parents, and children themselves that they will learn by observing and contributing where possible (Rogoff, Paradise, Mejía-Arauz, Correa-Chávez, & Angelillo, 2003). In contrast, cosmopolitan middle and high SES families with an extensive history of schooling focus the organization of children's activities on school learning and play while contributions to household chores often only involve taking care of their own things (Alcalá, Rogoff, Mejía-Arauz, Coppens, & Dexter, 2014; Mejía-Arauz, 2015; Mejía-Arauz, Keyser Ohrt, & Correa-Chávez, 2013). For example, ethnographic reports from 30 middle-class dual-career families in Los Angeles showed that although both children and parents were aware that parents needed help with household chores, children did not contribute to the household unless they were asked, and even when asked, children in the majority of the families resisted or refused to help (Klein, Graesch, & Izquierdo, 2009).

These contrasts in ways of generating involvement in family activities also point to different parental conceptions on how to orient children's development and education that may have repercussions for broader family and community life. Ochs and Izquierdo (2009) for example have proposed that the different patterns of child help stem from different moral socialization practices across cultural communities. Whereas some communities stress respectful awareness of others and self-reliance even in childhood, in many middle-class communities, socialization practices emphasize children's dependence on adults' decisions. We relate our findings on how children learn to collaborate and develop initiative in Indigenous families with child-rearing practices that are embedded in *LOPI* to family and community endeavors (Rogoff, 2014; Rogoff, Najafi, & Mejía-Arauz, 2014).

3. FAMILY ACTIVITIES IN CHERÁN AND GUADALAJARA

We interviewed 34 mothers in the P'urhépecha community of Cherán, as part of a larger study on 8- to 10-year-old children's interaction, attention, and communication patterns. Because we were interested in examining maternal education and associated sociocultural practices that could be related to children's patterns of interaction, we distinguished two groups in Cherán: one group with 9 mothers who had more than 10 years of school and the other group with 25 mothers who had 9 or less years of school. We also interviewed 18 middle-class mothers who had extensive experience with school and related urban practices in the city of Guadalajara, which we refer to as the *cosmopolitan* group.

Cherán is the largest P'urhépecha community in Mexico. It was founded over 600 years ago and is at present an important center of commerce for smaller Indigenous and rural communities in the area. Ninety-seven percent of Cherán's inhabitants consider themselves P'urhépecha due to the social organization, customs, rituals, and history of the community (INEGI, 2011). Of the economically active population, 27% work in agriculture or forestry, 25% work in sawmills, carpentry, crafts, or construction, and 48% work in trade or as professionals. Due in part to agricultural politics and policy, migration to the United States has been present in Cherán over generations such that most families in town (and in our sample) have at least one or two family members living in the United States.

Census information shows that over time families have come to rely less on small scale farming for subsistence and income generation (INEGI, 2011). However, most families continue to maintain small fields and also keep farm animals such as chickens, pigs, and other livestock, to provide additional resources (such as corn, meat, or funds based on selling the products) to contribute to family and community celebrations. The tradition of tending to these animals and land provides a valued opportunity for family members to work on something together. The maintenance of these agricultural subsistence traditions along with urban and international influences illustrates the diversity of cultural practices in Cherán.

Data was also collected in Guadalajara, the second largest city in Mexico with a population of 4.5 million habitants (INEGI, 2010). The city is known for being a commercial and industrialized business center. Many middle-class families in Guadalajara have extensive experience with Western schooling through several generations (Rogoff et al., 2014). Family schooling, types of occupation, and the demanding rhythm of the city are associated with the urban family organization of daily activities that includes extensive involvement of children in extracurricular activities particularly in middle and high SES families. Unlike in Cherán, migration to the United States is not common for middle-class families in Guadalajara, nor in other middle-class communities of Mexico.

Schooling is part of a constellation of cultural practices that relate to the ways in which parents raise their children (LeVine et al., 1991; Mejía-Arauz et al., 2013; Rogoff, Correa-Chávez, & Navichoc Cotuc, 2005). Participant mothers from Cherán had an average of 8 grades of school, and fathers 9 grades overall. In the Cherán low schooling group, about half of the 25 mothers had 0–6 grades of schooling and half had 7–9 grades; fathers' range of schooling was similar. In the Cherán high schooling group, about half of the 9 mothers had 10–14 grades and half had 16 or more (4 of the mothers with higher schooling had training as teachers); the fathers' schooling levels were similar to the mothers'. Some of the families in Cherán have professional and skilled labor occupations and others work in the fields and in forestry.

The 18 cosmopolitan participants were middle–high SES families. Mothers had an average of 15 grades of school (one mother had 9 grades of school, two had finished high school, and 13 had finished college); all fathers had college or more. Parents had professional occupations or some have their own businesses; of them, 49% of the mothers have formal jobs or their own business. This mirrors the current city statistic that 48% of women are currently involved in a paid occupation outside the home (INEGI, 2013).

The interview was conducted at the participants' homes using semistructured open-ended questions and was focused on the practices of the children, parents, and grandparents. In Cherán, besides the mother, often the target child and other family members were present and participated in the interview. Although the interview touched upon multiple topics, here we focus on how children collaborate in family activities, the ways that parents promote child engagement in household or other family work, and reports regarding the voluntary or compulsory nature of the activities.

4. COLLABORATION IN FAMILY WORK AMONG THE P'URHÉPECHA FAMILIES FROM CHERÁN

Most of the parents from both Cherán groups (87%) reported that their children collaborated in the running of the household in some way. As Table 1 shows, the range and complexity of work activities in which children participate differs among the two Cherán family types and the cosmopolitan group. We first report the patterns for the families that have less experience with school and continue to engage in many traditional Indigenous practices before turning to the families in Cherán that are more familiar with Western ways and have extensive experience of schooling and its associated practices.

Among mothers with 9 grades or less of schooling, 20 of the 25 of them (80%) reported that their 8- to 10-year-old child contributed by engaging in a wide range of work that benefited the entire family, such as clearing the table, washing dishes, sweeping or mopping, collecting firewood, caring for a sibling, feeding animals, running errands, washing clothes, and sewing. (See Table 1 for a complete list and the proportions of children involved.) Similarly, many of the children in this group contributed in small but meaningful ways to family businesses (17 children, 65%). These families reported that their children engaged collaboratively in 3–6 helping activities per day, sometimes more activities across multiple days, and very often out of their own initiative. This willingness to help can be seen in the following report by a mother from Cherán with 8 years of schooling, referring to her 10-year-old daughter:

> *Andrea sweeps with no need for us to ask her. Some times when I arrive home, even when no one has asked her to, she says: "Mami I already swept the house."*

Among Cherán families with limited schooling, children not only contributed, but some children also spontaneously piped up during their mother's interview to report that they were learning something by participating. For example, one 9-year-old boy told the interviewer that he takes care of his little sister, teaching her to walk by using a *rebozo* (a traditional shawl) looped under her arms to help her stand upright and teaching her to talk by speaking to her. He commented that he learned to do this by watching his mother and

Table 1 Types of Activities and Number (and Percentage) of Children That Participate in Them, According to Maternal Report

	Number and Percentage of Children Who Complete This Activity in		
Type of Activity	**P'urhépecha Families (Mothers 0–9 Years of School)**	**P'urhépecha Families (Mothers 10–16 Years of School)**	**Cosmopolitan Families**
Clearing table, washing dishes	9 (36%)	4 (44%)	13 (72%)
Cleaning their rooms, picking up their own clothes or toys	8 (32%)	5 (55%)	15 (83%)
Sweeping and mopping communal portions of house, picking up and washing clothes of others, folding others' laundry, making beds of others	13 (52%)	1 (11%)	1 (5%)
Help outside the home: gathering firewood or water, running errands for household goods, buying tortillas	6 (24%)	0	0
Elaborated help in the kitchen: making tortillas, preparing masa, preparing vegetables, heating food for self or others, simple food prep (e.g., eggs)	5 (20%)	0	1 (5%)
Simple help in the kitchen: washing the vegetables, preparing agua fresca, grating cheese	5 (20%)	2 (22%)	3 (17%)
Helping in the field: clearing fields; helping plan or cultivate plants, flowers, vegetables; help with logging work; caring for livestock	8 (32%)	1 (11%)	0

Continued

Table 1 Types of Activities and Number (and Percentage) of Children That Participate in Them, According to Maternal Report—cont'd

Type of Activity	Number and Percentage of Children Who Complete This Activity in		
	P'urhépecha Families (Mothers 0–9 Years of School)	**P'urhépecha Families (Mothers 10–16 Years of School)**	**Cosmopolitan Families**
Helping in family business, e.g., selling products or preparing food items for selling; sewing; keeping accounts for business, basic office work	17 (68%)	2 (22%)	5 (28%)
Taking care of siblings	5 (20%)	2 (22%)	5 (28%)
Taking care of sick relatives: preparing food, changing diapers, bathing others, changing bandages	4 (16%)	0	0

Note: Participation in the activity categories was not mutually exclusive; in many cases, children participated in multiple types of activities, so the totals are greater than the number of children.

older sister do the same. He compared this learning to "a chain" in which his mother, older sister, he, and his younger sister were all linked by their roles as teachers (mother, older sister, himself) and learners (older sister, himself, younger sister). By using the chain metaphor, he was able to express the fluid roles and relationships that are sometimes shared and sometimes redefined in learning situations.

When giving accounts such as this, the children usually showed pride for their contributions. In this case, the boy showed pride by jumping in the conversation, taking the time to comment on the learning and explaining his observations, as well as by sitting up a little taller and smiling as he spoke.

In contrast, in Cherán families with extensive schooling, families reported that their children typically only engaged in 0–3 helping activities per day, and in families that had their own businesses children's contribution to family business was rare (22%). As Table 1 illustrates, the most common task in which children from highly schooled Cherán families engaged was picking up their own clothes. Many parents seemed to encourage children in tasks concerning the individual child, rather than in work benefiting the family, as illustrated by this mother with 16 years of schooling talking about her 9-year-old child:

> *Well, with their clothes above all... I tell them "put your clothes away, I'm not telling you to put away your dad's clothes or pick up mine, but put your clothes away."*

Additionally some Cherán parents with extensive schooling who assigned tasks to their children that were less difficult and less responsible seemed to believe that was all that the children were capable of. For example in one highly schooled family, both parents indicated that their children should not be given responsibility for sibling care, even if the child sought it out, despite the fact that both parents reported helping to care for their siblings when they were young: The father recounted how he cared for his brother carrying him in a *rebozo* as he played marbles with his friends. However, neither he nor the mother (a teacher with 16 years of schooling) believed that their own children should be given that responsibility. The mother reported that her children asked to babysit or care for children, but that she considered it too much for them. Instead she asked them to engage in simpler tasks such as helping her carry the diaper bag.

Even when parents in highly schooled families liked the idea of incorporating children in collaborative participation, some reported not being able to find opportunities to do so. In a family where both parents are teachers (16 years of schooling), a mother commented that because her primary work is outside the home, this limits her ability to teach her child different activities and skills:

> *Well I would also like to teach him different activities... but like I said we don't have another kind of job where we can teach him... to work in that way... We try to keep him busy in the evenings with something... he goes to a basketball club.*

The quote from this mother, as well as the example of the parents who helped as children but now think it's too much to ask of their own children, illustrate that the pattern of children contributing in family work was common in Cherán until quite recently. This has been changing in families that have had many years of school and familiarity with Western child-rearing practices (see also Rogoff et al., 2014).

5. COSMOPOLITAN CHILDREN'S INVOLVEMENT IN WORK AT HOME

Constellations of socioeconomic factors and cultural practices in cosmopolitan cities are very different than in rural and Indigenous towns, and these have an important relation to children's development and in particular on their opportunities for collaborative participation (Mejía-Arauz, 2015; Rogoff et al., 2014). In contrast to rural and Indigenous towns, life for Mexican families in cosmopolitan areas is characterized by hectic schedules, long periods spent in car traffic and in the movement of the city, and formal jobs with inconvenient schedules for both parents. This often forces families to find other care options for children outside the family. Thus, children spend long hours in school or in extracurricular classes where they are often cared for by paid non-family members.

Adults have limited time to spend with their children since childhood has been segregated from the everyday life activities in which adults participate. Children's activities have thus been relegated to child-focused activities, as in other middle-class communities (Morelli, Rogoff, & Angelillo, 2003). For example, cosmopolitan parents from middle-class families report that children frequently engage in extracurricular activities in which they can develop artistic and sport skills (Alcalá et al., 2014; Mejía-Arauz, 2015). The structure of interaction in these afterschool activities usually includes an adult who guides the activity, and children are segregated by age and ruled by a structured schedule. Despite the strict structure and scheduling, many urban parents place their children in these extracurricular "training situations" with the hope that the children learn something that parents consider might be useful for the future.

With many hours invested in formal learning situations, cosmopolitan children have little time to spend in their homes casually interacting with their siblings, parents, or others. This lack of unstructured interaction limits children's opportunities for developing abilities for decision-making, for organizing their spare time, and identifying their own interests (Mejía-Arauz, 2015), and may limit children's opportunities for learning to develop initiative. Mothers report that the children seldom participate and almost never take initiative to help in family household chores; their contributions are generally limited to individual tasks that primarily benefit themselves (Alcalá et al., 2014).

This is corroborated in our own study, as 83% (15/18) of the cosmopolitan parents reported that their children's involvement in work is mostly limited to cleaning up their rooms and picking up their toys and clothes. Even when parents assigned chores that could be considered to benefit the whole family (in 44% of the families), the mothers cast these as a responsibility that the child must accomplish alone. In the two examples below, two cosmopolitan mothers who both have 16 years of schooling described their children's help as focused on self-care chores or, if benefiting others, it is still done solo:

> *Interviewer: Does he help in any of the household activities?*
> *Mother: Yes*
> *I: Like what?*
> *M: He has to clear the table. He [also] has to clean up his bedroom and put away his underwear (child is 10 years old)*

In another case:

> *Interviewer: Does your daughter help at home?*
> *Mother: Yes, she has to clean up her room, —something she doesn't always do, but at least when she comes back from school she has to finish cleaning up. And on weekends they (the siblings) take turns to wash the dishes. (Child is 11 years old)*

In contrast with the P'urhépecha families from Cherán, cosmopolitan families did not frequently engage with their children in activities where everyone contributed together toward the same goal or activity. We believe this lack of family engagement has implications for children's desire to participate, to contribute, and to develop initiative in family activities—an idea that we develop below.

6. INITIATIVE, AUTONOMY, AND LEARNING IN COLLABORATION

In many Indigenous communities of the Americas, parents and researchers report that children participate with initiative with others who are involved in the same activity who often support their participation and learning (Alcalá et al., 2014; Corona & Pérez, 2005; de Haan, 1999; Gaskins, 2010; Paradise & de Haan, 2009; Paradise & Rogoff, 2009; Urrieta, 2013; see also de León, 2015; García, 2015; Gutiérrez, Rosengren & Miller, 2015; Lorente Fernández, 2015; Martínez-Pérez, 2015). This is what Rogoff et al. (2014) call "collaborative initiative" and "pitching in"; it is engagement with initiative and purpose, to accomplish a task or fulfill a role, which involves being "eager *to contribute and belong* as valued members of their families and communities" (Rogoff, 2014, p. 74).

An emphasis on initiative in participation seems to be especially important in Indigenous American communities because it is a way of relating individual autonomy to the common good. In many Indigenous communities of the Americas, autonomy is "…a particular cultural understanding of interdependence and independence of participants in which autonomy complements and is congruent with interdependence" (Paradise & de Haan, 2009, p. 199). At the same time initiative is expected in collective work because all are responsible for the result, so if one sees that something is not going the way it should, he or she is expected to intervene, in accordance with his or her experience.

Initiative to participate as a form of autonomy and responsibility may include taking opportunities for learning as the child observes and takes part in ongoing interaction. This involves many facets of *LOPI* as children decide what to participate in and when to participate. In doing so, children can learn a valued community practice, become spontaneously engaged, and offer expert help when others need it. This is illustrated by a mother from Cherán with 6 years of schooling who told us about how her son learned the family business (selling meat that the family butchers and cooks) when he was 5 years old by accompanying the mother as she prepared *carnitas*. The son accompanied her and worked with her at small tasks, but wanted to participate more:

> *Mother: Well when we first started making the carnitas, already then I would cut the big pieces of meat and he would help me throw them into the big pot. It was just to throw them in the pot, but [the son] would sometimes grab the knife and want to cut the pieces himself.*
> *Interviewer: And you would let him?*
> *M: Well, yes. I would let him. I would say, "look from here you are going to slice here like this and not too small, like this," and yes, yes, he would do it. He would do it. Also with killing the pig (now that the child is 9 years old) I tell him "look, you are going to shave him like this, not like that," and he does it. "To shave him you are going to do this, to cut him up you are going to do that. Look when you cut the head you cut here…" and yes, he does it.*

[In another part of the interview]

> *M: My daughter's husband the other day had to slaughter a pig and he didn't know how. Then [the 9-year-old son] said "look this is how we are going to do it" and he helped him. Yes, he already knew.*

Initiative to help with responsibility is known in Mexico as being *acomedido*, a term used to refer to children or adults who engage in needed helping activities (see López, Ruvalcaba, & Rogoff, 2015). We saw many examples of this kind of helping in the interviews with the P'urhépecha mothers from Cherán who had fewer than 9 years of schooling, like in the following quote where the mother had 6 years of school and is referring to her 10-year-old son:

> *Sometimes in the evening he says: "Grandpa, you look tired, I´ll get the water for the horses", or "I´ll go buy their oats". That´s what I see. That's how he helps [his grandfather].*

In another family, a father explained how everybody in the family helps prepare the family meals. While the parents take care of the main preparations, the 10-year-old daughter starts preparing the *agua fresca* (beverage made of fresh fruits) on her own, while other siblings set up the table. The father says: "every young person uses their own initiative to see what is needed and provides help."

Even after a child has learned how to do a specific activity, continuing to collaborate with initiative can help children expand on their existing skills. In some families, the children were reported to see value in observing and participating, and to be aware of the role it played in their own learning. A mother from Cherán with 6 years of schooling recounted how her 10-year-old son helps his father in construction work, with initiative and interest in learning from this:

> *Interviewer: Does he help you here, or does he help his father?*
> *Mother: Yes. You see, he [the father] is a builder, and so all of that, all you see there he built.*
> *I: Really?*
> *M: He [the son] would come and on his own start bringing over bricks. There is a well below and he would help with bringing the cement, water, all that was there and needed. So yes, he would help him [the father].*
> *Later...*
> *I: And does he do this on his own, or do you have to tell him things so he does them?*
> *M: ...Yes, he does it out of his own choice, because sometimes he says, "If I can't continue studying, well, then this is what I'll do, what my father does. I'll learn to be a builder. And that's what I'll do if later I don't want to study." That's why he is always nearby offering to bring things, [the child says:] "What do you need? What can I bring you? That way I can see what you are doing and I can learn also."*

This kind of initiative, or being *acomedido*, is about more than simply providing help. As López et al. (2015) explained, being *acomedido* is part of a larger value system. These P'urhépecha families from Cherán expect their children to willingly get involved observing, pitching in, and contributing to ongoing work, and they also see it as an opportunity to learn new skills, help others in the family, and learn important community values.

7. GENERATING COLLABORATION, INITIATIVE, AND CONSIDERATENESS BY WORKING TOGETHER

We speculate that in families where children contribute with initiative in meaningful ways, productive work is rarely something children are compelled to do or are sent to do alone. Usually this contribution is done with a close family member and only later does the child carry it out without relying on the presence of others to be motivated to do the work or to be able to accomplish it. However, even after learners have mastered an activity, work is often seen as something that is accomplished *with* others.

It is striking that in the P'urhépecha families of Cherán (especially those with less experience with schooling and related practices), parents reported that they promoted their child's collaboration by engaging and *integrating them with other members of the family* as the adults participate in activities that are necessary for the household or in family businesses. Work in this case becomes co-laborative in the truest sense of the word as people co-labor, that is, *work together* as they engage in a joint project or activity. Families reported that children worked *with* the grandparent, mother, father, siblings, or other member of the extended family, as they all performed productive activities together. This is not about doing chores in the presence of a relative; it is about working together in a social organization of work and learning. For example, one mother with technical training as a nurse whose husband often works in the fields with their 10-year-old son told us:

Mother: He knows how to plant and take care of [plants], and he likes to plant, just like his father.
Interviewer: And how did you teach him about plants?
M: It was his father who taught him
I: And how did he do it?
M: Well, only watching, by watching him [the father], and because he [the son] found it very interesting to work with plants.

The mother then goes on to say that now that the son is older he continues to plant and care for the family's plants and flowers even when no one accompanies or helps him with this.

At other times, parents' requests for the collaboration of children in work seem to be structured in terms of doing something together or helping the adult in doing something that needs to be done while the adult engages in another complementary task that is needed at the same time. In the following example, a mother from Cherán with 6 years of schooling encourages the co-laboration of her 10-year-old son (and other children) by framing the *work as something to do together* by working side by side with one another:

> *[I'll say] "Help me my son, help me sweep," or "you already swept, now help me mop," and they help. I tell them* ***"while I do the other room you clean this one"*** *and so we do it like that.*

A similar example of framing child co-laboration as a joint endeavor is given by this mother with 8 years of schooling:

> *For example, right now I was chopping wood and he was piling it. But if we were cleaning the area he would grab a broom and a shovel and gather the trash, and possibly if tomorrow we were washing the area I would tell him grab the broom and you start washing here, you throw water on the place while I soap up the area.*

7.1 Co-Laborating and Developing Consideration for Others

The social and co-laborative nature of work is highlighted by the examples above, but sociability in family work also includes being attuned to the needs of others. This sensitivity to the needs of others is a key component of being *acomedido* (López, Najafi, Rogoff, & Mejía-Arauz, 2012; López et al., 2015), and also showing *respeto* for others (Ruvalcaba, Rogoff, López, Correa-Chávez, & Gutiérrez, 2015). P'urhépecha mothers underscored that this was an important way in which they engendered collaboration in their children: by expecting and asking children to be responsive to the needs of others. For example, a mother from Cherán with 8 years of schooling told us:

> *Sometimes, because I sew, my hands are too warm so I tell them "I cannot get wet, who washes the dishes?" And my daughter (who is 8 years old): "I'll do it mom".*

Adults' urging of children to attend to the needs of others may also be related to the finding that children with Indigenous history attend more to the activity of others in research settings even when they are not asked to do so (Correa-Chávez & Rogoff, 2009; López, Correa-Chávez, Rogoff, & Gutierrez, 2010; Silva, Correa-Chávez, & Rogoff, 2010; Silva, Shimpi, & Rogoff, 2015). This request to be attentive to the activity and needs of others in the environment generally is key in being *acomedido*, and the children appear to learn to be on the lookout for times when their help might be needed. This, coupled with the fact that family work is often framed as children engaging in activity with other members of their family, may further encourage children to think of helping if they see that someone is busy or is needing support for accomplishing a task. This appeared to be the case in one family from Cherán where the mother had 8 years of schooling:

> *Mother: Sometimes when they see that I am washing, the older one (10 years old) will tell the younger one (8 years old), "start hanging the clothes to dry or clean up." I'll see my older daughter sweeping and the younger one washing dishes in the kitchen…since I have the kitchen upstairs… she'll clean up and they'll tell me, "mom we already cleaned the kitchen while you were washing" or something like that [and I tell them] "that's good, thank you."*

These accounts reveal how parents gradually involve their children in co-laborative family work as valued joint activities with goals that go far beyond the simple completion of any one project or task. The ways parents involve their children seem to generate a willingness to participate as a way of becoming part of the group and also as a way of developing consideration of others. At the same time, children develop initiative and acquire skills, abilities, and knowledge through their interaction and involvement in activities organized socially.

8. CHORES AS AN INDIVIDUAL RESPONSIBILITY

The ways of involving children in family work and the way parents appreciate and recognize children's contributions contrast with the way in which cosmopolitan families from Guadalajara report on their children's involvement in family chores. When families assign children to take care only of their own things, or they organize their participation individually taking turns even in activities that are for the benefit of the whole family, this shifts from helping with work to solitary chores.

Figure 1 shows the contrast between the P'urhépecha families from Cherán and the cosmopolitan families from Guadalajara in the extent to which children are involved in shared work with other members of the family or are doing solitary chores. When we asked mothers to tell us how their children contributed to the family, 68% of the families from Cherán with 9 or fewer years of schooling reported examples of their children helping in which they were involved in shared activities with family. Among the cosmopolitan families only 22% of the families reported activities in which children were engaged with others; 49% of the reported activities involved solitary chores. The families from Cherán with high schooling are in between the other two groups in terms of children's engagement in both social work and solitary chores.

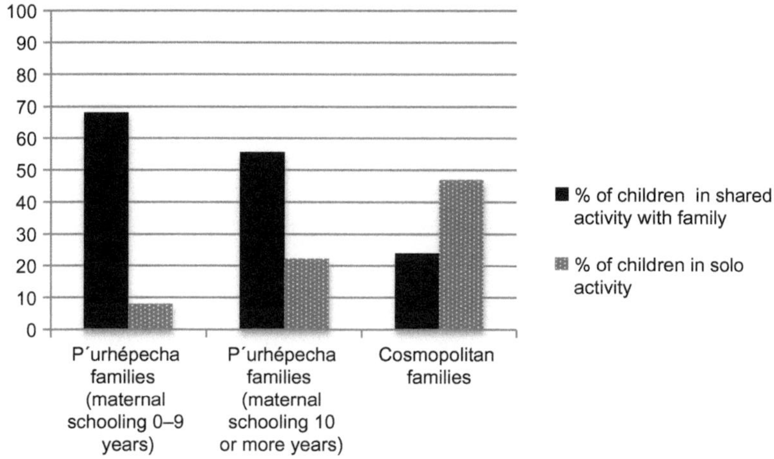

Figure 1 Percentage of children participating in shared family activity or solo. *Note*: The totals do not add up to 100% because in some interviews it was not clear if the child participated in the work or if the report was of what children should do generally (or this child should do in particular) and because some children did not help.

In the cosmopolitan families children do contribute, as they are expected to, by cleaning their rooms and helping in other household chores. However, this is done individually, and in many of the families, children are assigned "turns" for chores and these are assigned to the children as obligations.

We speculate that children may find the solitary activity unattractive and are therefore reluctant to do it. This may be one of the reasons parents employ tools such as chore charts to keep track of, and enforce, participation in chores. One such example was mentioned by a cosmopolitan mother and father talking about the work of their 10-year-old son (both parents had more than 16 years of schooling):

> *Father: Some days he has to wash the dishes after dinner...*
> *Mother & Father: (simultaneously) the dish-washing calendar (both laugh)*
> *Interviewer: He has a chore calendar?*
> *M: Yes, when to wash...*
> *F: Between him and his older sister they switch turns in the middle of the day.*

Another cosmopolitan mother with 16 years of schooling framed her daughters chores as concerning their own things and other house chores as obligatory assigned responsibilities:

> *Above all their responsibilities are around themselves and things that concern them, her homework [...] All of this concerning the house, I don't give her those kinds of responsibilities. The older one (14 years old), yes. She, for example is*

responsible for the dog because we have a dog. So ok, "did you feed your dog, walk her, keep her clean?" The older one does have more responsibilities around that area. Not the younger one (9 years old). Other than clearing her dishes or things like that, still very limited.

Even when children show their willingness to participate in household chores, some cosmopolitan parents emphasized that it is an obligation, in contrast to the language frequently used in the P'urhépecha community around children's participation in household chores as helping others in the family. For example, a cosmopolitan mother with 16 years of schooling commented that when her daughter was old enough (10 years), she asked her to be in charge of washing her school uniforms. But when the 8-year-old brother saw the older sister doing this, he wanted to do it as well, so the mother told him: "you are too little, you will do it later on," but the child said "I want to do it, I want to do it," so she told him

If you want to start doing it, this is not play, if you start you won't be able to get out of this chore later on. It will be your responsibility and if you don't do it then the consequence will be that you will not have clean uniforms during the week and this will also have consequences at school.

Young children in these middle-class families often do want to collaborate or help out spontaneously but this eventually fades (see Coppens & Rogoff, in preparation). This can be seen in a cosmopolitan mother's account, below, which also reports constantly having to monitor and regulate her 9-year-old daughter's behavior, which already seems to be focused solely on attending to her own things. The interviewer asks if chores are done spontaneously or the mother (with 16 years of schooling) has to request them:

When she was younger it was spontaneous. Lately, it's been about 2 years that it's been, "Angelica, your plate, Angelica, clean up that trash," and I make her go back for it... you see, for example, yesterday they left a wrapper here, I don't remember what it was, chips or I don't know what. I told the older one (14 years old), "and that wrapper there? To the trash can, it's off to the side." [The daughter responds] "It's Angelica's." Oh, well I called her [Angelica] and said "come over here, what about that wrapper?" [Angelica responds] "I forgot it." So it's about constantly being on top of her, no?

Not involving children in chores that are performed jointly or collaboratively and presenting their contribution to them as an individual obligation may contribute to work seeming unattractive to children. We speculate that it often "kills" an early willingness to collaborate.

9. PARENTS' CONCEPTIONS OF HOW COLLABORATION IN WORK IS PART OF EDUCATION AND DEVELOPMENT

The idea of co-laboration as a way of learning to work was a common theme among the P'urhépecha parents from Cherán with few years of school. This seemed to go beyond the idea of acquiring practical skills, as they referred to learning relevant social values as well as the emotional and cognitive skills necessary to be a member of the community. One mother with two years of schooling reported that her 10-year-old son sometimes helps at a mechanic's shop and earns thirty pesos (less than US$3), but what was important for this mother was that the child was learning to work and the responsibility involved. She emphasized that this learning to work was necessary in order to be successful in life.

Work is important for the P'urhépecha parents not only because it provides people with financial and natural resources needed to survive but also because it builds social relationships, which are also necessary to acquire resources. As such, work is the basis of survival. However, when parents (and others) in Cherán talk about work there are multiple layers of meaning.

In a separate study, when P'urhépecha teachers in Cherán were asked about the importance and meaning of work they mentioned that people who know how to work show that they are an active member of the community and they show their autonomy as well as their responsibility. By working, they also show their ability to maintain social relationships whether it be in a place of business or paid labor, or in a social community endeavor such as when making donations to communal celebrations. Within this broader definition, work is seen as something that dignifies human beings and makes one a member of the community (Keyser Ohrt, 2009; see also Cardoso, 2015). Local teachers proudly reported that Cherán is characterized as a community of hard workers (*gente trabajadora*), and that being labeled as lazy (someone who does not work) is one of the worst insults or labels a person could receive (Keyser Ohrt, 2009).

The value of work is reflected in our interviews and also in the work of other scholars who have discussed learning to work as the fundamental (or basic) goal of family and community learning and education among the P'urhépecha (Keyser Ohrt, 2015; Márquez Joaquín & Constancio Jiménez, 2007). Others have noted how among the P'urhépechas there are three stages of learning to become a community member (*educación comunitaria*) of which the third and final stage is "the indispensable skills involved in earning a living," or work (Aguirre Beltrán, 1952, p. 315).

However, with increased participation in schooling, this may be changing. Parents with more experience with school in Cherán emphasized that the main task for development in childhood is to meet the obligations that school demands, and that participating in household activity was secondary. The following quote from a Cherán mother with 16 years of schooling illustrates this:

> *When my older children were younger I would say to them, "your job now at your age is to go to school, and to do everything that they tell you to do in school."*

Parents with fewer years of school experience also valued school attendance and participation, but did not demand that children dedicate themselves exclusively to school to the exclusion of family work and community activity. Parents indicated that participation in work and community activity instills a sense of responsibility and initiative and also teaches children valuable skills that are useful for life.

Outside of school, children in Cherán are present in almost all daily activities and at fiestas where they take part with people of all ages. The celebrations in the community and in the family are particularly important for the education of children because in these situations, children learn social norms (such as consideration and reciprocity) and responsibilities by gender and age, and gain expertise (for example in roof building, furniture making, or cooking). From the parents' perspective, their children are gradually introduced and become full members of the community, with the primary goal being to reach the final level of being a community member: knowing how to work.

Another aspect involved in children's participation in family and community activities deals with learning responsibility, which as mentioned earlier is seen as an important aspect of work and involves considerateness to others. This is because in order to be a good worker a person must be responsible to their family and others who depend on them. Both responsibility and autonomy are a part of work because being responsible means knowing how to make decisions and respond to the needs of your work as well as the needs of your coworkers and people that depend on, or benefit from, your work. This conception of responsibility is different than in cosmopolitan, middle-class communities, where being responsible seems to refer to achieving and completing work assigned individually and less about consideration of others in family and community (see Rogoff et al., 2014).

Among the P'urhépecha of Cherán, "to be responsible" is one of the educational objectives from the moment that very small children begin to participate in activities, by sharing tasks or participating with a small part of the work to be done. The success of the activity depends on the responsibility of all participants. In this way, responsibility is linked with respect of others because if someone is responsible, they are not only looking out for their own needs but also for those of the social unit he or she is a part of (Keyser Ohrt, 2009; Rebeca Mejía-Arauz, unpublished manuscript).

Similar ideas about child education and development are seen among cosmopolitan parents and the parents from Cherán who have more experience with school practices and with urban settings. For both of these sets of parents, the main developmental task for children is to learn at school and to play (Mejía-Arauz, 2015). Contributing and collaborating at home, as mentioned before, primarily (or only) includes being responsible for the child's own things. For many of these parents, the idea of taking care of other household chores does not match their conception of childhood tasks, or of opportunities for learning, and they consider that children are too young or not developmentally ready for them (Mejía-Arauz et al., 2013; see also Alcalá et al., 2014). The restriction to later years of work that benefits others is shown in a cosmopolitan family by a mother with 13 years of schooling (father 16 years of schooling and child 11 years old):

Mother: His room, cleaning up the room, making his bed every day and… as far as responsibilities goes, it's just his room, to fold his clean clothes and put them away.
Father: But he is growing and as they grow they do a little bit more
M: He helps setting the table, usually
F: Does the dishes
M: Does the dishes; he has his turn once a week in the evening

Perhaps one of the biggest differences between the parents from Cherán with extensive schooling and the cosmopolitan parents is the idea that children's help at home should be voluntary in the case of the families from Cherán, whereas for cosmopolitan parents, children have a responsibility or "assignment" to help take care of their own things or to take turns in some household chore. A P'urhépecha father from Cherán with high schooling (16 years), but who values the Indigenous traditions of his community, told us how he requests help from his 10-year-old daughter:

Well the way I see it, you can't force them. I can't, I can't do it that way because it would be against my daughter's will. But on the other hand I point things out to her, right? "Daughter, if, if you can do this you're also helping us out." And yes, yes of course she also pitches in on household chores, but if you're asking if I tell her "You know what, you have to clear the table, and sweep your room, and you have to do this or that, you have to do your homework, and when I get back everything should be done?" I kind of see it like… nooo, no,no, no, we've never done that.

In contrast, the following quote from a cosmopolitan mother with 16 years of schooling, whose child is 10 years old, illustrates how cosmopolitan parents commonly talked about their children's involvement in household chores as assigned responsibilities:

Well, picking up his dirty clothes, not large tasks, more or less minimal ones…things like, things like… here in the house, maybe feed the dog, but not every day, only when I can't he does it, but I ask him. But he makes his bed, clears his dishes and toys; that is his responsibility.

10. WHEN SCHOOL WAYS REPLACE LOPI, IMPORTANT SKILLS AND VALUES ARE LOST

We have mentioned that the ability and motivation to "pitch in" is a fundamental organizer of learning in Indigenous American communities like Cherán and seems to be key in children's voluntary learning, which is valued in such Indigenous communities. However, this seems to be changing across generations and across families in the P'urhépecha town of our study and in urban areas.

It is interesting to note that highly schooled Indigenous parents, particularly those with teacher training, even though they were raised with the values and practices of their communities and learned by participating in family and community endeavors, have learned other concepts of education and have concepts of child development similar to those of cosmopolitan parents. There seems to be a generational change shown in these parents' ways of organizing their children's participation as individual contributions, disregarding potential opportunities to learn by co-laborating, and participating in accordance with community values. Their daily lives are instead spent working on a repertoire of individual skills that are supposed to serve them many years later. The aim is to prepare the children for adult life, but they are not integrated into the community with the skills and values that involve living with various age groups from infancy and engaging in activities that are of value to the family or the community during childhood.

The differences between families in the same community and the contrast with cosmopolitan families analyzed in this work show cultural and generational transformations in conceptions of child development, educational practices, and traditions. We believe it is useful to recognize these contrasts to identify their impact on children's development and learning and in turn their impact on the configuration of families, communities, and society.

11. FAMILY SOCIAL ORGANIZATION FOR CHILDREN'S DEVELOPMENT THROUGH CO-LABORATION

Our findings show how in this Indigenous American context, the social organization of the family incorporates and provides opportunities for children to participate at home with household work that is for the benefit of the whole family, sometimes even for the extended family and in the family business or parents' work. This corresponds with the central facet (facet 1) of LOPI, which refers to how community and family include children as contributors to the range of endeavors in which they engage.

The research we have presented here shows how the facets of LOPI are intertwined, supporting the idea that inclusion (facet 1) and collaborative engagement (facet 3) facilitate interested involvement of the learner (facet 2), and in the process, learning involves transformation of participation that includes transforming skills and knowledge, and also learning consideration and responsibility (facet 4), supported by children's contributions as well as by community expectations and the guidance of others (facet 5; Rogoff, 2014). The traditional social organization of the family and community in Cherán not only provides children with opportunities for contributing to the wellbeing of the family (facet 1) but is organized in a collaborative way (facet 3)—that is, doing productive work together or what we call co-laborating. This seems to facilitate children's eagerness to contribute (facet 2) by being able to be a contributing part of a group that values, expects, and guides their contributions (facet 5). In this process, the child learns important knowledge and skills for everyday living (facet 4).

Based on our interviews we suggest that the co-laborative nature and organization of interaction in which children are embedded may instill in children the desire to take initiative in contributing to family and community activity (see also Coppens & Alcalá, 2015) while at the same time teaching them to be considerate and care for others. In communities where children are embedded in family and community activity, children co-laborate by working alongside more experienced others contributing in small ways to accomplish complex tasks. The social nature of the interaction makes it markedly different from cleaning one's own room by oneself without any form of social interaction or feeling of contributing to a joint endeavor. The difference in the social context, practices, and ideas may help explain why in some communities children contribute in sophisticated and mature ways while in other communities parents struggle to get children to pick up their socks.

The contrasts we found among the three backgrounds suggest that it makes a difference when parents ask children to engage in joint activity—co-laborating—in contrast to asking them to perform a solitary chore. When children co-laborate with other members of the family without being compelled to do so, they seem to develop initiative that we and Rogoff and other colleagues call pitching in, offering their help spontaneously when it is needed.

The community goals of learning not only skills and knowledge but also important social and emotional aspects of child development as a member of the community can be seen in how the mothers included consideration for others and recognition of others' efforts in their emphasis on the importance of learning to work. The children for their part seemed to understand the important cultural values inherent in this learning and showed pride in their efforts when others recognized their contributions and considerateness.

In contrast, when parents assign their child to contribute to family household chores as an individual or solitary activity, as was the case in most of the cosmopolitan families we interviewed from Guadalajara, children do not seem to be eager to participate or learn. This is underscored by the fact that parents treat their child's participation more as an obligation than as contribution or help, keeping their children from experiencing their contributions and participation as integrated in the family and community.

Family and community forms of social organization that promote learning to collaborate with initiative as well as consideration and care for others have important social implications beyond the practical benefit for the family and the learning and development of skills for the child or persons involved in work. Through participation, children can learn values of respect, reciprocity, and commitment. In this way, household work can be organized not as solitary, compulsory assigned chores but as opportunity for contribution and for important social learning.

ACKNOWLEDGMENTS

Appreciative thanks to the parents, children, and schools of Cherán and Guadalajara who welcomed us and provided us with valuable information. We are especially grateful to the principals and to the third and fourth grade teachers for their help and patience with data collection and recruitment. Thanks also to Vanessa Toledo and Orquidea Ahumada for their work on coding and transcribing. We deeply appreciate the comments of Barbara Rogoff on previous versions of this chapter. Appreciation also to the National Science Foundation (grant 0837898) for sponsoring the international workshops on Learning by Observing and Pitching In. This research was approved by Clark University's IRB and we were given permission by the participating schools and families. Support for this work was provided by the Spencer Foundation [Grant #201000025] to M. C.-C. and R. M.-A.

REFERENCES

Aguirre Beltrán, G. (1952). Problemas de la población indígena de la Cuenca del Tepalcatepec. In *Serie Memorias del Instituto Nacional Indigenista: Vol. III*. Mexico: Instituto Nacional Indigenista.

Alcalá, L., Rogoff, B., Mejía-Arauz, R., Coppens, A., & Dexter, A. L. (2014). Children's initiative in contributions to family work in Indigenous-heritage and cosmopolitan communities in Mexico. *Human Development, 57*(2–3), 96–115.

Cancian, F. M. (1964). Interaction patterns in Zinacanteco families. *American Sociological Review, 29*(4), 540–550.

Cardoso, R. (2015). Learning and human dignity are built through observation and participation in work. *Advances in Child Development and Behavior, 49*.

Chamoux, M.-N. (1992). Aprendiendo de otro modo [Learning in another way]. In M.-N. Chamoux (Ed.), *Trabajo, Técnicas y Aprendizaje en el México Indígena [Work, technique, and learning in Indigenous Mexico]* (pp. 73–93). Mexico City: Centro de Investigaciones y Estudios Superiores en Antropología Social, Ediciones de la Casa Chata.

Coppens, A., & Alcalá, L. (2015). Supporting children's initiative: Appreciating family contributions or paying children for chores. *Advances in Child Development and Behavior, 49*.

Coppens, A. D., & Rogoff, B. (in preparation). *Parental guidance and children's development of collaborative initiative: Cultural contexts of children's prosocial development*. Unpublished manuscript. Santa Cruz, CA: University of California, Santa Cruz.

Corona, Y., & Pérez, C. (2005). El enriquecimiento de las relaciones comunitarias a través de la participación de los niños en la vida ceremonial. In *Conference on children and youth in emerging and transforming societies, Oslo, Norway*.

Correa-Chávez, M., & Rogoff, B. (2009). Children's attention to interactions directed to others: Guatemalan Mayan and European-American patterns. *Developmental Psychology, 45*, 630–641.

de Haan, M. (1999). *Learning as cultural practice*. Amsterdam: Thela Thelis.

de León, L. (2015). The hidden life behind 'observing' and 'pitching in': Mayan children's creation of learning ecologies by initiative and co-operative actions. *Advances in Child Development and Behavior, 49*.

García, F. A. (2015). Respect and autonomy in children's observation and participation in adults' activities. *Advances in Child Development and Behavior, 49*.

Gaskins, S. (2010). La vida cotidiana de los niños en un pueblo Maya: Un estudio monográfico de los roles y actividades construidos culturalmente [Children's daily lives in a Mayan village: A case study of culturally constructed roles and activities]. In L. de León Pasquel (Ed.), *Socialización, lenguajes y culturas infantiles: Estudios interdisciplinarios [Socialization, language, and child cultures: Interdisciplinary studies]* (pp. 37–76). México: CIESAS.

Gutiérrez, I. T., Rosengren, K. S., & Miller, P. J. (2015). Día de los Muertos: Learning about death through observing and pitching in. *Advances in Child Development and Behavior, 49*.

INEGI (Instituto Nacional de Estadística y Geografía [National Institute for Statistics and Geography]). (2010). *Censo de población y vivienda 2010—Estados Unidos Mexicanos Resultados Definitivos por Entidad y Municipio*. Mexico: INEGI.

INEGI (Instituto Nacional de Estadística y Geografía [National Institute for Statistics and Geography]). (2011). *Catálogo de localidades*. Downloaded on 28/09/2011 from http://cat.microrregiones.gob.mx/catloc/LocdeMun.aspx?tipo=clave&campo=loc&ent=16&mun=024.

INEGI (Instituto Nacional de Estadística y Geografía [National Institute for Statistics and Geography]). (2013). Resultados de la Encuesta Nacional de Ocupación y Empleo en el cuarto trimestre de 2013 para el Estado de Jalisco [National survey about employment results for Jalisco 2013]. *INEGI Boletín de Prensa, 64*(14), 1–12.

Keyser Ohrt, U. (2009). *Los sentidos del otro entre docentes de educación indígena de una comunidad P'urhepecha [Senses of "the other" among teachers in a P'urhepecha community]*. Ph.D dissertation, Mexico: Universidad Pedagógica Nacional.

Keyser Ohrt, U. (2015). Actividades colaborativas en la educación en y para el trabajo entre niñas y niños en una comunidad P'urhépecha. In R. Mejía-Arauz (Ed.), *Desarrollo Psicocultural de Niños Mexicanos*. Guadalajara, México: ITESO.

Klein, W., Graesch, A., & Izquierdo, C. (2009). Children and chores: A mixed-methods study of children's household work in Los Angeles families. *Anthropology of Work Review, 30*(3), 98–109.

Lancy, D. F. (2008). *The anthropology of childhood: Cherubs, chattel, and changelings*. Cambridge: Cambridge University Press.

LeVine, R. A., LeVine, S. E., Richman, A., Tapia Uribe, F. M., Correa, C. S., & Miller, P. M. (1991). Women's schooling and child care in the demographic transition: A Mexican case study. *Population and Development Review, 17*, 459–496.

López, A., Correa-Chávez, M., Rogoff, B., & Gutierrez, K. (2010). Attention to instruction directed to another by U.S. Mexican-heritage children of varying cultural backgrounds. *Developmental Psychology, 46*(3), 593–601.

López, A., Najafi, B., Rogoff, B., & Mejía-Arauz, R. (2012). Collaboration and helping as cultural practices. In J. Valsiner (Ed.), *Oxford handbook of cultural psychology* (pp. 869–884). NY: Oxford University Press.

López, A., Ruvalcaba, O., & Rogoff, B. (2015). Attentive helping as a cultural practice of Mexican-heritage families. In Y. M. Caldera & E. W. Mexican American (Eds.), *Children and families* (pp. 76–91). New York: Routledge.

Lorente Fernández, D. (2015). Children's everyday learning by assuming responsibility for others: Indigenous practices as a cultural heritage across generations. *Advances in Child Development and Behavior, 49*.

Márquez Joaquín, P., & Constancio Jiménez, J. (2007). Juchari mimixekua: (Libre determinación o control cultural). In *Jorhénguarhiri* (pp. 128–149). Zamora: Universidad Pedagógica Nacional. Unidad 162.

Martínez-Pérez, M. (2015). Adults' orientation of children—and children's initiative to pitch in—to everyday adult activities in a Tsotsil Maya community. *Advances in Child Development and Behavior, 49*.

Mejía-Arauz, R. (2015). Contraste en el desarrollo sociocognitivo de niños de contextos urbanos y rurales o indígenas de México. In R. Mejía-Arauz (Ed.), *El desarrollo Psicocultural de Niños Mexicanos*. Guadalajara, México: Editorial ITESO.

Mejía-Arauz, R., Keyser Ohrt, U., & Correa-Chávez, M. (2013). Transformaciones culturales y generacionales en la participación colaborativa de niñas y niños de una comunidad P'urhépecha [Cultural and generational transformations of children's collaboration in a P'urhépecha community]. *Revista Mexicana de Investigación Educativa, 18*(59), 1019–1045.

Morelli, G., Rogoff, B., & Angelillo, C. (2003). Cultural variation in young children's access to work or involvement in specialized child-focused activities. *International Journal of Behavioral Development, 27*, 264–274.

Ochs, E., & Izquierdo, C. (2009). Responsibility in childhood: Three developmental trajectories. *Ethos, 37*(4), 391–413.
Paradise, R., & de Haan, M. (2009). Responsibility and reciprocity: Social organization of Mazahua learning practices. *Anthropology and Education Quarterly, 40*(2), 187–204.
Paradise, R., & Rogoff, B. (2009). Side by side: Learning by observing and pitching in. *Ethos, 37*, 102–138.
Rogoff, B. (2003). *The cultural nature of human development*. New York: Oxford University Press.
Rogoff, B. (2014). Learning by observing and pitching in to family and community endeavors: An orientation. *Human Development, 57*(2–3), 69–81. In Rogoff, B., Alcalá, L., Coppens, A. D., López, A., Ruvalcaba, O., Silva, y K.
Rogoff, B., Correa-Chávez, M., & Navichoc Cotuc, M. (2005). A cultural-historical view of schooling in human development. In D. Pillemer & S. H. White (Eds.), *Developmental psychology and social change* (pp. 225–263). New York: Cambridge University Press.
Rogoff, B., Moore, L. C., Correa-Chávez, M., & Dexter, A. L. (2015). Children develop cultural repertoires through engaging in everyday routines and practices. In J. E. Grusec & P. D. Hastings (Eds.), *Handbook of socialization: Theory and research* (2nd ed., pp. 472–498). NY: The Guilford Press.
Rogoff, B., Najafi, B., & Mejía-Arauz, R. (2014). Constellations of cultural practices across generations: Indigenous American heritage and learning by observing and pitching in. *Human Development, 57*(2–3), 82–95.
Rogoff, B., Paradise, R., Mejía-Arauz, R., Correa-Chávez, M., & Angelillo, C. (2003). Firsthand learning through intent participation. *Annual Review of Psychology, 54*, 175–203.
Ruvalcaba, O., Rogoff, B., López, A., Correa-Chávez, M., & Gutiérrez, K. (2015). Children's avoidance of interrupting others' activities in requesting help: Cultural aspects of considerateness. *Advances in Child Development and Behavior, 49*.
Silva, K., Correa-Chávez, M., & Rogoff, B. (2010). Cultural variation in children's attention and learning in events not directed at them: Patterns in a U.S. Mexican community. *Child Development, 81*(3), 898–921.
Silva, K., Shimpi, P., & Rogoff, B. (2015). Young children's third-party attention in a quasi-naturalistic setting: Cultural differences. *Advances in Child Development and Behavior, 49*.
Urrieta, L., Jr. (2013). Familia and comunidad-based saberes: Learning in an Indigenous heritage community. *Anthropology and Education Quarterly, 44*, 320–335.

CHAPTER THREE

Children's Everyday Learning by Assuming Responsibility for Others: Indigenous Practices as a Cultural Heritage Across Generations

David Lorente Fernández[1]
National Institute of Anthropology and History of Mexico
[1]Corresponding author: e-mail address: david_lorente_fernandez@hotmail.com

Contents

Abstract

This chapter uses a comparative approach to examine the maintenance of Indigenous practices related with *Learning by Observing and Pitching In* in two generations—parent generation and current child generation—in a Central Mexican Nahua community. In spite of cultural changes and the increase of Western schooling experience, these

Advances in Child Development and Behavior, Volume 49
ISSN 0065-2407
http://dx.doi.org/10.1016/bs.acdb.2015.08.005

practices persist, to different degrees, as a Nahua cultural heritage with close historical relations to the key value of *cuidado* (stewardship). The chapter explores how children learn the value of *cuidado* in a variety of everyday activities, which include assuming responsibility in many social situations, primarily in cultivating corn, raising and protecting domestic animals, health practices, and participating in family ceremonial life.

The chapter focuses on three main points: (1) *Cuidado* (assuming responsibility for), in the Nahua socio-cultural context, refers to the concepts of protection and "raising" as well as fostering other beings, whether humans, plants, or animals, to reach their potential and fulfill their development. (2) Children learn *cuidado* by contributing to family endeavors: They develop attention and self-motivation; they are capable of responsible actions; and they are able to transform participation to achieve the status of a competent member of local society. (3) This collaborative participation allows children to continue the cultural tradition and to preserve a Nahua heritage at a deeper level in a community in which Nahuatl language and dress have disappeared, and people do not identify themselves as Indigenous.

1. INTRODUCTION

When I was a young girl, my mother gave me a special gift, a turkey. She told me nothing, but I knew I had to take care of it. The turkey is delicate, it has many needs. When I was older, I listened to an old lady saying: 'if a woman knows how to take care of a turkey, she knows how to take care of a baby.' Both [turkeys and babies] are needy.

María Peralta, 43 years old, August 2013

Children's learning, understood as an "informal" pedagogy, is a core aspect of the family and community life of Indigenous communities, or communities with an Indigenous tradition, in Mexico and other regions of the Americas. A distinctive feature of this kind of learning is that nothing is hidden from children, who are exposed to, and take part in, a wide variety of everyday situations that adults routinely deal with (Bolin, 2006; Chamoux, 1992, 2015; Gaskins, 1999; Good, 2001; Lorente Fernández, 2006, 2012; Merrill, 1988). Children learn through close observation and listening, behaviors that are aimed at participating in household and community endeavors; in this way, the children are motivated by the cultural values of the activity and act with initiative, autonomy, and responsibility, sometimes encouraged or guided by adults who facilitate or foster their participation. This cultural tradition has been described and labeled as *Learning by Observing and Pitching In* (LOPI) to family and community endeavors (Paradise & Rogoff, 2009; Rogoff, 2014; Rogoff et al., 2007; Rogoff, Paradise, Mejía-Arauz, Correa-Chávez, & Angelillo, 2003), an informal pedagogical model closely related to a variety of practices rooted in different Indigenous peoples of the Americas. LOPI encompasses different features, associated in each particular empirical and historical case with specific cultural styles. When cultural practices and changes are considered, it becomes possible to describe historical variations within, or among, communities regarding the organization of children's informal learning, and to analyze which concrete aspects of this learning persist or evolve from one generation to the next (López, Ruvalcaba, & Rogoff, 2015; Magazine & Ramírez, 2007; Mejía-Arauz, Keyser Ohrt, & Correa-Chávez, 2013; Rogoff, Najafi, & Mejía-Arauz, 2014).

In the overall tradition of Mesoamerican civilization (Bonfil Batalla, 1996), and in the Indigenous tradition of Nahua communities in particular (Chamoux, 1992; Good, 2011; Madsen, 1960; Sandstrom, 1991; Taggart, 1983, 2007), assuming responsibility for others (expressed as *cuidado* in Spanish) represents a cultural value system that is both a means for organizing children's learning along with the objective of this learning—the acquisition of the cultural value. In other words, assuming responsibility for others is, on the one hand, a guideline that orients and gives meaning to different practices that children take part in collaboratively in their day-to-day life, and on the other hand, a moral or philosophical value that adults expect children to learn precisely by participating in these activities.

Assuming responsibility, as a pedagogical resource and as a value, involves different facets of the Learning by Observing and Pitching In (LOPI) model: the development of keen attention, the incorporation of children into domestic activities, initiative in the participation aimed at taking on valued roles and becoming valued members of the family, learning aimed at transforming the participation and learning to collaborate with responsibility, guidance from more experienced people, coordination during the activity (Rogoff, 2014). In the *cuidado* system, children engage with motivation stemming from contribution to an important cultural value; they learn by collaborating with parents in "rearing" as well as fostering other natural and spiritual beings to reach their potential and fulfill their development, and they are guided by Nahua expectations connected to a local concept of life based on interdependence and reciprocity that governs social relations. *Cuidado*, associated sometimes with the concept of "rearing" or "raising," involves the interactional behavior of children with adults, or children with other children, that leads to the acquisition of both theoretical and practical knowledge. Practicing *cuidado* activates children's initiative, their individual autonomy, their responsibility, as well as coordination with others and the ability to learn through their interactions (Paradise & De Haan, 2009).

This chapter presents a descriptive analysis of how the children of a community with a Nahua Indigenous tradition (San Jerónio Amanalco), located in central Mexico just 40 km from the national capital, learn *cuidado*, i.e., to assume responsibility, understood as a pre-Columbian Indigenous value based on being responsible for helping other beings—human, animal, plants, or spirits—to fulfill their role in social life or in the Nahua universe.

The results presented in this chapter show three main interrelated aspects:

(1) How practices based on assuming responsibility are Indigenous patterns that transcend the notion of doing chores or taking care of things, as understood in the Western tradition.

(2) How children from the community learn these practices of assuming responsibility through an informal pedagogy related to *Learning by Observing and Pitching In*, which involves the development of responsibility, observation, and self-motivation within the process, adapted to different age groups.

(3) That the value of assuming responsibility through collaborative participation in domestic activities is passed on as a pre-Columbian Indigenous heritage, down to the present day.

The chapter demonstrates that assuming responsibility as a cultural value lives on today in a context of economic changes, parallel to the imposition of formal, school-based education that involves not only children's exposure to a culturally distinct learning tradition, but also the dedication of almost all their waking hours to school. The loss of the Nahuatl language due to social changes has not affected the transmission of the value of *cuidado*, which currently plays an important role in establishing community cohesion and defining local cultural identity. A comparative analysis of the last two generations shows that learning the value of assuming responsibility through collaborative participation has declined in certain activities of Nahua existence, but that there is still significant continuity between the two generations.

In the sections below, this chapter first examines the cultural value system of *cuidado*, and then shows the relationship between generational change and cultural continuity in the community under study, by describing the relationship between the age groups in terms of the Nahua classification and practices of assuming responsibility. The next section offers a comparative analysis of how the generations of parents and children have learned the practices of assuming responsibility as a cultural heritage in four types of activities (raising crops, raising domestic animals, attending to spiritual health, and attending to the souls of the dead by participating in family ceremonial life). Finally, by way of conclusion, the author proposes a systemization of the social organization of *cuidado* practices and their relationship with LOPI, along with an analysis of the continuity of learning practices in a context marked by the presence of school-based education and a conspicuous process of modernization.

2. THE CULTURAL VALUE SYSTEM OF *CUIDADO* OR ASSUMING RESPONSIBILITY

In order to point out its differences from the motivations and practices of the Western tradition, and to better understand what it is that children *do*, *how* they do it, and *why* they do it in their particular terms (Chamoux, 1992; 2015; Gaskins, 1999; Good, 2001; Gutiérrez & Rogoff, 2003; Paradise, 1996, 2002), it is helpful to consider *cuidado* in terms of Indigenous beliefs that belong to a larger Nahua socio-cultural context, which is seen as a coherent, integrated system.

Assuming responsibility, for Nahuas, is related to helping other beings to attain their optimal level of development, either in society or in the cosmos; it has to do with the value the Nahuas place on work and helping out around the house. But the idea of assuming responsibility, in the concept of *cuidado*, has an economic or productive dimension that goes beyond the Western idea of "doing chores." Assuming responsibility is rooted in Nahua cosmology and in the Indigenous idea that living and developing depend on the help and intervention of other agents: beings are not "self-made"; they do not develop autonomously. They depend on the actions and initiatives of other beings. This Nahua conception has been defined with the term "working together" (Good, 2005; Magazine, 2011; Sandstrom, 1991; Taggart, 1983), and with the expressions "regime of co-activity" or "coordination of different agents," which refer to analogous conceptions among other Indigenous groups of Mexico and the Americas (Pitrou, 2014).

For the Nahuas of the community, assuming responsibility implies a process and consists of a way of helping, of enabling a being to become what it presumably ought to be. For example, a woman spoke about corn in the following terms: "You have to treat it with joy and respect so that its soul is happy, it grows tall and produces a lot of ears to feed us human beings, because corn is our flesh. We need corn." In the Nahuas' conception, assuming responsibility consists of persuading beings to develop in the right direction, of orienting their "nature" and affecting their mood so that they respond to the caregiver's actions and fulfill themselves. It is about helping them to develop, to become, to attain a state of maturation, or to manifest their full potential by realizing their *essence* or their nature, which is like a seed, contained in them since birth.

It is said that beings are born with the potential to become what they are, but that they need the care of others to attain it. For example, newborn babies are considered to be tender and full of moisture; certain practices of assuming responsibility consist of "warming" babies in a steam bath so that they "dry out" and can eventually start to walk and begin their life as human beings. In the case of animals, raising them involves giving them food, protection, and good words, which serve to commit them in a bond of reciprocity in such a way that they later, in gratitude, offer their meat or other products as a service to human beings. In the case of the souls of the dead, assuming responsibility primarily means feeding them so that they can "live" in the other world, since it is believed that there is no food there and the dead depend on their relatives for survival; they in turn can help the living by assuring them health or making their fields fertile.

In this way, assuming responsibility is understood as having a double meaning of "protection" and "raising," but also "motivation" so that other beings, whether they be animals or humans, can attain fulfillment while behaving properly in social life or in the universe, by completing their respective roles.

In the Nahuatl language, there are different verbs to denote this act of assuming responsibility, depending on the living being involved in the action and on the ultimate purpose pursued in each act of *cuidado* (e.g., *huapahua* for children, *nahuatia* for livestock, etc.; Molina, 2004; Karttunen, 1992). Today, however, due to the economic transformations that have led to the decline in the use of the Indigenous language, these Nahuatl verbs have all been subsumed into the Spanish verb *cuidar*. But as the Nahuas use it in different contexts, the Spanish verb keeps the original semantic content of the different Indigenous verbs, which has not been lost.

Finally, it is useful to point out that assuming responsibility is closely related to the Nahuas' ideas of "life," which helps to discern a deeper meaning in the practices associated with this value. Nahuas use two different but complementary terms to refer to life. On the one hand there is *yoltoc*, which means "to be alive" and refers to life as a *state*, something intrinsic to beings considered to be infused with life; on the other hand there is *nemi*, which insinuates the idea of "developing over time," "advancing," "walking the path of life," thus conceiving of life as a *process*, as something that unfolds gradually (Chamoux, 2011; Good, 2011; Karttunen, 1992). It is in this sense of life as *nemi* or process that *cuidado* comes into play: it implies the accumulation of human beings' actions on other beings so that they develop by stages, in a continuous effort, by means of the Indigenous practices aimed at assuming responsibility for others. All beings in the world have their function in Nahua society and in the Nahua universe, but in order to fulfill it, it is not enough for them to simply be alive; they require incentives, help, and interaction, i.e., an ongoing human influence on them.

The relationship between the beings that interact in terms of *cuidado* tends to be, in the long run, mutual and reciprocal, and at the same time, beneficial. Each being contributes to the development and well-being of the other by responding and thus fulfilling higher ends in the Nahua worldview: a broad framework of reciprocal help and interdependence.

3. GENERATIONAL CHANGES AND CULTURAL CONTINUITY IN THE COMMUNITY OF SAN JERÓNIMO AMANALCO

The community of San Jerónimo Amanalco is located 40 km east of Mexico City and has roughly 6500 inhabitants (INEGI, 2011). It was founded before the arrival of the Spanish and despite the political and religious changes brought about by the conquest of Mexico, the community kept its Indigenous traditions practically intact until the final decades of the twentieth century. Community members spoke Nahuatl (the language of the Aztecs) and grew the Mesoamerican trio of crops—corn, beans, and squash—for consumption within the family. Cultural elements of Spanish origin, such as European domestic animals and the cult of Catholic saints, were integrated into the local Nahua Indigenous cosmology and practices, and for five centuries the community conserved its typically Mesoamerican social organization, traditions, and religious beliefs associated with the growing of corn, the veneration of the rain gods, and the household cult of the dead (Lorente Fernández, 2011, 2012).

Starting in 1970, however, cultural practices underwent increasing changes. The region's isolation was overcome when highways were built connecting the community to Mexico City, at that time already one of the largest cities in the world. The Nahuas began to work as wage earners in the city, exposing themselves to "modern" cosmopolitan life in the capital. At the same time, the modernizing program of the Mexican state reached the community in the form of newly built schools: children came into contact with pedagogical dynamics of Western education and values that arose in an urban milieu.

But the deepest changes stemmed from the educational policy of the Mexican state, which held that the language, beliefs, and practices of the Indigenous world should be eradicated as an obstacle to the country's development and modernization. All things "Indian" were seen as synonymous with backwardness and ignorance, the opposite of modern Mexico (Bonfil Batalla, 1996; Frye, 1996; Gamio, 1982). As of that moment, the Indigenous historical roots of the community were questioned by the inhabitants themselves, as they stopped identifying explicitly as Nahuas to avoid the cultural stigma, and began to align themselves with the more prestigious national *mestizo* culture. But different cultural practices that are identified with Mexican Indigenous communities persist locally even though their Nahua roots are not necessarily recognized (Lorente Fernández, 2011, 2012).

The most profound changes were experienced by the first generation that went to school (born between 1970 and 1995), called "the parent generation" in this chapter. Eighty-two percent of this generation went to school between the ages of 6 and 12 years—only 5.8 years on average—and almost no one finished elementary school. It was nonetheless a substantial change in comparison with the experience of their parents and previous generations, who did not go to school at all (SEP, 2013). These children did not learn the Nahuatl language because schooling was conducted in Spanish. They never dressed in the distinctive Indigenous clothing worn by their parents; after marrying they had fewer children (an average of 3) and got paying jobs or worked in sales or other kinds of informal employment. Many commuted daily to Mexico City, while only a few continued farming.

Nevertheless, these people were educated in the Indigenous tradition by their parents, who had no formal schooling, spoke Nahuatl and maintained important Indigenous values and practices, such as the respect (harmonious and mutual relations) and reciprocity that governed everyday life, growing corn for their own consumption, raising animals in their home, notions of health and illness, the rituals of the cult of the dead, and the existence of Indigenous myths and cosmology that gave meaning to daily life. In spite of their Nahua practices, these people do not identify themselves as Indigenous in order to avoid the stigma attached to the concept of "Indian" and they pass on to their children an elevated esteem of formal schooling as a path to a higher standard of living and a shield against discrimination in the urban setting. At the same time, with a kind of "cultural inertia," they instill a desire to observe closely, collaborate, and take part in highly valued household activities in order to belong to the local culture; these practices are included in the system of LOPI (Rogoff, 2014).

Those who belong to what this chapter calls the "child generation" (born between 1995 and 2010) are monolingual in Spanish and spend most of the day in school, reaching much higher grades than the parent generation did (primary and secondary school, which means that most attend school up to the age of 15). This increase is due in large part to the encouragement of their parents and the availability of schools in the community: five primary schools, one secondary school, and one high school (INEGI, 2011). Outside of school they do more homework and fewer household chores than their parents, but they continue to take an active part in certain highly esteemed and culturally familiar activities of Indigenous origin. As will be seen in this chapter, even though the children do not self-identify as Indigenous, they continue to reproduce Indigenous practices. They take the initiative to participate in them and consider them valuable because they observe the importance that the practices have for adults and because they feel that participation is the way to become valuable members of their family and their community—approaches that are central to LOPI.

This chapter shows the contrasts in the learning and in the application of *cuidado* as an aspect of Nahua Indigenous pedagogy between the two generations in question. In other words, it does a comparative analysis of the intergenerational variations within the community and relates them to the persistence of Indigenous practices in a context of change, and to the learning of *cuidado*-based practices through children's collaborative participation that develops attention, coordination with others, autonomy, and self-motivation in the process.

The data and findings presented in this chapter come from a wider long-term anthropological study that encompassed different periods of residency in the community between the years of 2005 and 2015. The method included an ethnographic approach and participant observation of the lives of the study families, which in practice consisted of accompanying their members in a variety of everyday activities and of closely documenting children's participation. Conversational interviews were also conducted with fathers, mothers, and children in their homes, using open-ended questions in Spanish (the primary language of all participants), focusing on the following topics: Indigenous practices, children's participation in family activities that imply assuming responsibility in the present and the past generations, schooling, and continuity/change in everyday life.

For the observation and the interviews, two samples were selected:

(1) The first group was made up of 48 families (48 mothers and 48 fathers) belonging to what we called the "parent generation" (born between 1970 and 1995).

(2) The second sample included 96 children (50 girls and 46 boys)—taken from the 48 families just mentioned (2 children per family)—who corresponded to what we have called the "child generation" (born between 1995 and 2010).

A comparative analysis of the samples from the two generations examines the continuities in the value of assuming responsibility, the children's collaboration in the Indigenous practices related to this cultural value system, and the way the children get involved and participate as a way of learning. These continuities occur, however, in a context of changes and certain variations in the "constellations of cultural practices" (Rogoff et al., 2014; see also Dehouve, 2007). That is to say, the persistent pre-Columbian Indigenous educational practices coexist with a process of change triggered by the increase of Western schooling, the professionalization and specialization of the parents' economic occupations, and the shift from a "rural" community to one undergoing urbanization.

4. CONTINUITY ACROSS TWO GENERATIONS: CHILDREN, NAHUA AGE GROUPS, AND *CUIDADO* PRACTICES

The results of the analysis show that even though Nahuatl is almost never spoken any more in the community's day-to-day life, what subsisted in the parent generation, and subsists currently in the child generation, is an Indigenous classification of age groups that associates and correlates children's age sequences with certain types of *cuidado* practices and degrees of involvement. This classification of age groups continues to be expressed using Nahuatl terms, which reveals its deep roots in the community and its relevance for local culture. The link between these age groups and the activities that involve assuming responsibility in which children learn by participating in accordance with their age reveals the historical depth of an Indigenous pedagogical tradition. It is relevant to point out that a very similar classification was used in the Nahuatl language by the Aztecs in pre-Columbian times, almost five centuries ago; evidence can be found in documents such as the Codex Mendoza (1978).

The classification is present in the community in the way people talk about children and the activities in which they are expected to collaborate, depending on their age, and in the answers that both parents and children gave in the interviews. The classification is as follows:

- *Piltziquitl*: "newborns," encompasses the first week of life. They assume no responsibility; others take responsibility for them.
- *Conetl*: "infants, breastfed children," up to the age of 2–3 years. Their primary activity is to observe.
- *Piltonconetl/susuhuato*: "older boys and girls," from the ages of 4–6 to 10 years.

  4 and 5-year-old boys make their first attempts at assuming responsibility in the fields.

  8 and 9-year-old boys assume responsibility for entire activities in planting.

  6-year-old boys begin to assume responsibility for a herd of sheep.

  4 and 5-year-old girls begin to assume responsibility for the house, domestic fowl, and younger siblings.

  6-year-old boys and girls begin to help with the responsibility for attending to their relatives' health.

  6-year-old boys and girls begin to assume partial responsibility for the souls of the dead when they set up household altars with offerings for the Day of the Dead.
- *Telpocatl/ixpocatl*: "boys and girls," from 10 to 15 years old.

  10-year-old boys assume firm responsibility for sheep and other animals (horses, mules, cows, if there are any); they also assume autonomous responsibility for fields with crops.

  11-year-old girls have a full set of skills for taking care of the house, younger siblings, and domestic fowl, including turkeys.

  11-year-old boys and girls participate with greater responsibility for attending to their relatives' health, and in the cult of the souls of the departed on the Day of the Dead.

The relationship between stewardship activities and the different stages of age groups can be developed in more detail by describing how the collaborative participation varies by age.

The value of stewardship begins to develop with observational learning, which starts as the child is exposed from an early age (2–3 years, in the *conetl* stage) to all the household activities that adults engage in. Learning Indigenous practices that fall under the heading of assuming responsibility depends on the gradual development of children's capacity for careful attention, and on the subsequent perfecting of this initial attention as it becomes more precise with the children's first experiences of participation (starting at the age of

4–5 years, the *piltonconetl* phase if it is a boy, the *susuhuato* phase if it is a girl). During the *conetl* stage, adults occasionally give children brief pieces of advice and moral orientation, and they urge them to be present in order to see all kinds of activities. A 28-year-old woman told her 3-and-a-half-year-old daughter: "Come with me out into the yard so you can see the eggs the turkey laid, and how we're going to take care of them so that the chicks hatch." At 2–3 years, participation consists of observation, and of learning to observe.

When children are considered ready to intervene (at the age of 4–5 years, the *piltonconetl* stage for boys and the *susuhuato* stage for girls), parents give them a verbal indication: "*cuida*" (look after, or watch over). The indication is brief, concise, specific: "They just tell them; they give them the order: 'you're going to do this,' that's all," a 30-year-old woman explained, remembering back to when she was 5: "We listen to how things are and we also watch; then one day they call on us to start participating." As children grow, the parents' request to carry out the activity fades away. An 8-year-old boy explained: "My mother didn't have to be running after us, because we knew we were supposed to do it. It was my role to tend the sheep together with my little brother; we were expected to do it." Starting at this age, stewardship combines individual autonomy with collaboration and responsibility (Paradise & De Haan, 2009). From 4–5 years to 10 years of age, children increase their participatory collaboration step by step, along with their mastery of technical skills and the knowledge involved in the different activities, and they gradually assume more and more responsibility.

Should the child disobey, complain, or resist collaborating, the ways of correcting the participation involve first of all a verbal intervention. A 32-year-old mother said: "If the boy does not want to do it, we speak to him, and we tell him why he needs to do it." The importance given by the Nahuas to the spoken word perhaps hearkens back to the advice and exhortations that the Aztecs gave their children to encourage them to work and behave properly (Sahagún, 1969). Only after persuasive language has failed do parents resort to scolding ("How lazy you are!"), and in exceptional cases, as a last resort, to physical punishment, and even then only between the ages of 6 and 10. Nahuas see this as the last option because they believe that responsibility should come from individual initiative, as a "natural" response, the fruit of the child's development: if it is not forthcoming, then parents can resort to physical punishment (Lewis, 1960; J. Taggart, personal communication, 2015). In cases of negligence, parents correct their children by exposing them to the failed results of their actions. For example, if a child neglects an animal and it dies, they confront her with the dead animal and make her responsible (as will be seen below in the case of the turkey).

10 to 15-year-olds (who belong to the *telpocatl* stage if they are boys and the *ixpocatl* stage if they are girls) have already acquired considerable autonomy in practices of assuming responsibility, and have developed full competencies in a range of activities. During this time, they distinguish themselves by mastering the skills considered distinctive of their gender roles, which implies contributions as useful members of the family as well as the capabilities needed to become involved in community life. This stage is considered in the community to be the last phase of "childhood" and concludes—around the ages of 15–17 years—with the marriage of the youth, who becomes a man (*tlacatl*) or woman (*sohuatl*).

During the different stages referred to here, assuming responsibility is embodied in the children's interactional behavior with other living beings, who could be considered the recipients of the care, and thus seem to possess less agency than the child providing the care. The apparent passivity of the being that is the object of stewardship enables children, depending on their age, to wield a certain active initiative, a certain autonomy, and to implement responsible action. From a pedagogical viewpoint, practicing stewardship could be related to an Indigenous learning dynamic that has been called "tacit collaboration" (Paradise, 1996). Tacit collaboration implies that a seemingly passive participant in an interaction actually plays a key role by evoking or encouraging an active response from the child involved, who takes initiative in order to adapt and coordinate her actions within the interaction, thereby demonstrating an ability to handle the situation on her own. In this way, in Indigenous stewardship practices, the receptive or seemingly passive attitude of the being receiving the care—whether it be, for example, corn, or a small flock of sheep, or a turkey, or a sick relative—is complemented by an active initiative on the part of the child, who takes responsibility. This experience stimulates in the child a sense of independence, interest in taking charge of the situation, and a tendency to adjust her actions and cooperate with others. The child's fluid coordination with the being receiving the care encourages her to give precise responses spontaneously, and this is the core of the learning dynamic.

For example, in the case of a flock of sheep—as will be seen below—the animals' relative passivity obliges the boy to deploy a whole array of actions in order to make them advance, stop, or to lead them in the right direction. He needs to control their reactions and respond to them with initiative. In the case of raising a turkey (as will also be seen below), the animal offers the girl social and interactional support for developing the ability to respond to the bird's attitude. Because turkeys tend to stop eating if they are not stimulated with words and singing, being in charge of a turkey means that the girls assumes a responsibility to respond to an interlocutor or "care recipient."

The dynamic of tacit collaboration established between the caring child and the object of his or her care also serves to stimulate "extensive" or "generative learning," a kind of fertile learning that leads in the long run to new and diverse forms of participation, to assuming more and more complex responsibilities. People say that learning stewardship by carrying out a concrete activity enables a child to acquire resources that prove to be useful and applicable in other situations, as the previous examples illustrate. The Nahuas see tending sheep as an indispensable activity before a boy can be entrusted with cows or horses. They feel that the skills that the child acquires by tending and herding sheep give him greater autonomy and mastery in the control of larger and more independent animals, and that the previous experience helps to reduce the risks he will run when dealing with stronger, more violent animals. In the same way, it is expressed explicitly in the community that raising and taking care of a turkey, with the very peculiar behaviors attributed to this bird, helps a girl to develop useful skills that will serve her well in the future when the time comes to care for a human baby.

It is clear then that Nahuas give importance to learning stewardship by carrying out activities in their "real," everyday context, and not in "made-up situations designed for children" or simulations. This has a number of implications: (1) children learn for life in real-life situations; (2) children develop self-motivation in order to attain real goals; (3) children grasp the purpose of the real-life activity; (4) sometimes this knowledge builds on other knowledge and the children perceive the cultural connections among different activities; and (5) at the same time that they acquire skills, when engaged in collective practices children also develop capacities for collaboration and coordination with other community members who are involved in the activity (Fortes, 1970; Mead, 1963; Rogoff et al., 2007). The following section contains a historical-comparative analysis of children's practices of learning the value of *cuidado* in the parent generation (1970–1995) and the current child generation (1995–2010). The analysis focuses on four primary settings of the community's day-to-day existence: stewardship of the *milpa* or cornfield, raising and protecting farm animals, Indigenous practices related to bodily health and balance, and attending to the souls of the departed during the Day of the Dead ceremony. The importance of learning from practice is described, as well as the value of assuming responsibility by participating in these activities, and the changes, variations and consistencies from one generation to the next are studied.

5. FOUR SETTINGS FOR PRACTICES WHERE THE VALUE OF STEWARDSHIP IS LEARNED AND RESPONSIBILITY FOR OTHERS IS ASSUMED: A PERSPECTIVE OF TWO GENERATIONS

5.1 Stewardship of the Milpa, or Cornfield

Traditionally in the community of San Jerónimo Amanalco it is considered an ethical imperative to cultivate the *milpa* so that it produces an abundant harvest of corn. This belief is common to other regions of Mexico with a Nahua tradition (Good, 2011; Madsen, 1960; Sandstrom, 1991; Taggart, 1983). Corn is valued as a staple because it constitutes the basis of the community's diet in the form of tortillas, and people believe that eating corn gives them "strength," "health," and "life."

Nahuas see corn as a living being who has a "soul" and is fragile, like a small child who frightens easily or grows sad and stops growing if it is not nurtured properly. It needs to be treated with affection and watched over constantly, since it requires human help in order to fulfill its potential and develop. Significantly, the growth stages of corn are explicitly compared with the different ages of human beings: the tender ear is said to be like a baby; the green ears that have attained their full size are like young people at the peak of their vitality, while dried ears are like old people (Good, 2011; Monaghan, 1995; Sandstrom, 1991, 2009; Taggart, 2007). This suggests a certain identification between corn and human beings in the Nahua world-view: both are said to have a soul, they follow a similar path to maturity, and they share needs and characteristics.

The farming cycle involves different activities: preparing the field, making the furrows, sowing the seeds, weeding, defending the cornfield from predators, and harvesting, and ancient Mesoamerican techniques are employed. The work is done by hand and with a wooden plow, drawn sometimes by animals, with no industrial machinery.

In the parent generation (1970–1995), there were numerous cornfields in the community and over 76% of the boys participated in fieldwork. They started at a very young age, before turning six. While their parents worked, the boys, seated to one side, played with sticks and other objects from the natural environment (making little houses, for example), but while playing they closely observed the different activities. Starting at age 6 they spontaneously approached to watch the details of how the father prepared the plow and hitched it to the draft animals, and they accompanied the father, walking behind him down the furrows, keeping quiet and observing closely. Observation "from the side of the cornfield" gave way to observation "from inside the cornfield," by accompanying a moving activity. Then they were assigned simple tasks: pulling some weeds, perhaps dropping a few seeds into the open furrows.

At the age of 8 or 9 participation in the activities stepped up to a higher level as the boys assumed greater responsibilities, following the different phases of the farming cycle. The boys helped to weed, sow, defend the cornfield from predators, harvest (pick the ears from the stalks) and store the harvest at home, but they were not yet allowed to plow or steer the draft animals, which required more experience and knowledge. Participation in the activity did not require many words, just a gesture or an indication of the right body posture. A number of fathers explained that boys learn by "remembering what they see," and "being there in the cornfield and coming up to look."

At night the boys were told what they would do the next day: "Let's see, son, tomorrow you'll go with me to the cornfield because we're going to sow," or "We're going to harvest the corn." The boy's motivation sprang from the idea of mutual help offered to the family: "if we all eat, we all work; if we live together, we all pitch in."

At the age of 10–11, boys were considered capable of taking care of a fully grown cornfield. They sometimes spent the night in the field to ward off predators who would eat the corn. Spending the night in the *milpa* required autonomy and responsibility, and the boy had to show previous mastery of the other techniques associated with the cornfield. From this age to age 15, boys received more detailed verbal indications right in the field as they carried our certain complex activities. The execution of these activities, within their actual context, was accompanied by brief comments: "My father would take me and say: 'This is how you plow,' 'This is how you hold the team'; then we would plant the seeds with a shovel, keeping a distance of five or ten centimeters between one and the next." The verbal explanation took a back seat to observation and participation as the boy collaborated with his father; in this way he mastered the activities required for stewardship of the *milpa*. This was a male setting, although the girls knew it from visiting the field every day to bring their fathers and brothers lunch. Everyone pitched in when it came to storing the harvest in the home. Because of the belief that corn "suffers" as people do it must be spoken to with affection and respect, and when storing great care must be taken to not bruise or drop the ears.

In the child generation (1995–2010), the number of cornfields dropped sharply as new homes went up in the fields to house the growing population. Compared with 76% of the parent generation, today only 14% of the boys participate in stewardship of the fields. Some accompany the fathers who still farm to the *milpa*, but the school schedule clashes with the prolonged periods and intermittent attention required by farm work. Work in the cornfield is no longer continuous as in the parents' time; it is limited to the breaks in the school calendar. Thus, boys' participation in these activities is reduced and restricted. "My husband used to plant fava and pinto beans and corn, but my children now know little about planting. He takes them on weekends and during school vacations." Parents with more years of schooling and with professional or specialized jobs want their children to spend as much time as possible on school activities. One father explained:

> *Things are different now. We're not going to teach my sons fieldwork anymore. As long as they want to study, we're willing to support them. We don't tell them to go plow because there's no more land. We have no more farmland to leave them. 'Their inheritance is their schooling.' That's all we can leave our children nowadays. (41-year-old father)*

However, the decline in farming activities and the reduced participation in them on the part of boys from the current generation has not diminished the learning of the value of stewardship. As will be seen below, boys continue to learn by participating in other settings, such as health-related practices or the cult of the souls of the departed in the Day of the Dead ceremony. Significantly, this last activity highlights the value of stewardship as it relates to growing corn, albeit in an implicit way. Boys whose families no longer work in the fields and who buy from their neighbors the corn they need to prepare offerings for the dead hear stories and instructions about the importance of stewarding corn and the close identification that the Nahuas see between this plant and human beings.

5.2 The Raising, Fostering, and Protection of Domestic Animals

In the community of San Jerónimo Amanalco, stewardship of the *milpa* was often associated with practices of taking care of certain animals by taking them out to graze in the fields. Both are considered male activities and are performed outside of the home. The animals most often cared for in this way are sheep. Taking care of sheep involves leading them to places where they can eat fresh grass, guiding them—i.e., exercising a certain amount of control over their movement—along the way so that they do not get lost, keeping them from destroying cornfields, taking them to drink clean water, and at night, keeping them sheltered, away from the elements and predators. The person in charge of their care must therefore make certain decisions and impose his will over the sheep's, as well as assume responsibility for any damage they cause to crops or any harm that comes to the sheep themselves.

In the parent generation (1970–1995), over 78% of the extended families had flocks of sheep and the boys were in charge of their stewardship. Without any previous training, a 6- to 7-year-old boy would one day receive his father's request to take care of the sheep. Of course he had already had the opportunity to observe other boys doing it as he walked around the town, and to notice details and techniques for controlling the animals, but he had never before taken charge by himself. The idea was that this activity had to be learned "on the job, by doing it"; "they send you out, you take the sheep out of the pen and you start walking," said one man as he remembered his childhood. Actually, as testimonies show, the stock of observations made by the boy in earlier years took shape and were "activated" as knowledge already acquired. This knowledge was put into practice when the activity called for it, as the boy took charge with initiative and responsibility, responding to the animals as "care receivers" whose behavior enabled the boy's learning through tacit collaboration, as explained above. Stewardship meant assuming responsibility suddenly, not gradually, for anywhere between 5 and 12 sheep, depending on the number of animals the family owned. From that point on, learning depended on trying out strategies for leading the sheep in one direction, herding them, or keeping them away from dangerous places. There was no help available for the boy, who found himself alone without supervision, dealing with the situation on the ground using his own resources, based on prior observation and on the sheep's actions and reactions.

Significantly, a good number of adult men explained that when they were boys, this was the first activity involving stewardship that was entrusted to them. They remembered the effort it took at their young age to pull it off outside the home, together with the realization of the animals' economic value and the risks they had to face and overcome, with no one nearby to turn to. Before giving them even more responsibilities, around the age of 10, parents checked to see if their sons had fulfilled the basic expectations of stewardship: whether they had lost animals through negligence or the attack of a predator, whether the sheep had been kept healthy, if they had grown and were well fed. They also checked to see if the boy knew how to get the sheep out of the pen, take them to the best places for grazing and drinking water, tie them up or lead them back into the pen at night for protection. If he did, they assumed that the boy was an expert steward, capable of taking charge, with full autonomy, of a flock of sheep.

The experienced boys later received increased responsibilities: they were allowed to take the sheep to more distant grazing grounds, on the mountainsides around the community, considered remote, inaccessible places, dangerous for both the flock and the shepherd. Others were given bigger flocks that combined their father's animals and their neighbors' flocks. Furthermore, these boys were entrusted with taking care of larger animals, when there were any, such as horses or cows (recorded in 68% of the cases), which called for even greater attention because they were considered more strong-willed than sheep. In Nahua eyes, sheep are "passive" while cows are "very tricky." From this viewpoint, the dynamic of tacit collaboration referred to earlier changes considerably, since the responses the boy must give to the cows' and horses' actions are more active, more resolute, than those called for by the sheep. The responsibility is greater, and learning continues to take place in the search for new responses to the actions of these animals that possess greater strength, independence, and initiative. However, as experience shows, some of the technical skills involved in taking care of horses and cows are built on the previous experience with sheep.

At the age of 12–13, boys expanded their work as stewards: with small amounts of money that they had saved, they started buying their own sheep, which they added to the family flock and thus began to acquire a first-hand understanding of the potential of these animals as capital in the household economy: a resource that can be exchanged or sold for cash when a need arises, or in case of a debt or an emergency. This practice of buying their own sheep was recorded in 74% of the fathers, who as boys stewarded the family flocks, meaning that it was a relatively common practice. The boys' initiative, which tended to emerge spontaneously, was regarded approvingly by adults, who let their sons manage their money for the purchase, or exchange their own sheep (or products derived from them, like wool), with freedom and autonomy. In this way the boys would accumulate a bit of capital, free of parental interference.

The female equivalent of shepherding, so to speak, was the domestic stewardship of poultry: chicken, ducks, and especially turkeys. Eighty-two percent of the girls in the parent generation engaged in this kind of activity. Chickens and ducks required feeding and little else, but raising turkeys was a more complex task. The smallest girls, age 2–3, would observe closely what happened in the yard, and how their mothers and older sisters treated the turkey. It was said that the turkey was a "delicate," "dependent" bird that could not survive without constant human intervention at all stages of its development. "Stewardship" consisted of taking charge of it, and helping it to fend for itself, to "complete itself." With turkeys the steward had to guide the animal and exercise the will that it lacked.

At the age of 4–5, the girls received corn kernels from their mothers to feed the adult turkeys by simply dropping the corn on the ground. At the age of 8–9, and with more resolve when they reached 10, girls were involved in the whole stewardship process: from having observed their mother, they knew that they had to feed the turkey chicks at certain times, as if they were nursing babies, and make them feel happy and loved by using the right words and songs, so that they would eat and be healthy. They also had to prepare shelters for them to take refuge from the rain, check their feet and head to prevent illness such as skin eruptions or "fever," apply home-made medicines if they got sick, and talk to them sweetly to keep them from being "sad" and losing their appetite, which could cause their death. The girls devoted many minutes of the day to protecting, watching over, spoiling, motivating, and stimulating the birds to live.

One important aspect of "raising" was explained verbally to older girls at the age of 11–12, and that was the way to help turkeys hatch. According to local belief, turkey chicks sometimes do not have the strength required to break their shells. Some women would keep track of the days of incubation. When the time came, they would put the eggs in hot water to soften the shells and thus make it easier for the chicks to hatch, or they even broke the shells themselves with their fingers. A 45-year-old woman recalled her experience at the age of 13: "My mother told me: 'You have to be careful. Count 4 weeks since the mother turkey began to brood so you can help the chicks hatch, and they don't die.'" The woman added:

> *But once I forgot to count the days and I put an egg in water. It didn't hatch! What if too much time had gone by? I broke the egg. Oh, the poor thing, it bled to death! It died. I was worried. My mother scolded me. 'I can't believe you forgot! You're so forgetful. Write it down if you forget, write it down! Look what you did to the poor animal! Look, look, you killed it! Poor thing!' And since then I've always counted the days of incubation, ever since then until now that I'm an adult. (39-year-old woman)*

This testimony shows that when learning about "raising" in its context, words are used first to give the girl a detailed explanation of the procedure and to warn about the negative consequences should she do things differently. But the mother also resorted to words to show her disapproval of the girl's negligence in two senses. First the mother reminded her of the need to "remember," i.e., to keep in mind and in her memory significant events, an ability that is indispensable for successfully completing and coordinating numerous household activities. Secondly, she used "scolding" words to underscore for her daughter the negative consequences of her irresponsibility in taking care of other living beings. Here, the use of direct verbal communication is clearly evident as the activity unfolds, used as a way to assess and give feedback about the adequacy of the contribution, with an eye to correcting the deficient participation and developing a correct sense of responsibility, under the guidance of the mother as a person with experience.

There is an additional aspect concerning learning about stewardship in raising turkeys. Two decades ago there still existed in the community the custom of giving a turkey to 15 to 6-year-old girls as preparation for motherhood. One woman told her story: "My boyfriend's mother gave me a turkey when I turned 15. It was no ordinary gift. I knew it had special meaning, because some time after she gave it to me, she said: 'What happened to the turkey? Are you taking care of it?' I'm sure it was a way to see how I would take care of her grandchild. And yes, when I had my children, I thought that a turkey is fragile and demanding, like a baby."

Nahuas believe, as seen in the above description of how this bird is perceived in the community, that the turkey's characteristics and the care it needs closely resemble the care that a baby needs. In this sense, the belief is that raising a turkey simulates raising a human being. Thus, the idea implicit in this testimony is as follows: giving a girl a turkey to raise as a kind of mock baby serves to both *familiarize* her with the process of raising a human baby by rehearsing motherhood in the process of caring for one of these birds that cannot fend for themselves, and to carefully *assess* the caring abilities that she will employ in the future (Lorente Fernández, 2015).

As the facet of assessment in the LOPI model proposes, the Nahua stewardship system includes in this case a way to assess the girl's progress in learning about raising other living beings. Unlike the kind of assessment that takes place in schools or with conventional teaching, assessment does not involve giving prizes or praise; it serves a number of purposes: it measures the girl's spontaneous interest in the activity (as reflected in the question posed in the quote: "Are you taking care of it?"); it also assesses the girl's individual initiative in dealing with the activity of raising, despite the fact that it was the adult who deliberately provided her with the element of learning (the turkey). Furthermore, the test, which consists of raising the animal, is aimed at promoting learning as it helps the girl learn the skills of raising poultry and the related value of stewardship. It is assumed that learning will happen as the girl develops skills in response to her continued exposure to this "care receiver"—the turkey—in a pedagogical dynamic in which the animal does its part by way of tacit collaboration. The use of the turkey in the assessment of knowledge about "raising" works for the Nahuas because, while the activity calls for responsibility, it is a relatively minor responsibility, and should mistakes be made, the risks involved are less consequential than what the activity is preparing the girl for: raising a human baby. To conclude, in this kind of assessment, "grades" or praise like "good job!" or "well done!" are not the point, because the turkey's development in itself represents evident and unmistakable feedback for the girl.

Today, in the child generation (1995–2010), the transformation of their parents' occupation to wage-earning jobs—a consequence of more formal schooling—seems to have resulted in fewer farm animals in the home. The flocks of sheep and poultry are less common, although they still exist in about 40% of the families. The proportion of boys in the community who steward their own sheep is 23%, compared to 78% in their parent generation, although the 53% of the boys, who have no sheep at home, engage in a meaningful learning experience by taking care of their neighbors' flocks. As for taking care of farm birds, 56% of the girls still engage in this activity (82% of their mothers did). Thus, the practice of assuming responsibility persists into the present generation, following the same informal learning patterns described above.

In some families, the time demanded by formal schooling seems to have redistributed the children's activities. As a 40-year-old man explained: "I look after the animals, because my children, well, my son works and the girl goes to school, so they don't time for anything except showering, getting ready, and making their bed. They don't have to help me with the animals. My daughter used to go to secondary school in the afternoon and she'd help me take care of the chickens: feeding them giving them water." A woman added: "Now we look after the older people: me, my husband, or my daughter-in-law. The kids go to school and come home late; by that time the animals have already been fed or sent out into the hills." In these families, however, assuming responsibility as part of LOPI has not disappeared altogether since the children continue to look after animals, but to a more limited extent, in their free time or on weekends.

5.3 The Indigenous Practices of Stewardship Related to Bodily Health and Balance

In the community of San Jerónimo Amanalco there are different household practices related to family members' physical and spiritual health, which is a key concern for Nahuas. Many of them are associated with the *temazcal*, the pre-Columbian steam bath, a tradition related to preventing disease or recovering health.

In the parent generation (1970–1995), most houses had a *temazcal*, which consists of a tiny building where steam is generated and people crouch inside lashing themselves with medicinal plants. According to the interviews, 87% of the children, after observing the preparation and use of *temazcales* from the age of 2–3, began to collaborate at the age of 8–10 in the preparation of these baths. A 38-year-old women explained, remembering the time when she was 9 years old:

> *You learn as a girl because you see how the adults clean it and set the fire... My mother would tell me: 'Clean out the ashes!' She'd have me sweep inside the temazcal, and then fetch water for the bath. I'd set it inside in a bucket, then I'd go out into the yard to pick medicinal plants for rubbing and cleaning the patients' bodies. I'd fetch the firewood, I helped my mother with that too... Not to light it of course, because I could have burned myself... (38-year-old woman)*

Aside from participating collaboratively in preparing the steam bath, 11 to 12-year-old boys and girls gradually became involved in practices of assuming health-related responsibility that date back to pre-Columbian times and persist to this day: (1) helping the human body grow strong and mature, or (2) recovering temperature balance when it has been lost to an illness (López-Austin, 1980; Madsen, 1960; McKeever Furst, 1995; Sandstrom, 1991). These treatments sought either to prepare people to fulfill their respective roles or to return them to a state of health that would allow them to continue fulfilling their roles.

(1) The first type of practices of assuming responsibility can clearly be seen in the case of newborn babies. When a baby is born, its body is considered to be "moist" or "soft," analogous to tender vegetables full of water. For Nahuas the process of maturation begins with "losing moisture," "drying out," and "hardening"; only then can babies undertake their motor development. As a 32-year-old woman said: "Babies are tender and with the heat of the *temazcal* they dry out and harden; then they can walk and move better." The testimony expresses the value of assuming responsibility associated with health practices revolving around the *temazcal*: developing physically as a human being, attaining a mature body, and achieving mobility are not natural, autonomous processes; they must be fostered with external support from other people.

11 to 12-year-old children participate in these practices by accompanying adults: they hold babies in their arms, they rub them in the steam bath with the right plants, or they control the bathwater temperature to keep the baby from receiving too much heat or steam, and they wrap them with clothes when they come out of the *temazcal*. They also help the mother during the bath if necessary, bringing her recepticles, plants, or dry clothes from outside when they are needed. Coordination is established with body gestures and brief comments such as "It's too hot" or "I need more water."

Nevertheless, the activity involves a Nahua conception of assuming responsibility that children can grasp without words, as suggested by the LOPI model: they are present during the activity and correct their acts on the basis of the mother's indications. The observations, specific indications and coordinated adjustments during the task make it clear that the *temazcal* is being used to move the baby in the right direction of development and completion by: accumulating heat, drying out, hardening, becoming able to walk, etc. The practices contribute to babies' unfolding or development, to their advancing in life and their maturation toward an optimal state of development. This recalls the practices of assuming responsibility related to growing corn—tender and fragile first, hardened later, and dry at the end. The Nahuas themselves point out this equivalence: "We are born tender and green, and thanks to the care we get, we mature and gradually dry out, the way plants do," said one woman. In the case of older children, this idea of assuming responsibility understood as collaboration in development goes beyond the physical aspect of the "drying-out" process and can be seen in the social dimension: the child's conversion into a relation-oriented person which is the Nahua ideal. This is not an autonomous or self-directed process it is fostered and encouraged by people close to the child who urge him or her to develop the capacity to form reciprocal relationships and links of interdependence (Lorente Fernández, 2012).

(2) Another health-related stewardship practice revolving around the *temazcal* has to do with illnesses that arise from an imbalance in body temperature. This care is generally afforded to older people suffering

> from rheumatism or joint pain. Nahuas believe that old people tend to "go cold" and become weak because they "lose heat." In these cases the prescribed treatment is to eliminate the "cold" that has taken up residence in their body, and to "revitalize" them with "heat" from a steam bath. Assuming responsibility implies keeping old people healthy; even though they are seen as heading toward the end of their life, their well-being is fundamental both for family order and for effective fulfillment of the roles they are expected to play due to their age—for example, coordinating the preparation of offerings for the Day of the Dead, as will be shown below.
>
> The interviews showed that, along with caring for babies, 87% of the parent generation had taken part as children in these practices that call for assuming responsibility for older relatives' health. Eleven- to 12-year-old children collaborated with their parents by helping the old people get in and out of the *temazcal*, checking the temperature and amount of steam in the bathhouse, rubbing the different parts of the body with the right plants since the old people often cannot reach them. These practices involved a gender-based division of labor: the girls helped their mothers and other relatives to bathe the old women, while the boys did the same with the old men.

An examination of the interview transcripts shows that participation in *temazcal*-based health care involved the acquisition of a kind of knowledge that went beyond the technical aspect or practical skills. By the age of 12–13 children had heard, in the context of the steam baths, many comments and brief explanations from their parents regarding the Nahua conception of the body and the different kinds of care required depending on the person's age. Thus, as described in the LOPI model, by "picking up" information through their participation and listening in the context of the activity, they had acquired a substantial understanding of the Nahuas' ideas about the functioning of the human body by being there, "on the scene," with no recourse to systematic explanations, memorization, or verbalized questions and answers. The participatory learning that comes out of these practices of assuming responsibility enabled the parent generation to reproduce and preserve pre-Columbian forms of health care that contributed to the correct performance of people's social roles.

In the child generation (1995–2010), despite the material changes, the situation remains very similar. The number of *temazcales* has declined—perhaps only one in every six households has one, the space having been used for building—but fewer *temazcales* does not mean less use, as people often borrow their neighbors' baths. Mothers communicate by sending cell-phone messages from one house to another: "Do you want to use the *temazcal*?" "Could you lend me some firewood?" Moreover, *temazcal* use includes a social dimension: sometimes family members who live in different houses, or close neighbors, share one, generally following a gender-based pattern. Most children today take *temazcal* baths and help to prepare them, either in their own home or a neighbor's. As one 10-year-old boy said, referring to the *temazcal* that his aunt still has: "When they ask me, I go and help them gather firewood, pick medicinal plants and sometimes light the fire." The participation follows the same dynamic described in the case of their parents, including the acquisition of Nahua conceptions about the nature of the body. One 12-year-old girl explained:

> *The temazcal is used when a woman has a baby, because childbirth makes a woman 'go cold' and she must be warmed up so that she gets her strength back and can continue working. Babies also take a bath to gain strength, but just a quick one—they aren't left inside too long. I helped bathe my little brother when he was born.*

An 11-year-old girl said:

> *You give people a temazcal bath when their bones, feet or knees hurt because they 'go cold.' I know that the temazcal has a place where you put the firewood, and you put a bucket with water so that it boils and you throw in special plants—camphor and huejote (a kind of willow). My mother sends me out to pick them and I make branches to rub the bodies of old people. I helped to bathe and take care of my grandmother when she got 'cold' in her feet.*

Significantly, the time demanded by going to school has not diminished children's participation in this activity because it is usually done at night or on weekends. The interviews show that 82% of today's children over the age of 11 collaborate and have acquired a deep understanding of the need to intervene in the physical development of small babies and old people, to help them develop, mature, and maintain their health so that they can fulfill their family functions. The Indigenous practices of assuming responsibility related to the *temazcal* elicit in today's children a strong sense of initiative and self-motivation to participate, and highlight the strength of local cultural expectations as guidelines for the members of the new generation. This provides a clear example of the interconnection among the different facets of the LOPI model.

5.4 Participation in Family Ceremonial Life: Assuming Responsibility for the Souls of the Departed in the Day of the Dead Celebration

The celebration of the "Day of the Dead" is one of the main social events in the community of San Jerónimo Amanalco. According to Nahua belief, the souls of the dead visit the world of the living for only 2 days a year, the 1st and 2nd of November. The living relatives must then feed the dead in an act of reciprocity, as a sign of gratitude for the help the dead gave to the family when they were alive. It is also said that in exchange for the food, the souls help the family with good luck, success at work, fertility in the fields, health, and prosperity (Lorente Fernández, 2012; see also Gutiérrez, Rosengren, & Miller, 2015).

The villagers steward the dead by feeding them. The dead, it is believed, consume only the "smell" and "taste" of the food, and on their altars the living offer plates of food, drinks, and fruit with an especially pleasing aroma. The dead's favorite food and the main ingredient of the offering is a kind of decorated bread with an intense, sweet aroma; all the family members help to prepare it.

In the parent generation (1970–1995), 94% prepared altars for the Day of the Dead when they were children, and they gathered in the grandparents' home to make the bread. The 2 to 3-year-olds would simply watch carefully as they walked around the father, mother, siblings, and grandparents who were engaged in the activity. At the age of 3–4, they got pieces of dough from their parents and older siblings, who said nothing to them as a way to stimulate their participation. In this way, the small children began to get involved in the key phase of the process: shaping the dough to make figures out of bread. First the children would cut off and flatten pieces of dough with rollers, give them to their mothers, who would shape them and decorate them with figures of animals or dolls, in a way that highlighted collaboration and coordination. 4 to 7-year-olds would participate with greater and greater skill in this stage of the process, sometimes even taking the mother's place and completing both stages of the shaping of the dough: first flattening it and then shaping and decorating the figures. They tended to make smaller and more misshapen figures than their parents did, but they would be gathered up with the rest to be baked in the oven and subsequently offered on the altars with the same solemnity as the bread the adults made. The children would put great effort into making their bread, knowing it was not a game: the dead would also consume the aroma of their bread, and the children's effort would make a contribution to their own well-being as well as the family's. Up to the age of 8–10 there was no gender distinction in the children's activities. When the boys turned 10–12, their participation extended to the two most complex stages of bread making: first, measuring out the precise amount of ingredients for making the dough that would be shaped into the decorative figures, and the final stage: putting the finished figures into the oven.

Throughout the whole bread-making process, the parents and grandparents would narrate the dreams they had in the previous days. The Nahuas believe that the dreams people have in the days prior to setting up the altars are especially important because the dead appear in them and pass on messages to the living, explaining that they need hot food with enticing aromas, and warning that there will be punishments if their requests are not met. The dreams are always similar, and sometimes dreams told by other people are repeated. These narrations, seemingly disconnected from the technical aspects of bread making but integrated into the overall activity, and not addressed directly to the children, served as a collective explanation or justification of the reason for baking bread and offering it on the altar.

By listening to these narrations as their participation progressed through different activities as they grew up, the children acquired cosmological knowledge of a philosophical-abstract nature about the needs and requirements of the dead, as well as the idea of stewardship through food. They also acquired a conception of responsibility that went beyond the responsibility toward living relatives and included people they had never met but who still belonged to the family. The children also received an implicit motivation regarding the need to steward the dead—the punishments or nightmares that the dead could inflict on them if they felt neglected. A 31-year-old woman recalled what she did as an 11-year-old girl: "I would help my parents make the bread by shaping animal figures and decorating them. The bread smelled very good because it had sugar. It's very important to look after and feed the souls of the dead so that things go well for us, and so that they help us in our lives, and give us good health. If you don't feed them well, you can have nightmares afterward."

In the child generation (1995–2010), participation in the Day of the Dead and in bread making has changed little. According to the interviews, 89% of the children participate in the same way as described in the parent generation; it helps that the Day of the Dead festivities are school holidays and they can spend all their time on the celebration. Furthermore, participation in this activity is a source of great joy and investment of resources on the adults' part, which seems to persuade the children of the compelling need to contribute in order to join into the family's ritual life.

The children take part in the bread making and learn the activity motivated by a desire for belonging and the stimulus of performing as socially valued family members. There is a close relationship between motivation, collaboration, and coordination in the activity, three key aspects of the LOPI model (Rogoff, 2014). The motivation comes from recognizing the "real" contribution of their actions to the collective effort, and seeing their own bread placed as an offering on the altar. The idea of cooperation and unity are associated symbolically with the activity's effectiveness. Thus, a 10-year-old boy explained: "The bread is important because *we make it all together*; it is the *shared effort* that helps to take care of our dead." The percentage of interviewed children referred to above demonstrated a clear conception of the dead, their needs, how to take responsibility for their feeding, and the idea that their relatives, after dying, come back to the world of the living, making it necessary to offer them care and attention as an act of reciprocity.

The value of interdependence is key for the Nahuas and is associated with the system of stewardship and reciprocity: just as the living take care of the dead, the dead also take care of the living in a circular Indigenous conception that considers the mutual dependence among different beings in the cosmos as indispensable for producing and perpetuating life.

6. CONCLUSIONS

6.1 Social Organization of Stewardship Practices, and Its Relation with the Tradition of *Learning by Observing and Pitching In*

The four practices described here, while they might seem heterogeneous, share a significant feature: by participating in them, children put into practice the fulfillment of responsibility and learn the value of stewardship. These are practices that are organically interrelated in such as way that the values and ways of acting and assuming responsibility learned in any one of them tacitly complement—and facilitate participate in—the others. They are four meaningful activities in the community that form a pedagogical "constellation" (Rogoff et al., 2014), and in spite of their differences, a close examination reveals a number of common threads in the structure of the participation and the social organization of learning.

The four activities provide evidence of the interconnection of a number of facets of the LOPI model. Children first learn through observation, by being an observer on the side (because they have free run of the house, the yard, and the surrounding areas where their relatives live, for example), or immersed in the activity's context (because they are deliberately taken to the place where it occurs, such as the cornfield, or the grandparents' house to make bread). This initial observation comprises the years from birth to the age of 2–3, and allows children to learn how to participate: by looking at processes, gestures, sequences of movements and periodicities. Observing offers a basis for participating, but participating (around the age of 4–5) enables children to continue maturing and fine-tuning their observation, and diversifying their attention.

Observing while participating in the activity contributes to coordinating with others (see Mejía-Arauz, Correa-Chavez, Keyser Ohrt, and Aceves-Azuara, 2015)—while working in the cornfield, for example, or making bread for the Day of the Dead. Additionally, observing while participating enables children to adapt to the attitudes of the being who is receiving their care and for whom responsibility is being exercised.

Observation, however, does not mean only immediate attention to the action at hand; it is also "memory," or the capacity to "recall" and predict phases of the process that stretch over time (planting–harvesting, turkey eggs, etc.). The maturation of observation-memory skills coincides with children's involvement with the overall development of the entire activity, which occurs around the age of 10–11 in the four activities.

Children are self-motivated to act: they know that assuming responsibility is a key contribution to the family and a cultural value, and they look for a chance to participate. Adults seem to have a very clear idea of when, and where, children are ready to assume an important responsibility—the activity is important and mistakes bring with them economic losses, or children can do real damage to plants, animals, or other culturally relevant beings. After spending time and getting involved with other relatives, it is assumed that children are ready to steward with greater autonomy. This tends to happen around the age of 6. At this point, oral communication comes into play in the form of a request to take care of (cornfield, sheep, *temazcal*). Children receive the request and carry out the activity in question with considerable initiative (as has been also noted in other Mexican communities by Alcalá, Rogoff, Mejía-Arauz, Coppens, & Dexter, 2014).

Words and oral communication are used, starting with the initial request made by an adult, in three well-defined ways: (1) As specific instructions accompanying the activity. (2) As a kind of information that "emerges" during the spontaneous process among the adults and gives the children a chance to indirectly learn theoretical–philosophical knowledge about cosmology in the Nahua tradition (*milpa*, animals, *temazcal*, the dead); i.e., children listen or observe as "third parties" (Correa-Chávez & Rogoff, 2009; Good, 2001; Lorente Fernández, 2006) or as interlocutors who are seemingly uninvolved in the adults' conversation in the context of the activity. These comments are never disconnected from the activity being carried out, even though they might allude to similar cases, dreams, past experiences, stories, and they might include mythical knowledge or abstract spiritual knowledge that the children can pick up (Jordan, 1989; Merrill, 1988). And (3) words are also used as a kind of correction through scolding and showing, and making explicit, the calamitous consequences of negligence or distraction (raising animals, feeding the dead). In this particular way of communicating, however, verbal explanation is not used to give detailed lessons or to teach what stewardship is outside of the activity. This is a characteristic that distinguishes the learning of this Indigenous value from the formal transmission of knowledge that takes place in schools in the community that children attend every day and where they are exposed to a Western tradition of learning.

Even though practicing the value of stewardship is something that children desire, because they help their families, demonstrate socially valued skills and abilities, generate a benefit for others and contribute to the production of "life" by participating in the development of fulfillment of other beings, sometimes adults make a conscious effort to instill the desire to learn in children by stimulating their will with short pieces of advice or, in rare instances of disobedience or defiance of authority, by warning or scolding.

The different characteristics of children's learning through participation to assume responsibility that are analyzed above (the development of keen observation, children's self-motivation to contribute and become a useful member of the family, coordination with other participants combined with autonomy, specific oral communication during the activity including shared references, and the forms of assessment) are consistent with the tradition of *Learning by Observing and Pitching In to family and community endeavors* (Rogoff, 2014).

6.2 Continuities in a Context of Change: Learning and the Value of Stewardship in the Face of Increased Formal Schooling and Modernization

When the stewardship practices of the parent generation (1970–1995) are compared with those of the child generation (1995–2010), clear differences can be discerned. A very high percentage of the parents in their childhood participated in the four kind of activities described here, while their children participate less in the first two and in a high proportion in the last two. This situation leads to the question Why? What conditions have changed from one generation to the next to explain, at the same time, the change and the continuity? An in-depth analysis of the ethnographic observations and the content of the interviews offers some meaningful results regarding this historical–cultural process or dynamic.

The parent generation had a low level of formal schooling (5.8 years on average), i.e., their experience of this pedagogical system was limited. And their time in school was sprinkled with absences because their parents, who had received no formal schooling whatsoever, often took them out of school to take part in collaborative family activities. In this way, they participated without restrictions in *cuidado* practices.

The parent generation, whose learning took place primarily through observation and participation in family activities tied to cultural values of the Nahua tradition (respect as harmonious and mutual relations, reciprocity, helpfulness), came to give high esteem to formal schooling as a path to a better standard of living, to attain a higher social status, and to avoid the stigma assigned to their Indigenous heritage (to avoid being called "Indians," an insult that insinuates backwardness and ignorance; Bonfil Batalla, 1996; Frye, 1996; Lorente Fernández, 2012). As a result, the parent generation modified their conceptions of childhood education and transformed some practices for raising their children, looking to improve their prospects in life. They decided to orient their children's everyday activities around the school, defined as "their obligation," by saying: "Children need to study; otherwise they'll be the same or worse off than we are." To encourage their attendance, they "relieved" them of household chores and began to take charge themselves of the activities that their children used to do, as seen in the testimonies quoted above regarding the raising of farm animals ("Now it's us, the older people, who take care of that"). This promotion of schooling and release from household chores can be recognized in the following examples.

> *Q: Do the girls take charge of any activity around the house?*
> *A: They devote their time to studying more than anything else; if they have time, they help us with the tortillas; well, they play with the corn dough, or with their toy brooms they start sweeping. They help us in whatever they want to do. And we wash their clothes and do everything else. (32-year-old mother, with daughters age 7 and 9)*
> *Q: Do your daughters have any obligation to take care of farm animals?*

A: Not any more. In the morning they get ready to go to school. When they come back they pick up their things and do their homework. They focus on studying, and if they have any free time, I have them help me bring the chickens to the henhouse from the outside (37-year-old mother with daughters age 9 and 11).

Nevertheless, dedicating most of their time to school (where the educational program leads to a certain dissociation from the local social and cultural context because the curriculum does not recognize the community's Indigenous historical roots; Lorente Fernández, 2012), did not mean that the children utterly abandoned their participation in certain specific household activities. Parallel to school attendance, the parents facilitated the children's incorporation into culturally valued but not necessarily productive activities that belong to the more private and domestic sphere, i.e., they take place in the most intimate domain of the household and involve other family members in a dynamic involving strong emotions and sociability (stewardship of bodily health and preparation for the Day of the Dead, as opposed to stewardship of the cornfield and farm animals). These activities involve the pursuit of collective well-being and are valuable for the group's cultural reproduction at a profound level. While they happen sporadically at specific times and are not everyday activities, that does not make them any less meaningful, nor are they superficial in the children's experience.

Through the desired involvement, the learning in context, the adults' guidance, and the conversations they have among themselves during the activity, the children's active participation in the practices of assuming responsibility leads to the acquisition of a cultural value system rooted in a pre-Columbian Indigenous tradition. This value involves assisting the development of other living beings so that they can advance in their existence, perform their functions and play their assigned roles in society and the cosmos. It is necessary to convey affection to them, speak to them properly, look after their soul, and provide them with the right food in order to enable them to attain their realization and behave properly, within a conception that assumes that living beings maintain relations of reciprocity and interdependence among themselves and with their human caregivers. The care receiver in the long run gives thanks or favors to their human stewards by offering them help in different settings of their existence and contributing to the overall prosperity of the Nahua universe.

The children, persuaded by the intrinsic importance that adults assign to the activities that involve assuming responsibility, show initiative and eagerness to participate in them, as well as pride in the responsibilities that they assume; they get involved collaboratively in the awareness that the activities represent an important way to perform as family and community members. They also develop autonomy and an ability to transform the participation that leads to assuming greater and greater responsibilities by taking care of more fragile or complex beings. The interrelation of these aspects in learning to assume responsibilities directly links this participatory and pedagogical dynamic to the tradition of LOPI (Rogoff, 2014), which continues to be a living practice in the community.

Parents do not seem to perceive the contradiction or opposition between this participatory orientation in some stewardship practices and school attendance; on the contrary, they encourage them both as parallel, co-existing forms of social participation. They do not find conflicts or incompatibility between the two at a mental or conceptual level, and it helps that neither times nor schedules clash: school attendance is every day, while the other activities are not; when they occur, it is usually at night, in the afternoon or during school vacation, and children can remain home or at the most, head over to neighbors' houses. This double participation—school and collaboration—is considered appropriate by parents and allows the children to acquire an Indigenous value system of pre-Columbian origin and to preserve a profound intergenerational Nahua heritage in a context of Western schooling and without resorting to the Indigenous language (Frye, 1996; Lorente Fernández, 2012; Madsen, 1960; Magazine, 2011; Magazine & Ramírez, 2007).

This research has shown how four practices associated with assuming responsibilities have been transmitted to the children's generation and continue to be practiced today. They exist, however, to different degrees. When it comes to the stewardship of bodily health as it relates to assuming responsibility for human beings, and the practices associated with the stewardship of the dead, who are believed to help other beings from beyond the grave, children still participate widely, and engage in the informal, participatory kind of learning described above. The practices involved in growing corn and raising farm animals have declined in the current generation due to economic transformations, but they have not disappeared entirely and they do not seem to have diminished the value of assuming responsibility. Even though some children do not engage in them, they readily understand their Indigenous logic and transfer key aspects of this cultural value system that they have learned from other household activities: the ideas of helpfulness, mutual relations, reciprocity, and the Nahua conception of life as a "process" that implies the joint participation of different agents in the development of living beings.

The maintenance of the value of stewardship in the community of San Jerónimo Amanalco is perhaps representative of a more widespread situation in different regions of Mesoamerica, in which Indigenous practices live on despite the presence of seemingly conflicting institutions, such as Western-style schooling and certain government programs and policies, and the existence of generational changes (López et al., 2015; Mejía-Arauz et al., 2013; Paradise & De Haan, 2009; Rogoff et al., 2014; see also Dehouve, 2007). The inculturated appearance and loss of visible features of Indigenous identity, such as language and dress, merely conceal from the view of outside observers the vigorous roots of organically integrated Indigenous practices that continue to be reproduced through a process of *Learning by Observing and Pitching In to family and community endeavors* as a part of an ancient Indigenous heritage.

ACKNOWLEDGMENTS

I express my gratitude for the participation of the families, children, and schools of the village of San Jerónimo Amanalco. I would also like to thank the National Institute of Anthropology and History of Mexico for the financing granted as part of project n° 3186. Thanks to Barbara Rogoff, Maricela Correa-Chávez, and Rebeca Mejía-Arauz for their comments on an earlier version of this chapter, and to Ana Delgado Rodríguez for her reading and editorial suggestions. Funding for the writing of this chapter came from the National Science Foundation (0837898).

REFERENCES

Alcalá, L., Rogoff, B., Mejía-Arauz, R., Coppens, A., & Dexter, A. L. (2014). Children's initiative in contributions to family work in Indigenous-heritage and Cosmopolitan Communities in Mexico. *Human Development*, *57*, 96–115.

Bolin, I. (2006). *Growing up in a culture of respect*. Austin: University of Texas Press.

Bonfil Batalla, G. (1996 [1987]). *Mexico profundo: Reclaiming a civilization*. Austin: University of Texas Press.

Chamoux, M. N. (1992). *Trabajo, técnicas y aprendizaje en el México indígena*. México: Centro de Investigaciones y Estudios Superiores en Antropología Social, Centro de Estudios Mexicanos y Centroamericanos.

Chamoux, M. N. (2011). Persona, animacidad, fuerza. In P. Pitrou, M. C. Valverde Valdés, & J. Neurath (Eds.), *La noción de vida en Mesoamérica* (pp. 155–180). México: Universidad Nacional Autónoma de México, Centro de Estudios Mexicanos y Centroamericanos.

Chamoux, M.-N. (2015). Conceptions of Educational Practices among the Nahuas of Mexico: Past and present. *Advances in Child Development and Behavior*, *49*, 253–271.

Codex Mendoza, Aztec Manuscript. (1978). *Commentaries by Kurt Ross. Miller Graphics*. Spain: Productions Liber, S. A. CH-Fribourg.

Correa-Chávez, M., & Rogoff, B. (2009). Children's attention to interactions directed to others: Guatemalan Mayan and European American patterns. *Developmental Psychology*, *45*, 630–641.

Dehouve, D. (2007). *La ofrenda sacrificial entre los tlapanecos de Guerrero*. México: Plaza y Valdés, Instituto Nacional de Antropología e Historia.

Fortes, M. (1970 [1938]). Social and psychological aspects of education in Taleland. In M. Fortes (Ed.), *Time and social structure* (pp. 201–259). New York: University of London, The Athlone Press.
Frye, D. (1996). *Indians into Mexicans: History and identity in a Mexican town*. Austin: University of Texas Press.
Gamio, M. (1982 [1916]). *Forjando patria*. Porrúa: México.
Gaskins, S. (1999). Children's daily lives in a Mayan village: A case study of culturally constructed roles and activities. In A. Göncü (Ed.), *Children's engagement in the world: Sociocultural perspectives* (pp. 25–62). New York: Cambridge University Press.
Good, C. (2001). El ritual y la reproducción de la cultura: Ceremonias agrícolas, los muertos y la expresión estética entre los nahuas de Guerrero. In J. Broda & F. Báez-Jorge (Eds.), *Cosmovisión, ritual e identidad de los pueblos indígenas de México* (pp. 239–297). México: Conaculta, Fondo de Cultura Económica.
Good, C. (2005). Ejes conceptuales entre los nahuas de Guerrero: Expresión de un modelo fenomenológico mesoamericano. *Estudios de Cultura Nahuatl*, *36*, 87–113.
Good, C. (2011). Una teoría náhuatl del trabajo y la fuerza: Sus implicaciones para el concepto de la persona y la noción de la vida. In P. Pitrou, M. C. Valverde Valdés, & J. Neurath (Eds.), *La noción de vida en Mesoamérica* (pp. 181–203). México: Universidad Nacional Autónoma de México, Centro de Estudios Mexicanos y Centroamericanos.
Gutiérrez, K., & Rogoff, B. (2003). Cultural ways of learning: Individual traits or repertories of practice. *Educational Researcher*, *32*, 19–25.
Gutiérrez, I. T., Rosengren, K. S., & Miller, P. J. (2015). *Día de los Muertos*: Learning About Death Through Observing and Pitching. In *Advances in Child Development and Behavior*.
INEGI (Instituto Nacional de Estadística, Geografía e Informática). (2011). *Catálogo de localidades*. Retrieved from http://www.microrregiones.gob.mx/catloc/contenido.aspx?refnac=150990024.
Jordan, B. (1989). Cosmopolitical obstetrics: Some insights from the training of traditional midwives. *Social Science and Medicine*, *28*(9), 925–944.
Karttunen, F. (1992). *An analytical dictionary of Nahuatl*. Norman: University of Oklahoma Press.
Lewis, O. (1960). *Tepoztlan, village in Mexico*. New York: Holt, Rinehart & Winston.
López, A., Ruvalcaba, O., & Rogoff, B. (2015). Attentive helping as a cultural practice of Mexican-Heritage families. In Y. M. Caldera & E. M. Lindsey (Eds.), *Mexican American children and families: Multidisciplinary perspectives* (pp. 76–91). New York: Routledge.
López-Austin, A. (1980). *The human body and ideology: Concepts of the ancient Nahuas: Vol. I* Salt Lake City: University of Utah Press.
Lorente Fernández, D. (2006). Infancia nahua y transmisión de la cosmovisión: Los *ahuaques* o espíritus pluviales en la Sierra de Texcoco (México). *Boletín de Antropología Universidad de Antioquia*, *20*(37), 152–168.
Lorente Fernández, D. (2011). *La razzia cósmica: Una concepción nahua sobre el clima. Deidades del agua y graniceros en la Sierra de Texcoco*. México: Centro de Investigaciones y Estudios Superiores en Antropología Social, Universidad Iberoamericana.
Lorente Fernández, D. (2012). 'Ser respetuoso es ser persona': El niño y la pedagogía moral de los nahuas del centro de México. *Revista de Dialectología y Tradiciones Populares*, *67*(2), 431–452.
Lorente Fernández, D. (2015). Una etnografía del guajolote: de su crianza humanizada a la personificación ritual en la Sierra de Texcoco. *Scripta Ethnologica*, *37*. in press.
Madsen, W. (1960). *The Virgin's children. Life in an Aztec village today*. Austin: University of Texas Press.
Magazine, R. (2011). 'We All Put on the Fiesta Together': Interdependence and the production of active subjectivity through cargos in a highland Mexican village. *Journal of Latin American and Caribbean Anthropology*, *16*(2), 296–314.
Magazine, R., & Ramírez, M. A. (2007). Continuity and change in san Pedro Tlalcuapan, Mexico: Childhood, social reproduction, and transnational migration. In J. Cole &

D. Durham (Eds.), *Generations and Globalization: Family, Youth and Age in the New World Economy* (pp. 52–73). Bloomington: Indiana University Press.
McKeever Furst, J. L. (1995). *The natural history of the soul in ancient Mexico*. New Haven: Yale University Press.
Mead, M. (1963). Socialization and enculturation. *Current Anthropology*, *4*(2), 184–188.
Mejía-Arauz, R., Correa-Chávez, M., Keyser Ohrt, U., & Aceves-Azuara, I. (2015). Collaborative work or individual chores: The role of family social organization in children's learning to collaborate and develop initiative. *Advances in Child Development and Behavior*, *49*, 25–51.
Mejía-Arauz, R., Keyser Ohrt, U., & Correa-Chávez, M. (2013). Transformaciones culturales y generacionales en la participación colaborativa de niñas y niños de una comunidad p'urhépecha. *Revista Mexicana de Investigación Educativa*, *18*(59), 1019–1045.
Merrill, W. L. (1988). *Raramuri souls: Knowledge and social process in Northern Mexico*. Washington, D.C.: Smithsonian Institution Press.
Molina, F. A. d. (2004 [1571]). *Vocabulario en lengua castellana y mexicana y mexicana y castellana*. México: Porrúa.
Monaghan, J. (1995). *The covenants with earth and rain: Exchange, sacrifice, and revelation in Mixtec sociality*. Norman: University of Oklahoma Press.
Paradise, R. (1996). Passivity or tacit collaboration: Mazahua interaction in cultural context. *Learning and Instruction*, *6*(4), 379–389.
Paradise, R. (2002). Finding ways to study culture in context. *Human Development*, *45*(4), 229–236.
Paradise, R., & De Haan, M. (2009). Responsibility and reciprocity: Social organization of Mazahua learning practices. *Anthropology & Education Quarterly*, *40*(2), 187–204.
Paradise, R., & Rogoff, B. (2009). Side by side. *Ethos*, *37*, 102–138.
Pitrou, P. (2014). Life as a process of making in the Mixe Highlands (Oaxaca, Mexico): Towards a 'general pragmatics' of life. *Journal of the Royal Anthropological Institute*, *21*(1), 86–105.
Rogoff, B. (2014). Learning by observing and pitching in to family and community endeavors: An orientation. *Human Development*, *57*, 69–81.
Rogoff, B., Moore, L., Najafi, B., Dexter, A., Correa-Chávez, M., & Solís, J. (2007). Children's development of cultural repertories through participation in everyday routines and practices. In J. E. Grusec & P. D. Hastings (Eds.), *Handbook of Socialization* (pp. 490–515). New York: Guilford.
Rogoff, B., Najafi, B., & Mejía-Arauz, R. (2014). Constellations of cultural practices across generations: Indigenous American heritage and learning by observing and pitching in. *Human Development*, *57*, 82–95.
Rogoff, B., Paradise, R., Mejía-Arauz, R., Correa-Chávez, M., & Angelillo, C. (2003). Firsthand learning through intent participation. *Annual Review of Psychology*, *54*, 175–203.
Sahagún, F. B. d. (1969). *Florentine Codex: General history of the things of New Spain. Book 6: Rhetoric and moral philosophy*. Translated from the Aztec original into English by A. J. O. Anderson and C. E. Dibble, Santa Fe, New Mexico: School of American Research and University of Utah.
Sandstrom, A. R. (1991). *Corn is our blood: Culture and ethnic identity in a contemporary Aztec Indian village*. Norman: University of Oklahoma Press.
Sandstrom, A. R. (2009). The weeping baby and the Nahua corn spirit. The human body as key symbol in the Huasteca Veracruzana, Mexico. In C. T. Halperin, K. A. Faust, R. Taube, & A. Giguet (Eds.), *Mesoamerican figurines*. Florida: University Press of Florida.
Secretaría de Educación Pública (SEP). (2013). Censo de escuelas, maestros y alumnos de educación básica y especial. Atlas Educativo. Retrieved from http://www.cemabe.inegi.org.mx.
Taggart, J. (1983). *Nahuat myth and social structure*. Austin: Texas University Press.
Taggart, J. (2007). *Remembering victoria. A tragic Nahuat love story*. Austin: University of Texas Press.

CHAPTER FOUR

Supporting Children's Initiative: Appreciating Family Contributions or Paying Children for Chores

Andrew D. Coppens*[,1], Lucía Alcalá[†]
*Department of Education, University of New Hampshire, Durham, New Hampshire, USA
[†]Departamento de Cultura y Educación, Universidad Intercultural Maya, de Quintana Roo, Mexico
[1]Corresponding author: e-mail address: andrew.coppens@unh.edu

Contents

Abstract

Collaborative initiative is an important aspect of *Learning by Observing and Pitching In* (*LOPI*), and many interrelated family and community practices in *LOPI* may support children's initiative. In this chapter, we examine two cultural ways of supporting children's helpfulness and responsibility that draw on different cultural paradigms for organizing children's participation in everyday work in U.S. Mexican-heritage and European American communities. European American university students reported having received allowances as a contractual enticement to do assigned chores. In contrast, although U.S. Mexican-heritage university students reported having received pocket

Advances in Child Development and Behavior, Volume 49
ISSN 0065-2407
http://dx.doi.org/10.1016/bs.acdb.2015.10.002

money from their families, this was as a gift, noncontingent on completed chores or good behavior. They reported that this noncontingent support for children's responsibility focuses children on collaborating with the family, and contributing to shared work with initiative, consistent with *LOPI*, in which children are integrated in family and community endeavors and are eager to contribute. The chapter challenges traditional dichotomies in motivational theory that attempt to specify the "source" of children's motivation to learn and help within either individuals or social contexts.

1. INTRODUCTION

In this chapter, we examine a cultural paradigm in which children's collaborative initiative may be supported, in part, by allowing children to contribute to family endeavors, without compelling them by means of contingent rewards to do chores. In this paradigm, adults occasionally give children gifts, not to incentivize children's compliance with assigned responsibilities, but to share resources and show appreciation of children's generally responsible roles as contributors with others in family and community work.

We examined families' use of noncontingent gifts in relation to a paradigm of organizing children's learning and participation in everyday work that emphasizes children's integration in mature family and community endeavors, called *Learning by Observing and Pitching In* (*LOPI*; Rogoff, 2014; Rogoff, Moore, Correa-Chávez, & Dexter, 2015). *LOPI* ways of involving children in mature endeavors include flexible leadership and shared responsibilities between adults and children and trust regarding children's ability and motivation to accomplish goals and activities of shared importance to the child, family, and community. Children's learning is facilitated by their access and keen attention to ongoing work, and children undertake efforts to collaboratively advance family endeavors with initiative.

Noncontingent support for children's collaborative initiative in *LOPI* contrasts with a cultural paradigm that is characterized by children's segregation from mature productive work. In this paradigm, common in many middle-class communities (Morelli, Rogoff, & Angelillo, 2003; Rogoff et al., 2014), adults appear to use contractually negotiated rewards and payment to incentivize and control children's contributions in activities in which children are not already taking part (Alcalá, Rogoff, Mejía-Arauz, Coppens, & Dexter, 2014).

In the following sections, we first review aspects of the *LOPI* paradigm that may support children's collaborative initiative in making responsible contributions to family and community endeavors. Specifically, we examine giving children *domingos*, a practice in some Mexican communities where families give noncontingent gifts to children, often on Sunday (*domingo*) when the family gathers, generally appreciating their roles in the family and sharing available resources. We argue that giving gifts noncontingently, as in *domingos*, fits with the kinds of support for children's collaborative initiative that *LOPI* describes.

To help explain the relation between *domingos* and *LOPI*, we then examine contrasting approaches in middle-class communities, where children's contributions are rarely made with initiative and where children are commonly involved in everyday work mostly under contractual arrangements emphasizing contingencies. Although many studies note the difficulties of middle-class parents in inducing their children to help at home (see Goodnow, 1988; Montemayor, 1983; Ochs & Kremer-Sadlik, 2013), middle-class cultural practices using contingency and contracts to induce children's compliance are not central areas of focus in much of this research. We noticed this paradigm of contingency in our previous work with middle-class Mexican families, which was made visible by the contrasting reports of Mexican mothers from a nearby community with Indigenous history, who instead emphasized collaborative initiative in children's extensive and voluntary help at home and occasionally mentioned the use of *domingos* (Alcalá et al., 2014).

Overall, the present chapter explores the contrast between using contingent, contractual inducements for compliance in attempts to encourage children's help versus including children as contributors in shared family work, and providing occasional noncontingent gifts that appreciate children's collaborative involvement. We report our interviews with U.S. Mexican-heritage and European American college students regarding the use of *domingos* versus contingent allowances, and the students' speculations regarding developmental benefits of these cultural practices for children's development of responsibility and helpfulness at home.

2. ASPECTS OF *LEARNING BY OBSERVING AND PITCHING IN (LOPI)* SUPPORTING CHILDREN'S COLLABORATIVE INITIATIVE

Key aspects of the *LOPI* model may support children's collaborative initiative. These include children's integration as meaningful contributors in mature endeavors, adult support for children's autonomy in finding ways to be helpful, and cultural values and expectations that guide children toward responsibly contributing without assignments or payments for helping. Each of these aspects is examined below.

2.1 Children's Integration and Initiative in Mature Family and Community Endeavors

Children's collaborative initiative may be supported by their integration in mature family and community endeavors in many Indigenous and Indigenous-heritage communities of the Americas (Morelli et al., 2003; Paradise & Rogoff, 2009; Rogoff, 2003, 2014). Many children in these communities are allowed to participate in the full range of productive work, including household work, sibling and child caregiving, and parents' paid jobs (Alcalá et al., 2014; Coppens, Alcalá, Mejía-Arauz, & Rogoff, 2014, 2015), and their participation is allowed even before they are fully competent (Urrieta, 2013). Children's extensive contributions with others in productive endeavors of shared importance to their families and communities have been widely reported in numerous ethnographic studies, summarized in various articles on *LOPI* (e.g., Paradise & Rogoff, 2009; Rogoff, 2003; Rogoff et al., 2015).

Our previous work has brought to the fore the voluntary nature of these children's extensive contributions to household work. In many Mexican and Mexican-heritage communities where children are integrated as contributing members in family and community endeavors, they regularly notice work that needs to be done and take initiative to help, sometimes independently taking on work that benefits the family, as a regular responsibility. For example, children in an Indigenous-heritage community of México made extensive, complex household work contributions for the benefit of the whole family, helping and collaborating under their own initiative (Alcalá et al., 2014; Coppens, Alcalá, et al., 2014; Coppens et al., 2015). Mothers in this community stressed that children's collaborative contributions were rooted in children's desire to be helpful—children's helpfulness was "born within them" ("*les nace*," Coppens et al., 2015). In this and other Indigenous communities of the Americas, children's agency and autonomy are commonly valued and supported (Martínez-Pérez, 2014, 2015/this volume; Paradise & de Haan, 2009; Paradise & Rogoff, 2009). Children developing the ability to "see" and to "hear, listen to it" are considered central aspects of children's development in some Maya communities in México, where parents see an intelligent child as one who has developed observational skills and is responsible and respectful (Cervera Montejano, in press; Chavajay, 1993).

Adults or older children are also attentive to children's interests in helping, and support children's involvement by "helping the child to help" (Coppens & Rogoff, in preparation; Gaskins, 1999), with the shared goal of completing the task (Martínez-Pérez, 2014). These parents also emphasize that children cannot be forced to help and to be attentive. The child needs to first show eagerness to collaborate, and then parents and community members guide and support their initiative in making a contribution.

2.2 Parents Support Children's Autonomous Helping and Avoid Controlling Children's Involvement

The noncontingent and noncoercive aspect of many Indigenous-heritage Mexican children's initiative in helping the family is consistent with the *LOPI* paradigm, where children's autonomy is central—children's help is expected, as it is expected from any other family member, but not obligated. The motivation to contribute may be closely related to children working toward a common goal that benefits the family and/or community (Alcalá et al., 2014; Coppens, Alcalá, et al., 2014; Mejía-Arauz, Correa-Chávez, Keyser Ohrt, & Acevez-Azuara, 2015/this volume; Paradise, 2005; Pelletier, 1970).

In several Mexican Maya communities, mothers voiced the view that the learning process cannot be imposed on a child, but it can be supported. They responded to researchers' requests for their child's participation in research by saying, "it is up to them." Mothers emphasized the importance of children's will to participate, over their own wishes, and children's decisions were respected even for activities that mothers might not approve of (e.g., bird catching, Jiménez, 2012; see also Cervera Montejano, in press; de Haan, 1999). Tzotzil Mayan 2-year-olds are allowed to regulate the pace, timing, and organization of their help and participation in various activities, such as helping mom make tortillas or *desgranar maiz* [thresh corn] to feed the family animals (Martínez-Pérez, 2014). Mothers or older siblings support young children's initiative using gestures, verbal instructions, and modeling the task, to help the 2-year-olds to learn to make a productive contribution. Work in this community was rarely done individually; other members are regularly present and children are allowed and trusted to make decisions regarding their own activities and interests. Mothers assume that children are learning and developing the understanding of the social and material world around them (see also Mejía-Arauz et al., 2015/this volume).

In two studies, each asking whether children helping without being asked was important for children's development, many Indigenous-heritage Mexican mothers and U.S. Mexican-heritage mothers reported that children's contributions should not be forced; help should come from "within" the child (Alcalá & Rogoff, in preparation; Coppens & Rogoff, in preparation). For example, one U.S. Mexican-heritage mother responded,

> *It is important because that way, one knows that helping is coming from them and that there's no need to be telling them, 'Take the trash out, mop, clean.' And that they by themselves are starting to help. Alcalá and Rogoff (in preparation)*

Another stated,

> *For me, it is very important... to help, spontaneously help with something. There are kids that don't do that. I am very pleased that when we go to México, that my daughter pitches in. She helps my mom clean her house, clean the bathroom, sweep, and I like that they see how they can help. Alcalá and Rogoff (in preparation)*

Interestingly, children from Indigenous-heritage Mexican families also agreed that helping the family without being asked is important (Coppens, Alcalá, et al., 2014). For example, a 9-year-old child in an Indigenous-heritage Mexican community playfully explained that contributing without initiative is not that helpful:

> *Child: Their mom washes their clothes for them, washes... the dishes... it's just like my sister [laughs].*
> *Interviewer: So, you think it's bad that their mom washes their clothes for them?*
> *Child: Yeah, it's just like my sister... [continues laughing] they have to tell her what to do. Coppens, Alcalá, et al. (2014, p. 120)*

With children of younger ages, U.S. Mexican-heritage mothers also emphasized autonomy as a support for children learning to collaborate with others and contribute with initiative in productive family endeavors. Almost all (90%) of U.S. Mexican-heritage mothers with a 2- to 3-year old or a 6- to 7-year old reported involving children collaboratively in shared work at home and emphasized supporting children's initiative by *not obliging or insisting* on their contributions (Coppens & Rogoff, in preparation). This collaborative, autonomy-supportive approach was rare among middle-class European American mothers of young children, who either avoided children's involvement in everyday work at home altogether (especially at age 2–3) or controlled children's involvement with assigned tasks (Coppens & Rogoff, in preparation). Many middle-class European American mothers, when interviewed about children helping without being asked, did not see children helping without being asked as important or reacted that it is unrealistic. For example,

I like that! [laughs] It's nice when it happens and yet I try to remind myself that when you're 8 years old or 11 years old, you're in your own world and not thinking, 'Oh, mommy needs help right now.' Alcalá and Rogoff (in preparation)

Not at this age [3]. That would be miraculous. It has happened, and I was like, 'Oh my gosh! You cleaned that up, that's amazing!'... At 3, I'm not really expecting it. Don't they have like an immature prefrontal cortex or something, and they cannot plan ahead. I don't know. Coppens and Rogoff (in preparation)

2.3 Cultural Values and Expectations That Emphasize Children Helping Without Being Asked

Many Mexican-heritage families support children's collaborative initiative in contributing to family and community endeavors by encouraging them to be *acomedida/o*. A child that is *acomedida/o* is attentive to the needs of others, identifies when help is needed, and helps voluntarily and spontaneously (see López, Rogoff, Najafi, & Mejía-Arauz, 2012; López et al., 2015).

The cultural value of being *acomedida/o* fits with aspects of *LOPI* and may guide how many Mexican-heritage children take initiative to help in work at home. As children are integrated into community activities, they have opportunities to be attentive and to pitch in when appropriate. Being *acomedida/o* requires initiative on the part of the person trying to help, "not waiting to be asked to help, but taking the initiative to do it" (López et al., 2015, p. 82). Mexican-heritage parents described being *acomedida/o* as a "very complex process, you almost have to guess what others are thinking. Being alert; always being ready to do what is needed" (p. 82).

Encouraging children to be *acomedida/o* is expecting that children are more than just helpful: "If one is obliged to help, help will not be given in a generous spirit. But [being *acomedida/o*] has to be more voluntary, it needs to emerge from oneself" (López et al., 2015, p.81). This cultural value elevates what is expected of helpfulness beyond simply doing requested or assigned tasks. In general, Mexican-heritage mothers found little merit in children helping only when asked (Alcalá et al., 2014). These mothers held the view that encouraging children's help with motivational incentives discouraged children from *voluntarily* attending to ongoing work to find ways to be helpful. For children to help under their own initiative, awareness that help is needed is required, which seems to develop from children's meaningful integration in shared family and community endeavors.

In summary, supports for children's initiative in *LOPI* may include children's integration in the full range of family and community activities, values and practices guiding children toward being *acomedida/o*, and the avoidance of attempts to control children's involvement by incentivizing compliance.

We explore *domingos* as a practice that makes clear the noncontingent, noncontractual way that *LOPI* supports children's involvement and initiative in family and community endeavors in many Indigenous and Indigenous-heritage Mexican communities.

3. ATTEMPTS TO CONTROL CHILDREN'S COMPLIANCE IN DIVIDED AND ASSIGNED FAMILY WORK

Many middle-class families may attempt to control children's compliance in completing assigned chores through contingent incentives. In this approach, the assignment of work creates (and/or reflects) principles of "ownership" regarding who is assumed to be responsibility for that work. Chore assignments based on "ownership" create a contractual relationship between parents and children, and if-then negotiations may be used to incentivize children's compliance with doing "their own" assigned work. These ways of organizing and motivating children's involvement in everyday work may undermine children's initiative and narrowly delimit the range of their involvement. This approach represents a paradigm of childhood and family life that contrasts with the *LOPI* model; it is characterized by children's segregation from mature family and community endeavors, where adults and children work from contrasting agendas (Rogoff et al., 2014).

Our previous work found that children in middle-class communities in México and the United States made minimal contributions to work that benefitted the family as a whole, and children seldom helped without having their involvement assigned to them. Even in self-focused tasks (which contrast with shared family work in that they pertain to the child's own things and spaces and only benefit the child), requests and assignments for children's help often required contingent consequences for compliance (Alcalá et al., 2014; Coppens, Alcalá, et al., 2014; Coppens et al., 2015; Coppens & Rogoff, in preparation). This pattern is similar in numerous middle-class communities and appears to be related to a paradigm of divided, individualized work between adults and children (Goodnow, 1996; Goodnow & Delaney, 1989; Klein & Goodwin, 2013; Klein, Graesch, & Izquierdo, 2009; Ochs & Kremer-Sadlik, 2013). Ochs and Izquierdo (2009) note that among the 30 U.S. middle-class families that they observed extensively, no child routinely assumed responsibility for household tasks without effortful appeals by parents for help, and children contributed little to the practical running of the household.

Implicit or explicit rules and assigned work distributions may delimit children's responsibilities in ways that segregate their involvement from other contributors, and may relate to children's minimal contributions and initiative. This divided, individualized way of understanding and delegating responsibilities may nonetheless be understood normatively as "working as a team" in middle-class families (Coppens, Alcalá, et al., 2014). Middle-class Mexican children and parents often divided family work according to implicit rules such as "*a cada quien lo suyo*" ["to each their own" work] (see also Warton & Goodnow, 1991), and middle-class Mexican mothers endorsed these "fairness" rules spontaneously in their reports of children's contributions (Coppens et al., 2015).

A form of controlling children's involvement is for parents to take on roles that focus on motivating children to do the household work that they assign (see Coppens & Rogoff, in preparation). Many middle-class parents incentivize children's completion of assigned household work with contingent rewards, such as receiving an allowance (Alcalá et al., 2014). Around half to three-quarters of children in middle-class European-heritage communities receive an allowance on a regular basis. For example, 74% of U.S. ninth graders (Mortimer, Dennehy, Lee, & Finch, 1994), approximately 60% of Australian children (Feather, 1991), and more than 75% of Canadian children received allowances (Kerr & Cheadle, 1997). In a recent U.S. market research study of over 1000 families with an 8- to 14-year-old child (about 3/4 were middle-class European-heritage), 70% of children received a regular allowance (T. Rowe Price, 2015). In some middle-class families, children are paid an additional amount to do extra jobs around the house (Warton & Goodnow, 1995).

Contingent chores may be central to how many middle-class children get allowances and may relate to implicit rules that govern how many middle-class families distribute and enforce household responsibilities. It seems pertinent to point out that parental chore assignments involving implicit ideas about the ownership and contractual division of responsibilities are, in principle, no less contingent than negotiating payment for children's help with a one-time "extra" job. Money is tied to work done, to earning it. Interestingly, we are aware of at least one patent filed for "chore charts" described as "a device and process for modifying behavior of children," where assigned chores and good behaviors are each given a specific dollar amount to be paid to children (U.S. Patent No. 5,573,404, 1996). Smartphone/tablet mobile applications are also numerous and widely available for parents to "get kids to do their chores" (Coppens & Rogoff, 2014), with contingent payment as a central feature of most of them.

4. *DOMINGOS* AS PART OF *LOPI*, A PARADIGM SUPPORTING CHILDREN'S COLLABORATIVE INITIATIVE

Domingos, and *LOPI*, contrast with approaches to organizing children's involvement in everyday family and community work where contingencies divide family roles into those responsible for assigning children's work and motivating their contributions, and those who are asked to execute proscribed tasks in individual domains.

The concept of "fairness" is one example of a difference between the *LOPI* paradigm and other cultural approaches that emphasize children's involvement in divided, individual endeavors. In an Indigenous-heritage community of Guadalajara, mothers viewed "fairness" rules—implicit contingent agreements about who should be responsible for doing what in the home (Goodnow, 1998)—as threatening to children's autonomy in shared family endeavors. Almost half of these mothers explicitly protested interview questions containing this "fairness" idea, and instead emphasized children's initiative and autonomy in helping and contributing (Coppens et al., 2015).

Very limited evidence exists on the prevalence of *domingos*. In prior work where children in an Indigenous-heritage community of México made extensive family household work contributions largely under their own initiative, children were often reported to receive *domingos* that explicitly were not contingent on chore completion. Instead, mothers reported giving *domingos* to children as a way to share the family's resources, similar to a birthday or Christmas present (Alcalá et al., 2014; Coppens, Alcalá, et al., 2014; Coppens et al., 2015).

Although *domingos* appear to be especially common in some regions of México, the cultural values that undergird *domingos* may more widespread among Indigenous American communities. For example, in the Yucatan Peninsula, children are commonly given a *gastada*—pocket money for a treat during or after school—that is not contingent on children's chores, behavior, or school performance (Jiménez, personal communication). These children are often given small, noncontingent amounts of money based on family economic resources, and they are just expected to help at home, unrelated to the *gastada*.

Domingos might connect to *cargo* systems of reciprocal networks of exchange that are characteristic of Indigenous communities of Mesoamerica (Topete Lara & Díaz Araya, 2014). In these systems, exchange is based on "giving and receiving, asking and providing" (Velázquez Galdino, 2014), and the act of soliciting goods or services involves no implicit contingency. When a request is attended to and provided (partially or entirely), a system of *cargo* and reciprocity draws from and helps to reinforce a community network that guarantees the provision. Brayboy (2013) explains the crucial difference between this kind of reciprocity, which appears related to how *domingos* fit with *LOPI*, and Western notions of economic give-and-take:

> *Reciprocity here is not... simply a quid pro quo. It is more deeply rooted in the nature of relationships and responsibility because it calls for those who have something to give, to do so willingly and without an expectation that they will receive something monetary in return. Those individuals give, because they can and because they are responsible for maintaining their relationships with the peoples and places around them (p. 8)*

In a Nahua community of México, children's part in reciprocal systems of family relationships relates to the expectation that children help with household work in their immediate and extended family, and often with other community members (Ramírez Sánchez, 2007). This expectation continues until they marry and leave the house, at which point parents provide the newlyweds with a small property and some resources so they can establish their own family, which allows for the parents to be cared in old age by their children.

This widespread ethos of reciprocity—or *cosmovisión* of circulating productive energy (Good Eshelman, 2005)—is central to social relations in many Indigenous communities of México and suggests understanding *domingos* as a cultural practice that helps to build long-term relationships and strengthens the community as a whole. Children's family contributions are regarded as the basis for learning to engage in these kinds of reciprocal interactions in the community and as conducive to the preservation of important cultural values (Corona Caraveo & Pérez, 2007; Good Eshelman, 2005; Ramírez Sánchez, 2007; Urrieta, 2013).

Next, we present findings regarding how U.S. Mexican-heritage and European American university students describe *domingos* and allowances in relation to children helping at home, as well as how they describe the potential developmental benefits of these two contrasting practices.

5. USE OF *DOMINGOS* VERSUS ALLOWANCES IN RELATION TO CHILDREN'S HELP AT HOME

Our prior work suggests that the cultural practices of giving *domingos* versus allowances relate to children's initiative in work at home. The present chapter extends those observations with analyses and data that connect family pocket giving practices to a model of learning described as *LOPI.* We examine the relation of those monetary practices to cultural values regarding adult–child relations as being based on mutuality and reciprocity versus being based on controlling children's participation.

5.1 Cultural Differences in Giving Children Domingos Versus Allowances

We interviewed U.S. college students of European American and Mexican-heritage backgrounds about their childhood experience of receiving an allowance or a *domingo*, and what their views were on these practices. Drawing on these data and existing literature (note that none existed regarding *domingos*), we defined these two practices as follows:

Allowances: Money or gifts (including privileges and outings) regularly and contractually given to a child, contingent on doing chores, getting good grades, or behaving well. It is pay for those things, or those things come with "strings attached".

Domingos: Noncontingent money or gifts given to the child regularly by any family member (usually by adults and on Sundays) emphasizing family togetherness and appreciation of the child's contributions to shared family endeavors.

Participants were 28 European American (14 female) and 30 U.S. Mexican-heritage college students (27 female) who completed an open-ended questionnaire and participated in a 1-h focus group discussion about their responses, in a class activity during a regular meeting of their upper-level university course on culture and human development. (Students of other backgrounds participated in the activity in the class, but their responses are not analyzed here.) We asked how students' families had handled giving them pocket money, when they were 7- to 12-year-old children, and their views on the developmental benefits of these practices. Among European American students, both parents were of European descent and were raised in the United States or Canada. In the U.S. Mexican-heritage group, both parents were of Mexican descent; the students were mostly either immigrants themselves or children of immigrants.

Half of the U.S. Mexican-heritage students and none of the European American students reported regularly receiving *domingos*. Most of the European American students (79%) reported receiving allowances but only 12% of the U.S. Mexican-heritage students had. In addition, sporadic noncontingent gifts (that were neither allowances nor *domingos*) were reported by some students (European American students 19%; U.S. Mexican-heritage students, 37%). Taken together, between-community differences in these frequencies were statistically significant, $\chi^2(2) = 35.11$, $p < 0.001$.

The U.S. Mexican-heritage students reported that giving *domingos* was something that families and communities did to show appreciation to their children and godchildren. Seven of the 15 U.S. Mexican-heritage students that received a *domingo* reported that it usually was given by grandparents or godparents, reflecting the importance of the extended family in child-rearing practices and the expectation that children's contributions include the extended family (see also Ramírez Sánchez, 2007). In contrast to the use of *domingos* by extended family members among U.S. Mexican-heritage students, allowances were reported to be given exclusively by parents. No European American students reported receiving pocket money from extended family members.

Many U.S. Mexican-heritage students who received *domingos* described this practice as creating opportunities for family and community togetherness. For example,

> *Every other Sunday, mainly when it was payday, in my community, we would go out and be with the family. The kids tended to get a toy [with their* domingo*] or something that week that they had been wanting. It was just a time when family would come together, and there would be some extra income.*

Domingos traditionally are given in the form of cash, but U.S. Mexican-heritage students often reported receiving *domingos* in the form of a toy or a special meal or outing—the underlying meaning remained the same.

5.2 Cultural Values, Goals, and Assumed Benefits of Domingos and Allowances

We also asked students about the potential developmental benefits of either *domingos* (noncontingent gifts) or allowances (contractual payments for chores or good behavior).

The responses of U.S. Mexican-heritage students repeatedly emphasized that *domingos* as a cultural practice were neither contingent, not needing to be "earned," nor were they an entitlement that is "just given" to children. Descriptions of *domingos* were situated alongside children "naturally" doing what is expected and not as part of prespecified contractual arrangements meant to get children to do chores, schoolwork, or to behave.

These cultural expectations may be experienced as complimentary to children's autonomy in finding ways to be helpful (e.g., Pelletier, 1970).

Cultural expectations are powerful sources of guidance for children's learning and development and have received insufficient attention (Rogoff, 2003). They are an aspect of the support system for children's learning, along with specific guidance by other people, in the *LOPI* model (Rogoff, 2014).

U.S. Mexican-heritage students commonly referenced the importance of helping without expecting anything in return, and that children doing things for the family to get money was problematic because it discourages children from doing what is expected of them or can cause family competition. For example, one U.S. Mexican-heritage student reported,

> *Kids should do things because they want to, with the encouragement and guidance of a parent/elder sibling.... I personally was never given money for doing what was expected of me.*

U.S. Mexican-heritage students described *domingos* in relation to mutual family goals and benefits for individuals in coordination with the family. One student reported that noncontingent *domingos* "teach children responsibility and [to] help the community; [it's] not just for their own [benefit]." Other students stated, "to teach us responsibility and the expectations of our community, such as learning to be hardworking and respectful." Some reported that parents used *domingos* to teach children to show appreciation and to share with others what they had. For example,

> *It was never just like, 'oh, Ana's gonna get this, but you guys aren't.' It was like, when I would get something, my brother and my sister would get [it too]... Like, [my parents] would never just take like my sister somewhere because she got an A. It was like, 'okay, well when you're able to, we're all gonna go out.'*

In contrast, European American students commonly assumed that if children were not contingently earning the pocket money they received through (usually) assigned chores, the money was an entitlement with no expectation that children would help around the house. Most of these students reported that "just giving" money to children without contingencies was developmentally inappropriate—children need to learn that money "does not grow on trees." "Earning it"—even just by not fighting with a sibling, in one student's example—was central to their assumed developmental benefits of receiving a contractual allowance, because that is "how the real world works." European American students commonly described allowances as related to individual benefits that would serve the child in the future, such as learning how to handle money responsibly, working for money, and gaining financial independence. One European American student reported,

> *I think that the culture of the US heavily relies on independence and self worth... with how good one's job is or how much money they are making, or if they can work hard. If a child learns to "earn it," it will probably be easier for that child to develop in this economic environment where working hard is very important. Also helps them appreciate the money they earn.*

Overall, European American students suggested that contingencies were *necessary* for learning and emphasized the developmental value of children needing to *earn* pocket money in contractual arrangements. Without contingencies, these students seemed to assume that children would be unmotivated to learn what they needed to. In fact, many European American students found it difficult to understand how noncontingent *domingos* could support learning and development at all—contingency was assumed to be a requirement for children learning to be responsible. One European American student stated this clearly during a focus group discussion: "I have no idea what a *domingo* is [it had come up in conversation], but simply handing money to children on a regular basis is detrimental to their character."

This clearly contrasts with the idea that *domingos* help to build long-term reciprocal relationships within the family and community, as reported by many U.S. Mexican-heritage students. As previously stated, by giving *domingos*, U.S. Mexican-heritage students reported that their parents were supporting children in learning to "Be respectful and be caring to your elderly and help whenever help is needed." These are key aspects of reciprocal relationships in many Indigenous families and communities.

The views of most U.S. Mexican-heritage students that received *domingos* were that contingencies *undermined* children's learning and reciprocal family collaboration. One student clearly stated that money should not be used to get children to help, "Children should not have to rely on money or a certain gift to do something; it should be out of their will..." In these students' views, the use of contingent rewards changes the nature of the relationship from one based in collaboration and joint purpose, to a relationship that is adversarial between members of the family and/or community. A U.S. Mexican-heritage student reported that equal treatment within the family members was important:

> *My little brother wasn't the greatest at school but grandma still gave him equal amount as me. It doesn't matter of achievement. She simply gave because she loved us both equally. I think "earning it" causes competition and pins siblings against each other.*

Another student of this background mentioned, "I believe there are benefits [of giving *domingos*] because it shows children to be responsible to their family and their needs without expecting anything in return." The reports of noncontingent *domingos* among U.S. Mexican-heritage students fit a cultural pattern of childhood and family life characterized by *LOPI*, especially regarding children's integration, autonomy, and helpfulness in mature endeavors.

6. DISTINCT CULTURAL APPROACHES TO ENCOURAGING CHILDREN'S LEARNING AND HELPFULNESS

In the exploratory study we discuss above, in Indigenous-heritage Mexican families of our three previous studies (Alcalá et al., 2014; Coppens, Alcalá, et al., 2014; Coppens et al., 2015) and in extensive ethnographic research throughout Indigenous communities of the Americas, *domingos* (or other noncontingent pocket giving practices) seem to be associated with other features of *LOPI*. These features include involving children in family activities as contributing participants and the appreciation and expectation of children's initiative. Together, these related cultural practices seem to (1) appreciate and reciprocate children's contributions to the family; (2) emphasize children's autonomy and valued role in mutual endeavors of shared importance; and (3) support permeability across collaborative family activities, from household work to weekend leisure activities (see also Kremer-Sadlik, Fatigante, & Fasulo, 2008).

Along with key features of LOPI, the absence of controlling efforts in the form of contingent rewards may support children's collaborative initiative in making helpful, prosocial contributions to everyday family and community productive endeavors. In many of the communities where *domingos* are commonly reported and where children have regular and meaningful access to family and community work, children regularly take initiative to observe and contribute (Paradise & Rogoff, 2009). This possible association between noncontingent gifts acknowledging children's help and responsibility, *LOPI*, and children's initiative raises important issues in theorizing how children become motivated to learn and develop a sense of responsibility to take part in ongoing activities.

7. *DOMINGOS, LOPI,* AND EXPANDING MOTIVATIONAL THEORIES WITH CULTURAL RESEARCH

LOPI may support a motivational paradigm that is not well described by theories that dichotomize into "internal" and "external" origins or sources of children's motivations. The extensive helpfulness and collaborative initiative of many Indigenous and Indigenous-heritage Mexican children does not seem to be "intrinsic" to them personally but instead may relate inseparably to how their participation in everyday endeavors is organized and supported (Paradise, 2005; Paradise & Rogoff, 2009; Rogoff et al., 2014). We speculate that *LOPI*—a theoretical model of children's learning within the collaborative social organization of shared family work common to many Indigenous and Indigenous-heritage communities of the Americas—imbues everyday work with a level of sociality and complexity that is interesting and highly motivating for children. In superficial or material terms, household tasks are not especially complex, at least not for older children. Yet, *sharing in and accomplishing this work with others* can be highly engaging, particularly when children can figure out what needs to be done and how to be helpful. Having regular opportunities to share social purposes seems to powerfully support children and adolescents' learning and motivation (Damon, 2009; Fuligni, 2001; Fuligni & Telzer, 2013; Mejía-Arauz, et al., 2015/this volume; Walton & Cohen, 2011; Yeager & Bundick, 2009).

Theoretical attempts to locate "sources" of children's motivation may assume children's segregation from productive cultural activities and/or, more broadly, a division between individuals and the social world (see Rogoff, 2003 for discussions of sociocultural approaches that emphasize the mutual constitution of individuals and the social and cultural world). Evidence from communities that routinely and meaningfully integrate children in mature family and community endeavors—the central feature of *LOPI*—challenges motivational theories to unify personal and social aspects of cultural activity.

Theories that reflect a division between individual children and mature cultural activities may stem from communities (commonly, middle-class) where children are characteristically segregated from mature endeavors. Decades of social psychological research on motivation suggest that the cultural paradigm in which middle-class children do assigned chores for allowances is not effective for motivating children's collaboration and contributions (see also Goodnow, 1996; Klein & Goodwin, 2013; Klein et al., 2009; Ochs & Izquierdo, 2009; Ochs & Kremer-Sadlik, 2013). These children's low motivation for helping and contributing might be explained by the extent to which children experience contingent chore assignments as autonomy limiting (Iyengar & Lepper, 1999), and to the extent that pocket money and gifts are configured as "extrinsic" rewards (Deci, Koestner, & Ryan, 1999a; Lepper, Greene, & Nisbett, 1973; Zhou, Ma, & Deci,

2009). In what may be the most in-depth study of U.S. middle-class family life to date, Klein and Goodwin (2013) note,

> *Across the [study] families* there was no positive correlation attributed to receiving an allowance for tasks and the quantity of household work children performed. ... *When children's participation is tied to avoiding occasional parental threats or to personal benefits such as monetary or material rewards, children may be less likely to become intrinsically motivated to help others (italics added, p. 114).*

The separation of child and adult roles, in contrast to the integration of children in family and community activities as in *LOPI*, may be responsible for an emphasis on the necessity of adult control for children's responsible development. Middle-class parents seem to assume that a parent's role is to "instill" this helpfulness orientation because helping with chores does not come naturally to children. Relatedly, many middle-class European American parents claim that it is unrealistic to expect children to help if no one asked them to help (Alcalá et al., 2014; Coppens & Rogoff, in preparation; López et al., 2015). By contrast, many U.S. Mexican-heritage mothers see their role as supporters of their child's helpfulness by avoiding coercion, to support autonomy (Coppens & Rogoff, in preparation).

An important question regarding cultural ecologies of children's everyday learning in middle-class communities relates to whether assigning chores to a child, in a way that undermines autonomy with contingencies and delimits the child's responsibilities to simple self-focused tasks, reduces for children the activities' potential social interest and cognitive complexity. This would help to explain why extrinsic rewards are needed to motivate many middle-class children to make even minimal contributions. Deci, Koestner, and Ryan (1999b) propose that children can become motivated to take part and help in these activities that they find uninteresting, through "extrinsic contingencies" that are eventually internalized and integrated. Many middle-class parents may approach children's development of helpfulness and responsibility in ways that fit this theoretical view (Coppens & Rogoff, in preparation). However, ours and others' previous work does not support the prediction of an "internalization" pathway from contingently assigned chores to self-determination in children's helpfulness in work that benefits others (Alcalá et al., 2014; Coppens, Alcalá, et al., 2014; Coppens et al., 2015; Ochs & Kremer-Sadlik, 2013). Most of the middle-class children in our prior work, across a range of ages, seldom took initiative to help and commonly required contingent assignments and requests to make even minimal contributions.

The *LOPI* approach to involving children in everyday household work, supported by noncontingent gifts to acknowledge children's learning and participation, and appreciative gestures that maintain children's autonomy may create rich developmental opportunities for children (Coppens, Silva, et al., 2014). Children's integration into collaborative productive activities as contributors may support long-term dispositions for learning and motivation, in addition to accomplishing goals related to economic socialization and learning financial responsibility (Orellana, 2009; Robles, 2012; Rogoff, 2003). Giving *domingos* to children noncontingently—sharing family resources to show appreciation for everyone's contributions, as a small regular shared celebration—allows children to take part and pitch in to family endeavors (whether economic or otherwise) in ways that seem to support children's initiative in making contributions to everyday family and community work, and learning to become responsible contributing members of their family and community.

ACKNOWLEDGMENTS

We are grateful to the University of California Santa Cruz students who participated in conversations and provided information about these topics.

REFERENCES

Alcalá, L., & Rogoff, B. (in preparation). *Collaboration as shared thinking or dividing roles: Cultural differences*. Santa Cruz, CA: University of California, Santa Cruz (unpublished manuscript).

Alcalá, L., Rogoff, B., Mejía-Arauz, R., Coppens, A. D., & Dexter, A. L. (2014). Children's initiative in contributions to family work in Indigenous-heritage and cosmopolitan communities in Mexico. *Human Development, 57*(2–3), 96–115. http://dx.doi.org/10.1159/000356763.

Brayboy, B. M. J. (2013). Tidemarks and legacies: Building on the past and moving to the future. *Anthropology and Education Quarterly, 44*, 1–10.

Cervera Montejano, M. D. (in press). Studying Yucatec Maya children through the eyes of their mothers. In V. Pache, E. Guillermet, & C-E. de Suremain (Eds.), *Production politique et institutionnelle de l'enfance autour du monde—Politics and institutional production of childhood around the world*. Liège, Bélgica: Presses Universitaires de Liège.

Chavajay, P. (1993). Afterward: Independent analyses of cultural variations and similarities in San Pedro and Salt Lake. In Rogoff, B., Mistry, J., Göncü, A., & Mosier, C. (Eds.), *Monographs of the Society for Research in Child Development, 58*, 162–165.

Coppens, A. D., Alcalá, L., Mejía-Arauz, R., & Rogoff, B. (2014). Children's initiative in family household work in Mexico. *Human Development, 57*(2–3), 116–130. http://dx.doi.org/10.1159/000356768.

Coppens, A. D., Alcalá, L., Mejía-Arauz, R., & Rogoff, B. (2015). Two cultural paradigms of children's contributions in family work. In S. Punch, R. M. Vanderbeck, & T. Skelton (Eds.), *Familial and Friendship Relations and Spatial Socialities: Vol. 5*. Heidelberg: Springer.

Coppens, A. D., & Rogoff, B. (2014). A puzzle for some parents: "How do I get my kids to do their chores?". Presented at the *11th International Conference of the Learning Sciences,* Boulder, CO.

Coppens, A. D., & Rogoff, B. (in preparation). *Parents' socialization practices and cultural values in support of children's development of collaborative initiative.* Santa Cruz, CA: University of California, Santa Cruz (unpublished manuscript).

Coppens, A. D., Silva, K. G., Ruvalcaba, O., Alcalá, L., López, A., & Rogoff, B. (2014). Learning by observing and pitching in: Benefits and processes of expanding repertoires. *Human Development, 57*(2–3), 150–161. http://dx.doi.org/10.1159/000356770.

Corona Caraveo, Y., & Pérez, C. (2007). The sense of belonging: The importance of child participation in the ritual life for the recreation of the culture of the indigenous peoples. In T. Wyller & U. S. Nayar (Eds.), *The given child: The religions' contributions to children's citizenship* (pp. 125–158). Oakville, CT: Vandenhoeck & Ruprecht.

Damon, W. (2009). *The path to purpose.* New York, NY: Simon and Schuster.

Deci, E. L., Koestner, R., & Ryan, R. M. (1999a). A meta-analytic review of experiments examining the effects of extrinsic rewards on intrinsic motivation. *Psychological Bulletin, 125*(6), 627–668.

Deci, E. L., Koestner, R., & Ryan, R. M. (1999b). The undermining effect is a reality after all: Extrinsic rewards, task interest, and self-determination. *Psychological Bulletin, 125*(6), 692–700.

de Haan, M. (1999). *Learning as cultural practice: How children learn in a Mexican Mazahua community.* Amsterdam, The Netherlands: Thela Thelis.

Feather, N. T. (1991). Variables relating to the allocation of pocket money to children: Parental reasons and values. *British Journal of Social Psychology, 30,* 221–234.

Fuligni, A. J. (2001). Family obligation and the academic motivation of adolescents from Asian, Latin American, and European backgrounds. *New Directions for Child and Adolescent Development, 94,* 61–75.

Fuligni, A. J., & Telzer, E. H. (2013). Another way family can get in the head and under the skin: The neurobiology of helping the family. *Child Development Perspectives,* 7(3), 138–142. http://dx.doi.org/10.1111/cdep.12029.

Gaskins, S. (1999). Children's daily lives in a Mayan village: A case study of culturally constructed roles and activities. In A. Göncü (Ed.), *Children's engagement in the world* (pp. 25–61). Cambridge: Cambridge University Press.

Good Eshelman, C. (2005). Ejes conceptuales entre los Nahuas de Guerrero: Expresión de un modelo fenomenológico mesoamericano. *Estudios de Cultura Náhuatl, 36,* 87–113.

Goodnow, J. J. (1988). Children's household work: Its nature and its functions. *Psychological Bulletin, 103*(1), 5–26.

Goodnow, J. J., & Delaney, S. (1989). Children's household work: Task differences, styles of assignment, and links to family relationships. *Journal of Applied Developmental Psychology, 10,* 209–226.

Goodnow, J. J. (1996). Collaborative rules: How are people supposed to work with one another? In P. B. Bates & U. M. Staudinger (Eds.), *Interactive minds: Life-span perspectives on the social foundation of cognition* (pp. 163–197). Cambridge: Cambridge University Press.

Goodnow, J. J. (1998). Beyond the overall balance: The significance of particular tasks and procedures for perceptions of fairness in distributions of household work. *Social Justice Research, 11*(3), 359–376.

Iyengar, S. S., & Lepper, M. R. (1999). Rethinking the value of choice: A cultural perspective on intrinsic motivation. *Journal of Personality and Social Psychology, 76*(3), 349–366.

Jiménez, D. P. (2012). *Concepciones infantiles sobre el proceso salud-enfermedad en una comunidad maya de Quintana Roo.* Masters' thesis, Maestría en Ciencias en la especialidad de Ecología Humana, Department of Human Ecology, Cinvestav, IPN, Mérida, México.

Kerr, M., & Cheadle, T. (1997). Allocation of allowances and associated family practices. *Children's Social and Economic Education, 2*, 1–11.
Klein, W., & Goodwin, M. H. (2013). Chores. In E. Ochs & T. Kremer-Sadlik (Eds.), *Fast-forward family: Home, work, and relationships in middle-class America* (pp. 111–129). Berkeley, CA: University of California Press.
Klein, W., Graesch, A. P., & Izquierdo, C. (2009). Children and chores: A mixed-methods study of children's household work in Los Angeles families. *Anthropology of Work Review, 30*(3), 98–109. http://dx.doi.org/10.1111/j.1548-1417.2009.01030.x.
Kremer-Sadlik, T., Fatigante, M., & Fasulo, A. (2008). Discourses on family time: The cultural interpretation of family togetherness in Los Angeles and Rome. *Ethos, 36*(3), 283–309.
Lepper, M. R., Greene, D., & Nisbett, R. E. (1973). Undermining children's intrinsic interest with extrinsic rewards: A test of the "overjustification" hypothesis. *Journal of Personality and Social Psychology, 28*, 129–137.
López, A., Rogoff, B., Najafi, B., & Mejía-Arauz, R. (2012). Collaboration and helping as cultural practices. In J. Valsiner (Ed.), *The Oxford handbook of culture and psychology* (pp. 869–884). New York, NY: Oxford University Press.
López, A., Ruvalcaba, O., & Rogoff, B. (2015). Attentive helping as a cultural practice of Mexican-heritage families. In Y. M. Caldera & E. W. Lindsey (Eds.), *Mexican American children and families* (pp. 76–91). New York, NY: Routledge.
Martínez-Pérez, M. (2014). Children's initiative and multimodal learning in action and interaction: A study of socialization among the Mayas Tzotzil of Huixtán. *Methaodos Revista de Ciencias Sociales, 2*(2), 256–274.
Martínez-Pérez, M. (2015). Adults' orientation of children—and children's initiative to pitch in—to everyday adult activities in a Tsotsil Maya community. *Advances in Child Development and Behavior, 49*, 113–135.
Mejía-Arauz, R., Correa-Chávez, M., Keyser-Ohrt, U., & Aceves-Azuara, I. (2015). Collaborative work or individual chores: The role of family social organization in children's learning to collaborate and develop initiative. *Advances in Child Development and Behavior*, 49, 25–51.
Montemayor, R. (1983). Parents and adolescents in conflict: All families some of the time and some families all of the time. *Journal of Early Adolescence, 3*, 83–103.
Morelli, G. A., Rogoff, B., & Angelillo, C. (2003). Cultural variation in young children's access to work or involvement in specialized child-focused activities. *International Journal of Behavioral Development, 27*(3), 264–274.
Mortimer, J. T., Dennehy, K., Lee, C., & Finch, M. D. (1994). Economic socialization in the American family: The prevalence, distribution, and consequences of allowance arrangements. *Family Relations, 43*(1), 23–29.
Ochs, E., & Izquierdo, C. (2009). Responsibility in childhood: Three developmental trajectories. *Ethos, 37*(4), 391–413. http://dx.doi.org/10.1111/j.1548-1352.2009.01066.x.
Ochs, E., & Kremer-Sadlik, T. (Eds.), (2013). *Fast-forward family: Home, work, and relationships in middle-class America*. Berkeley, CA: University of California Press.
Orellana, M. F. (2009). *Translating childhoods*. Piscataway, NJ: Rutgers University Press.
Paradise, R. (2005). Motivación e iniciativa en el aprendizaje informal. *Revista Electrónica Sinéctica, 26*, 12–21.
Paradise, R., & de Haan, M. (2009). Responsibility and reciprocity: Social organization of Mazahua learning practices. *Anthropology and Education Quarterly, 40*(2), 187–204. http://doi.org/10.1111/j.1548-1492.2009.01035.x.
Paradise, R., & Rogoff, B. (2009). Side by side: Learning by observing and pitching in. *Ethos, 37*(1), 102–138.
Pelletier, W. (1970). Childhood in an Indian village. In S. Repo (Ed.), *This book is about schools*. New York, NY: Pantheon Books.

Ramírez Sánchez, M. A. (2007). "Helping at home": The concept of childhood and work among the Nahuas of Tlaxcala, Mexico. In B. Hungerland, M. Liebel, B. Milne, & A. Wihstutz (Eds.), *Working to be someone: Child focused research and practice with working children* (pp. 87–95). London: Jessica Kingsley Publishers.

Robles, A. (2012). Participación de niños indígenas mazahuas en la organización familiar del trabajo. *Papeles de Trabajo Sobre Cultura, Educación y Desarrollo Humano, 8*, 1–11.

Rogoff, B. (2003). *The cultural nature of human development*. New York, NY: Oxford University Press.

Rogoff, B. (2014). Learning by observing and pitching in to family and community endeavors: An orientation. *Human Development, 57*(2–3), 69–81. http://dx.doi.org/10.1159/000356757.

Rogoff, B., Alcalá, L., Coppens, A. D., López, A., Ruvalcaba, O., & Silva, K. G. (Eds.). (2014). Learning by observing and pitching in to family and community endeavors. Special issue of *Human Development, 57*(2–3).

Rogoff, B., Moore, L. C., Correa-Chávez, M., & Dexter, A. L. (2015). Children develop cultural repertoires through engaging in everyday routines and practices. In J. E. Grusec & P. D. Hastings (Eds.), *Handbook of socialization: Theory and research* (2nd ed., pp. 472–498). New York, NY: The Guilford Press.

Stawski II, W. S. (1996). *U.S. Patent No. 5,573,404*. Washington, DC: U.S. Patent and Trademark Office.

Topete Lara, H., & Díaz Araya, A. (2014). Sistema de cargos y organización social en Mesoamérica. *Diálogo Andino, 43*, 3–7. http://dx.doi.org/10.4067/S0719-26812014000100001.

T. Rowe Price. (2015). *Parents, kids & money survey summary*. Baltimore, MD: T. Rowe Price Investment Services, Inc. Retrieved from, https://corporate.troweprice.com/Money-Confident-Kids/Site/Media/Resources/Articles/2015-pkm-survey-results-summary.

Urrieta, L., Jr. (2013). Familia and comunidad-based saberes: Learning in an indigenous heritage community. *Anthropology and Education Quarterly, 44*(3), 320–335. http://dx.doi.org/10.1111/aeq.12028.

Velázquez Galdino, Y. (2014). El intercambio de "ayuda": Economía y organización social entre los nahuas de la Sierra Norte de Puebla [The exchange of 'help': Economy and social organization among the nahuas of Sierra Norte de Puebla, México.]. *Diálogo Andino, 43*, 41–50.

Walton, G. M., & Cohen, G. L. (2011). Sharing motivation. In D. Dunning (Ed.), *Social motivation* (pp. 79–101). New York, NY: Psychology Press.

Warton, P. M., & Goodnow, J. J. (1991). The nature of responsibility: Children's understanding of 'your job'. *Child Development, 62*(1), 156–165.

Warton, P. M., & Goodnow, J. J. (1995). Money and children's household jobs: Parents' views of their interconnections. *International Journal of Behavioral Development, 18*(2), 335–350.

Yeager, D. S., & Bundick, M. J. (2009). The role of purposeful work goals in promoting meaning in life and in schoolwork during adolescence. *Journal of Adolescent Research, 24*(4), 423–452.

Zhou, M., Ma, W. J., & Deci, E. L. (2009). The importance of autonomy for rural Chinese children's motivation for learning. *Learning and Individual Differences, 19*, 492–498.

CHAPTER FIVE

Adults' Orientation of Children—And Children's Initiative to Pitch In—To Everyday Adult Activities in a Tsotsil Maya Community

Margarita Martínez-Pérez[1]
Centro de Investigación y Estudios Superiores en Antropología Social (CIESAS) and Universidad de Ciencias y Artes de Chiapas (UNICACH)
[1]Corresponding author: e-mail address: maggieagle@yahoo.com.mx

Contents

Abstract

This chapter examines how 2-year-old children attempt to actively participate in adult work in a Mayan community in Chiapas, Mexico, and how adults contribute and accommodate to the contributions. As children enter into activities and adults orient and reorient the activity to direct the children, teaching from expert to novice is generated by children's agency in co-participatory interactions. The chapter enriches the LOPI model by focusing on the structure of participation and communication, social and community organization, and the evaluation that occurs in the activity itself.

1. INTRODUCTION

In this chapter, I analyze how Chamula Tsotsil children (approximately 2–3 years old) take the initiative to pitch in to activities carried out by their family members. Specifically, I examine how learning processes are produced in situated activity. I demonstrate how the child generates this

Advances in Child Development and Behavior, Volume 49
ISSN 0065-2407
http://dx.doi.org/10.1016/bs.acdb.2015.09.002

process in co-participative interactions, how they insert themselves into the process, and how adults orient and reorient the activity to guide the child.

This work draws on different disciplines. I build on studies of community learning that have underscored the important role played by "observation, perception, and keen attention" and have distinguished how verbal language is directly relevant to carrying out the activity itself, unlike language often used in school in a manner disconnected from the action's context (Gaskins & Paradise, 2010; Paradise & Rogoff, 2009; Rogoff, 1990 [1993], 2003, 2014; Rogoff, Paradise, Mejía-Arauz, Correa-Chávez, & Angelillo, 2003 [2010]).

I also build on work that is situated within the framework of linguistic anthropology, in particular in the tradition of language socialization which sees socialization as interactional and not a one-way process. In this view, children play different participatory roles and are actively involved in the transformation of their competences (de León, 2005; Ochs & Schieffelin, 1984 [2010], 2011; Schieffelin & Ochs, 1986) as well as the co-construction of the interactive organization of action within situated activity (Goodwin, 1990, 2007).

In order to interweave both perspectives, I take as my starting point an "activity theory" approach as the core of learning and socialization (Lave, 1996 [2001], 2011; Lave & Wenger, 1991; Leontiev, 1981; Rogoff, 1990 [1993], 2003; Vygotsky, 1978). In this way, the unit of analysis is situated activity, understood as instances of action with spatially and temporally organized structure (Goodwin, 1990, 2006a).

The activities analyzed in this chapter reflect examples of the model of "Learning by Observing and Pitching In" (Rogoff, 2014), formerly known as Learning through "Intent Community Participation (ICP)," developed by Rogoff et al. (2003 [2010]). The model describes this form of learning in seven facets displayed as a prism (for a more detailed explanation see Rogoff, 2014): the organization of learning in the community, the motivation, the social organization, the learning goal, the use of broad and keen attention, the forms of communication, and the ways of evaluation. These facets are together posited to be holistically and intrinsically connected.

Although work using this model has already shown that children learn by taking initiative, through the use of observation, keen attention, and with their active participation and pitching in as the activity unfolds (Alcalá, Rogoff, Mejía-Arauz, & Coppens, 2014; Coppens, Alcalá, Mejía-Arauz, & Rogoff, 2014; Correa-Chavez, Roberts, & Martínez-Pérez, 2011; Paradise & Gaskins, 2010; Paradise & Rogoff, 2009; Rogoff, 2014;

Rogoff et al., 2003 [2010]); in this chapter, I am interested in showing that the initiative taken by small children is not only related to "observing and taking part in the task." Rather it starts with actions that involve other participants, who "break down" the tasks by means of an interactional sequence that is supported by different communicative resources that characterize the Tsotsil culture of this study.

With this purpose in mind, I start by briefly introducing the community that was studied, along with the ethnographic context of children's socialization and participation in valued activities of everyday life. Subsequently, I present three examples of family activities that show children's initiative to "explore" and "pitch in" to chores. Finally, I relate the findings of this chapter to the LOPI model.

2. THE STUDY AND THE COMMUNITY

This study was conducted in a Mayan community called Ichintón, located in the Highlands of the state of Chiapas; this Tsotsil-speaking community belongs to the municipality of San Juan Chamula in southern Mexico and has a population of approximately 1000 inhabitants (Rural Medical Unit, 2015).

This chapter is part of a larger project that looks at the process of socialization of language and attention. It is based on longitudinal, ethnographic, and linguistic research of a focal family and four complementary families. The cases used here were drawn from a database that was generated as a result of an ethnographic analysis of the focal family's interactions in their everyday activities. The fieldwork started in 2008 and lasted until 2012, during this time 88 hours of video footage of natural interactions were recorded. In addition, the research has been enriched by the autobiographical and participatory experience of the researcher, as she is a member of this community.

Because of Mexico's economic instability, since the 1990s San Juan Chamula has seen a larger percentage of its population emigrate to the United States to work as day laborers than most other municipalities in the country. Despite the high rate of emigration over the past two decades, the everyday lives of the families under study and of the community in general continue to revolve around certain activities. The economic activity of this community, and of the municipality overall, is based primarily on agriculture and the sale of vegetables to supply the local market of San Cristóbal de las Casas, the main economic center for many neighboring communities and municipalities. Most men work as farmers or construction workers, some trade in vegetables and craftwork, and a few work as truck and bus drivers.

The women in the community perform a wide variety of household activities, ranging from taking care of the children to housekeeping, planting and harvesting corn and beans, and carrying firewood. They also engage in weaving and embroidering activities, as well as taking care of the wool-producing sheep (which involves shearing the sheep, carding, and spinning the wool) to create each family's traditional garments.

In all of these everyday activities, children are always included alongside adults, sometimes accompanying and observing, other times actively participating and collaborating. This means that during most of their waking hours, children have the chance to observe while adults carry out their myriad activities. As they grow up, children gradually develop the motivation to work collectively and collaboratively, getting involved through their own initiative and pitching in to these everyday activities alongside adults, as they develop responsibility and independence.

3. CHILDREN'S INITIATIVE IN THREE EVERYDAY ACTIVITIES

The fragments of three observations from everyday life that are analyzed in this chapter show us children's initiative to "explore" and "pitch in" (Martínez-Pérez, 2015):

Activity 1: Mar (3 years old) takes the initiative to wash clothes even though her mother (45 years old) and sister (23 years old) are not washing clothes at the time; however, just across from her house she can see a group of women washing clothes (at the community washboards), which might have motivated the girl's initiative.

Activity 2: The grandmother (69 years old) is shelling beans, and Beto (1 year 9 months old) takes the initiative to join and "help" her.

Activity 3: Beto (3 years old) watches his father (46 years old) prepare and put a cement floor in place, which motivates his initiative to take part in the activity.

It is interesting to point out that in all three activities, the adults display some rejection of the children's initiative. However, this rejection strengthens the children's motivation and insistence, until they succeed in being incorporated explicitly and implicitly into the activity. The apparent rejection by the adult is actually a deliberate provocation used by parents to encourage participation and to help children develop interactive skills for reaching agreements, setting limits, and defining values and social responsibility associated with each activity.

3.1 Activity 1. "Mar Washes clothes"

This activity shows the initiative of a 3-year-old girl named Mar to "wash clothes." The interaction occurred over a period of 7 min and 41 s, and involved 116 verbal and nonverbal interactional turns. For 1 min, she tried to insist and convince her mother to let her carry out the activity. Mar's initiative and insistence generated a co-participative interaction with the mother and later the sister, to guide and accompany Mar in carrying out the activity.

Unlike Activities 2 and 3 (described below) in which the child gets involved in an activity that is already underway, in this case the girl starts it by herself: neither her mother nor her older sisters are washing clothes. In fact, both the mother and the sister are embroidering blouses; another sister is taking care of the baby, and while the mother works on the blouse, she sustains a casual conversation with the researcher. We did spot a group of women across the street washing clothes, which may have triggered the girl's interest in the activity.

Below, I describe the people involved in the event and then examine the interaction.

Participants:

Mother	(45 years old) monolingual in Tsotsil.
Estela	(23 years old) slightly bilingual (Tsotsil-Spanish).
Mar	(3 years old) monolingual in Tsotsil.

Context: Before Mar takes the initiative, the mother is sitting in the patio of the house embroidering a blouse. As she embroiders, she has a stick in her hand to scare off the chickens that leave their droppings on the patio floor where they are sitting. After a brief moment, the baby that was being taken care of by one of the other daughters starts crying, and the mother takes him in her arms to breast feed him while maintaining a casual conversation with the researcher. Suddenly, Mar comes out of the house with a piece of clothing in her hand and tells her mother that she wants to wash it. The mother looks at the sweater and tells her to wash it, but then immediately shifts her position and tends to the baby in her arms while continuing the conversation with the researcher. However, Mar expresses her wish to wash the sweater right there on the patio floor, but this time the mother does not respond, and so the girl insists verbally along with body language to catch her mother's attention. When the mother finally responds, she tells her to go to the public water faucet at the community washboards (across from the house), but the girl insists with different verbal resources, gestures, tantrums, and whining to get permission to wash right there at home. The mother also responds with her own verbal resources, threats, provocations of fear, and hand and head gestures to convince Mar not to wash there, and that if she insists, she can go to the community washboards, but that someone could steal her. Such a threat in this context has the function of dissuading the girl's participation. However, this only served to strengthen the girl's resolve, until the mother agreed to let her to wash the sweater in the patio.

After accepting, the mother and oldest sister engage in the activity by providing the girl with guidance: finding the materials she needs, showing her the concrete actions to perform the task, all the way to the activity's final process, which is hanging the sweater out to dry.

Fragment 1 shows the initiative that Mar took on her own and the wealth of communicative resources she used to convince her mother both to let her carry out the activity and to let her do it in that particular place.

3.1.1 Fragment 1: Mar's Initiative

The interaction begins:

1. Mar → mother: *Mama ta jchuk' jech to vi*
   "Mom, I'm going to wash this (sweater), look"
   ((Mar shows her mother the sweater)) Image 1
2. Mother → Mar: ((The mother looks at what Mar is pointing out))

Image 1 Mar asks for permission to wash the sweater.

3. Mother → Mar: *batan* "go away" ((the mother tends to the baby and continues the casual conversation with the researcher)) (2.3)[1]

4. Mar → Mother: *li' ta jchuk'*
"I'm going to wash it here"
(10.21)

5. Mother: ((No response))

6. Mar → Mother: *chichuk'umaj*
"I'm going to wash"

((A slight grumbling intonation is used, with associated hand and feet movement))
(1.98)

7. Mother: ((No response))

8. Mar → Mother: *ma chichuk'umaj*
"Mom, I'm going to wash"
(0.29)

9. Mother: ((No response))

10. Mar → Mother: *ma chichuk'umaj*
"Mom, I'm going to wash"
((Mar stamps her feet quickly, signaling a tantrum))
(0.14)

This sequential segment shows that the girl made a verbal request (Turn 1) along with the display of the sweater in her hand directed toward her mother. Despite her young age, the girl shows her initiative with great insistence in an interactional, active, and agentive process (Ochs & Schieffelin, 2011) based on an array of verbal resources juxtaposed with a series of embodied actions such as stamping her feet (tantrum) and expressing emotions (whining) (Goodwin, 2007). These strategies serve to intensify her request until she achieves her objective: to get her mother's permission to perform the activity.

In the turns, I omitted the mother resorts to threats and provocations of fear to discourage Mar's participation, while she continues to take care of the baby.

This fragment relates to the approach to learning described by LOPI (facet 2), in that the learner is anxious to pitch in and collaborate in the activity (Rogoff, 2014) on her own initiative.

After Mar finally succeeds in convincing her mother, fragment 2 shows the active involvement of the mother and the sister in helping the girl recognize the materials needed for the activity. At that moment, the mother

[1] Duration of silent periods in milliseconds.

stops talking to me and focuses her attention on Mar's actions. The older sister supports her younger sister while she continues to embroider the blouse, as the researcher observes the interaction and the adult conversation stops.

3.1.2 Fragment 2. Guidance and Support in Finding the Work Materials

46. Sister → Mar: *chech-o tal a-anfora ne*
"drag your bucket over here"
(3.81)
47. Mar: ((Mar brings bucket filled with water))
48. Sister → Mar: *ich'-o me tal a-boch un*
"bring your cup"
(3.96)
49. Mar: ((Mar brings the cup))
51. Mother → Mar: *ba ich'o tal a-xavon*
"go get your soap"
((With a head gesture the mother indicates where the soap is))
(1.6)

The mother and sister both help Mar find the materials she needs to carry out the activity. The girl actively pitches in and follows the instructions given by the adults. Mar's initiative prompts the adults to provide guidance, the purpose (possibly unconscious and implicit) of which is to transform the girl's participation. In other words, it is for Mar to identify and recognize the materials she needs to actually wash, and not to limit herself to mere play and entertainment.

Once the required materials are identified, fragment 3 shows how the adults (mother and sister) guide and accompany the girl in the specific actions implied in washing the sweater.

3.1.3 Fragment 3. Guidance and Support in Concrete Actions to Execute the Activity

55. Mar: ((The girl washes the sweater with enthusiasm))
56. Mother: ((The mother focuses on the girl's actions))
57. Mother → Mar: *lek me xachuk'umaj un, ak'bo ya'lel un*
"wash it well, pour more water on it" CORRECTION
59. Mother → Mar: *t'uxubtaso lek' achuk'ob un, t'uxubtaso*
"get the sweater wet, get it wet"
(0.74)

64. Sister → Mar: *juxo lek, t'uxi xa, lek xajux o, bu me ti sjabonale juxbo leko*
"scrub it hard, it's already wet, scrub it hard where the soap is"

EXPLANATION AND CORRECTION

100. Sister → Mar: *lich'o lek' ta silla, eso, votsilano me*
"hang it on the chair, that's right, squeeze it (the sweater), into a ball"
(1.49)

101. Sister → Mar: ((The sister helps pour the water on the sweater))

102. Sister → Mar: *votsilano, vi*
"squeeze it into a ball, watch ((she observes))"
(8.6)

Fragment 3 shows the activity's social organization. The adults' (mother and sister) joint collaboration guides Mar smoothly with instructions that make use of specific verbs related to washing, so that Mar recognizes the actions required for this activity: get the sweater wet, scrub it, squeeze it into a ball so that the soap is well distributed, and rinse it with just the right amount of water, without wasting it. The adults' explanations and corrections are interspersed throughout the activity itself, which are part of a positive approach that leads to pitching in and the transformation of the participation from the starting point of the child's own initiative.

Finally, fragment 4 shows the agentive role played by Mar, illustrated in the communicative exchanges with her mother, who gives a series of instructions to conclude the activity. The mother tells Mar that the sweater is ready to dry. We see that the mother even guides her to the last part of the task—hanging the sweater out to dry.

3.1.4 Fragment 4. Final Process in the Activity (Hanging the Sweater)

103. Mother → Mar: *ba k'io o*
"go hang it"
(0.27)

104. Mar → Mother: ((No response))

105. Mother → Mar: *ba ki'o le' le'* (☞) ((*she signals with her head*)) *and* ((she points with her finger))
"go hang it up, over there ((pointing where to hang it))"

106. Mar → Mother: *sk'an to xlaj*
"I haven't finished yet"
(0.02)

EXPLANATION

107. Mother → Mar: *lek' xa xkile*
"I think that's enough"
(0.13)

108. Mother → Mar: *ak'bo xa echeluk*
"wet it one more time"

109. Mar → Mother: *sk'an to xkil*
"It's not done yet"

EXPLANATION

110. Mar → Mother: *oto* = (*oy to*) *xavon* ((eye contact and smile))
"it still has soap"

In the end, the mother cannot convince the girl, so she shifts her attention to something else (de León, 2011; Goodwin, 2006b; Tulbert & Goodwin, 2011). This attention shift consisted of ignoring the girl and going back to the task she was performing before Mar's initiative—embroidering a blouse. After a few minutes, the girl finally decides to hang the sweater, thus concluding the activity.

Fragment 4 shows how the mother allows the girl to see that the sweater has been scrubbed and rinsed enough, that there is no soap left on it, so the sweater is ready to be hung out to dry and the process has been completed. However, the girl does not respond to her mother's instruction, and she refuses to finish the activity. In (Turn 105), the mother indicates with head and finger gestures where to hang the sweater out to dry. The use of gestures juxtaposed with a verbal indication serves to emphasize the mother's request. This triggers a communicative exchange of explanations by Mar, who gives her reasons for not hanging the sweater yet: (Turns 106 and 110) she has not finished the activity and (Turn 111) "it still has soap."

This last fragment gives evidence of an interactive process between the girl and her mother in carrying out the activity. The girl does not play a passive role, but actively pitches in, assigning meaning and making her own decision at the conclusion of the activity. This is consistent with the perspectives of other studies that point out that children are active agents in their own socialization and learning processes (de León, 2005, 2011; Rogoff et al., 2003 [2010]; Schieffelin & Ochs, 1986). It also ties into the LOPI model, indicating that learners pitch in to the goals of their family and community, and that their motivation to take initiative is based on mutual responsibility (Alcalá et al., 2014; Coppens et al., 2014; Rogoff, 2014).

The interactive nature of Activity 1 shows a connection with most of the LOPI facets. Although I looked at these connections separately, I agree wholeheartedly with the idea that each facet is holistically related and interconnected with the others (Rogoff, 2014; Rogoff et al., 2003 [2010]). They are like a woven textile or a back strap loom, where all the threads are juxtaposed and interwoven into a single piece, as is demonstrated in the interrelational nature of the data presented in this chapter.

The facets of LOPI observed here were:

a. Facet 2: Mar is eager to pitch in to the activity.

b. Facet 3: The activity's social organization emerges collaboratively and in joint coordination with others. The girl's initiative prompts the adults to pitch in to the activity.

c. Facet 4: The interaction aims at transforming the girl's participation, including getting her to recognize the materials and concrete actions needed to execute the activity as well as supporting her initiative.

d. Facet 6: Using verbal and nonverbal communicative resources, the mother and sister guide and accompany the girl in carrying out the activity. For her part, Mar actively contributes to her own learning process in each step of the activity that she executes.

e. Facet 7: The adults' explanations and evaluations are inserted and interspersed in the activity as Mar performs each action, for the purpose of developing Mar's understanding about washing.

3.2 Activity 2: "Beto Shelling beans"

This activity lasted 10 min and 49 s. In this chapter, I analyze only a few fragments of the whole interaction.

The child, Beto (1 year 9 months old), is playing around his grandmother when she begins to clean dry bean pods and extract the seeds. Being exposed to the activity triggers the boy's interest to explore and "pitch in" to "help" the adult. Beto's initiative and participation gives his grandmother the opportunity to teach him how to distinguish rotten pods from good ones. In addition, the grandmother shows him that the beans are not to be thrown away, only the hull goes into the wastebasket.

Context: The grandmother (69 years old) is shelling beans. Her grandson Beto (1 year 9 months old) joins in the activity and imitates his grandmother's actions. The grandmother does not say anything to the boy and continues performing the activity. The boy starts vocalizing, and the grandmother responds with the interjection sequence *umm* "what," while both shell the beans and throw the hulls into the wastebasket.

Beto crushes the bean hull while he throws it into the wastebasket. During this process, he notices that there is a pod in the wastebasket. He takes it out and tries to shell it, but cannot open the pod. He then asks for his grandmother's help. The grandmother takes the bean pod, notices that it is rotten, and begins explaining this to the boy through a series of demonstrations. Finally the boy seems to understand, and he continues helping his grandmother (obviously, the "helping" is from his own perspective).

Now the boy grabs a handful of beans in their shell and almost throws them into the trash. When his grandmother notices this, she takes the handful from his hands, which leads to a series of explanations of how the beans are not to be thrown away, only the hulls.

3.2.1 Fragment 1: Initiative

1. Beto: ((Directly gets involved in the activity to pitch in))
(9 Turns are omitted) Image 2
11. Beto: ((Grandmother and grandson carry out the activity))
12. Beto: ((The boy throws the hull into the wastebasket, imitating his grandmother's actions))

Fragment 1 shows how this 1-year-9-month-old boy takes initiative to "pitch in" and help his grandmother shell beans. Unlike Activity 1, in which the initiative is expressed verbally and with gestures, Beto's initiative occurs through direct involvement, without the use of verbal language.

After Beto gets directly involved, fragment 2 shows how his initiative opens a window for interaction and an exchange of communication between him and his grandmother to distinguish a rotten bean pod from a good one.

Image 2 Beto and his grandmother shelling beans.

3.2.2 *Fragment 2. The Grandmother Helps Beto Distinguish a Rotten Bean Pod from a Good One*

(3 Turns are omitted)

16. Beto: ((Beto notices a bean pod in the wastebasket, takes it out and sits down to try and shell it, but fails in his attempt))

17. Beto → Grandmother: ((Then he holds out his hand and shows it to his grandmother))

18. Grandmother → Beto: ((The grandmother takes the bean pod to shell it))

19. Beto → Grandmother: ((The boy smiles at the sight of his grandmother shelling the bean pod))

20. Grandmother → Beto: ((The grandmother sees that it is rotten and shows this to Beto)),
av-i = (*avil*)
B2-look
"Look"

DEMONSTRATION

21. Beto → Grandmother: *hee-hee-hee* ((smile))

22. Grandmother → Beto: *O!*, *k'o' xa* ((throws the shell in the trash))
"oh, it's rotten"

EXPLANATION

23. Beto: ((Beto looks at the pod that his grandmother threw into the trash))

24. Grandmother → Beto: ((The grandmother once again picks up the pod and puts it in front of Beto, to show him that the beans are not good))

25. Beto → Grandmother: *¿ja'*?
"What?"

26. Grandmother → Beto: ↑*k'o' xa*
↑ "it's rotten"

27. ((Grandmother and Beto line up their bodies and face toward the rotten bean pod that the grandmother is holding)).

28. Grandmother → Beto: *k'o' xa vi*
"look, it's rotten"

DEMONSTRATION
EXPLANATION

29. Beto → Grandmother: ((ignoring))

30. Grandmother → Beto: *k'o' xa*
"it's rotten"

31. Beto → Grandmother: ((ignoring))

32. Grandmother → Beto: *k'o' xa:::*
"it's rotten"

Beto shells the beans imitating his grandmother's actions. After a couple of minutes, he notices a bean pod among the hulls in the wastebasket. He picks it up and tries to shell it (Turn 16), but fails because a rotten bean pod is very hard to shell. In view of his failure, he asks his grandmother for help. The grandmother picks up the bean pod and notices it is rotten. She then puts the pod in front of Beto (Turn 20) for him to look at closely, and explains that it is rotten, before tossing it into the wastebasket (Turn 22). Beto looks at the pod in the wastebasket (Turn 23). When she realizes this, the grandmother picks up the bean pod again, puts it in Beto's view for him to notice that it is rotten. The boy responds with a vocalization that sounds like a question (Turn 24), which prompts a series of repetitions from the grandmother, who tries to make Beto understand that the pod was tossed because of its bad, "rotten" state.

We can see how Beto's initiative to "help" and "pitch in to" the activity performed by his grandmother triggers a series of explanations during the activity so that Beto learns to distinguish a good bean pod from a rotten one.

Fragment 3 shows how the grandmother helps Beto realize an essential aspect of bean shelling, which is that the beans are not be thrown away, only the hulls. The grandmother's explanation was a result of the boy's mistake during his collaboration in the activity.

3.2.3 Fragment 3. The Grandmother Helps Beto Realize That Only the Hulls Are Thrown Away

33. Beto: ((Takes a handful of beans and throws them into the wastebasket))

34. Grandmother → Beto: *mu xa jop*
"stop taking them (handfuls)"

35. Beto → Grandmother: ((Beto continues to place handfuls of bean pods into the wastebasket)).

36. Grandmother → Beto: ((The grandmother takes the bean pods from the boy's hand))
mo'oj xa li sat, mo'oj
"not the beans, don't (throw them away)"
(5 Turns are omitted)

42. Beto: ((Continues putting beans in the wastebasket))

43. Grandmother → Beto: *mo'oj xa me sat-e*
"I told you, not the beans"

44. Beto → Grandmother: ((ignoring))

45. Grandmother → Beto: *mo'oj xa*
"stop"

46. Grandmother → Beto: *ja' li spate*
"(only) the hulls"

FOCUS POINT FOR DEMONSTRATION

Beto's mistake (Turn 33) of taking a handful of beans and throwing them into the trash prompted the verbal intervention and correction by the grandmother. The grandmother corrects Beto by telling him not to take handfuls of beans, but Beto disobeys her. Then, (in Turn 26) the grandmother takes the beans out of Beto's hand before he throws them into the trash and repeats her explanation, saying that beans are not to be thrown away, and (in Turn 46) she draws attention to the fact that only the hulls should be thrown away.

With regards to such repetition, de León states that "recycling is used to fine-tune perception, calibrate attention and train the children with didactic explanations in tasks in which they are not yet competent" (2011:101). Thus, the series of repetitions used by the grandmother have the same function of contributing to competence development without dissuading the child from taking on an agentive role.

Despite Beto's age, his grandmother does not block his participation, and this produces guidance and correction in two aspects of the activity:

1. She helps him distinguish a rotten bean pod from a good one.

2. That the bean hull is tossed into the trash, but not the beans themselves.

This example shows how adults help to transform little children's participation, which will eventually enable them to actively belong, contribute and pitch in to family and community activities.

This also shows us the nature of children's interactions at an early age, how they gradually get involved in the activity of their own initiative, and how adults do not ignore the child's participation; on the contrary, they accompany them smoothly and collaboratively unless the child is excluded from the activity for not showing cooperation. However the question of exclusion can also depend on other factors, such as the level of specialization or how dangerous the activity is.

This example relates to the following facets of the LOPI model:

Facet 1: Despite his young age, Beto is eager to pitch in and be a part of everyday activities, which can be seen in the way the boy takes initiative to imitate his grandmother.

Facet 2: The grandmother gets involved when she notices Beto's initiative. Her contribution includes patience so that Beto can participate in the activity.

Facet 4: The grandmother's purpose is to transform Beto's participation by guiding him and correcting his mistakes.

Facet 5: The boy will learn and develop his sense of responsibility and independence by pitching in to these activities. Learning by doing will allow the boy to develop his skills and fine-tune his attention, so that he can not only take part in the execution, preservation and innovation of social practices, but also be a competent member of the Tsotsil community.

Facet 6: The grandmother guides and orients the boy using verbal resources such as instructions, requests, demonstrations, and focus points along with gestures and eye contact inserted into the process of carrying out the activity. The boy observes her actions closely. Sometimes both use only body movements, face alignment, and eye contact to maintain their focus on the same thing.

Facet 7: Explanations serve as feedback regarding the boy's competence. As previously shown, the grandmother's evaluation is aimed at correcting the child using his mistake as a starting point.

3.3 Activity 3. "Beto (Age 3) Takes Initiative in Construction"

Finally, we look at the third and last activity, which revolves around construction work. This activity requires a higher degree of competence due to its level of specialization, but in spite of this, little children are not discouraged from participating and pitching in.

Participants:

Father, 46 years old, who speaks to Beto in Spanish

Beto, 3 years old, who speaks to his father in Spanish or Tsotsil

Context: The father went to install a cement floor in his friend's shed, and Beto accompanied him. When his father began mixing cement and started to work, Beto grabbed one of his father's tools and started to help him. After smearing some cement on the ground, he tells his father that he is finished and asks for another area to continue working, but his request is denied due to his young age and the level of specialization and care that the activity demands.

3.3.1 Fragment 1: Initiative

1.	Beto:	((Beto grabs an old tool and imitates his father's actions)) (11.51)
2.	Beto → Father:	((Beto stops for a moment)) ready, daddy

"Daddy, I'm finished"
(2.51)
3. Father → Beto: ((No response))
4. Beto → Father: it's ready, daddy
"daddy, I'm finished"
5. Father → Beto: [Is it finished, son?
6. Beto → Father: it's ready
(0.02)
7. Father → Beto: Hmmm, so fast!
(13.25)
(4 Turns are omitted)

This fragment shows Beto's initiative to pitch in to the activity. While observing his father's actions, the boy becomes eager to help. After helping for 1 min, he stands up and tells his father that he is finished with the activity. We notice that the father is concentrated on working and ignores his son, so Beto repeats that he is finished with the activity. The father responds with a question, and the boy says yes, which prompts the father to respond with an exclamation, showing surprise at how fast he has finished. This communicative exchange (Turns 2–7) shows that the boy wants to continue helping, but somewhere else and switching tools as his father does. However, his father tries to evade Beto's intentions with questions and exclamations. There is an implicit rejection by the father.

Fragment 2 shows the boy's insistence to pitch in to the activity, but he now wants to use the tool that his father is using. At this age, the boy is motivated by the agility of his father's every action, and seems to think that the tool is the cause. Hence, he energetically requests the tool through a series of communication resources directed at his father, which in turn produces a series of justifications about why the boy is not included in the activity.

3.3.2 Fragment 2. Beto's Initiative and Insistence

12. Beto → Father: *tsak tal le'*
"pass me that"
(2.68)
13. Father → Beto: ((The father continues working and ignores Beto's request))
14. Beto → Father: *tsak tal le' papi, tsak tal le' papi:::*
"pass me that, daddy, pass me that!!"
((Beto extends his hand to emphasize his request))
(1.41)
15. Father → Beto: ((The father continues working and does not respond))

16. Beto → Father: *tsak tal vu'un le' papi, papi* ↑
"Give that (the tool) to me, daddy, daddy"
((He raises his voice to get what he wants))
(1.59)
17. Father → Beto: ((Does not respond and continues working))
18. Beto → Father: ((Beto crouches and gets closer, trying to reach for the tool))
19. Father → Beto: No, no, no, no
(0.81)
20. Father → Beto: leave that, go outside, go outside
21. Beto → Father: *tsak tal, ya pue, akbun ya pue*
give me, come on, give me, come on
22. Father → You're almost there, son, maybe one more year.
(2 Turns are omitted)

When the boy's verbal request is ignored by his father, he intensifies his request; in addition to repetitions (Turn 14), there is a juxtaposition of several communicative resources to intensify the boy's request, such as reaching for the tool as a shared reference, but he adds the vocative *daddy* to appeal directly to his father; he also elongates the vowels to show emotion as one more persuasion strategy. When he does not get an answer (in Turn 16), Beto raises his voice when saying the word *daddy* and repeats it to intensify his request. We see that far from losing motivation, the boy becomes more and more attracted to the activity, seeing it as a challenge, insisting further and strengthening his will to participate in the activity. In the end (Turn 22), it is interesting to note the father's explanation to his son: that the child is too young.

3.3.3 Fragment 3. Beto's Reinvolvement in the Activity

25. Beto: ((Beto directly grabs a tool like the one his father has and pitches in to the activity)) Image 3
26. Father → Beto: ((The father says nothing, he only smiles at the boy's action and implicitly lets him continue))
27. Beto: ((Beto is excited about leveling out the cement on the ground))
28. Father → Beto: ((The father observes Beto's actions and corrects him))
(20.34)
29. Father → Beto: Baby, not like that.
30. Beto → Father: ((Beto does not respond and continues pitching in))
(2.61)

Image 3 Beto grabs a similar tool and joins the activity directly.

31. Father → Beto: Are you working hard and quickly? That shows spirit. (1.05) — EVALUATION

32. Father → Beto: That's enough (8.69)

33. Beto: ((Beto steps on the fresh cement)) — EXPLANATION AND EVALUATION

34. Father → Beto: Baby, heeey, you stepped on it, get off (0.2)

35. Father → Beto: Your foot is full of mud (2.83) Not that way (5.38)

36. Father → Beto: They fix it and you ruin it.

37. Beto: ((Beto disengages from the activity briefly)) (0.39)

(7 Turns are omitted)

45. Beto → Father: Ready, daddy, ready

46. Father → Beto: We're leaving now (.) Your mom is looking for you. (0.02)

((The father kept justifying why Beto could not join in the activity until he finished his work, then he justified leaving quickly, before Beto could reengage in the activity)).

In response to his father's rejection in fragment 2, fragment 3 shows Beto grabbing a tool and getting directly involved in the activity. This suggests that his father's rejection is really just a provocation to increase his motivation. In fact, this reinforces the boy's direct involvement and we see that the father, far from being upset, smiles at the child's action (Turn 26). However, given the boy's age and the activity's level of specialization, it is clear that the boy is not competent in the activity, which is why the father intervenes (in Turn 29) to correct Beto's actions. The father (in Turn 32) tells him that he "has done enough" and implicitly ends his participation in the activity, although Beto continues working with enthusiasm. Finally, (in Turn 33) Beto does something serious, stepping on the fresh cement and ruining finished work, which brings about the definitive end of his participation in the activity (Turn 34). We observe that the father gives Beto explanations and evaluations (Turns 35 and 36) "your foot is all covered in mud," "that's wrong," and "they fix it and you ruin it" so that the boy realizes what he has done. This last aspect shows how the father contributes to what de León (2011) calls the socialization of attention. It also shows the care that needs to be taken in this activity with a child's limitations, which relates to facet 5 of the LOPI model, which stresses guidance enabling the learner to observe and pitch in that contributes to the construction of shared activity in future endeavors.

Finally, (in Turn 45) Beto once again asks to join in the activity, and the father (in Turn 36) justifies his rejection inventing that they are leaving because "your mom is looking for you." Thus, the father tries to shift the boy's attention to avoid his participation in the activity. This is a very valuable example, since it shows how adults use a series of explanations or justifications to keep children from participating in activities where they are not competent enough to pitch in. We see that parents generally do not make an explicit rejection, since Tsotsil parenting ideology consists of not discouraging children's participation, but rather reinforcing their motivation and directing it toward the development of a sense of responsibility, reliability, and awareness of others.

4. CONTRIBUTIONS TO THE LOPI MODEL

The interactive nature of the relationship between little children and adults shows a ritualized game of requesting and rejecting. This appears to be related to de León's observation (2005) about the provocation of fear among the Tsotsil people of Zinacantán as a way to strengthen their ch'ulel (soul or essence) and strengthen the character of Tsotsil infants. The adults' apparent dismissal of a child's initiatives in these three examples serves as a kind of provocation that strengthens the children's motivation to pitch in to the activity as responsible and competent members. This relates to Ochs and Izquierdo's conception that "socialization practices that promote children's attention to the activity of others is a first step toward social awareness; social responsiveness and self-reliance in practical matters that affirm the worth of others and give dignity to the child's own place within the family and community" (2009:405).

It is important to emphasize that even though each activity analyzed here would seem to be divided into several parts, ultimately it is a single interaction serving as a project aimed at transforming the child's participation in family and community activities. This is consistent with the LOPI model (Rogoff, 2014): LOPI may be divided into seven facets, but they all make up a whole and contribute to the same family and community objectives.

One of the main contributions of this chapter to the LOPI model is to show the interactional nature of little children's dealings with adults and the wealth of communicative resources used between them in the interaction process when an activity is being carried out. Verbal language as well as pointing gestures serve to involve the participants' vision and attention interactively (Goodwin 2000; 2010), focusing on the creation and recreation of interaction frameworks and shared objects of attention. These are already considered in the LOPI model, but the data in this chapter underscore the nature of juxtaposed communicative resources used in the child's initiative-taking and insistence, as well as the activity's social organization consisting of the guidance and accompaniment provided by adults in their interactions with small children.

Previous work by Alcalá et al. (2014) has pointed out that mothers with an Indigenous American heritage report that children pitch in to household activities on their own initiative. Similarly Coppens et al. (2014) report children's own expectations of taking initiative in their contribution to household and community tasks, which are based on a sense of mutual responsibility. However, it has not been shown how small children's initiative actually unfolds and how their insistence draws adults in to break down the activity's execution into interactional sequences. This study shows that the initiative of very young children is sometimes requested verbally as in Activity 1, sometimes by direct incorporation (Activity 2), or on occasion by a combination of both (verbal request and direct incorporation) as shown in Activity 3.

The cases presented in this chapter not only show small children's initiative and how they express it, but also presents the diversity of communicative resources they use to insist and become involved in the activity, as well as to prompt adults to guide and accompany them in carrying out the activity. The chapter points out how the activity works like a magnet for children, who cannot resist and insist on pitching in. For this, children make use of different verbal and nonverbal resources. They even get emotionally involved, venting their tension and frustration when they are not allowed to pitch in to the activities, until they convince adults to let them participate. Thus, these results expand and enrich the ideas set forth in the LOPI model (Rogoff, 2014) and previous research on children's initiative in helping at home. The data presented in this chapter on the processes of very young Tsotsil children's initiative and the support of adults may help us understand the early basis of the sophisticated ways older Indigenous American children contribute to household and community activities later in life.

REFERENCES

Alcalá, L., Rogoff, B., Mejía-Arauz, R., & Coppens, A. D. (2014). Children's initiative in contributions to family work in indigenous-heritage and cosmopolitan communities in Mexico. *Human Development, 57*, 96–115.

Coppens, A. D., Alcalá, L., Mejía-Arauz, R., & Rogoff, B. (2014). Children's initiative in family household work in Mexico. *Human Development, 57*, 116–130.

Correa-Chavez, M., Roberts, L. D. A., & Martínez-Pérez, M. (2011). Cultural patterns in children's learning through keen observation and participation in their communities. In J. Benson (Ed.), *Advances in child development and behavior* (pp. 209–241). Vol. 40. Burlington, MA: Academic Press.

de León, L. (2005). *La llegada del alma. Lenguaje, infancia y socialización entre los tzotziles de Zinacantán* (p. 396). México: CIESAS-INAH-CONACULTA.

de León, L. (2011). Calibrando" la atención: directivos, adiestramiento, y responsabilidad en el trabajo doméstico de los niños mayas zinacantecos. In S. Frisancho, M. T. Moreno, P. Ruíz-Bravo, & V. Zavala (Eds.), *Aprendizaje, cultura y desarrollo. Una aproximación interdisciplinaria* (pp. 81–110). Lima: Universidad Pontificia Católica del Perú.

Gaskins, S., & Paradise, R. (2010). Learning through observation in daily life. In D. F. Lancy, J. Bock, & S. Gaskins (Eds.), *The anthropology of learning in childhood* (pp. 85–117). Lanham, MD: Alta Mira Press.

Goodwin, M. H. (1990). *He said, she said: Talks as social organization among black children*. Bloomington, IN: Indiana University Press.

Goodwin, C. (2000). Action and embodiment within situated human interaction. *Journal of Pragmatics, 32*, 1489–1522.

Goodwin, M. H. (2006a). *The hidden life of girls: Games of stance, status, and exclusion*. Oxford: Blackwell.

Goodwin, M. H. (2006b). Participation, affect, and trajectory in family directive/response sequences. *Text and Talk, 26*(4/5), 513–542. Special issue entitled family discourse, framing family. Deborah Tannen and Marjorie H. Goodwin (eds.).

Goodwin, C. (2007). Participation, stance and affect in the organization of activities. *Discourse & Society, 18*(1), 53–73.

Goodwin, C. (2010). Multimodality in human interaction. *Calidoscopio, 8*(2), 85–98.

Lave, J. (2001). La práctica del aprendizaje. Chaiklin Seth and Lave Jane (comp.) (1996 [2001]). Estudiar la prácticas. Perspectivas sobre actividad y contexto. Ediciones Amorrortu.

Lave, J. (2011). *Apprenticeship in critical ethnographic practice*. Chicago, IL: Chicago University Press.

Lave, J., & Wenger, E. (1991). *Situated learning. Legitimated peripherical participation*. Cambridge: Cambridge University Press.

Leontiev, A. N. (1981). The problem of activity in psychology. In J. V. Wertssch (Ed.), *The concept of activity in soviet psychology*. Armonk, NY: Sharpe.

Martínez-Pérez, M. (2015). *Xchanel-xchanubtasel: lenguaje, acción y enseñanza en actividades valoradas entre los mayas de San Juan Chamula*. Tesis de doctorado en Lingüística Indoamericana del CIESAS.

Ochs, E., & Izquierdo, C. (2009). Responsibility in childhood: Three developmental trajectories. *Ethos, 37*(4), 391–413.

Ochs, E., & Schieffelin, B. B. (1984). Language acquisition and socialization: Three developmental stories and their implications. In R. Levine & R. Schweder (Eds.), *Culture theory: Essay on mind, self and emotion*. Cambridge: Cambridge University Press. Versión en español "Adquisición del lenguaje y socialización: tres historias de desarrollo y sus implicaciones". Traducción de Alejandro Curiel Ramírez del Prado. En de León, Lourdes (2010), Socialización, lenguajes y culturas infantiles: estudios interdisciplinarios. México. CIESAS.

Ochs, E., & Schieffelin, B. B. (2011). The theory of language socialization. In A. Duranti, E. E. Ochs, & B. B. Schieffelin (Eds.), *The handbook of language socialization* (pp. 1–21). Malden, MA: Blackwell.

Paradise, R., & Rogoff, B. (2009). Side by side: Learning by observing and pitching in. *Ethos, 37*(1), 102–138.

Rogoff, B. (1990 [1993]). *Aprendices del pensamiento. El desarrollo cognitivo en elcontexto social. Traducción de Pilar Lacasa* (p. 301). Barcelona, España: Editorial Paidós.

Rogoff, B. (2003). *The cultural nature of human development*. New York, NY: University Press.

Rogoff, B. (2014). Learning by observing and pitching in to family and community endeavors: An orientation. *Human Development, 57*, 69–81.

Rogoff, B., Paradise, R., Mejía-Arauz, R., Correa-Chávez, M., & Angelillo, C. (2003). Firsthand learning through intent participation. *Annual Review of Psychology, 54*(1), 175–203. Versión en español "El aprendizaje por medio de la participación intensa en comunidades". Traducción de Guadalupe Correa. En de León, Lourdes (2010), Socialización, lenguajes y culturas infantiles: estudios interdisciplinarios. México. CIESAS.

Schieffelin, B., & Ochs, E. (1986). *Language socialization across cultures*. Cambridge: Cambridge University Press.

Tulbert, E., & Goodwin, M. H. (2011). Choreographies of attention: Multimodality in a routine family activity. In J. Streeck, C. Goodwin, & C. LeBaron (Eds.), *Embodied interaction: Language and body in the material world* (pp. 79–92). Cambridge: Cambridge University Press.

Vygotsky, L. S. (1978). *Mind in society*. New York, NY: Cambridge University Press.

CHAPTER SIX

Respect and Autonomy in Children's Observation and Participation in Adults' Activities

Fernando A. García[1]
Program for the Formation of Bilingual Teachers in the Peruvian Amazonia (FORMABIAP) and the Ministry of Education of Peru, Lima, Peru
[1]Corresponding author: e-mail address: fgarcia20@yahoo.com

Contents

Abstract

This chapter examines Peruvian Quechua children's learning by observing and pitching in. The children concentrate attentively when they observe the activities of the adults and they exercise autonomy in the context of adults' encouragement of measured behaviors while always showing respectful silence in the presence of their elders.

1. INTRODUCTION

This chapter examines the development of autonomy and respect among children in a Peruvian Indigenous community where children carefully observe adults' activities while collaborating with them in different ways, depending on their age. The line of argument is that these children, in spite of the adults' constant indications to them to keep quiet and behave modestly in the presence of adults, display levels of autonomy that allow them to undertake actions and learn in ways that benefit themselves and their families. These ways of learning through observation and the development

Advances in Child Development and Behavior, Volume 49
ISSN 0065-2407
http://dx.doi.org/10.1016/bs.acdb.2015.10.003

of autonomy are grounded on the one hand in the Aucará community's family education traditions, and on the other, in the challenges that each member of the community faces in preparing for participation in local life and in other contexts outside the community.

Learning through observation and the encouragement of initiative, within a framework of participation and with an emphasis on involving children in family and community activities, are key features of the learning model proposed under the name *Learning by Observing and Pitching In* (LOPI; Rogoff, 2014). This chapter offers a point of view that demonstrates the holistic integration of these features of LOPI in a certain way of learning.

In this chapter, I analyze children's learning through observation and participation in the activities of a Peruvian Quechua community that offers children frequent opportunities to be present in most of the activities that their family and community undertake. By participating in their family's significant activities, they act with interest and motivation to contribute to the successful completion of these activities. Motivation linked to significant family activities leads to meaningful learning gained by dealing with the challenges that these activities entail. In this varied sociocultural framework, it is remarkable that local education emerges with an orientation toward forming respectful people who learn and develop by observing in silence, with certain restrictions imposed by adults that nevertheless do not frustrate or inhibit their capacities for taking initiative.

In the first part of this chapter, I present the ancient context of the Quechua locality that I come from and where I made my observations of how adults help children develop as persons following the ideal of "being like people."

The second part of the chapter analyzes the notions of *respect* and *autonomy* as they are understood in the Quechua language and used in the discursive practices of the people living in the community of Aucará. In the community's social practices and discourse, the two notions show a certain complementarity, rather than contradiction, within the framework of the formation of an ideal, fully developed person according to local visions.

The third part of the chapter looks at children's observation of, and participation in, their parents' day-to-day work. In this participation, children clearly receive care and protection from the adults in the form of emotional and physical proximity with family members and acquaintances. It is also evident that children play a role in family and community activities and conduct themselves in a way that shows respect for the interactions among adults, by keeping quiet and remaining calm. This sociocultural framework is the space where the children's autonomy develops through their participation in the family and community's meaningful activities.

The next section presents the community's conceptions about learning through the care and upbringing that parents offer their children so they develop as fully as possible, in accordance with their notions of human formation. This section focuses on the fact that the data presented on childcare, based on observations of everyday life, are highly consistent with the conceptions and ideas that parents express about children's overall development in the perspective of "becoming people."

The last part looks at the way children develop the capacity for autonomy in the opportunities for participation and learning that parents procure for them in day-to-day life. The argument is that the care and appreciation that adults offer serve to ensure the children's comprehensive development and enable them to acquire capabilities for autonomy in carrying out their initiatives, within a scaffolding of social rules that adults enforce so that children will be respectful toward their elders.

2. LEARNING TO "BE LIKE PEOPLE" IN THE QUECHUA REGION

The locality of Aucará,[1] where the data presented here were gathered, is a Quechua-speaking community in the southern Andes of Peru, a settlement with ancient pre-Inca historical roots (García, 2007). As its ancestors did, this community of roughly one thousand inhabitants earns its living primarily through agriculture for self-consumption, corn, and potatoes being the most important crops. Local life requires active members who take initiative to help work in the fields and raise small farm animals as the main source of their subsistence. For most of the families, monetary income is also important as they interact more and more with the market and cities.

In Aucará, for as long as people can remember, education within the family follows the traditions of the Andean peoples. One distinctive feature of this community, in addition to its system for forming persons on the basis of respect, is the conception expressed by parents, grandparents, and older siblings about how to form the new generations. They speak of

[1] The locality of Aucará, which belongs to the Farming Community of Aucará, is located in the district of Aucará, in the province of Lucanas, in the Ayacucho region, and in the southern sector of the Peruvian Andes. This community occupies a collectively owned territory, which includes a Communal Directorate, elected in a communal assembly, and a local municipal government, chosen in elections regulated by the national electoral institution.

comprehensive processes based on upbringing, care and the correct accommodation of children's capacities so that they can be like people (*runa hina kay*),[2] are prepared to "make their way through life," devote themselves to the well-being of their family, which naturally includes them as well, and contribute to the prosperity of their community.

In this conception, the capacities for autonomy that people develop in these contexts center on their personal competencies, and yet they also involve taking part with a certain degree of autonomy in their family's meaningful activities and contributing in this way, through their personal achievements, to both their family's and their own well-being. In other words, personal autonomy develops for the purpose of dealing with social challenges; it is not an autonomy detached from the individual's life and that of his or her family, as will be argued below.

Within this sociocultural framework, children develop by participating in the community's everyday activities, carefully observing adults and older children as they go about their tasks, at times with great concentration, other times more casually, but always with an interest in contributing. At the same time, they maintain the attitude of respect instilled by their elders, consisting of remaining quiet and not interrupting interactions among their elders, within a scaffolding of mutual respect between adults and children. Their participation in activities that focus on the family's subsistence is based in part on self-interest, which means that they find motivation in what they do. Nevertheless, some tasks involve personal efforts that children do not entirely enjoy, but have to be done because they contribute to the children's well-being and that of their family.

Children's participation in their community's activities and the quality of the learning they achieve in this process have been amply documented in studies of Indigenous communities throughout the Americas (Gaskins & Paradise, 2010; Paradise & Rogoff, 2009; Rogoff, 1993, 2003; Rogoff et al., 2007). These studies highlight, aside from the children's initiative in achieving their learning and their involvement in activities that are meaningful for the family, the role that parents play and the value of communal traditions as particular sociocultural realities where child development

[2] *Runa hina kay* literally means "being like people" in the Quechua of Aucará. A justification of this concept can be found in García (2007). Grim-Feinberg (2013, p. 104) mentions that one way to translate *runa hina kay* into Spanish is "pórtate como gente," which she translates into English as "behave like a human being!", a recommendation often heard by the researcher when parents correct their children for breaking the norms of the Aucará community. *Runa* means "people."

occurs. This chapter contributes to this line of research by looking at LOPI as it occurs in the Quechua community of Aucará.

A case similar to the traditions of child development and education found in Aucará has been documented by Bolin (2006) in a Quechua population in the high Andes of Peru. She has identified in this population the value of family educational conceptions for raising well-adjusted children who are fully satisfied with being useful to their family and their community, in a region where extreme environmental conditions and the marginalization of its inhabitants make for harsh living conditions. The author argues that in the community of Chillihuani, parents, older siblings, and grandparents manage to raise persons with a strong sense of respect for all forms of life, and that this generalized respect and the satisfaction of enjoying all that has been bestowed on them is a guarantee for carrying on their lives within the ancient traditions handed down by their ancestors.

A study conducted in Aucará also recognizes respect as a fundamental orientation of this community in the care and upbringing of children. Grim-Feinberg (2013) highlights the expression in Spanish that she heard regularly, "Pórtate como gente" (behave like people) as an expression close to the Quechua recommendation *runa hina kay* (be like people) reported in my own research (García, 2007). Furthermore, Grim-Feinberg comments that the meaning the community members express regarding respect is related to the idea of "minding" in the sense of "paying attention" or "listening," implying a relationship between people who communicate with one another and in this exchange pay full attention to their communication. In this way, the author maintains that children in Aucará are motivated to act respectfully in their families through affective bonds and a desire for belonging.

3. QUECHUA NOTIONS OF RESPECT AND AUTONOMY

Although the notion of "respect" has a range of manifestations and meanings in different Indigenous communities, it has been shown to be an important notion when it comes to raising children. For example, in some Indigenous communities, respect has been identified with children's autonomy (Rogoff, 2003). In communities of the Amazon jungle in Peru, children's learning seems to involve respect for elders and their knowledge (Aikman, 2003). In Mazahua families in Mexico, Paradise (1987) recognizes respect for children in the care, seriousness, and appreciation shown toward babies. In Indigenous communities of the Texcoco Hills in Mexico, Lorente

Fernández (2006) reports that children are respectful when they answer their parents correctly, eat the food that their parents have prepared for them, and help around the house. Taggart (2003) has reported that the Nahuas of northern Puebla, Mexico, instill respect by forming children "as human beings" who show mercy, respond with consideration, and are obedient.

In the Quechua language, the equivalent of "respect" is *yupaychay* [to consider] according to Cerrón-Palomino (1994) and Soto (1976). Moreover, *uyakay*,[3] understood as "listening," is closely related to the notion of "minding" in the sense of listening and paying attention (Grim-Feinberg, 2013). Thus, *uyakay* and "minding" are part of the respectful behavior demanded of children in the community of Aucará. Quechua discourse in this locality also makes use of the term *rispitay* [from the Spanish "respetar," meaning "to respect"].

In the community of Aucará, *respect* implies observing different behaviors and attitudes that constitute the type of family education used locally. When it comes to children, respect means behaving modestly and quietly, especially in the presence of adults, and for adults, it means speaking softly in the presence of strangers or people with some kind of important status in the locality. Children are constantly taught to greet their elders, often using kinship terms like "uncle," "mom," or "dad," as a way to show closeness or affection for people who are not blood relatives. Along these same lines, for both adults and children respect involves speaking cordially and politely to other people and displaying humility before them.

Other facets of respect in this community have to do with the "minding" that children are expected to show to their parents and other adults by paying attention and listening to them. Likewise, adults can "mind" children in the sense of listening to them and putting themselves in their shoes, as reported by Grim-Feinberg (2013). Adults and children are expected to feel embarrassed when they fail to follow the norms of respect in the presence of others, or when they fail to display the qualities of "being like people," *runa hina kay*.

These notions of respect in the community might seem to clash with the meanings of "autonomy" that are conventionally understood as independence. Particularly, "obedience" as a manifestation of respect that is demanded of children would seem to contradict the development of levels of personal autonomy in family education as practiced in this community.

---

[3] *Uyakuy* is related to *uya* [face] and to [listen]. So when *uyakuy* is translated as "obeying," the intention is to imply primarily listening, not submitting to the other. This word also contains the suffix *-ku* implying benefit for the verb's subject.

The opposite is true; however, in this community's family educational practices, being obedient is not at odds with the development of capacities for agency that go into the formation of children's *autonomy*. In Aucará, the development of autonomy also entails the development of children's initiative as they participate by collaborating in the family's activities. Adults encourage the development of children's initiatives when they consist of "doing" something to contribute to the success of the activity; less encouragement is given for verbal initiatives. The formation of a fully developed person who displays the qualities of "being people" focuses on the cultivation of personal autonomy not only for participating and learning in pursuit of personal interests within the family's everyday activities but also for personal growth depending on his or her particular capabilities.

This individual development toward the ideal of a complete, well-rounded person who is "like people" is not supposed to be aimed at the individualistic well-being of a subject who is detached from family and community ties. The development of autonomy in this community is about progressively wielding more and more capabilities of agency aimed at well-being and a good life for one's family and oneself. It is about the formation of personal responsibility for respecting all human and nonhuman beings with whom one lives in the local setting and beyond. In other words, this community looks for children to develop levels of autonomy that will enable them to attain individual plenitude, what Bonfil Batalla (2003: 70) calls *individual realization*, which is reached by means of service to the community, and this service to the community benefits everyone, including the individual.

4. CHILDREN'S PARTICIPATION BY OBSERVING ACTIVITIES

The types of activities that are meaningful to the community, primarily cultivating corn and potatoes, and raising farm animals, require daily attention from adults, in different proportions depending on the season—rainy or dry. In this context, children from a very young age accompany their parents in carrying out these activities. However, the obligation to send children to school starting at the age of five is depriving children of this fundamental stage of their early childhood that allows them to spend time with their parents and learn from life itself the capacities and values that are fundamental for local life.

When parents take their children with them as they go about their everyday activities, especially when the mother carries her small child on her back, children are in constant contact with their caregivers. In this context, children have access to most adult activities with very few restrictions, which gives them the chance to participate in the most meaningful activities of the family and community. For this same reason, children's access to the spaces where adults interact requires certain rules that govern children's behavior. Children are asked to keep quiet and calm in the presence of adults, a kind of *respect* that is encouraged in this community (García, 2007).

By participating in most of the family and community activities, children have chances to closely observe the activities, practices, and social events that take place in the family and the community. They constantly participate alongside their parents and other adults, they observe intensely, they listen to varied discourse, they imitate adults and play at communal activities with other children from the family or with neighbors.

I illustrate this kind of proximity with my observations of a 2-year-old girl interacting with her mother and other adults. The quality of the emotions experienced by this girl was clear to see, along with the autonomous games she played, always in visual and emotional contact with her mother, within the context of a family from Aucará sowing corn (García, 2007). As the family planted, the girl experienced all the incidents and difficulties that the work entailed for the adults, as she observed her mother and the other adults with different kinds of attention. Sometimes, she paid close attention to her mother and the men plowing with a team of oxen; other times, she watched them out of the corner of her eye and paid more attention to her games. Other times, when the adults took a break from their work, she sat protected by her mother in the shade of an apple tree, or when she was left alone under the tree, she organized her own games with things from nature that she found on the ground. This girl showed capacities for agency in organizing her own games or seeking the protection of her mother's skirts when she felt threatened by a lamb grazing in the cornfield, always in the care of her mother, who did her work and simultaneously kept an eye on her daughter.

Although the little girl was clearly alone playing and wandering around the apple tree most of the day, she was always listening to the adults' animated conversation and under her mother's watchful eye. After the adults took a few breaks, the little girl continued playing a while longer until she fell asleep on the blankets under the tree. When the time came to return home, the mother picked the sleeping girl up, put her on her back, and headed back with the others. The little girl woke up along the way and from her mother's back watched what was going on and listened to the adults talking and singing the ritual planting songs called *harawi*.[4]

In the scenes described above, the 2-year-old girl has an intense experience of corn planting day, the family's most important activity not only because corn is a regional staple but also because the ritual serves to reaffirm and deepen the family and *compadrazgo* bonds in the annual act of reproducing corn in the bosom of the earth. According the Aucará traditions, the patron spirit of sowing deeply appreciates the presence of the extended family, including children, and of the closest *compadres*, and bears in mind their contribution as a *kuyay* [appreciation] that must be returned to the giver when he does his own planting.

Even though the little girl was playing in the field most of the day without intervening verbally in the adults' interactions, her presence beside the adults gave her intimate proximity to the productive activity and the meanings that people share about social life and the ancestral values bound up in planting corn and collaborating as a group. The little girl witnesses the adults' intense emotions throughout the day, meaning she has a front row seat to the efforts the adults make to share work within a demonstration of appreciation for the other, the joy of undertaking the activity jointly, the feeling of satisfaction for having complied with the social and spiritual rules of planting with the permission and the protection of the *Apus*.[5] Thanks are given to the Apus with a toast in their honor and with the ritual songs of respect for their protection, all with the pleasant tone of an ordinary conversation, but at the same time showing a certain fear of powerful beings.

Surrounded by this tone of respect children experience and learn attitudes from a very young age. This affective tone can be recognized as well among the Hopi people, where children also learn the norms of their society and good manners in the warmth and security of the intimacy of their family and community (Eggan, 1974).

Due to the obligation to send 3 year olds to preschool, many children no longer have the opportunity to experiences these interactions at planting time, when different local practices, visions, meanings, and know-how, handed down from previous generations, are mobilized and incorporated

[4] *Harawi*: Ritual song that women sing during and after planting. The songs have a meaning that is full of affection by highlighting the collaboration among family members and *compadres* and by asking the protective beings to permit future plantings in the same conditions of collaboration and reciprocity.

[5] *Apu*: Protective being, deity, who is the origin and caregiver of the sources of life in the environment. It can be a hill, a lake, a river.

into other cultural contexts. Nevertheless, there are still some children who can participate in these meaningful activities of their family, usually because their mother decides to include them, or because it is easier to take them along when there are no adults or older siblings available to look after them. If schools understood the importance of these experiences in children's lives, it would reach agreements with the parents so that the children could attend school depending on their age, and with time off to participate in the family and community's most important agricultural activities, which follow a clearly established calendar.

Within the framework of this warmth and affection, children learn and develop in ordinary life, under the care of their parents, participating in the family and community's everyday activities, having access to the guidance of experts in carrying out these activities and to stories and discourse, feeling useful to the family by contributing to tasks on which their subsistence depends. They feel protected by a family that lets them feel the emotions of sharing fieldwork, with the help and protection of the Apus, considered the "owners" of the local environment and of life. The belief that the Apus are the owners of life does not refer only to the sense of proprietary rights, but primarily to their attributes of creators and protectors of *Pacha*,[6] time and space experienced as a whole.

5. LEARNING IN THE FRAMEWORK OF CARETAKING AND UPBRINGING AS EXPERIENCED BY CHILDREN

In Aucará, children develop under their parents' watchful eye. The close, intimate protection that children receive includes on the one hand the care they need to survive the inclemencies of a physical and geographical environment located 3200 m above sea level. On the other hand, it includes comprehensive protection that ensures the integrity of the children's physical and emotional health, the proper cultivation of empathy with other people and with natural powers, and the development of respect for all living beings.

The care and protection offered to children allow them to develop their full personality in harmony with their socio-natural environment. Within this development framework that adults procure for children, learning takes

[6] *Pacha*: Time and space conceived jointly and holistically. Quechua concept that shows the consistency of Indigenous thought, as it wisely groups into one category both the moment of the occurrence of the actions and the natural, geographical, and social context in which they occur. *Kay Pacha* is these present circumstances, the present world with all its existences and actors.

place through participation in the adults' activities. In local activities, adults and older children face challenges and problems that they must solve, and smaller children closely observe these problem-solving processes. Learning for life is achieved by experiencing life itself, and in this way, children are prepared for the kinds of challenges they will most likely face in their locality and community. At other times, these same children will also be prepared for life in other contexts; for this reason, the parents demand the support of schools so that children learn competencies for other realities outside of their community.

The farming community of Aucará is remarkable for the coexistence of ancestral values and practices with other conceptions brought in from cities. For the parents with the strongest roots in this community, this coexistence is not an irreconcilable contradiction. The ancestral formation in respect for one's elders and appreciation for family members as a guarantee of a full life, within a framework of reciprocity among relatives and *compadres*, also includes the aspiration to go to school in order to achieve "professional" status as a way to be prepared for the demands of life in the cities and other contexts outside of the community.

The interactions between children and their caregivers in the context of the family's day-to-day activities show the protection, care, and emotional and physical closeness that children receive from their adult caregivers, primarily mothers, grandmothers, aunts, and sisters, starting from the very youngest childhood. Bolin (2006) describes very similar interactions in the Peruvian Quechua community of Chillihuani in the Cusco region, although in this community, the care given is even more intense because of the extreme climate conditions of the high altitude where the community is located, and also because the main livelihood in the region is herding.

In spite of the evident differences imposed by the distinct ecological conditions in which they live their lives, in both communities, the same kind of respect is cultivated toward all those making up the social and geographic environment, and toward all the beings that inhabit the space–time encompassed in the Quechua notion of *Pacha*. The type of formation offered to children is based on the esteem given to each member of the family; on adults who give good examples in real-life situations, showing indulgence for others and gratitude for gifts received with the conviction to reciprocate; and on the beings that protect natural resources.

These kinds of learning experienced in the community of Aucará are reflected in the meaning conveyed by the Quechua language, this population's ancestral language, regarding the idea of learning. In this language, "learning" is *yachay*, a term that is also used for the idea of "inhabiting and living." For the speakers of this language, the notion of "learning" is related to "inhabiting living," which is consistent with the kinds of learning that revolve around the community's day-to-day activities. Unlike in Spanish, the notion of "teaching" is not expressed with a separate word in Quechua; it is constructed out of the word for "learning": *yachachiy* (with the causative morpheme *-chi*) can be translated as "making learning."

The way of conceptualizing learning also occurs in other Indigenous communities, for example, among the Nasa people of Colombia (Ramos & Rojas, 2003). In the Nasa communities, people do not focus so much on the role of teaching as on the process of learning that the learner goes through.

These forms of learning as experienced in the community and the conceptions of learning as codified in the original languages of the communities suggest a human group that conceives of children's development as ongoing learning for life, learning that is pursued to deal with immediate challenges as well as with challenges from other spaces beyond the community that learners will need to navigate in order the enhance their condition of "people." This development of children is grounded in the kind of participation that parents set up for them, a generalized participation in most of the family and community's meaningful activities that includes certain norms of respect such as not interrupting adults' interactions. It is a way to support children's learning that has been described in the conceptual model of Leaning by Observing and Pitching In (Rogoff, 2014).

This type of participation enables children to observe adults' activities with greater concentration, which allows them gradual autonomous learning of their elders' social and economic practices. These observations also serve as the basis for games and imitations that children engage in when adults are not present. When they protect the cornfields from birds, or when they take the flocks out to graze (activities that children usually carry out once they are allowed to go to these places in the company of an older child), children organize their games or imitations by recreating scenes and interactions that they have observed in adults. In this way, children autonomously develop capacities for agency that at the same time, adhere to the norms of respect and focus on personal well-being that will contribute to a good life for the family.

Parents and grandparents, aside from the care that they give, constantly instill in children—in ordinary conversations, in ritualized nighttime and early morning stories, and by example—the importance of being "good people." A grandmother, for example, reflecting on "proper people," mentioned that they should ingratiate themselves, speak softly and not in a disagreeable tone as "common savages" [*millapa chusku indio*[7]] do:

> *Proper people should make themselves appreciated,* ***be soft in their speech****. Those that speak like common savages are contemptible. They don't understand, they are willful, and they're the ones who feel superior to others.*

This grandmother's expressions emphasize the expectation to "make oneself appreciated" in the sense of eliciting affection and also as a manifestation of reciprocity, meanings evoked in the notion of *kuyay* [appreciation] recognized also by Isbell (2005). Likewise, disapproval is expressed for people who "give themselves airs," i.e., locals who consider themselves superior to ordinary people from the community.

In addition to these expectations to "make oneself appreciated" and act modestly, there is the need to form children to be obedient and hardworking. In the conception of Quechua-speaking parents, *uyakuy* is a way to show "respect" as it expresses the idea of "listening for one's own benefit." It implies "minding" in the sense of paying attention to someone else. Obeying implies listening and paying attention to an adult. It does not suggest submission to the adult because learners have the autonomy to listen, although their obligation is to listen to the experts in order to assure proper learning. Thus, listening to adults and working hard are two more expectations that adults convey to children so that they grow into complete, well-rounded persons.

6. THE DEVELOPMENT OF CAPACITIES FOR AUTONOMY

Although parents believe that children by themselves should learn the capacities needed to be useful to their family, this expectation of autonomous development is accompanied by intense care for children's physical and spiritual well-being, to ensure that they develop the right way until they become adults with responsibilities for their family and community.

In the previous sections, we have seen that children, in the sociocultural framework of the community, have the possibility to observe their family and community's activities closely by keeping quiet and concentrating on the actions. This generates autonomous capacities for personal development

[7] Literally, "disagreeable, savage, uncivilized."

in the framework of social rules for respectful behavior and in the process of situated learning that contributes to family life.

Children's capacity for agency develops in the framework of the family's well-being. By achieving effective and meaningful learning that has a direct impact on daily life, by solving personal and family problems in order to meet immediate needs as well as the social aspirations of the family and community, children develop their autonomy by gradually wielding capacities for agency that help to sustain life itself.

Consequently, the development of this autonomy is not a process undertaken by a person free of social ties; it is the development of a person rooted in her primary life-sustaining activities and in the framework of her social roles that contribute to the well-being of the family and immediate community group.

The levels of autonomy and freedom that children wield when they participate in family and community activities expand when they play with other children or carry out their family responsibilities in the fields or taking care of farm animals. There they deploy their autonomy and potential by imitating adults and playing the roles of man and woman, in accordance with the aspirations and concrete life of their families and community.

In play, children do not just have fun; they also reinforce their learning by imitating adults, and they develop their creativity at their own pace. At the same time, they experience the satisfaction of helping their family and deploy their imagination related to worlds of well-being or conflict situations, on the basis of adults' discourse and the everyday interactions that they have observed and experienced.

The autonomy that the children develop is not an autonomy of "free will," without limits, but rather an autonomy that is bounded by the social norms of their family and community. Since these social norms focus on respect for adults for the purpose of attaining personal and collective well-being, which are inextricably bound up together, the norms that guide the development of autonomy make this capacity a strength for individuals to deal with local challenges and those of other spaces outside of the community.

The observations described in this chapter, taken from the specific realities of an Indigenous community in the Andes of southern Peru, serve to demonstrate the conceptual model of Learning by Observing and Pitching In (Rogoff, 2014). This contribution highlights the notions of children's participation in family and community activities, in which mutual respect between adults and children is demonstrated. This respect is expressed in children's discreet and silent behavior when they take initiative in family and community activities and when they listen to adults in order to make their contribution to the family more efficient, and when they pay attention to adults in order to wield their autonomy and initiative in learning processes while at the same time contributing to meaningful activities in their family.

REFERENCES

Aikman, S. (2003). *La educación indígena en Sudamérica: Interculturalidad y bilingüismo en Madre de Dios, Perú*. Lima: Instituto de Estudios Peruanos.

Bolin, I. (2006). *Growing up in a culture of respect: Child rearing in Highland Peru*. Austin, TX: University of Texas Press.

Bonfil Batalla, G. (2003). *México profundo. Una civilización negada*. México, DF: Grijalbo.

Cerrón-Palomino, R. (1994). Quechua sureño. Diccionario unificado. *Biblioteca Básica Peruana V*. Lima: Biblioteca Nacional del Perú.

Eggan, D. (1974). Instruction and affect in Hopi cultural continuity. In G. Spindler (Ed.), *Education and cultural process* (pp. 311–332). New York, NY: Holt, Rinehart & Winston, Inc.

García, F. (2007). *Runa hina kay. La educación familiar y comunitaria orientada al respeto en una comunidad quechua*. Tesis de Doctor en Ciencias, México, DF: Departamento de Investigaciones Educativas del Centro de Investigación y de Estudios Avanzados del IPN.

Gaskins, S., & Paradise, R. (2010). Learning through observation in daily life. In D. F. Lancy, J. Bock, & S. Gaskins (Eds.), *The anthropology of learning in childhood* (pp. 89–95). Lanham, MD: Alta Mira Press.

Grim-Feinberg, K. (2013). *Cultural models of respectful subjectivity among primary school children in post-conflict Ayacucho, Peru: An embodied learning analysis*. Doctoral dissertation, Urbana, IL: Graduate College of the University of Illinois at Urbana-Champaign.

Isbell, B. J. (2005). *Para defendernos: Ecología y ritual en un pueblo andino*. Cuzco: CBC.

Lorente Fernández, D. (2006). *La razzia cósmica: Una concepción nahua sobre el clima (el complejo ahuaques-tesiftero en la Sierra de Texcoco, México*. Tesis de Maestría en Antropología Social, México, DF: Universidad Iberoamericana.

Paradise, R. (1987). *Learning through interaction: The experience and development of the Mazahua self in the context of the market*. Unpublished doctoral dissertation, University of Pennsylvania.

Paradise, R., & Rogoff, B. (2009). Side by side: Learning by observing and pitching. *Ethos, 37*(1), 102–138.

Ramos, A., & Rojas, T. (2003). Educación escolar, vida comunitaria y uso de las lenguas: Reflexiones sobre el proceso en el pueblo nasa (páez). In *Ponencia presentada en el 51° Congreso Internacional del Americanistas. Santiago de Chile, 14–18 de julio 2003*.

Rogoff, B. (1993). *Aprendices del pensamiento. El desarrollo cognitivo en el contexto social*. Barcelona: Paidós.

Rogoff, B. (2003). *The cultural nature of human development*. New York, NY: Oxford University Press.

Rogoff, B. (2014). Learning by observing and pitching in to family and community endeavors: An orientation. *Human Development, 57*, 69–81.

Rogoff, B., Moore, L., Najafi, B., Dexter, A., Correa-Chávez, M., & Solís, J. (2007). Children's development of cultural repertoires through participation in everyday routines and practices. In J. Grusec & P. Hastings (Eds.), *Handbook of socialization: Theory and research* (pp. 490–515). New York, NY: The Guilford Press.

Soto, C. (1976). *Diccionario Quechua Ayacucho-Chanca*. Lima: Ministerio de Educación/ Instituto de Estudios Peruanos.

Taggart, J. (2003). Como los niños aztecas aprenden a ser adultos: Inculcando el respeto hoy en día en una comunidad mexicana. In *Ponencia presentada en la III Reunión del Grupo de Trabajo de Familia e Infancia del Consejo Latinoamericano de Ciencias Sociales. Valdivia, Chile, 29 de setiembre al 1 de octubre de 2003*.

CHAPTER SEVEN

Mayan Children's Creation of Learning Ecologies by Initiative and Cooperative Action

Lourdes de León[1]
CIESAS, Mexico City, Mexico
[1]Corresponding author: e-mail address: lourdesdeleonp@gmail.com

Contents

Abstract

This chapter examines Mayan children's initiatives in creating their own learning environments in collaboration with others as they engage in culturally relevant endeavors of family and community life. To this end, I carry out a fine-grained ethnographic and linguistic analysis of the interactional emergence of *learning ecologies*. Erickson defines learning ecology as a socioecological system where participants mutually influence one another through verbal and nonverbal actions, as well as through other forms of semiotic communication (2010, 254). In analyzing learning ecologies, I adopt a "theory of action" approach, taking into account multimodal communication (e.g., talk, gesture, gaze, body positioning), participants' sociospatial organization, embodied action, objects, tools, and other culturally relevant materials brought together to build action (Goodwin, 2000, 2013; Hutchins, 1995).

I use *microethnographic analysis* (Erickson, 1992) to bring to the surface central aspects of children's agentive roles in learning through "cooperative actions" (Goodwin, 2013) and "hands-on" experience (Ingold, 2007) the skills of competent members of their community. I examine three distinct Learning Ecologies created by children's initiatives among the Mayan children that I observed: (i) children requesting guidance to collaborate in a task, (ii) older children working on their own initiative with

Advances in Child Development and Behavior, Volume 49
ISSN 0065-2407
http://dx.doi.org/10.1016/bs.acdb.2015.10.006

subsequent monitoring and correction from competent members, and (iii) children with near competence in a task with occasional monitoring and no guidance. I argue that these findings enrich and add power to models of family- and community-based learning such as Learning by Observing and Pitching In (Rogoff, 2014).

1. INTRODUCTION

This chapter examines Mayan children's agentive roles in creating their own learning environments in collaboration with others as they engage in and practice culturally relevant endeavors of family and community life.

Studies of children's learning in families and communities in the Americas have highlighted children's observational skills and spontaneous willingness to engage in family and community endeavors (de León, 2011, submitted for publication; Gaskins, 1999, 2000; Greenfield, 1984, 2004; Martínez Pérez, (2015a); Mejía-Arauz, Rogoff, Dexter, & Najafi, 2007; Maurer, 1977; Paoli, 2003; Paradise & Rogoff, 2009; Rogoff, 1990, 2003, 2011, 2014; Rogoff et al., 2007, among others). In these sociocultural contexts, children's lives are very much highly structured around "the primacy of adult work" (Gaskins, 1999) and parents encourage and expect children to contribute and learn by keenly attending to culturally valued activities. Skilled observation requires the child's active management of attention to household activities normally organized in multiparty interactions (Chavajay & Rogoff, 1999; de León, 1998, 2011, 2012a, 2012b; Rogoff, 2003).

Evidence of children's learning by skillfully observing is revealed by their *initiative* to engage in routine activities without being told (Alcalá, Rogoff, Mejía-Arauz, Coppens, & Dexter, 2014; Coppens, Alcalá, Mejía-Arauz, & Rogoff, 2014; de León, 2011, submitted for publication; Rogoff, 2014). Children's *initiative* or "eagerness to contribute and belong as a valued member of their family and communities" (Rogoff, 2014, 73) is a crucial element in the learning model referred to as "Learning by Observing and Pitching In" (LOPI) to families and communities (Rogoff, 2014). This model has been defined as "a multifaceted process where motivation, social interaction, goals of learning, attention, communication, and language are socially and cognitively interrelated in a holistic way" (Rogoff, 2014, 73).

One cross-cutting theme in LOPI is "*children's initiative in contributing responsibly* to ongoing activities of their families and communities together with other people's support for children's initiative through collaborative guidance" (2014, 73). Yet, we need to further document how children's *initiative* emerges and unfolds in the moment-to-moment interactions of family and community life. What is involved for the child to display initiative to collaborate? How may a child's initiative create a learning environment? What elements conspire to make a learning environment unfold in everyday activities?

In this chapter, I carry out a fine-grained ethnographic and linguistic analysis of learning events in a Mayan community to reveal "hidden" or undocumented aspects of the interactional and situated nature of children's initiative and role to recruit others to aid in their own learning processes in family- and community-based learning (de León, submitted for publication; Martínez Pérez, 2015b).

To this end, I document Mayan children's agentive roles in involving others in initiating actions that are part of the routine activities of their everyday lives, and discuss how these actions bring about a *situated learning ecology*. I take as a point of departure Erickson's definition of a learning ecology as a socioecological system where participants mutually influence one another through verbal and nonverbal actions as well as other forms of semiotic communication (Erickson, 2010, 254). In order to examine participants' engagement in situated learning ecologies, I adopt a "theory of action" approach taking into account the mutual elaboration of diverse semiotic resources, including multimodal communication (e.g., talk, gesture, gaze, body), participants' sociospatial organization, embodied action, objects, tools, and other culturally relevant materials brought together to build action (Goodwin, 2000, 2013; Hindmarsh, Reynolds, & Dunne, 2011; Mondada, 2012; Streeck, 2015; Streeck, Goodwin, & LeBaron, 2012).

I embrace the view that human action is intrinsically cooperative in character and central to human sociality (Bruner, 1962; Enfield & Levinson, 2006; Goodwin, 2013; Ingold, 2001; John-Steiner, 1985; Rogoff, 1990; Sacks, Schegloff, & Jefferson, 1974; Streeck, 2015; Vygotsky, 1978, 1987). In this context, I argue that one central aspect of children's learning is shaped by taking initiative to engage in cooperative actions through which they gradually "inhabit the actions" (Goodwin, 2013, 15) of the competent members of their community.

To this end, I provide an interactional microanalysis of a collection of different goal-oriented activities in which the Mayan children of the study participate in their everyday lives (e.g., preparing flowers for a Day of the Dead altar, knitting, and splitting wood). Then I examine the processes of creating situated learning ecologies. I conclude with observations on how my analysis of learning ecologies offers new insights to the LOPI model.

2. THE STUDY

This study was conducted in the Mayan hamlet of Nabenchauk, a Tzotzil-speaking community of around 5000 inhabitants in the municipality of Zinacantán, Chiapas in the South of Mexico. (The total number of inhabitants of Zinacantán is approximately 30,000, and there are about 300,000 Tzotzil speakers.) In the context of contemporary indigenous Chiapas, Zinacantán has a relatively self-sufficient economy based on corn and flower industry, transportation, commerce, and increasing out-migration. Although most children attend elementary school, where Spanish is the primary language, they are socialized in a predominantly Tzotzil-speaking environment, where adult work organizes family life.

The present analysis is rooted in three decades of linguistic and anthropological research in the Highlands of Chiapas (de León, 1998, 2005a, 2005b, 2007, 2010, 2011, 2012a, 2012b, submitted for publication). Over this period, a longitudinal ethnographic and linguistic study of one focal family and eight complementary families was undertaken. The corpus for this study consists of everyday interactions of the focal family at home and in their agricultural fields. The everyday life of this family is typical of agricultural families in this community, which, in fact, constitute a large majority in the community.

For this study, I analyze a collection of activities involving four children of the focal family at different ages along the longitudinal line in which the research has taken place.

The research combines ethnomethodology, talk-in-interaction, and language socialization approaches (Duranti, Ochs, & Schieffelin, 2012; Garfinkel, 1967; Goodwin, 2006, 2007; Ochs, 1988; Ochs & Schieffelin, 1984; Schieffelin, 1990).

It takes situated activities as units of analysis (Goffman, 1982; Goodwin, 1990, 2006) within a broader approach derived from activity theory. Here, notions of activity and goal-directed action are central (Leontyev, 1979; Rogoff, 1990, 2003; Vygotsky, 1978).

3. CHILDREN'S COOPERATION AND LEARNING IN SITUATED LEARNING ECOLOGIES

Scholars studying learning ecologies cross-culturally have noted the importance in some communities of children's agency and self-motivation in learning without instruction (Fortes, 1970; Lancy, 2010; Mead, 1970; Philips, 1983). This phenomenon has been examined in its various guises, including learning by: (i) observation, involving "keen" or "open attention" (Gaskins & Paradise, 2010; Lancy, 2010, 2012; Odden & Rochat, 2004; Rogoff, Paradise, Mejía-Arauz, Correa-Chávez, & Angelillo, 2003); (ii) "pitching in" (Paradise & Rogoff, 2009; Rogoff, 2003, 2014); (iii) overhearing (de León, 1998, 2012a, 2012b); (iv) "intent community participation" (Rogoff et al., 2007, 2003); and more recently, (v) "LOPI" in family and community (Rogoff, 2014).

LOPI is a multidimensional model that comprises seven interrelated "facets" represented as a *prism* (Rogoff, 2014, 73). These facets are

1. Learner's incorporation and contribution to family/community endeavors.
2. Learner's eagerness to contribute and belong.
3. Collaborative organization of endeavors.
4. Transformation of participation is the goal of learning.
5. Learning by means of wide, keen attention, and contribution with guidance by other people or community values.
6. Communication based on coordination of shared reference and "nonverbal (and verbal) conversation."
7. Assessment appraising support from others for the activity, along with the learner's mastery, in order to aid the learner's contributions during the endeavor.

The model provides an abstract representation of a learning ecology. In this chapter, I examine how such ecology "comes to life"—in Vygotsky's term, its *microgenesis* (1978)—by looking in detail how it emerges from children's self-initiated actions as they engage in goal-oriented activities.

The active role of children in engaging in learning experiences has been addressed in the tradition of sociocultural studies for several decades (see Erickson, 1996; Greenfield, 1984; John-Steiner, 1985; Maynard, 2002, 2004; Rogoff, 1990; Rogoff & Lave, 1984; Vygotsky, 1978, 1987, among others). These scholars have argued that children's cognitive development takes place through their interaction with other competent members of society who mediate activity through intellectual practices and tools (especially language) (Vygotsky, 1978, 1987).

Within anthropology, Ingold has more recently argued that: "In reality children are involved, as much as are their teachers, as active and creative participants in the learning process. They participate by making their own contribution to shaping the contexts in which learning occurs and knowledge is generated" (2007, 113). We may ask, however, how do children create and "shape" these learning contexts?

In analyzing learning-in-doing situations, such as with archeologists and geologists in the field, Goodwin has argued that human sociality is established and sustained by human action: "human action is intrinsically *co-operative* in character, *as each party builds upon structure provided by others* (my emphasis)" (2013, 16). This process is cumulative and is created and lodged endogenously within particular communities (2013, 9; see also Ingold, 2001; Streeck, 2015).

In this study, I argue that one central aspect of children's knowledge and learning is shaped by taking initiative to engage in cooperative actions on "structures provided by others" in a field of practice (Goodwin, 2013). Following Goodwin, by "cooperative actions" I mean that children operate, use, and reuse structures or "substrates" from their predecessors through direct or "hands-on" experience as they engage in culturally relevant activities. Learning thus takes place in everyday life in good part through direct experience, that is, by observing, practicing, or enacting, in collaboration with other agents.

As Ingold observes: "[...] it is above all through the 'hands on' experience of engaging with others in practical situations of everyday life that learning takes place. Children learn not to gain entry to the social world but to make their way *within* it" (my emphasis) (Ingold, 2007, 113). In my own long-term ethnographic research in the Mayan highlands of Chiapas, México, I have witnessed how children "make their way within their social world" through eagerly engaging in "hands-on" experience. In fact, children actively create their own learning environments through practicing the cooperative actions of others they have witnessed attentively. I have observed this happening in two basic ways:

(1) *Children take initiative to practice actions through "hands-on" experience* with culturally relevant objects used by competent family members in previously observed activities. I have encountered many situations in which young children engage in exploratory practices such as a 2-year-old trying to weave with his mother's loom, the same

2-year-old boy digging a hole and inserting a flower stem to "plant" a flower, a 3-year-old girl using a hoe to weed a plot of vegetables, another 4-year-old boy trying to fix a chair with a hammer, and the same boy trying to embroider his sister's appliqué (de León, 2005a, submitted for publication). This process of exploratory practice is what I refer to as "the missing link" between "observing" and "pitching in" in the LOPI model. In fact, I would argue that it is one of the leading forces of "taking initiative." Lancy has referred to this particular kind of process as a form of "autonomous learning" (Lancy, 2010); Ingold refers to it as a form of "self-discovery": "To know things you have to grow into them, and them grow in you, so that they become a part of who you are" [...] "It is, in short, by watching, listening and feeling—by paying attention to what the world has to tell us—that we learn" (2013, 1).

It is nevertheless important to acknowledge that autonomous learning and self-discovery are inherently social, since they involve learning by observing and listening to other competent members of the community. However, it is through emulating the actions of others that practice ripens into a form of knowledge or skill. Goodwin (2013) explains this as an aspect of cooperation, which involves "operating" on a structure provided by others.

(2) *Children take initiative to cooperate with others* (as in (1)) and thereby create the conditions of a *situated learning ecology*. This interactional process may involve a child's expectation or request to have a competent participant guide him or her, yet the potential guide may or may not be willing to engage. In Zinacantán, this interactional process normally occurs with younger children (aged 2–5). With older children, competent participants seem less inclined to monitor and intervene unless it is for correcting specific aspects of the task since there is the expectation that the child already knows or does not need to be told.

Overall, the child's cooperative actions may trigger the spatial and social reconfiguration of participants to mutually engage in joint attention around the child's activity (de León, 1998, 2012a, 2012b; Goffman, 1981; Johnson, 2015, submitted for publication). The sociospatial organization toward a shared focus of attention is what Goffman referred to as an "ecological huddle" (1964, 135). Goodwin succinctly defined this configuration as "a public, shared focus of visual and cognitive attention that is created by the mutual orientation of the participants' bodies" (Goodwin, 2007, based on Goffman, 1964). This notion relates to Erickson's notion of "learning ecology": "an ecosystem of mutual influence among participants where talk is not privileged over non-verbal action and other semiotic media" (Erickson, 2010, 254). Whereas Erickson's notion of learning ecology comprises the larger, learning ecosystem, the "ecological huddle" is the interactionally emerging cognitive and social shared focus of attention of participants toward the ongoing actions.

As participants engage in joint attention, the learning process is co-constructed not through talk alone but, rather, through the mutual elaboration of diverse semiotic resources, including talk, spatial formations, embodied action, and objects, such as tools or materials.

In such a situation, the competent participant's engagement to guide the child may involve three possible learning ecologies, among others:

Learning Ecology 1: Incorporating the child in the ongoing task, at his or her level of competence, only if considered a priority by the competent participant (see example below of Cande (age 4) preparing flowers for the Day of the Dead).

Learning Ecology 2: Providing multimodal commentary, assessment, correction, or demonstration in the course of ongoing action to the not-yet-competent child (see example below of Xun, age 9, knitting a scarf).

Learning Ecology 3: Occasional monitoring of the child's activity (see example below of Joel, age 8, splitting wood with a machete).

Since the learning ecology involves an interactional process among participants, the learner's engagement may involve insistence on participating through actions, questions, and/or requests for guidance or explanation (see example below of Learning Ecology 1), which is normally the case with younger children (Martínez Pérez, 2015b). I have also found instances of older children taking initiative through attentive observation as they engage in a new activity through trial and error. This may bring other participants to monitor, correct verbally, or offer demonstrations. The child then corrects the sources of trouble through listening and attentive observation; at the end, he or she completes the task by him or herself (see example below of Learning Ecology 2).

In what follows, I would like to examine three examples that illustrate these different instantiations of a learning ecology. I start with an event involving a 5-year-old and go progressively to show more complex activities involving older learners. The following example focuses on a young participant actively requesting guidance in order to collaborate in a task.

3.1 Learning Ecology 1: The Child Takes Initiative to Contribute to an Ongoing Task

The family has been very busy preparing for the approaching Day of the Dead rituals on November 1st and 2nd. This special religious holiday has deep roots in Mexican society, especially among the Indigenous populations, where the whole community focuses on "welcoming" their dead ancestors back to the house with food and flower offerings. The preparations involved some members of the Hernández household going to the flower fields and to the market to get the flowers needed for the altar: marigolds, chrysanthemums, and red velvet celosia flowers. These are normally combined in flower arrangements that are placed on the altar and then taken to the cemetery as offerings for the dead relatives.

In this particular event, mother (with baby on back, Figure 1)[1] and Aunt Luisa bring fresh flowers into the house and place them on a working table in order to make the flower arrangements (Figure 2). They proceed to examine the flowers and discard the ones that are damaged or withered, placing them on the floor by the side of the table.

Figure 1 Mother brings flowers in.

[1] All figures are based on drawings from my original videotaped images from my own database. For reasons of indoor recording in poorly lighted spaces, I chose to have some of the original images transferred to drawings. I thank Herlinda Contreras for her invaluable help.

Figure 2 Aunt Luisa sets flowers on the table.

Cande, who is about to turn 5 years old, sits on a mat by the side of the adults' working area. As she observes the ongoing interaction, she picks up some flowers from the pile of discarded ones. She examines them, noticing all have broken stems and puts them by her side in a little pile and tries to put together some bouquets. As her Aunt Luisa notices she is handling the damaged flowers, she tells her to pluck off the petals and to stick them in a basket. The petals, her aunt tells her, will be used to decorate the family graves as well as the Day of the Dead altar. Cande smiles in delight to be properly included in the ongoing task (Figure 3).

Figure 3 Cande works on a mat by the side of the table.

Mother and Aunt keep on bringing buckets of fresh flowers into the house as Aunt Luisa starts making arrangements. Cande has been attentively observing the ongoing activities family members have been intensely carrying out. With her own initiative and cooperative actions with the damaged flowers, she was able to engage by plucking off petals, but she still wants to be more actively engaged as "part of the action." To this end, she asks her mother if there are still more flowers with broken stems (line 1). Her mother does not respond, but her aunt hands her a few more damaged flowers (line 2) (Figure 4).

1 Cande: Me' a ti mi oy k'aseme
Mom, are there broken ones?
2 Aunt: *((approaches and gives Cande flowers with broken stems))*

Figure 4 Aunt Luisa gives Cande more flowers with broken stems.

3 Mother→Cande: Mi o k'asem, tuch'o.
(If there are) broken ones, pull off (the broken stem).
4 Cande→Mother: Je, tuk' xaval, mu xka'i lek k'op.
Speak clearly, I don't understand you well.
5 Me' ta la jtik' si-ok.
Mom, do I put the stem in here?
((she points to a bucket by her side))
6 Mother: *((does not reply as she is focused on organizing the flowers))*
7 Cande→Mother: K'u chaval, li o k'asem le'e.
What do you think?, are there (more) broken (flowers) there?
((she gazes at the table to search for more flowers))
8 Mother: *((no answer))*
9 Cande: Me', (ch)ba(t) xa kak' ta mukenal.
Mom, I will take them to the cemetery.
10 Mother: *((no answer))*

In this example, the child attentively observes what is going on, she listens as a third party to what other participants are engaged in, what the activity is about, and eagerly takes initiative to contribute by working on the damaged flowers.

By her insistence, she eagerly attempts to transform the ongoing participation structure to *find her way* as a ratified participant in the activity from periphery to focality (de León, 2012a, 2012b, 103). At her own initiative, she starts to collect the damaged flowers and tries to make bouquets with them. This brings her aunt's attention, who ratifies Cande as a participant by telling her to pluck off petals and put them in a basket. In line 1, Cande tries to transform the organization of the ongoing dyadic participation structure between mother and aunt by asking her mother about the broken stems expressing her intention and eagerness to work on them. In line 2, her aunt replies to her request by giving her some discarded flowers, engaging in a momentary "ecological huddle,"—an emerging and temporally unfolding visual and cognitive shared focus of attention—without any verbal commentary. In line 3, in overlap with the aunt's action, her mother answers her question telling her from afar to "break off" the stems. However, Cande does not understand her mother and asks her to repeat her reply, saying *tuk' xaval!* "Speak clearly!"—explicitly demanding guidance (line 4). In lines 5 and 7, she again requests guidance about where to put the broken stems and if there are more of them. She gets no reply.

Throughout all the interaction, Cande is actively requesting how to fine-tune her actions in order to transform her marginal participation status and truly collaborate in the task. By taking initiative to contribute, she has been trying all along to "choreograph" (Tulbert & Goodwin, 2011) her mother's attention in order to engage her in her own situated learning ecology. Cande guides her own fine-tuning of attention by asking, then insisting, and finally recycling her questions and directives to her mother. Line 2 shows how Aunt Luisa aligns by momentarily sharing a joint focus of attention as she hands her the requested flowers, but the ecological huddle quickly dissolves as both she and Cande's mother continue focusing on their joint endeavor. Overall, the young girl creates a learning ecology by making her way within the activity, through "hands-on" experience with the broken flowers, by her eagerness to carry on the relevant cooperative actions, and by her insistence on guidance.

In line 8, she tries another strategy to legitimize participation to get her mother to pay attention to her initiative: She announces that she "will be taking [the flowers] to the cemetery." This last line shows how she frames the activity as a "legitimate one"—at least, to her mother's eyes, and also indexes her emerging cultural understanding of the *kind* of activity in which she and the family are engaged. It not just about flowers, it is about flowers specifically for the cemetery and for an important occasion. Through her different strategies to transform the ongoing participation structure, she strives to "inhabit the actions" (Goodwin, 2013; Streeck, 2015, see Heidegger, 1926) of the competent actors of her community in order to engage as a competent actor. By doing so, she shows signs of having learned at least some aspects of the task, through her own observation, initiative, cooperative actions, request for guidance, and transformation of participation.[2]

Regarding participation, I should clarify: there are two levels of analysis of participation here, derived from two approaches that are congenial: (i) *The talk-in-interaction approach* analyzes the child's participatory status as it *interactionally* emerges as a result of being ratified by adults as part of the participation structure within the ongoing activity. The interactional organization of participants in the specific learning ecology is also consistent with Erickson's notion of "ecosystem of mutual influence among participants" (2010, 254). (ii) *A LOPI perspective* which argues, at a larger scale, that the child learns by "transforming participation" (Facet 4 of the LOPI prism) (Rogoff, 2014, 74):"[s]uch transformation involves learning to collaborate with consideration and responsibility, as well as gaining information and skills" (Rogoff, 2014, 74, see also Rogoff, 1997, 1998). Both levels are evidently related, although they occur at different scales, the first one reveals the *interactional microgenesis* of participation in the emerging learning process, and the second one the by-product of larger processes such as the ones documented in the LOPI model.

Overall, the child has created *through her own initiative* a situated learning ecology in collaboration with others. However, initiative does not suffice; one central aspect of the situated learning ecology analyzed here involves the child transforming her participation status in the ongoing interaction. She succeeds in this by engaging other participants in shared frames of attention as she requests guidance to fine-tune her cooperative actions on the relevant materials of the activity.

[2] In analyzing participation, I use the Goffmanian model of "footing" (1974, 1981) redefined by Goodwin in terms of "participation" as the "temporally unfolding process through which separate parties demonstrate to each other their ongoing understanding of events as they are engaged in by building actions that contribute to the further progression of these very same events" (Goodwin, 2007, 12; see also Goodwin & Goodwin, 2004). I further adapted this analytical tool as a language acquisition and socialization model that departs from dyadic models of language learning. In de León (2012a), I use it to explain how children may learn language by overhearing and how their multimodal actions evidence their participation status. In the context of the present analysis, I extend my premises to learning events, not necessarily limited to language learning.

3.2 Learning Ecology 2: Providing Guidance as a Result of the Learner's Initiative

In this section, I outline another learning event, this time created by Xun (age 9), Cande's young brother, but occurring some years later (2003). My interest here is not to provide a detailed microanalysis of the full interaction (for details, see de León, submitted for publication), but to show the unfolding nature of an emergent learning ecology, in this case with an older child. In this particular example, the learner starts his own exploratory actions but is still not competent in the task he engages in. A nearby sibling notices what he is doing, criticizes his efforts, and eventually guides him to correct the sources of trouble so he can accomplish the task *on his own*, after intense engaged practice.

The situation is as follows: for several days, Xun has attentively observed his elder sister Cande (now age 15) knitting a scarf with a small wooden loom given to her at school (Figure 5).

Figure 5 Cande knits a scarf.

He is usually very keen on learning new skills and eager to try, but his sister has no interest in teaching him; so without any guidance, he grabs an extra wooden loom that happens to be in the house and sets it up with some leftover yarn he found (Figure 6).

After about 10 min, his sister Mary (11), already an experienced knitter who had been embroidering by his side sitting on the same bed, looks at him, noticing the yarn is tangled because he didn't set up the loom in

Figure 6 Xun starts setting up the knitting loom.

the correct way. She criticizes: *ma'uk yech chapas chak le'e*, "that's not the way to do it."

Setting up a knitting loom involves tying the yarn to the first peg or nail on the side. The next step is to wrap the yarn around subsequent pegs in a cursive "e" pattern and continue wrapping until the pattern reaches the desired length. In the following sequence, Mary evaluates Xun's errors, which consisted of not having systematically wrapped the yarn in a cursive "e" pattern and also of having skipped some pegs. This causes the yarn to get tangled and difficult to repair (Figures 7–10).

1 Mary: ((She is embroidering and briefly turns towards Xun's weaving))

Figure 7 That's not the way to do it (lines 1 and 2).

2 Mary: ma'uk yech chapas chak le'e.
That is not the way to do it.
3 *((goes back to her own embroidering))*
4 Xun: *((keeps on doing stitches on the loom looking confused))*
5 Mary: *((looks again at Xun's knitting, she leaves her own embroidery, and gets close to Xun's piece of work))*

Xun's initiative to start the knitting project is followed by the occasional monitoring and the negative assessment (line 2) of his sister. In lines 6 and 7, Mary gets close to Xun's piece of work and examines it. Here, both participants engage in an ecological huddle jointly focusing their attention to identify the source of the trouble in Xun's work. In line 6, Mary "calibrates" or fine-tunes Xun's attention (de León, 2011; Goodwin & Cekaite, 2012) to the way the yarn should be wrapped on the right peg, with a correction "you wrap it here,"[3] followed by another negative assessment (it is not like this) as she points at the trouble source.

6 Mary: cha'chuk to [li'e, ma'uk yech le'a.
you wrap it [here, it is not like this.
7 [((*points at stitch*))

Figure 8 You wrap it here, it is not like this (lines 6, 7).

[3] I examine how these multimodal "correctional directive trajectories" interactively unfold in everyday goal-oriented activities. (See Martínez Pérez, 2015b for an analysis of related "orientational directives" in Mayan Chamulan families. Martínez looks at larger directive trajectories, whereas I just focus on correction.) See also Jefferson (1974), Johnson (2015), Hindmarsh et al. (2011), and Lindwall and Ekström (2012) for an analysis of corrections in interaction.

8 *((Mary does next stitch)*

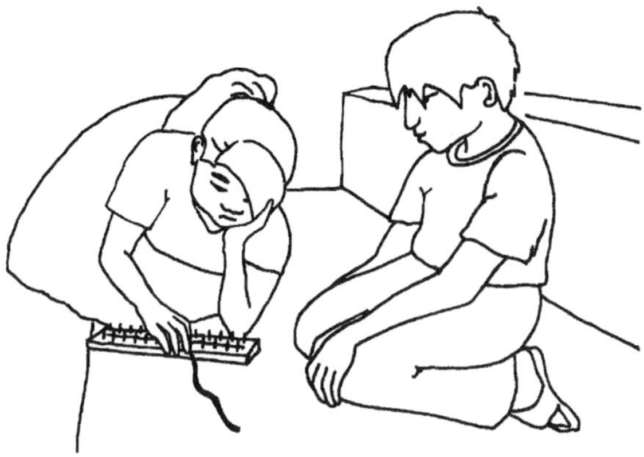

Figure 9 Mary does next stitch (line 8).

((Lines 9–12 deleted. They include more instructions in action))

13 Xun: *((pays attention to Mary's subsequent actions as he leans back against the wall))*

In lines 14–21 (deleted here), Mary points out the other sources of trouble and shows Xun, by demonstration with specific actions, how to wrap the yarn onto the loom. Xun tries one stitch at the beginning of Mary's guidance, but the rest of the time he just gazes attentively at her demonstrations. At the end of Mary's guidance, he picks up the loom and examines it with intense focus.

22 *((Xun picks up loom and examines it))*

Figure 10 Xun picks up loom (line 22).

Right after he picks up the loom and examines it, Mary and their younger brother make fun of Xun's flawed attempts. Ignoring them, he pulls the yarn off, undoes the whole knitting, and starts all over again. He continues knitting by himself that evening and the following morning appears in the kitchen with his first noble attempt, a long knitted strip, which although far from perfect, he proudly shows to all the family. The family acknowledges his efforts, although they do not consider the piece as a real scarf (Figure 11).

Figure 11 Xun shows "scarf" to family members.

In this particular learning ecology, Mary's multimodal corrections that were used to guide Xun to fix the faulty stitches were necessary for him to be able to repair the knitting project. In this case, multimodal guidance consisted of assessments, corrections, demonstrations, pointing at trouble spots, and offering explanations, lodged in multimodal "action packages" (Goodwin, 2007). All of this to point out the breaches in Xun's knitting project and to suggest ways to fix them.

I argue here that the notion of "multimodal action package" helps to understand the multimodal nature of guidance in situated learning activities such as the ones included in the LOPI model, which focuses on coordination of shared reference and "nonverbal (and verbal) conversation," in Facet 6 (Rogoff, 2014; see also Martínez Pérez, 2015b). The communicative resources such as talk and gesture associated with ongoing actions interactionally emerge in the guiding process as the learner keenly listens and attends in order to go back to the job through "hands-on" experience. The final knitted strip is the evidence of the effectiveness of the multimodal guidance in the situated learning ecology, but also, in critical ways, to the learner's active attentional engagement in the unfolding interaction. Overall, the learner is an agent in helping to cocreate or contribute to an effective learning ecology in the field of a culturally relevant practice.

3.3 Learning Ecology 3: Occasional Monitoring of the Near Competent Child

In this third learning ecology, the focal participant is Joel, the youngest sibling of the family when he was 8 years old. He starts on his own initiative to split a special kind of oily wood called *toj* to produce kindling required to make open fires, especially for cooking in the kitchen. Although girls can also do it, this is considered a boys' work.

Boys are expected to learn the skill, as many others, by observation and practice. In fact, I have never witnessed a boy being guided in how to chop or split wood, in spite of the risks involved. By contrast, I have seen young children with knives, machetes, and other tools (e.g., hoes and hammers) experimenting on their own without adult intervention, unless somebody notices they are about to seriously hurt themselves. In using these tools, children are evidently trying to emulate adults' use of them, as a result of their observational learning. As I mentioned before, I have seen very young children hammering broken chairs, using a hoe to weed, peeling a peach with a small knife, etc.

This scene differs from the previous events I analyzed in that here Joel already displays near full competence in a skill he has evidently learned through keen observation and "hands-on" experience by his own initiative. I analyze this scene in two parts—first, Joel's "hands-on" experience with the machete and then the emergence of a situated learning ecology as Joel's siblings happen to monitor his efforts.

(i) "Hands-on" Experience: Joel Splits Wood with a Machete

As I discussed before, "hands-on" experience is a form of self-discovery or exploratory cooperative action that clearly reveals previous attentional engagement in practices of competent family members.

In order to illustrate how the particular event unfolds, Figures 12 and 13 show Joel splitting wood on his own.

Figure 12 Joel splits wood with a machete.

Joel shows mastery of the use of the tool by standing the long piece of wood vertically on a firm surface, by placing the machete blade on top of the wood, by driving it downwards, and then by holding the higher part of the kindling to finish splitting it.

In Figure 13, Joel changes the machete to his left hand and then searches for a log, which he will use to hammer the machete down to break off the kindling, just as a competent adult would do it.

Figure 13 Joel looks for a log to "hammer" his machete down.

Joel's cooperative actions reveal a kind of self-guided process of enskilment (Ingold, 2001) that is the outcome of his own awareness and agency in a field of practice he has evidently participated in as an observer from different perspectives. His actions reveal self-guided processes of fine-tuning of attention that depend on the "intimate coupling of perception and action" (Ingold, 2011, 58, see also Gibson, 1979) in the emergent task. By practicing on his own what he has keenly observed, he is his own creator of his learning experience. Nevertheless, his actions are not of an isolated individual, they "are invoking ways of knowing" (Goodwin, 2013, 15) of the community that he is a member of. With respect to this, Goodwin further elaborates:

> *Action is fashioned in part by performing operations on this substrate. This combinatorial process makes it possible for actors to systematically incorporate structure and meaning built by others into the interior organization of their own action. By doing so they can invoke forms of knowing that would be impossible for them to display as isolated individuals.* Human beings inhabit each other's actions.
>
> ***(2013, 15, my emphasis)***

Joel's apparent solitary actions reveal he already dwells within the actions of the competent members of his community (Streeck, 2015). His use of historically constituted tools and the skills associated with them is part of a larger "cognitive ecology" (Hutchins, 1995) which is socially organized. His actions to break off the *toj* pieces display a sense of flow, in which practitioner, tool, and material become one, as Ingold observed in his analysis of an expert carpenter sawing a plank (Ingold, 2011, 58). With Joel, his machete becomes more than an object *per se*, it is an extension of his arm and hand, as he performs the relevant actions on the kindling to split it.

Joel's gradual mastery of the machete in accomplishing this task clearly reveals how one central part of learning involves a process of embodying of skills associated with tools, in this case with the machete.[4] Joel's skill with the machete is inscribed within a field of activity of cutting and splitting wood, activities he has clearly learned over time through observation of competent members of his community and through his own exploratory practice (Bourdieu, 1977; Vygotsky, 1978, 1987).

As he practices, he creates the conditions for his own "education of attention" (Ingold, 2001, see de León, submitted for publication). Evidence of this is that he provides solutions to ongoing challenges that emerge in the task. For example, when he feels the wood's resistance, he shifts the wood to his left hand so he can use another log as a hammer to force the machete down more strongly to split off more kindling. He then collects the thin pieces from the ground and brings them to the kitchen—further evidence that his efforts yield a product that is central in social activity (e.g., cooking food in an open fire).

Both his actions and his solutions to the difficulties that emerge as he successfully splits the wood instantiate what he has learned through careful

[4] See Heidegger, 1926, and Streeck (2015) for the embodiment of tools.

observation of competent members of his community. Furthermore, they also reveal how he emerges as a practitioner *becoming* a member of a community of practice: "If the person is both member of a community and agent of activity, the concept of the person closely links meaning and action in the world" (Lave & Wenger, 1991, 122).

(ii) Emergence of a Situated Learning Ecology: Joel's Siblings Happen to Monitor

As Joel works on his own, his two older siblings happen to pass by the courtyard area where he has been working and they get close to take a look at what he is doing (Figures 14 and 15).

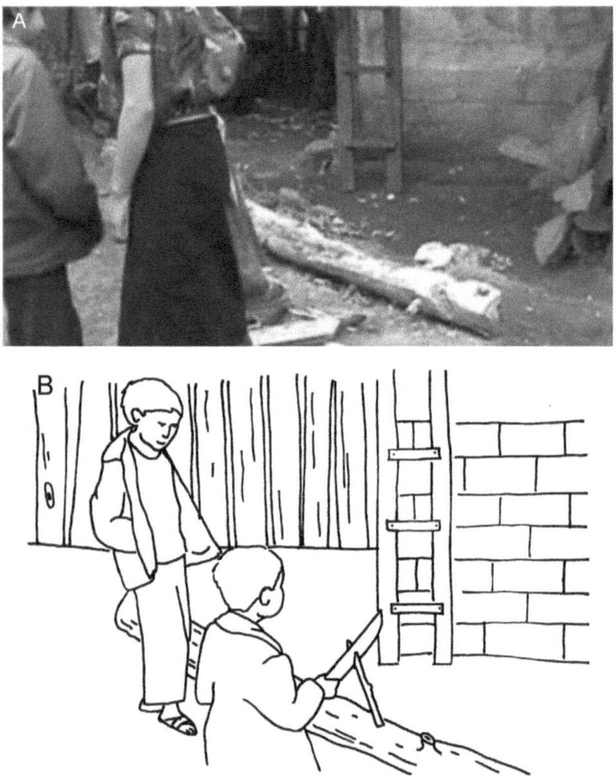

Figure 14 Emergence of (A) an "ecological huddle" and (B) a learning ecology.

There are no verbal interchanges but what emerges here is, as in the previous events, an "ecological huddle" reflecting visual and cognitive attention of the participants toward a shared focus of attention (Goodwin, 2007). The lack of verbal interchanges expressing guidance or criticism indicates his elder siblings' positive assessment of Joel's performance in the cutting task. The ecological huddle unfolds for a brief moment as siblings monitor Joel's actions but begins dissolving as they start walking away from his working area. At this moment, he turns his gaze to make eye contact with his sister and smiles at her as she leaves the area (Figure 15).

Figure 15 Joel makes eye contact with his sister.

The face-to-face alignment between the two siblings and Joel's smile confirms the ongoing intersubjective alignment between the two of them. The lack of further multimodal commentary between them indicates further approval of Joel's performance. If he had been doing the task poorly by damaging the wood or the machete, he would have been told to correct his technique or to stop altogether. Children are strongly warned from an early age not to damage household goods.

The emergence of the ecological huddle through the participants' sociospatial engagement and the nonverbal validation or approval of Joel's actions, without further commentary, is another example of a situated learning ecology. In this case, there is no unfolding of commentary or guidance as the boy shows mastery of the skill. However, it involves monitoring, sociospatial organization of participants toward a shared focus of attention, validation, and eye contact in showing interactional and cognitive engagement.

4. CONCLUSIONS

This chapter has examined the interactional emergence of learning ecologies as a result of Zinacantec Mayan children's initiatives to engage in culturally relevant goal-oriented activities.

Initiative is a central aspect of LOPI; "*children's initiative in contributing responsibly* to ongoing activities of their families and communities" is a cross-cutting theme of all seven facets of LOPI (Rogoff, 2014, 73, see also Alcalá et al., 2014; Coppens et al., 2014). In analyzing forms of initiative at a fine-grained scale, I found a variety of self-initiated actions—evidently nourished by previous observational learning—such as the child actively engaging in a task and requesting guidance, or experimenting with new skills by doing, attending, and practicing through gradual appropriation of tools and materials. These different actions lead by children reveal the "microinteractional" emergence of "initiative" related, at a larger scale, to the process of wanting to belong, to participate, and to collaborate in a responsible way in family and community endeavors.

Along this line, it should be emphasized that the activities and actions analyzed here are not those of an isolated individual, they are rather "invoking ways of knowing" of the community children belong to (Goodwin, 2013, 15). As children operate on structures built by others, they gradually dwell or inhabit the actions of competent members of their communities (Goodwin, 2013, 15).

The analysis of Mayan children's initiatives was carried out with three complementary perspectives:

(i) Looking at a variety of children's self-initiated goal-oriented activities and examining their specificities (see also de León, submitted for publication; Martínez Pérez, 2015b).

(ii) Analyzing the nature of children's forms of cooperative actions and practice through "hands-on" experience with objects, tools, and relevant materials of culturally valued activities.

(iii) Examining at a microethnographic level how learning ecologies emerge and unfold in the moment-to-moment interaction as a result of the child's initiative.

In looking at (ii), I have argued for the importance of documenting the child's initiative to engage in "hands-on" experience in order to instantiate skills of competent members he/she has witnessed in his family and community. The three examples illustrating Learning Ecologies document how children gain access to activities by engaging with others at different levels, through observation, actions, and through the gradual appropriation of relevant materials or tools.

In Learning Ecology 1, Cande engages by collecting discarded flowers and imbuing them with cultural meaning as a result of her own observation, initiative, and practice. Her appraisal of the actions of others and of the significance of their activities is the result of her being attentive and eager to participate. Cande's engagement by asking, requesting, and insisting to be guided creates a situated learning ecology; it also reveals her agency in transforming her participation in order to learn.

In Learning Ecology 2, Xun ventures to start a new project—knitting a scarf. In order to have a direct, hands-on experience of an activity, he was willing to do it on his own, relying on his own attentional skills. His initiative attracted his sister's attention and guidance, creating as a result a situated learning ecology. The learning outcome—producing a long knitted strip—resulted from his observational skills, his cooperative actions employing tools and materials from his community, his attention to his sister's multimodal guidance, and finally, his own initiative and determination to complete the project. His project is evidently driven by his will to become a legitimate member of a community of practice by producing a socially valued piece of work. In spite of criticisms and social censoring at some points of the task, he proved to himself and the rest of the family that he could be an accomplished learner.

In Learning Ecology 3, Joel's mastery of the use of a machete to split wood derived from his power of attention and practice in developing a skill he has learnt by observing, participating, and wanting to collaborate. His near mastery of the skill was briefly acknowledged and validated by his siblings, who had monitored his activity before they left the scene. What is relevant in this activity is Joel's "synergical" skill with the tool, again, as a result of his own initiative, his previous observational learning, and his desire to contribute to the larger activity of producing kindling for cooking.

In these three ecologies, we find that through practice, the skillful use of objects (e.g., flowers), tools (e.g., loom, machete), and/or materials (e.g., yarn) is developed through the child's agency, awareness, and motivation. Here, the notion of "cooperative action" (Goodwin, 2013) is central to the analysis. It explains why children's apparently isolated practices are rather evidence of how they gradually become agents of the actions of competent members of their communities and consequently of their cognitive ecologies (Hutchins, 1995). They accomplish this by their own active engagement and embodiment of actions, tools, and relevant materials that historically go with them.

Further, a key aspect of "initiative," as documented in this study, is that the child's actions transform the social organization of participation and create environments for learning—what I have referred to as situated learning ecologies. Here, I provided a talk-in-interaction and a "theory of action"

(Goodwin, 2013) analysis of the temporal unfolding of the "ecosystem of mutual influence among participants where talk is not privileged over non-verbal action and other semiotic media" (Erickson, 2010, 254). To this end, I examined the interactional moment-to-moment emergence of the ecosystems in question by looking at how participants socially organize themselves in an "ecological huddle" (Goffman, 1964) to share a visual and cognitive focus of attention on the activity in question.

Overall, the close examination of three learning ecologies against the background of long-term ethnographic research in learning and socialization in the Mayan community of study (de León, 1998, 2005a, 2005b, 2007, 2011, 2012a, 2012b, submitted for publication) reveals the centrality of children's initiative in their learning processes, in resonance with the LOPI model.

This study, however, has shown that the child's "eagerness to contribute and belong" (Facet 2 in LOPI) involves an underlying aspect that is fundamental to understanding the child's "readiness" to engage in order to be included in family endeavors. This hidden aspect is part of the larger "package" of initiative that goes between observing and pitching in. It involves "unpacking" children's initiatives at a microlevel and documenting the emergent and situated nature of children's agency in creating their own learning environments.

I have argued that it is not an isolated process as apparently suggested by some scholars who have described it as "autonomous learning" (Lancy, 2010; Odden & Rochat, 2004). It rather involves motivation to keenly attend, explore, discover, and understand, through the practice of inhabiting others' actions, what it is like to *belong* to a community. The practice also involves finely tuning attention in working with tools, objects, and materials through cooperative actions and co-construction of knowledge. In sum, the child becomes a leading force in transforming the social organization of participation in order to have others guide his or her own "education of attention" (de León, submitted for publication; Ingold, 2001).

I would like to point out here that, in the community of study, although children's initiative is pervasive across activities, competent members are not always immediately responsive to or supportive of the child's initiative. Guidance is, in fact, not always available and the child sometimes has to openly demand it at the risk of rejection. Assessments can also be framed against social expectations that a child, especially at a certain age, should already have mastered a skill without being taught.

Overall, LOPI provides a holistic learning model that accurately integrates the different facets of learning in families and communities, as documented here. This study, however, adds to this model the richness and power of "unpacking" children's initiatives at a microlevel in the co-construction and transformation of knowledge and practice.

Ingold has argued that "[...] in the growth of human knowledge, the contribution that each generation makes to the next is not an accumulated stock of representations but an education of attention" (Ingold, 2001, 113). I would add here that the education of attention is a dynamically emerging process, led in important ways by the child's initiative to collaborate. In this sense, learning is an interactional and intergenerational accomplishment involving, in important ways, the young generation guiding their own education of attention by their own agency and practice.

A final point here is whether the findings here extend to children in general or just to the Mayan children of the study. I would argue that children's initiative to collaborate, to explore, and practice actions learned from others is a human trait (Tomasello, 2009) that is present in all cultures.

However, different trajectories and cultures of socialization may produce several outcomes. One main one, I would think, is the effect of segregating children from community life by sending them to school and thus separating them from adult work (Rogoff et al., 2003). The middle-class child-centric organization of family life involves radically different attentional ecologies with children having their own spaces and times to play, to do school homework, to engage in self-care activities, and to minimally contribute, as a result, to family endeavors (Ochs & Izquierdo, 2009; Ochs & Kemer-Sadlik, 2013). If our Mayan children had toys, leisure time, and adults playing with them, they would probably pay less attention to the activities where looms, machetes, or flowers come to life.

In spite of these arguments, I would argue that the capacity of children's initiative to create and shape learning environments is human and manifests in different ways in different cultural environments (Goodwin and Cekaite, 2012; Johnson, 2015, submitted for publication). Its connection, however, with culturally relevant endeavors may perhaps be more fluid in family- and community-based learning. More comparative research with the microethnographic lens used here may shed light into this question.

ACKNOWLEDGMENTS

The research and fieldwork for this chapter were supported by CONACyT Grant #133492. I eternally thank the Martínez family in Nabenchauk, Zinacantán for all the inspiring moments I have spent with them. Pseudonyms were used to protect collaborators' confidentiality and data collection follows protocols from CIESAS, México.

Some of the ideas developed here stem from workshops with Barbara Rogoff and colleagues of the research group on "Intent community participation." I thank Barbara for organizing these very rich and generous intellectual spaces to share work in a collaborative environment. I also thank her and Maricela Correa-Chávez for very helpful editorial suggestions and comments to a previous draft. I would also like to acknowledge Chuck and Candy Goodwin's inspiration and thoughtful comments on many of the ideas presented here, especially within the context of the Symposium on Cooperation at UCLA (February 2015). Special thanks to Elinor Ochs and Tanya Stivers for their invitation to this outstanding conference. Last, but not least, my gratitude to Lance Brunner for his inspiring, generous, and always helpful editorial help. Any misconceptions remain my own responsibility.

REFERENCES

Alcalá, L., Rogoff, B., Mejía-Arauz, R., Coppens, A. D., & Dexter, L. A. (2014). Children's initiative in contributions to family work in indigenous-heritage and cosmopolitan communities in Mexico. In B. Rogoff (Ed.), *Human Development: 57 (2–3). Learning by observing and pitching in to family and community endeavors: An orientation* (pp. 69–81).

Bourdieu, P. (1977). *Outline of a theory of practice*. Cambridge: Cambridge University Press.

Bruner, J. (1962). Introduction. In L. S. Vygotsky (Ed.), *Thought and language* (pp. v–x). Cambridge, MA: MIT Press.

Chavajay, P., & Rogoff, B. (1999). Cultural variation in management of attention by children and their caregivers. *Developmental Psychology, 35*(4), 1079–1090.

Coppens, A., Alcalá, L., Mejía-Arauz, R., & Rogoff, B. (2014). Children's initiative in family household work in Mexico. In B. Rogoff (Ed.), *Human Development: 57(2–3). Learning by observing and pitching in to family and community endeavors: An orientation* (pp. 69–81).

de León, L. (1998). The emergent participant: Interactive patterns in the socialization of Tzotzil (Mayan) infants. *Journal of Linguistic Anthropology, 3*(2–3), 131–161.

de León, L. (2005a). *La Llegada del Alma: Lenguaje, Infancia y Socialización entre los Mayas de Zinacantán. (The arrival of the soul: Language, infancy, and socialization among the Maya of Zinacantán)*. México: CIESAS-INAH-CONACULTA.

de León, L. (2005b). Intent participation and the nature of participation structures: A look from a Chiapas Mayan community everyday life. In *Document presented at the presidential workshop on intent participation, Santa Cruz, CA, June 15–16.*

de León, L. (2007). Parallelism, metalinguistic play, and the interactive emergence of Tzotzil (Mayan) siblings' culture. *Research on Language and Social Interaction, 40*(4), 405–436.

de León, L. (2010). The ecology of children's observational learning in a Mayan household: A look at autonomous learning practices. In *Poster presented at the international indigenous language policy research conference, American Indian Language Policy Research and Teacher Training Center, College of Education, University of New México, April 26–27, 2010.*

de León, L. (2011). Calibrando" la Atención: Directivos, Adiestramiento y Responsabilidad en el Trabajo Doméstico de los Niños Mayas Zinacantecos ("Calibrating" attention: Directives, enskilment, and responsibility in household chores among Mayan Zinacantec children). In V. Zavala & S. Frisancho (Eds.), *Aprendizaje, Cultura y Desarrollo (Learning, culture and development)*. Lima, Perú: Fondo Editorial de la Universidad Católica Pontificia.

de León, L. (2012a). Multiparty participation frameworks in language socialization. In A. Duranti, B. B. Schieffelin, & E. Ochs (Eds.), *Handbook of language socialization* (pp. 81–112). Malden, MA: Blackwell.

de León, L. (2012b). 'The *j'ik'al* is coming!' Triadic directives and emotion in the socialization of Zinacantec Mayan children. Maya daily lives. In A. Breton & P. Nondédéo (Eds.), *Proceedings of the 13th European Maya conference (Paris, December 5–6, 2008), Acta Mesoamericana no 21*. Markt Schwaben: Verlag Anton Saurwein.

de León, L. (submitted for publication). Emerging learning ecologies: Mayan children's initiative and correctional directives in their everyday enskilment practices. In A. Kyratzis & S. J. Johnson (Guest Eds.), Multimodal and multilingual resources in children's framing of situated learning activities. *Linguistics and education* (special issue).

Duranti, A., Ochs, E., & Schieffelin, B. B. (Eds.), (2012). *Handbook of language socialization*. Malden, MA: Blackwell.

Enfield, N. J., & Levinson, S. C. (Eds.), (2006). *Roots of human sociality*. London: Berg Press.

Erickson, F. (1992). Ethnographic microanalysis of interaction. In M. LeCompte, W. L. Millroy, & J. Preissle (Eds.), *The handbook of qualitative research in education* (pp. 201–255). San Diego: Academic Press.

Erickson, F. (1996). Going for the zone: the social and cognitive ecology of teacher-student interaction in classroom conversations. In D. Hicks (Ed.), *Discourse, learning, and schooling* (p. 29). Cambridge: Cambridge University Press.

Erickson, F. (2010). The neglected listener: Issues of theory and practice in transcription from video in interaction analysis. In J. Streeck (Ed.), *New adventures in language and interaction*. Amsterdam: John Benjamins Publishing Company.

Fortes, M. (1970). Social and psychological aspects of education in Taleland. In J. Middleton (Ed.), *From child to adult* (pp. 14–74).Garden City, NY: Natural History Press (1938).

Garfinkel, H. (1967). *Studies in ethnomethodology*. Englewood Cliffs, NJ: Prentice Hall.

Gaskins, S. (1999). How Mayan parental theories come into play. In S. Harkness & C. M. Super (Eds.), *Parent's cultural belief systems: Their origins, expressions, and consequences* (pp. 345–363). New York: The Guilford Press.

Gaskins, S. (2000). Children's daily activities in a Mayan village: A culturally grounded description. *Cross-Cultural Research*, *34*(4), 375–389.

Gaskins, S., & Paradise, R. (2010). Learning through observation in daily life. In F. David, J. B. Lancy, & S. Gaskins (Eds.), *The anthropology of learning in childhood* (pp. 85–117). Lanham, MD: AltaMira Press.

Gibson, J. J. (1979). *The ecological approach to visual perception*. Boston: Houghton Mifflin.

Goffman, E. (1964). The neglected situation. In J. J. Gumperz & D. Hymes (Eds.), *American Anthropologist: 66 (6), Pt. 2. The ethnography of communication* (pp. 133–136) (special issue).

Goffman, E. (1974). *Frame analysis: An essay on the organization of experience*. New York: Harper & Row.

Goffman, E. (1981). *Forms of talk*. Philadelphia, PA: University of Pennsylvania Press.

Goffman, E. (1982). The interaction order: American Sociological Association presidential address. *American Sociological Review*, *48*(1 (Feb. 1983)), 1–17.

Goodwin, M. (1990). *He-said-she-said: Talk as social organization among black children*. Bloomington: Indiana University Press.

Goodwin, C. (2000). Action and embodiment within situated human interaction. *Journal of Pragmatics*, *32*, 1489–1522.

Goodwin, M. H. (2006). Participation, affect, and trajectory in family directive/response sequences. *Text & Talk*, *26*(4–5), 513–541.

Goodwin, C. (2007). Participation, stance and affect in the organization of activities. *Discourse & Society*, *18*(1), 53–73.

Goodwin, C. (2013). The co-operative transformative organization of human action and knowledge. *Journal of Pragmatics on Multimodal Interaction*, *46*(special issue), 8–23.

Goodwin, M. H., & Cekaite, A. (2012). Calibration in directive/response sequences in family interaction. *Journal of Pragmatics*, *46*(1), 179–194.

Goodwin, C., & Goodwin, M. H. (2004). Participation. In A. Duranti (Ed.), *A companion to linguistic anthropology* (pp. 222–244). Oxford: Basil Blackwell.
Greenfield, P. M. (1984). A study of the teacher in the activities of everyday life. In B. Rogoff & J. Lave (Eds.), *Everyday cognition* (pp. 117–138). Cambridge: Harvard University Press.
Greenfield, P. M. (2004). *Weaving generations together: Evolving creativity in the Maya of Chiapas*. Santa Fe: SAR Press.
Heidegger, M. (1926). *Being and time*. New York: Harper & Row.
Hindmarsh, J., Reynolds, P., & Dunne, S. (2011). Exhibiting understanding: The body in apprenticeship. *Journal of Pragmatics*, *43*(2), 489–503.
Hutchins, E. (1995). *Cognition in the wild*. Cambridge, MA: MIT Press.
Ingold, T. (2001). From the transmission of representations to the education of attention. In H. Whitehouse (Ed.), *The debated mind: Evolutionary psychology versus ethnography* (pp. 113–153). Oxford: Berg.
Ingold, T. (2007). The social child. In A. Fogel, J. King Barbara, & G. Shanker Stuart (Eds.), *Human development in the twenty-first century* (pp. 112–119). Cambridge: Cambridge University Press.
Ingold, T. (2011). *Being alive: Essays on movement, knowledge and perception*. London: Routledge.
Ingold, T. (2013). *Making: Anthropology, archeology, art and architecture*. London: Routledge.
Jefferson, G. (1974). Error correction as an interactional resource. *Language in Society*, *3*(02), 181–199.
Johnson, S. J. (2015). *The social and cognitive worlds of young children reading together*. Unpublished Phd. Dissertation, UCLA, Department of Education.
Johnson, S. J. (submitted for publication). Multimodality and footing in peer correction. In A. Kyratzis & S. J. Johnson (Guest Eds.), Multimodal and multilingual resources in children's framing of situated learning activities. *Linguistics and Education* (special issue).
John-Steiner, V. (1985). *Notebooks of the mind: Explorations in thinking*. New York: Harper & Row.
Lancy, D. F. (2010). Learning 'from nobody': The limited role of teaching in folk models of children's development. *Childhood in the Past*, *3*(1), 79–106.
Lancy, D. F. (2012). The chore curriculum. In G. Spittler & M. Bourdillion (Eds.), *African children at work: Working and learning in growing up* (pp. 23–57). Berlin: Lit Verlag.
Lave, J., & Wenger, E. (1991). *Situated learning. Legitimate peripheral participation*. Cambridge: University of Cambridge Press.
Leontyev, A. N. (1979). The problem of activity in psychology. In J. V. Wertsch (Ed.), *The concept of activity in Soviet psychology* (pp. 37–71). Armonk, NY: M.E. Sharpe.
Lindwall, O., & Ekström, A. (2012). Instruction-in-interaction: The teaching and learning of a manual skill. *Human Studies*, *35*(1), 27–49.
Martınez Pérez, M. (2015a). Xchanel-xchanubtasel: Lenguaje, acción y enseñanza en actividades cotidianas entre los mayas de San Juan Chamula. Ph.D. thesis. CIESAS, México: Graduate Program in Indoamerican Linguistics.
Martínez Pérez, M. (2015b). Adults' Orientation of Children – and Children's Initiative to Pitch In – to Everyday Adult Activities in a Tsotsil Maya Community. *Advances in Child development and Behavior*, *49*, 113–135.
Maurer, E. (1977). ¿Aprender o enseñar?: La educación en Takinwits, poblado tseltal de Chiapas. *Revista del Centro de Estudios Educativos*, 7(1), 84–103. México.
Maynard, A. E. (2002). Cultural teaching: The development of teaching skills in Maya sibling interactions. *Child Development*, *73*(3), 969–982.
Maynard, A. E. (2004). Cultures of teaching in childhood: Formal schooling and Maya sibling teaching at home. *Cognitive Development*, *19*(4), 517–535.

Mead, M. (1970). Our educational emphases in primitive perspective. In J. Middleton (Ed.), *From child to adult* (pp. 1–13). Garden City, NY: Natural History Press.

Mejía-Arauz, R., Rogoff, B., Dexter, A., & Najafi, B. (2007). Cultural variation in children's social organization. *Child Development*, *78*, 1001–1014.

Mondada, L. (2012). The organization of concurrent courses of action in surgical demonstrations. In J. Streeck, C. Goodwin, & C. LeBaron (Eds.), *Embodied interaction: Language and body in the material world*. Cambridge: Cambridge University Press.

Ochs, E. (1988). *Culture and language development: Language acquisition and language socialization in a Samoan village*. Cambridge: Cambridge University Press.

Ochs, E., & Izquierdo, C. (2009). Responsibility in childhood: Three developmental trajectories. *Ethos*, *37*(4), 391–413.

Ochs, E., & Kemer-Sadlik, T. (2013). *Fast-forward family: Home, work, and relationships in middle class America*. Berkeley: University of California Press.

Ochs, E., & Schieffelin, B. B. (1984). Language acquisition and socialization: Three developmental stories and their implications. In R. A. Shweder & R. A. Levine (Eds.), *Culture theory: Essays on mind, self, and emotion* (pp. 276–322). Cambridge: Cambridge University Press.

Odden, H., & Rochat, P. (2004). Observational learning and enculturation. *Educational and Child Psychology*, *21*(1), 39–50.

Paoli, A. (2003). *Educación, autonomía, y lekil kuxlejal*. Mexico City: Universidad Autónoma Metropolitana.

Paradise, R., & Rogoff, B. (2009). Side by side. Learning by observing and pitching in. *Ethos*, *37*(1), 102–138.

Philips, S. (1983). *The invisible culture: Communication in classroom and community on the warm springs Indian reservation*. New York: Longman.

Rogoff, B. (1990). *Apprenticeship in thinking: Cognitive development in social context*. New York: Oxford University Press.

Rogoff, B. (1997). Evaluating development in the process of participation. In E. Amsel & A. Renninger (Eds.), *Change and development* (pp. 265–285). Hillsdale: Erlbaum.

Rogoff, B. (1998). Cognition as a collaborative process. In W. Damon (Series Ed.), D. Kuhn & R. S. Siegler (Vol. Eds.), *Cognition, language, and perception: Vol. 2. Handbook of child psychology* (5th ed., pp. 679–744). New York: Wiley.

Rogoff, B. (2003). *The cultural nature of human development*. New York: Oxford University Press.

Rogoff, B. (2011). *Developing destinies: A Mayan midwife and town*. New York: Oxford University Press.

Rogoff, B. (2014). Learning by observing and pitching in to family and community endeavors: An orientation. *Human Development*, *57*(2–3), 69–81.

Rogoff, B., & Lave, J. (Eds.), (1984). *Everyday cognition: Its development in social context* (pp. 95–116). Cambridge, MA: Harvard University Press.

Rogoff, B., Moore, L., Najafi, B., Dexter, A., Correa-Chávez, M., & Solis, J. (2007). Children's development of cultural repertoires through participation in everyday routines and practices. In J. E. Grusec & P. D. Hastings (Eds.), *Handbook of socialization: Theory and research* (pp. 490–515). New York: The Guilford Press.

Rogoff, B., Paradise, R., Mejía-Arauz, R., Correa-Chávez, M., & Angelillo, C. (2003). Firsthand learning through intent participation. *Annual Review of Psychology*, *54*(1), 175–203.

Sacks, H., Schegloff, E., & Jefferson, G. (1974). A simplest systematics for the organization of turn-taking for conversation. *Language*, *50*(4), 696–735.

Schieffelin, B. (1990). *The give and take of everyday life: Language socialization of Kaluli children*. Cambridge: Cambridge University Press.

Streeck, J. (2015). Embodied communication. *Annual Reviews of Anthropology*, *44*, 419–438.

Streeck, J., Goodwin, C., & LeBaron, C. (2012). Embodied interaction in the material world: An introduction. In J. Streeck, C. Goodwin, & C. LeBaron (Eds.), *Embodied interaction: Language and body in the material world*. Cambridge: Cambridge University Press.

Tomasello, M. (2009). *Why we cooperate*. Cambridge, MA: MIT Press.

Tulbert, E., & Goodwin, M. H. (2011). Choreographies of attention: Multimodality in a routine family activity. In J. Streeck, C. Goodwin, & C. LeBaron (Eds.), *Embodied interaction: Language and body in the material world* (pp. 79–92). Cambridge: Cambridge University Press.

Vygotsky, L. S. (1978). *Mind in society: The development of higher psychological processes*. Cambridge, MA: Harvard University Press.

Vygotsky, I. S. (1987). Thinking and speech. In R. W. Rieber & A. S. Carton (Eds.), *The collected works of L. S. Vygotsky (N. Minick, Trans.)* (pp. 37–285). New York: Plenum.

CHAPTER EIGHT

Children's Avoidance of Interrupting Others' Activities in Requesting Help: Cultural Aspects of Considerateness

Omar Ruvalcaba*[,1,2], Barbara Rogoff*, Angélica López[†], Maricela Correa-Chávez[‡], Kris Gutiérrez[§,3]

*University of California, Santa Cruz, California, USA
[†]Psychology Department, University of California, Santa Cruz and Marymount California University
[‡]University of California, Los Angeles
[§]University of California, Los Angeles, California, USA
[2]Corresponding author: e-mail address: omar.ruvalcaba@csun.edu

Contents

[1] Now at California State University Northridge, Sierra Hall 305, 18111 Nordhoff St, Northridge CA 91330.
[3] Now at University of California Berkeley.

Advances in Child Development and Behavior, Volume 49
ISSN 0065-2407
http://dx.doi.org/10.1016/bs.acdb.2015.10.005

Abstract

To be able to collaborate skillfully, people need to coordinate well with others, taking into account how their actions fit with those of their partners. This is a key aspect of an approach to learning called *Learning by Observing and Pitching In*, hypothesized to be common in many Indigenous-heritage communities of the Americas. This chapter considers cultural values that emphasize considerateness and awareness of how one's actions impact others such as the Mexican cultural value of *respeto* and cultural differences in children's efforts to avoid interrupting others' activity.

US Mexican-heritage children showed more evidence of avoiding interrupting the ongoing activity of an adult when they requested help, compared with European American children from families with extensive schooling experience. Most of the Mexican-heritage children's requests for help that gave evidence of avoiding interruption were made nonverbally, which may facilitate unobtrusive requests. There were no significant differences among children from two US Mexican-heritage backgrounds varying in experience with Western schooling and likely experience with Indigenous-American practices, suggesting that the Mexican cultural value of *respeto* and associated considerateness is widespread even among US Mexican-heritage families with extensive experience with Western schooling and life in the United States.

In this chapter, we examine cultural aspects of children's efforts to avoid interrupting other people's activities, as a collaborative skill. Children's considerateness and awareness of their impact on the activities of others are likely to be helpful for coordinating effectively with others.

Coordinating skillfully with others and awareness of how one's actions impact collaboration are central to a conceptual model describing a way of organizing learning that is posited to be particularly prevalent in many Indigenous-heritage communities of the Americas: *Learning by Observing and Pitching In* (Learning by Observing and Pitching In (LOPI); Rogoff, 2014; formerly "*intent community participation,*" Rogoff, Moore, Najafi, Dexter, Correa-Chavez & Solis, 2007). This model for organizing children's learning emphasizes collaboration among children and adults, with mutual responsibility and flexibility. This includes avoiding interruptions of others' ongoing efforts.

We examined whether US Mexican-heritage children were more likely to show efforts to avoid interrupting the instruction and other activity of an adult than European American children from families with extensive school experience, when requesting help from an adult in constructing a toy. Such a finding would fit with the LOPI model and with research suggesting greater mutuality and collaboration among many Mexican-heritage children than among middle-class European American children (Kagan & Madsen, 1971; López, Ruvalcaba & Rogoff, 2015; Paradise & de Haan, 2009; Rogoff, Najafi, & Mejía-Arauz, 2014). We were also interested in whether the US Mexican-heritage children's requests for help that show such considerateness would more commonly be made nonverbally than verbally, in line with suggestions (reviewed below) that nonverbal communication facilitates smooth collaboration.

We first examine cultural values related to considerateness in collaboration, suggestions in the literature of cultural differences in children's requests for help with considerateness, and possibilities of unobtrusive nonverbal communication in coordination with others. We then present evidence that US Mexican-heritage children more commonly displayed a form of considerateness by attempting to avoid interrupting an adult's activity when requesting help during instruction, compared with European American children.

1. CULTURAL VALUES RELATED TO CONSIDERATENESS IN COLLABORATION

The values and practices of many Latino and Indigenous American communities, and the LOPI model, emphasize mutual considerateness for the direction of the group as a basis of social relations and collaboration (Basso, 1979; de Haan, 2001; Espinoza-Herold, 2007; Good Eshelman, 2013; Henne, 2009; Lamphere, 1977; Paoli, 2003; Paradise, 1996; Rogoff, 2014; Stearns, 1986; Taggart, 2003). The value systems of these communities often encourage children (and adults) to be responsible and considerate in shared endeavors, to think of the impact of their actions on others, and to avoid creating distractions, interruptions, or extra work for others (García, 2015; Lorente Fernández, 2006, 2010; Paradise, 2004).

Such consideration is an aspect of one version of the Mexican cultural value of *respeto* (Guilamo-Ramos et al., 2007; Valdés, 1996). This term does not translate exactly to the English term *respect*, and in Spanish has several distinct—somewhat incompatible—meanings. Although the term *respeto* sometimes refers to deference to authority and status hierarchies, we focus on a version of *respeto* that is based on nonauthoritarian mutual responsibility. We are not addressing the form of *respeto* that stresses hierarchy and authority, which has been attributed to colonization and to interactions within the socioeconomic hierarchy of Latin American countries (Garcia, 1996; Vigil, 1998).

The mutual form of *respeto* involves considerateness of the direction of the group's shared endeavors, not just consideration for other individuals as individuals (R. Mejía-Arauz, personal communication, March 2012). The mutual form of *respeto* includes nonhierarchical asymmetries in leadership roles, such as between collaborating adults and children—leadership is flexibly based on who can get things done, not based on rigid hierarchies.

This mutual value system has been noted especially in Indigenous and Indigenous-heritage communities of the Americas (Bolin, 2006; Flores, Urrieta, Chamoux, Lorente Fernández, & López, 2015; Henne, 2009; Lorente Fernández, 2006, 2010, 2015; Paradise, 2004; Paradise & de Haan, 2009; Pelletier, 1970; García, 2015). In Mexico, parents whose children show *respeto* are often commended; children's displays of *respeto* or lack of it (*falta de respeto*) may be considered a reflection on the parents' child rearing and on the family itself (Calzada, Fernández & Cortes, 2010; de Guzman et al., 2012).

In *respeto*, and in LOPI, children are expected to learn to distinguish when it is appropriate to participate, request help, and pitch in without disrupting ongoing activities of the group (López, Nafaji, Rogoff & Mejía-Arauz, 2012). Mexican-heritage and Indigenous Peruvian families socialize *respeto* through practices such as guiding looks, taps on the shoulder, nudges, and nods to encourage children to show *respeto*, and reminders that *respeto* is a form of caring that can be conveyed through considerateness and measured participation (Delgado-Gaitan, 1994; García, 2015).

Despite the emphasis on this value system in a number of Indigenous-heritage communities of the Americas, it is important to examine whether children from distinct communities actually differ in this form of considerateness. Although value systems emphasizing considerateness may be emphasized by adults in particular communities, adults' values may or may not translate to children's actual behavior. Further, the existence of a labeled cultural value (e.g., *respeto*) does not preclude the existence of the same kind and extent of considerateness among children from communities where this way of acting is not labeled with a particular term or explicit values.

Hence, we are interested in examining whether there are cultural differences in how children handle a situation in which they need an adult's help—do they differ in the extent to which they request help with explicit efforts to avoid interrupting the adult? We examine occasions when children are eager to request help—when they do so with efforts to avoid interrupting, they are not shyly avoiding the adult but rather they are carefully timing their request in a way that takes into account whether the adult is busy with something else. Requesting help with this type of considerateness involves assessing an appropriate moment to make a request, and then skillfully timing the request to fit into the flow of the ongoing activity, to avoid interrupting others or redirecting others' attention. In addition, we examine variability across two US Mexican-heritage communities, rather than assuming uniformity in application of a value system such as *respeto* or an approach to learning such as LOPI across whole national or ethnic groups.

2. CULTURAL DIFFERENCES IN CHILDREN'S REQUESTS FOR HELP WITH CONSIDERATENESS

Little attention has been given to cultural differences in children's considerateness in requesting help from adults, despite the importance of help-seeking for learning in and out of classrooms (Garland & Zigler, 1994; Nelson-LeGall, 1985; Nelson-Le Gall & Resnick, 1998; Srebnik & Cauce, 1996). The most relevant research is an observation that Native Hawaiian children commonly asked for help unobtrusively by standing quietly by their teachers, an approach that resembles the use of *respeto* (Gallimore, Boggs & Jordan, 1974). It is telling (and poignant) that the Native Hawaiian children's non-Native teachers often did not detect these requests for help.

A few studies focusing on cultural differences in children's disruption of adults are consistent with the idea that Indigenous-heritage children of the Americas may be more likely to avoid interrupting others' activities. These studies indicate that Indigenous-heritage Mexican and Guatemalan Mayan children seldom disrupted adults' ongoing interactions in home life and were less likely to interrupt others in teaching situations than European American middle-class children (Correa-Chávez & Rogoff, 2009; de Haan, 1999, 2001; Gaskins, 2000; Mejía-Arauz, Rogoff & Paradise, 2005; Paradise, 1994, 1996; Rogoff, Mistry, Göncü & Mosier, 1993; Silva, Correa-Chávez & Rogoff, 2010; Silva, Shimpi & Rogoff, 2015).

Our study is the first, as far as we know, to systematically examine cultural differences in evidence of children's explicit efforts to avoid interrupting adults' activities. Based on the emphasis on considerateness in LOPI as well as in the Mexican value system that includes *respeto*, we expected US Mexican-heritage children to more often show signs of considerateness for others' activities by explicitly attempting to avoid interruption in requesting help from an adult, compared with European American children from families with extensive schooling experience.

3. UNOBTRUSIVE NONVERBAL COMMUNICATION IN COORDINATING WITH OTHERS

We also examined whether children's requests that gave evidence of avoiding interrupting others' activities were particularly likely to employ nonverbal means. Although verbal communication can show considerateness (Henne, 2009), unobtrusive qualities of nonverbal communication may be especially conducive to collaboration and less disruptive than verbal communication (Philips, 1983). LOPI and an emphasis on *respeto* in collaborative endeavors may prompt Mexican-heritage children to request help nonverbally, to avoid interrupting ongoing endeavors. Our study contributes to substantiating whether considerately avoiding interruption and an emphasis on nonverbal coordination fit as defining features of the conceptual model focusing on LOPI to ongoing endeavors of the family and community (Rogoff, 2014).

Extensive use of nonverbal communication has been noted in many Mexican-heritage and Indigenous communities of the Americas, in which children more often used subtle nonverbal communication than middle-class European American children (Ellis & Gauvain, 1992; Mejia-Arauz, Roberts & Rogoff, 2012; Mejía-Arauz, Rogoff, Dexter & Najafi, 2007; Rogoff et al., 1993). For example, US Mexican-heritage children asked for help in folding a paper figure through nonverbal means more often than did middle-class European American children, who more often asked for help verbally, sometimes insistently (Mejía-Arauz et al., 2005).

4. EXPERIENCE WITH CULTURAL PRACTICES IN INDIGENOUS MEXICAN HERITAGE AND WESTERN SCHOOLING

We examined whether 44 US Mexican-heritage children—especially those whose families are likely to be familiar with Indigenous Mexican practices—would more often make efforts to coordinate their requests with an adult's ongoing activity and to avoid interrupting the adult, compared with 36 European American children from families with extensive schooling experience. The potential collaborative and unobtrusive qualities of nonverbal communication also led us to expect that the US Mexican-heritage children's requests for help that evidenced efforts to avoid interrupting would be made mostly nonverbally.

Our comparison with European American children from families with extensive schooling experience is based on the fact that this cultural group has been treated as the "norm" in studies of children's learning. However, rather than treating their approaches as the norm, we examine their approaches as those of a cultural group with experiences that may contrast in important ways with US Mexican-heritage children. In particular, this cultural group's extensive experience over several generations with the Western cultural institution of schooling (Bronfenbrenner, McClennan, Wethington, Moen, & Ceci, 1996) may discourage collaboration and the considerateness that facilitates coordination with others.

It is not our aim to single out schooling as the "active ingredient" that creates the potential cultural differences. Extensive experience in Western schooling is associated with a plethora of cultural differences in experiences and characteristics, including occupations, family structure, language, daily activities, and resources, among many others that also contribute to cultural patterns in child development (Rogoff et al., 2014). Extensive schooling is a defining feature of middle-class life, with all the characteristics associated with that cultural community.

European American ESE (Extensive School Experience) participants all had mothers with extensive experience with Western schooling (with a minimum of 12 grades and an average of 17 grades of schooling). The families were living in California; all these mothers were born in the United States. Most of them were stay-at-home mothers; the others worked as professor, writer, lawyer, and teacher. European American fathers' work included computer work, contractor, probation officer, therapist, engineer, and doctor.

The Mexican-heritage children were from immigrant families in California, mostly from rural regions of Mexico with historically Indigenous communities where limited schooling is associated with likely retention of Indigenous practices. Most of the children were born in the US and had mothers who were born in Mexico. We compared two backgrounds among the Mexican-heritage children:

- *US Mexican-heritage ESE* included 18 children whose families had extensive experience with Western schooling (mothers $M = 14$ grades, minimum 12). Mothers worked as housewife, teacher's aide, analyst, and customer service representative; fathers' occupations included driver, construction worker, police officer, and hotel worker.
- *US Mexican-heritage EIP* (likely experience with Indigenous-American practices) included 26 children whose families likely had more experience with Indigenous practices (and whose mothers had an average of 8 grades of schooling, maximum 11). Mothers' occupations included cook, factory worker, housekeeper, and stay-at-home mother; fathers worked as painters, gardeners, mechanics, cooks, and busboys.

The inference regarding likely experience with Indigenous practices is indirect, based on the historical association of limited schooling with Indigenous heritage in many rural areas of Mexico. Families with limited Western schooling who have come to California from rural Indigenous regions of Mexico (where access to Western schooling has been minimal) have been more likely to maintain some Indigenous practices than people who have had extensive access to Western schooling and practices (Buriel, 1993; Bonfil Batalla, 1996; Frye, 1996; López et al., 2012; Rogoff et al., 2014; Vigil, 1998).

The use of this indirect inference of experience with Indigenous American practices is necessary because many families from Mexico that engage in Indigenous Mexican practices and have Indigenous heritage do not claim it, due to strong discrimination against Indigenous people in Mexico for a number of centuries (Lorente Fernández, 2006; Urrieta, 2003). For example, the Mexican nationalistic movement of the early 1900s championed Spanish values and attempted to weed out Indigenous values and practices (Vasconcelos, 1997). In some Mexican communities, when adults' or children's actions are interpreted as being too humble or speaking softly, they are chastised for acting or speaking in ways that reflect Indigenous ways (Urrieta, 2003), such as in derogatory statements like *no seas tan 'Indio'* [*don't be so 'Indian'*]. Nonetheless, an Indigenous history is common in most Mexican families, especially in rural Mexico, in both Indigenous and Mestizo (mixed Indigenous and Spanish heritage) communities, as well as among Mexican immigrants to the US, whose roots are often in Indigenous or Indigenous-heritage communities (Bonfil Batalla, 1996; López et al., 2012; Rogoff et al., 2014).

Previous findings suggest that extensive Western schooling is associated with reduced use of Indigenous American practices among families with Indigenous American heritage (Chavajay & Rogoff, 2002; Correa-Chávez, Rogoff & Mejía-Arauz, 2005; Crago, Annahatak & Ningiuruvik, 1993; Mejía-Arauz et al., 2005; Rogoff et al., 1993, 2014). We therefore expected children from Mexican-heritage ESE families to less often evidence efforts to avoid interrupting, in their requests for help, than children from Mexican-heritage EIP families.

The expectation that children from Mexican-heritage EIP families would be especially likely to show efforts to avoid interruption is based on research reporting that many Indigenous communities of the Americas emphasize values akin to *respeto*, focusing on considerateness, reciprocity, and avoiding drawing attention away from community work toward individual concerns (Bolin, 2006; Good Eshelman, 2013; Guilamo-Ramos et al., 2007; Hill, 2010; Lorente Fernández, 2006, 2010; Matul &

Cabrera, 2007; Paoli, 2003; Valdés, 1996; García, 2015). Although *respeto* is a Spanish word, the underlying concept appears to be widespread in Indigenous-heritage communities of North as well as Central and perhaps South America (Basso, 1979; Henne, 2009; Lamphere, 1977; Taggart, 2003; Wieder & Pratt, 1990), including in ancient Nahua (Aztec) documents (Chamoux, 2015) and in current usage in Nahua-heritage and Quechua communities of Mexico and Peru (Chamoux, 2015; García, 2015; Lorente Fernández, 2015). Learning considerateness may be a feature of childrearing in Indigenous communities of the Americas.

5. THE SITUATION: REQUESTING HELP TO MAKE A TOY

We examined how children requested help, in a toy-building activity in which a research assistant followed a script in instructing children in how to make a toy, in a spare room at the children's school. The children averaged 8 years of age; they were sibling pairs between 6 and 11 years of age.[1] We made use of videotapes collected for two prior studies that examined a different question (Correa-Chávez & Rogoff, 2009; López et al., 2010). The design of the original studies involved two sessions for each child; because no differences in overall pattern of children's types of requests for help were observed between the two sessions, our analysis combines them.

In following the script for the toy-building session, the "Toy Lady" (a bilingual research assistant of the same ethnicity as the children) first guided the older child in building a toy mouse. If the child had difficulty, she gave the child an opportunity to request help before assisting. Meanwhile, the younger sibling waited at another table, with a distracter object, for a turn to build a different toy (an origami frog). When the older sibling finished making the mouse, the siblings switched seats, and the Toy Lady guided the younger sibling in building the frog.[2]

When each child returned individually about 10 days later to pick up the toy they had made, she or he was unexpectedly offered the chance to make the other toy. The Toy Lady mentioned that she had extra materials and asked the child if they would like to make the other toy

---

[1] There were 14 boys and 12 girls in the Mexican-heritage EIP background, 6 boys and 12 girls in the Mexican-heritage ESE background, and 11 boys and 25 girls in the European American ESE background.

[2] The procedure precludes making age comparisons, because age, order of instruction, and specific toy were not counterbalanced, to reduce variability in the data.

while she finished her work (reading a book or crocheting): "I have to finish this [shows her book or crochet], so you can go ahead and get started, but let me know if you need help." The Toy Lady then sat back and began to read or crochet. If the child requested help, the Toy Lady followed a script specifying a graduated series of hints and help, which involved pausing before helping.

6. CODING CHILDREN'S EFFORTS TO AVOID INTERRUPTING

A bilingual Mexican-heritage research assistant blind to the hypotheses coded whether or not the children's requests for help explicitly showed evidence of avoiding interruption. If avoidance of interruption was not shown, she coded the request as using neutral means, or in some cases showing obtrusiveness (which would be unlikely in these one-on-one interactions without competition for resources or for an adult's attention). She also coded whether the requests were made mostly verbally or using solely nonverbal means.[3]

Requests for help that evidence *avoidance of interrupting* the Toy Lady's ongoing activity show restraint, courteous timing, and efforts to fit with the cadence of her actions. Such requests involve waiting patiently, checking to see that the Toy Lady was not busy or about to say something, to avoid interrupting before asking for help. For example, one child looked up at the Toy Lady and slightly nudged the toy toward her, while attempting to make eye contact. The Toy Lady did not acknowledge this request; she was busy showing the child the next step in building the toy. The child patiently waited for the Toy Lady to look up and then nudged the toy toward her again.

It is important to note that evidence of *avoiding interruption* of others' activities is distinct from avoiding *involvement* due to shyness, timidity, anxiety, or lack of self-confidence to request help. *Avoiding interruption* of others' activities involves careful observation of others' pace in order to make requests at an appropriate juncture in others' activity.

[3] Reliability between a bilingual research assistant, who blindly coded 100% of the data, and the first author, who coded 40% of the data was excellent: evidence of avoidance of interruption $r=0.94$, neutral $r=0.95$, obtrusiveness $r=0.85$, mostly verbal $r=0.92$, and solely nonverbal $r=0.81$.

Neutral requests are straightforward requests for assistance that do not clearly evidence considerateness for the adult's activity. They also do not show obtrusiveness.

Obtrusive requests demand attention or information, pushing for an immediate response even though the request interrupts another's activity. For example, a child repeatedly, and without pause, asked, "Like this? Like this? Like this?" while the Toy Lady was finishing a step, thereby insisting on attention and not allowing time for her to respond between requests. In another example, a child jerked the Toy Lady's sleeve several times while the Toy Lady read her book.

All requests for help were also coded as either using *solely nonverbal* communication or *mostly verbal* communication, which could include some supportive nonverbal communication such as nodding, pointing, and leaning forward. (Solely verbal requests seldom occurred, so they were not distinguished from requests that were mostly verbal.)

7. THE TWO MEXICAN-HERITAGE BACKGROUNDS WERE SIMILAR[4]

To our surprise, the two Mexican backgrounds—those whose families had extensive Western schooling experience and those whose families likely had experience with Indigenous-American practices—did not differ significantly in evidence of avoiding interruption of the adult's activity (or use of neutral means or obtrusiveness) in their requests for help. They also did not differ in their proportion of mostly verbal and solely nonverbal requests for help. We examined the data upside down and backwards to check the surprising lack of differences. We had expected that avoidance of interruption and emphasis on nonverbal communication would be attenuated among Mexican-heritage children whose families had more contact with Western institutions such as school.

One explanation for the similarity between the two Mexican backgrounds is that the value system of *respeto* might be a resilient practice that survives generations even in new settings, despite competing cultural practices such as a US and Western schooling emphasis on extensive verbal

[4] Analyses employed proportions of the total number of requests for help because of the varying amount of help requested by the children. (An analysis of the raw numbers gave the same patterns as reported for proportions.) Controlling for children's age yielded the same patterns of results, so we report results without controlling for age. No gender differences were found.

expression (which is often assumed in the US to reflect an ability to think critically, Kim & Markus, 2002). Despite such pressures, or perhaps in response to them, the cultural value of *respeto* may have been retained over generations by Mexican-heritage families. Many US Mexican-heritage families have integrated in US circumstances without losing some cultural values of their ancestry (Buriel, 1993; Laura Ochoa, 1999; Solórzano & Delgado-Bernal, 2001).

In addition, our two Mexican-heritage samples do not represent the range of Mexican populations. For example, if we had included Mexican-heritage families from elite, professional communities in our comparison, we might well have found differences among Mexican populations in avoidance of interruption and use of nonverbal communication.

Another possible explanation for the lack of differences between the two Mexican-heritage backgrounds is that although *Learning by Observing and Pitching In* and the value of *respeto* may have origins in Indigenous communities, historically in Mexico there have been very few communities that have not had contact with Indigenous and Indigenous-heritage communities. When communities are in contact, values and practices may be adopted in several directions, not just by the less dominant group (Buriel, 1993). Indigenous-origin practices have blended into all Mexican communities for centuries, ever since initial contact (Bonfil Batalla, 1996; Wright, 1992). Thus, a practice that may have been especially emphasized in Indigenous Mexican communities may have spread to other Mexican populations.

8. US MEXICAN-HERITAGE CHILDREN MORE COMMONLY AVOIDED INTERRUPTION OF THE ADULT'S ACTIVITY THAN THE EUROPEAN AMERICAN ESE CHILDREN

Our research question focused on avoidance of interruption of the adult's activity on the occasions when children requested help. As background, we note that there was no significant difference in the overall number of requests for help made by the US Mexican-heritage and European American ESE children, among those who made any requests (*Ms* = 10.5 and 7.9 requests, SDs = 7.0 and 9.4, for the individual children of each background, combining the two Mexican-heritage backgrounds). There was only one pair in which neither sibling made a request for help; this European American ESE pair was excluded from analysis, because there were thus no occasions on which they could display efforts to avoid interrupting.

For both cultural backgrounds, the most common way of requesting help was neutrally, just plainly asking for help, without explicit evidence of considerateness for the adult's activity (for 59.4% of the US Mexican-heritage children's requests and 92.9% of the European American ESE children's requests, SDs = 31.7% and 11.0%, for the individual children of each background) (see Figure 1).

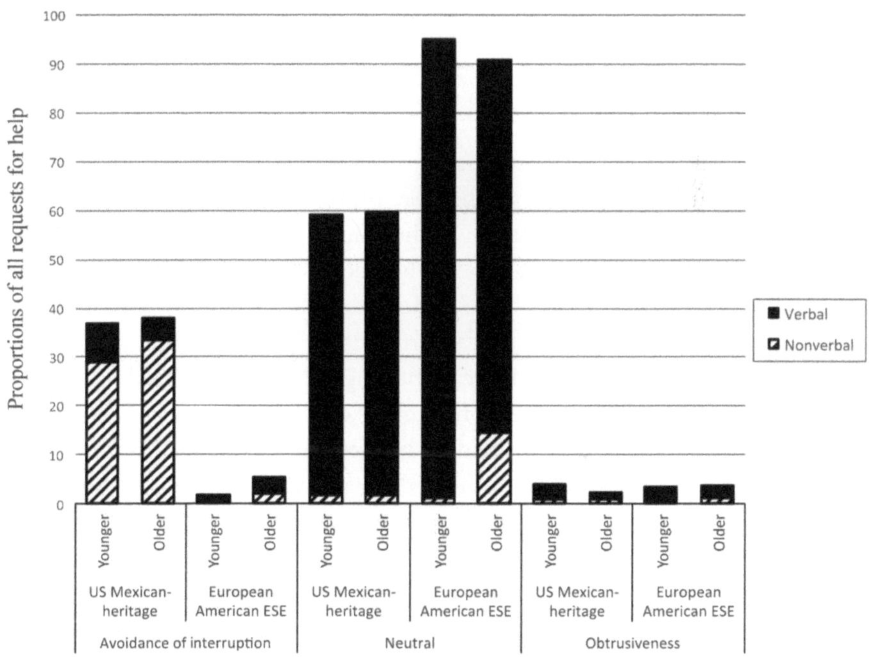

Figure 1 Percentage of requests for help that evidenced avoidance of interruption of the adult's activity versus were neutral or showed obtrusiveness, using mostly verbal or solely nonverbal means, by US Mexican-heritage and European American ESE children. Younger and older siblings in the pair are shown separately.

A very small proportion of the children's requests in both backgrounds were made with *obtrusiveness* (3.2% and 3.6%, respectively, SDs = 7.5%, 6.2%). Obtrusiveness would probably be more common in situations in which children have competition for materials or adult assistance.

The US Mexican-heritage children requested help with evidence of avoidance of interrupting the adult's activity 10 times as often as the European American ESE children. The individual children gave this evidence of considerateness in an average of 37.4% versus 3.6% of their requests for help, respectively, (SDs = 7.5% and 6.2%).

As expected, the US Mexican-heritage children significantly more often gave evidence of avoiding interruption in their requests for help, compared with the European American ESE children. The difference was significant in an ANOVA with the two siblings treated as a repeated measure, $F\,(1, 37) = 37.3$, $p < 0.001$, partial $\eta_2 = 0.50$.[5]

9. MOST REQUESTS AVOIDING INTERRUPTION WERE NONVERBAL AMONG US MEXICAN-HERITAGE CHILDREN

Requests that avoid interruption of the adult's activity do not *require* nonverbal means. However, as expected, most of the requests that showed evidence of avoiding interruption of the adult's activity by US Mexican-heritage children were made solely nonverbally (average = 78.5%, SD = 32.9), among the 37 (of 44) US Mexican-heritage children who made requests that showed avoidance of interruption. (These requests amounted to an average of 31.3% of US Mexican-heritage children's overall requests of any sort, SD = 30.3). Correspondingly, only an average of 21.5% (SD = 32.9%) of their requests evidencing avoidance of interruption were made mostly verbally (which amounted to an average of 6.1% of the US Mexican-heritage children's overall requests of any sort, SD = 11.0).

The idea that requests that avoid interruption are not necessarily nonverbal is supported by the fact that the European American ESE children's requests that evidenced avoidance of interruption were not heavily nonverbal (with an average of only 40% of being nonverbal, among the five

[5] To compare the extent of avoidance of interruption statistically, we used a repeated measures Analysis of Variance to avoid possible non-interdependence in the siblings' data, because the two siblings were each present for the other's first session with the Toy Lady. We had to make an adjustment for the seven pairs in which one of the siblings did not make a request for help (six European American ESE pairs and one US Mexican-heritage pair). In order to avoid losing the data from these pairs for the repeated measures ANOVA, we extrapolated from the sibling's data to use for the sibling who made no requests for help. Siblings within pairs held similar patterns in general and the pattern was similar when we examined only the data in which both siblings made requests, so this appeared to be a good solution. (The means, standard deviations and *t*-test reported in this paper are based on each individual child's performance; we only used extrapolated numbers in the ANOVA. The means are similar whether the extrapolated numbers are included or not.)

European American ESE children who made requests that evidenced avoidance of interruption).

The idea that nonverbal means were especially associated with considerateness of other people's activities by the US Mexican-heritage children is supported by the fact that their requests that did *not* evidence avoidance of interruption were usually made with mostly verbal means, as shown in Figure 1. The US Mexican-heritage children's primary means of making requests overall was mostly verbal (66.2% of their total requests). At the same time, they used nonverbal means much more often overall than the European American ESE children, more than three times as often, in 33.8% versus 9.7% of all of their requests for help (SDs = 31.6, 20.3), a significant difference, $t(71.7) = 4.38$, $p < 0.001$; CI 95% [14%, 38%]. Their use of nonverbal means was especially common when making requests with evidence of avoiding interruption.

Guided by *respeto* and by LOPI, children may learn to use skilled nonverbal communication to avoid interrupting or distracting others from ongoing endeavors. A key facet of the LOPI model involves the use of articulate nonverbal conversation in shared endeavors, allowing efficient and subtle reference to ongoing events. Our findings suggest that these value systems, emphasizing considerateness of the direction of the group and mutual responsibility, may help explain previous research noting that a number of Mexican-heritage and Indigenous communities of the Americas emphasize the use of nonverbal communication (Correa-Chávez, 2011; Lipka, 1991; Mejía-Arauz et al., 2007, 2012; Modiano, 1973; Paradise, 1996; Philips, 1983; Roberts & Rogoff, 2012; Rogoff et al., 1993).

10. VALUES AND CONTEXTS: WHEN *RESPETO* GOES TO SCHOOL

Considerateness and nonverbal communication may be effective strategies for requesting help in many Mexican- and Indigenous-heritage communities, where community members are consistently attentive to ongoing events and are expected to be aware of the direction of the group and of what is needed by others (Alcalá, Coppens, Mejía-Arauz, Roberts & Rogoff, 2014; Chavajay & Rogoff, 1999; Correa-Chávez & Rogoff, 2009; López et al., 2010, 2015; Rogoff et al., 1993; Silva et al., 2010; Silva et al., 2015). Attentiveness among adults in these communities may help them notice children's subtle nonverbal requests for help.

Unfortunately, the skills involved in considerate requests for help may go unnoticed or be misinterpreted by teachers who privilege other ways of seeking help, and who often differ in their nonverbal repertoires from those of the children (Greenbaum & Greenbaum, 1983; Nelson-Le Gall & Jones, 1991; Paradise, Mejía Arauz, Silva, Dexter & Rogoff, 2014). Some teachers see Mexican-heritage children's values and practices, such as wanting to help family and peers, as obstacles to success (Valenzuela, 1999).

Adults inexperienced with *respeto* may also see children's considerateness as hesitation that reflects shyness, disinterest, or passivity, when children are in fact skillfully trying to participate in a considerate way. *Respeto*, unlike shyness, is not a form of avoidance, timidity, or anxiety; it is vibrant involvement in an activity with awareness of how individual actions impact the cadence of the activity.

Even for college students, cultural differences in avoidance of interruption may get in the way of receiving help or be misinterpreted. This shows in responses of students who were asked to evaluate a vignette in which a student went to a professor's office for help but noticed that the professor was busy, so the student walked by the door several times instead of asking the question, before deciding to head home and not ask the question (Ruvalcaba, 2013). A US Mexican-heritage student's response referenced both a value of not interrupting someone who is busy and an expectation that the professor would respond to the nonverbal action of walking back and forth outside the door as a request for help unless extremely busy,

> *If he passed by that many times, I'm sure the teacher will email back, like when he has time or something.... But if he has an urgent, urgent question, there should be somebody else to ask, maybe a TA or another student or something, but not exactly the teacher if he's THAT busy.*
> *[Interviewer: What factors do you think influenced this student's actions?]*
> *The factor of respect, because he doesn't want to interrupt, he just keeps passing by. You just don't, like,.... I would feel that way!*

A European American student criticized the hypothetical student's response:

> *I just think that's stupid.... If they're busy with their own stuff, they have their door open, and I just think it's kinda like, whoa, what are you thinking, like, you're going way out of your way [to get there]. Like, what's so important about this person? I know they're a teacher, but what's so much more important about them than you?*
> *[Interviewer: What factors do you think influenced this student's actions?]*
> *Like, personally, I just think, like, they didn't think highly of themself.*

Mutual consideration of one's effect on others' activities is central to *respeto* and to skilled collaboration in the LOPI model. Promoting more mutually considerate relations in learning settings can help to design more equitable opportunities for learning, as both a tool and an outcome of mutuality of consideration among children and adults, learners and teachers (DiGiacomo & Gutiérrez, 2015).

11. CONSIDERATE COORDINATION OF ACTIVITIES AS SOCIAL/COGNITIVE SKILL

We argue that considerate avoidance of interruption is a prosocial skill that draws on and encourages development of attention, perspective-taking and sensitivity to others' intentions, planning, and self-control. Considerate requests for help require attentiveness and perspective-taking to avoid interrupting or disrupting the flow of the activity. Learning how to do this is a key aspect of children's development, in *Learning by Observing and Pitching In*. The US Mexican-heritage children in our study often carefully observed the Toy Lady before requesting help, apparently judging whether she intended to speak, and avoiding interrupting or overlapping their requests for help with her instructions or other activity. Showing considerateness required restraint and planning and a sensitivity to another's ongoing activity.

Recognition of the cultural value of *respeto*, and how it may appear in Mexican-heritage children's requests for help, can benefit communication and instruction for children from these backgrounds. At the same time, it may benefit children from backgrounds emphasizing *respeto* to learn to request help less unobtrusively for occasions in which they interact with people who are likely to miss subtle requests. It is valuable for everyone to enlarge their repertoires of practice (Gutiérrez & Rogoff, 2003) to be able to do things in more than one way.

Likewise, European American children and adults can enlarge their repertoires of practice to include considerate avoidance of interruption and to use subtle nonverbal communication. Considerate avoidance of interruption and nonverbal communication are tools for coordinating with others—they could be a resource for people from all backgrounds.

ACKNOWLEDGMENTS

Author note: We are grateful to the students, parents, and teachers from Moffett Elementary School as well as its principal Joann Isken, and the students, parents, teachers, and principal of Gault School for their participation in this research. For assistance, we thank Mayra Moreno, Pam Hernandez, and Edith Gurrola. We also appreciate comments from Margarita Azmitia, Maureen Callahan, and Su-hua Wang.

Funding for this research came from the National Science Foundation (0837898), the National Institute of Child Health and Human Development (T32HD046432), the UCSC Foundation Chair, the Ford Foundation, the Spencer Foundation, and AERA/IES and UC LMRI postdoctoral fellowships.

REFERENCES

Alcalá, L., Coppens, A., Mejía-Arauz, R., Roberts, A. L. D., & Rogoff, B. (2014). Children's initiative in contributions to family work in Indigenous-heritage and cosmopolitan communities in Mexico. *Human Development, 57*, 96–115.

Basso, K. H. (1979). *Portraits of "the Whiteman"* New York: Cambridge University Press.

Bolin, I. (2006). *Growing up in a culture of respect.* Austin, TX: University of Texas Press.

Bonfil Batalla, G. (1996). *México profundo.* Austin, TX: University of Texas Press.

Bronfenbrenner, U., McClelland, P., Wethington, E., Moen, P., & Ceci, S. J. (1996). *The state of Americans.* New York: Free Press.

Buriel, R. (1993). Acculturation, respect for cultural differences, and biculturalism among three generations of Mexican American and Euro American school children. *Journal of Genetic Psychology, 154*, 531–543.

Calzada, E. J., Fernández, Y., & Cortes, D. E. (2010). Incorporating the cultural value of *respeto* into a framework of Latino parenting. *Cultural Diversity and Ethnic Minority Psychology, 16*, 77–86.

Chamoux, M. N. (2015). Conceptions of educational practices among the Nahuas of Mexico: Past and present. *Advances in Child Development and Behavior, 49*, 253–271.

Chavajay, P., & Rogoff, B. (1999). Cultural variation in management of attention by children and their caregivers. *Developmental Psychology, 35*, 1079–1090.

Chavajay, P., & Rogoff, B. (2002). Schooling and traditional collaborative social organization of problem solving by Mayan mothers and children. *Developmental Psychology, 38*, 55–66.

Correa-Chávez, M. (2011). *The organization of interaction and communication in US Mexican heritage siblings' joint activity.* Worcester, MA: Clark University. Paper submitted for publication.

Correa-Chávez, M., & Rogoff, B. (2009). Children's attention to interactions directed to others. *Developmental Psychology, 45*, 630–641.

Correa-Chávez, M., Rogoff, B., & Mejía-Arauz, R. (2005). Cultural patterns in attending to two events at once. *Child Development, 76*, 664–678.

Crago, M. B., Annahatak, B., & Ningiuruvik, L. (1993). Changing patterns of language socialization in Inuit homes. *Anthropology and Education Quarterly, 24*, 205–223.

de Guzman, M. R. T., Brown, J., Carlo, G., & Knight, G. P. (2012). What does it mean to be prosocial? *Psychology and Developing Societies, 24*(2), 239–268.

de Haan, M. (1999). *Learning as cultural practice.* Amsterdam, the Netherlands: Thela Thesis.

de Haan, M. (2001). Intersubjectivity in models of learning and teaching. In S. Chaiklin (Ed.), *The theory and practice of cultural-historical psychology* (pp. 174–199). Aarhus, Denmark: Aarhus University Press.

Delgado-Gaitan, C. (1994). Socializing young children in Mexican-American families. In P. M. Greenfield & R. R. Cocking (Eds.), *Cross-cultural roots of minority child development.* Mahwah, NJ: Lawrence Erlbaum Associates, Inc.

DiGiacomo, D., & Gutiérrez, K. (2015). Relational equity as a design tool within making and tinkering activities. *Mind, Culture, & Activity, 00*, 1–15, (accepted).

Ellis, S., & Gauvain, M. (1992). Social and cultural influences on children's collaborative interaction. In L. T. Winegar & J. Valsiner (Eds.), *Research and methodology: Vol. 2. Children's development within social context* (pp. 155–180). Hillsdale, NJ: Erlbaum.

Espinoza-Herold, M. (2007). Stepping beyond *Sí se puede: Dichos* as a cultural resource in mother-daughter interaction in a Latino family. *Anthropology and Education Quarterly, 38*, 260–277.

Flores, R., Urrieta, L., Jr., Chamoux, M.-N., Lorente Fernández, D., & López, A. (2015). Using history to analyze the learning by observing and pitching in practices of contemporary mesoamerican societies. *Advances in Child Development and Behavior, 49*, 315–340.

Frye, D. (1996). *Indians into Mexicans.* Austin, TX: University of Texas Press.

Gallimore, R., Boggs, J. W., & Jordan, C. (1974). *Culture, behavior, and education.* Beverly Hills: Sage.

García, F. A. (2015). Respect and autonomy in children's observation and participation in adults' activities. *Advances in Child Development and Behavior, 49*, 137–151.

Garcia, W. (1996). *Respeto*: A Mexican base for interpersonal relationships. In W. Gudykunst, S. Ting-Toomey, & T. Nishida (Eds.), *Communication in personal relationships across cultures* (pp. 137–155). Thousand Oaks, CA: Sage.

Garland, A. F., & Zigler, E. F. (1994). Psychological correlates of help-seeking attitudes among children and adolescents. *American Journal of Orthopsychiatry, 64*, 586–593.

Gaskins, S. (2000). Children's daily activities in a Mayan village. *Cross-Cultural Research, 34*, 375–389.

Good Eshelman, C. (2013). Valores fundamentales en la tradición intelectual indígena de México. In G. Quinteros & Y. Corona (Eds.), *Las prácticas sociales del lenguaje en contextos de tradición indígena* (pp. 59–74). Xochimilco, MX: Universidad Autónoma Metropolitana.

Greenbaum, P. E., & Greenbaum, S. D. (1983). Cultural differences, nonverbal regulation, and classroom interaction. *Peabody Journal of Education, 61*, 16–33.

Guilamo-Ramos, V., Dittus, P., Jaccard, J., Johansson, A., Bouris, A., & Acosta, N. (2007). Parenting practices among Dominican and Puerto Rican mothers. *Social Work, 52*, 17–30.

Gutiérrez, K., & Rogoff, B. (2003). Cultural ways of learning: Individual traits or repertoires of practice. *Educational Researcher, 32*, 19–25.

Henne, R. B. (2009). Verbal artistry. *Anthropology and Education Quarterly, 40*, 331–349.

Hill, J. H. (2010). Today there is no respect. *Pragmatics, 2*, 263–280.

Kagan, S., & Madsen, M. C. (1971). Cooperation and competition of Mexican, Mexican-American, and Anglo-American children of two ages under four instructional sets. *Developmental Psychology, 5*, 32–39.

Kim, H. S., & Markus, H. R. (2002). Freedom of speech and freedom of silence. In R. A. Shweder, M. Minow, & H. R. Markus (Eds.), *Engaging cultural differences* (pp. 432–452). New York: Russell Sage Foundation.

Lamphere, L. (1977). *To run after them.* Tucson, AZ: University of Arizona Press.

Laura Ochoa, G. (1999). Everyday ways of resistance and cooperation: Mexican American women building puentes with immigrants. *A Journal of Women Studies, 20*, 1–20.

Lipka, J. (1991). Toward a culturally based pedagogy: A case study of one Yup'ik Eskimo teacher. *Anthropology and Education Quarterly, 22*, 203–223.

López, A., Correa-Chávez, M., Rogoff, B., & Gutiérrez, K. (2010). Attention to instruction directed to another by US Mexican-heritage children of varying cultural backgrounds. *Developmental Psychology, 46*, 593–601.

López, A., Nafaji, B., Rogoff, B., & Mejía-Arauz, R. (2012). Helping and collaborating as cultural practices. In Valsiner (Ed.), *The Oxford handbook of culture and psychology* (pp. 869–884). New York: Oxford.

López, A., Ruvalcaba, O., & Rogoff, B. (2015). Attentive helping as a cultural practice of Mexican-heritage families. In Y. M. Caldera & E. Lindsey (Eds.), *Handbook of Mexican American children and families* (pp. 76–91). New York: Routledge.

Lorente Fernández, D. (2006). Infancia nahua y transmisión de la cosmovisión. *Boletín de Antropología Universidad de Antioquia, 20*, 152–168.

Lorente y Fernández, D. (2010). Trayectoria metodológica de una investigación etnográfica en Mexico. *Revista Española de Antropología Americana, 40*(1), 85–100.

Lorente Fernández, D. (2015). Children's everyday learning by assuming responsibility for others: Indigenous practices as a cultural heritage across generations. *Advances in Child Development and Behavior, 49*, 53–89.

Matul, D., & Cabrera, E. (2007). *Cosmovisión Maya*. Guatemala: Liga Maya de Guatemala.

Mejia-Arauz, R., Roberts, A. D., & Rogoff, B. (2012). Cultural variation in balance of *nonverbal conversation* and talk. *International Perspectives in Psychology, 1*, 207–220.

Mejía-Arauz, R., Rogoff, B., Dexter, A., & Najafi, B. (2007). Cultural variation in children's social organization. *Child Development, 78*, 1001–1014.

Mejía-Arauz, R., Rogoff, B., & Paradise, R. (2005). Cultural variation in children's observation during a demonstration. *International Journal of Behavioral Development, 29*, 282–291.

Modiano, N. (1973). *Indian education in the Chiapas Highlands*. New York: Holt, Rinehart & Winston.

Nelson-Le Gall, S., & Jones, E. (1991). Classroom help-seeking behavior of African-American children. *Education and Urban* Society, 24(1), 27–40.

Nelson-Le Gall, S., & Resnick, L. B. (1998). Help seeking, achievement motivation, and the social practice of intelligence in school. In S. Karabenick (Ed.), *Strategic help seeking: Implications for learning and teaching* (pp. 39–60). Mahwah, NJ: Erlbaum.

Nelson-LeGall, S. (1985). Help-seeking behavior in learning. *Review of Research in Education, 35*, 55–90.

Paoli, A. (2003). *Educación, autonomía y lekil kuxlejal: Aproximaciones sociolingüísticas a la sabiduría de los Tseltales*. Mexico City: Universidad Autónoma Metropolitana Xochimilco.

Paradise, R. (1994). Interactional style and nonverbal meaning: Mazahua children learning how to be separate-but-together. *Anthropology and Education Quarterly, 25*, 156–172.

Paradise, R. (1996). Passivity or tacit collaboration Mazahua interaction in cultural context. *Learning and Interaction, 6*, 379–389.

Paradise, R. (2004). Interculturalidad como *respeto* mutuo. *Educación 2001, Revista mexicana de educación, 104*, 59–62.

Paradise, R., & de Haan, M. (2009). Responsibility and reciprocity: Social organization of Mazahua learning practices. *Anthropology and Education Quarterly, 40*, 187–204.

Paradise, R., Mejía Arauz, R., Silva, K., Dexter, A. L. D., & Rogoff, B. (2014). One, two, three, eyes on me! Attempting control versus guiding in support of initiative. *Human Development, 57*, 131–149.

Pelletier, W. (1970). Childhood in an Indian village. In S. Repo (Ed.), *This book is about schools* (pp. 18–31). New York: Pantheon Books.

Philips, S. H. (1983). *The invisible culture*. New York: Longman.

Roberts, A. L. D., & Rogoff, B. (2012). Children's reflections on two cultural ways of working together. *International Journal of Educational Psychology, 1*, 73–99.

Rogoff, B. (2014). Learning by observing and pitching in to family and community endeavors: An orientation. *Human Development, 57*, 69–81.

Rogoff, B., Mistry, J. J., Göncü, A., & Mosier, C. (1993). Guided participation in cultural activity by toddlers and caregivers. *Monographs of the SRCD, 58*, 1–174.

Rogoff, B., Moore, L., Najafi, B., Dexter, A., Correa-Chavez, M., & Solis, J. (2007). Children's development of cultural repertoires through participation in everyday routines and practices. In J. Grusec & P. Hastings (Eds.), *Handbook of socialization* (pp. 225–263). New York: Guilford.

Rogoff, B., Najafi, B., & Mejía-Arauz, R. (2014). Constellations of cultural practices across generations: Indigenous American heritage and learning by observing and pitching in. *Human Development, 57*, 82–95.

Ruvalcaba, O. (2013). More than one way to participate: Latina/o university student approaches to classroom participation. In *Presented at the Society for Research in Child Development, Seattle.*

Silva, K., Correa-Chávez, M., & Rogoff, R. (2010). Mexican heritage children's attention and learning from interactions directed to others. *Child Development, 81*, 898–912.

Solórzano, D., & Delgado-Bernal, D. (2001). Examining transformational resistance through a critical race and LatCrit Theory Framework. *Urban Education, 36*, 308–342.

Srebnik, D., & Cauce, A. (1996). Help-seeking pathways for children and adolescents. *Journal of Emotional and Behavioral Disorders, 4*, 210–220.

Stearns, R. D. (1986). Using ethnography to link school and community in rural Yucatan. *Anthropology & Education Quarterly, 17*, 6–24.

Taggart, J. (2003). Como los niños aztecas aprenden a ser adultos. *Grupo de Trabajo de Familia e Infancia del Consejo Latinoamericano de Ciencias Sociales*. Valdivia, Chile.

Urrieta, L. (2003). Las identidades también lloran: Identities also cry: Exploring the human side of Indigenous Latina/o identities. *Educational Studies, 34*, 147–168.

Valdés, G. (1996). *Con respeto*. New York: Teachers College Press.

Valenzuela, A. (1999). *Subtractive schooling*. New York: State University of New York Press.

Vasconcelos, J. (1997). *La raza cosmica*. Baltimore, MD: Johns Hopkins University Press.

Vigil, J. D. (1998). *From Indians to Chicanos*. Prospect Heights, IL: Waveland Press.

Wieder, D. L., & Pratt, S. (1990). On being a recognizable Indian among Indians. In D. Carbaugh (Ed.), *Cultural communication and intercultural contact* (pp. 45–64). Hillsdale, NJ: Erlbaum.

Wright, R. (1992). *Stolen continents: The Americas through Indian eyes since 1492*. Boston: Houghton Mifflin.

CHAPTER NINE

Young Children's Attention to What's Going On: Cultural Differences

Katie G. Silva*, Priya M. Shimpi*,†, Barbara Rogoff*,1
*University of California, Santa Cruz, California, USA
†Mills College, Oakland, California, USA
[1]Corresponding author: e-mail address: brogoff@ucsc.edu

Contents

Abstract

This chapter examines children' attention to surrounding events in which they are not directly involved, a way of learning that fits with the cultural approach of *Learning by Observing and Pitching In*. Research in instructional settings has found that attention to surrounding events is more common among Indigenous Guatemalan Mayan and some US Mexican-heritage children than among middle-class children from several ethnic backgrounds. We examine this phenomenon in a quasi-naturalistic setting to see if the cultural

Advances in Child Development and Behavior, Volume 49
ISSN 0065-2407
http://dx.doi.org/10.1016/bs.acdb.2015.10.007

variation in young children's attention to surrounding events in which they were not directly involved extends beyond instructional settings. During a home visit focused on their younger sibling, 19 Guatemalan Mayan and 18 middle-class European American 3- to 5-year olds were nearby but not addressed, as their mother helped their toddler sibling operate novel objects. The Guatemalan Mayan children more frequently attended to this nearby interaction and other third-party activities, whereas the middle-class European American children more often attended to their own activities in which they were directly involved or they fussed or showed off. The results support the idea that in some Indigenous communities of the Americas where young children are included in a broad range of family and community endeavors, children may be especially inclined to attend to ongoing events, even if they are not directly involved or addressed, compared to European American children whose families have extensive experience in Western school ways.

1. INTRODUCTION

This chapter examines cultural variation in young children's attentiveness when they have the opportunity to observe others but are not directly addressed (*third-party attention*). Wide, keen observation of ongoing events is hypothesized to be a key feature of a learning tradition emphasizing children's inclusion in family and community activities, which Rogoff and colleagues refer to as *Learning by Observing and Pitching In* (*LOPI*; previously, *Intent Community Participation*; Rogoff, 2014; Rogoff, Paradise, Mejía-Arauz, Correa-Chávez, & Angelillo, 2003; see also Paradise & Rogoff, 2009).

Several ethnographic observations remark on children's attentiveness to surrounding activities in communities where children have access to a wide range of community activities, particularly in many Indigenous communities of the Americas (Chamoux, 1992; de Haan, 1999; de Leon, 2000; Gaskins & Paradise, 2010; Suina & Smolkin, 1994; Cardoso (2015), García (2015), Martínez-Pérez (2015). The ethnographic studies often imply that attention to surrounding events is more common and valued in Indigenous American communities than in middle-class communities, like those of most of the ethnographers themselves.

However, very few studies systematically compare children's observation of surrounding events across cultural communities. The few exceptions, discussed below, are limited to a highly scripted instructional setting. In this chapter, we report findings from a comparative study in a quasi-naturalistic home setting, where we examined whether 3- to 5-year-old Guatemalan Mayan children would attend more to nearby parent–sibling interactions and other surrounding events than middle-class European American children.

It is plausible that in middle-class European American communities, where children are often segregated from important community events, children may attend less to surrounding events in which they are not directly involved than in communities where children are included in many mature activities (Morelli, Rogoff, & Angelillo, 2003; Rogoff et al., 2014; see also Cardoso (2015). Mejía Arauz, Correa-Chavez, Keyser Ohrt, Acevez-Azuara (2015). Middle-class children are extensively involved in Western schooling and preschooling, which contributes to the segregation of children from the range of community activities and often prioritizes a narrow attentional focus. In addition, teachers, as well as parents with extensive schooling themselves, often engage in child-focused interactions in which they closely manage young children's attention and discourage attention to surrounding events (Harkness, 1977; Laosa, 1982; Martini, 1996; Ochs & Schieffelin, 1984; Paradise, Mejía-Arauz, Silva, Roberts, & Rogoff, 2014; Philips, 1972; Rogoff, Mistry, Goncu, & Mosier, 1993). Hence, middle-class European American children may learn to take others' lead about what to pay attention to and may be less likely to attend spontaneously to interactions that are not directed to them (Paradise et al., 2014).

Although middle-class children do learn by attending to interactions that are not directed to them (Matheson, Moore, & Akhtar, 2013; Phillips, Seston, & Kelemen, 2012; Shimpi, Akhtar, & Moore, 2013; Shneidman, Sootsman-Buresh, Shimpi, Knight-Schwarz, & Woodward, 2009), observing surrounding events may be even more important for children from cultural communities with greater opportunities to observe, and the nature of their third-party attention may be distinct. The idea of a differing learning pattern is supported by findings that a sample of primarily European American children learned better from direct teaching situations, whereas Yucatec Mayan children learned just as well from observing others' interactions (Shneidman, Todd, & Woodward, 2013).

However, the research on cultural differences in *learning* from third-party events requires verifying whether there are reliable cultural differences in *attentiveness* to surrounding events. The three studies that have found cultural differences in third-party attentiveness are limited in generalizability in that all three have been carried out exclusively in one setting: explicitly instructional, highly scripted situations (Correa-Chávez & Rogoff, 2009; López, Correa-Chávez, & Rogoff, 2010; Silva, Correa-Chávez, & Rogoff, 2010). In all three of these studies, a child was asked to wait nearby to be taught how to make a toy while a research assistant followed a script to teach the child's sibling how to make a different toy, in a rented room or a spare room of the children's school. The waiting child's attention was coded for the extent to which the child paid attention to the nearby instructional interaction of the sibling and research assistant. Mayan and Mexican-heritage children from families with likely experience with Indigenous practices (and limited schooling) showed more attention to the third-party instruction than did children whose mothers had extensive experience in Western schooling and related practices—whether Mayan, Mexican-heritage, or middle-class European American.

Extensive research on the importance of context indicates that it would be dangerous to generalize about cultural differences in children's third-party attention based solely on studies in one setting. Many aspects of everyday life differ from the scripted instructional settings of the previous research.

The present study provides evidence that cultural differences in third-party attention extend beyond instructional settings, by observing young children who were casually present for family interactions in their home, and with younger children than in previous studies, which focused on 5- to 11-year olds. Generality of this attentional pattern in Indigenous-heritage communities lends support to the idea that wide, keen attention is an important feature of the LOPI way of organizing children's learning.

2. THIRD-PARTY ATTENTION IN A QUASI-NATURALISTIC SETTING

We examined the attention of Mayan and middle-class European American 3- to 5-year olds who were present in a conversational home visit that was focused on their mothers and toddler siblings. Our quasi-naturalistic setting differed from the staged instructional setting of the three prior comparative studies in many ways that may be important for developing a more general understanding of cultural differences in children's attentiveness. The children were at home and were not led to expect to be the target of instruction or even of interaction during any part of the session. Indeed, they were not specifically addressed nor asked to do anything in particular by the visiting researchers, and the researchers themselves did not anticipate studying the attention of the 3- to 5-year olds. The children were free to wander away (but seldom did so).

The adult involved in the third-party interaction was the child's mother (rather than a researcher following a script), who was simply asked to help the child's toddler sibling operate novel objects but not directed to interact (or not) with the 3- to 5-year old in any way. The surroundings included the child's home life as it would occur during a friendly visit of strangers. If the child's home included other people, they were free to be present or come and go without constraint by the researchers, and ordinary surrounding events went on (e.g., phones rang, trucks drove by on the street, neighbors called out, and so on).

The previous comparative studies of third-party attention controlled the situation as much as possible to create a rather standardized situation. In contrast, the goal of the present study was to examine a setting that was similar in some ways for all participants but which maintained many aspects of the child's ordinary home experience during a visit by strangers conversing with their mother.[1] Of course, many aspects of the visit are out-of-the-ordinary, such as the focus on the toddler sibling, the videotaping, the conversational interview led by strangers, and the novel objects handed to the mother to operate with the toddler sibling.

We expected that in this quasi-naturalistic situation with young children, Mayan children would show more attention to the third-party interaction between their mother and sibling and more time alert to other third-party activities than would middle-class European American children, who would spend more time focused solely on their own activities even when other activities were going on. This expectation is predicted by the conceptual framework of *Learning by Observing and Pitching In* (Rogoff, 2014) and would be consistent with the findings of the prior scripted studies of third-party attention with children in middle childhood.

[1] One might argue that standardization of all aspects of a situation is important for comparisons. However, standardization of features does not ensure that a situation is standard in the experience of the participants. Allowing a great deal of the variation that is normal within the child's home life may actually provide a more standard procedure, in terms of familiarity of the setting to the child. This classic issue regarding standardization of actions versus meanings is built into cultural comparisons (Cole & Means, 1981; Shweder, 1979; Sostek et al., 1981) because it is part of the definition of culture that many practices vary, often in systematic ways.

3. THE CHILDREN AND THEIR COMMUNITIES

The children we observed were 19 Guatemalan Maya and 18 middle-class European American 3- to 5-year olds (averaging 4.1 years in both communities), in roughly equal numbers of girls and boys. They were observed during a home visit that involved an interview and object exploration focused on their mother and their toddler sibling (who was 14–20 months old, averaging 17 months in both communities).

The two communities varied in many ways, including experience with Indigenous ways of life, family histories of extensive Western formal schooling, distinct occupations, varying family size, rural or urban settings, and many aspects of daily life. These are features of distinct cultural constellations, with many interrelated and inseparable aspects (Rogoff, 2011; Rogoff & Angelillo, 2002; Rogoff et al., 2014). Our aim is not to test the "effect" of specific aspects of the children's lives such as inclusion in community life or family history of schooling, but to examine a multifaceted pattern in which these two aspects may be especially important. Although children's opportunities to observe and participate in community life and experience with Western schooling are hypothesized to be particularly important aspects related to children's use of attention (Rogoff, 2003), we do not believe that these are free-standing "factors"; rather they are part of whole constellations of cultural practices.

Mayan participants were from San Pedro la Laguna, Guatemala, a Mayan agriculture-based town of about 8000 in 1991 when the observations were conducted. In the intervening two decades, formal schooling has become more extensive, occupations now include many salaried jobs, and many other changes have occurred (Rogoff, 2011; Rogoff, Correa-Chávez, & Navichoc Cotuc, 2005). "Old" data are particularly valuable for this research, because they allow access to more traditional Mayan learning practices that are in danger of disappearing with all the changes of recent decades. In particular, attentiveness to surrounding events may be disrupted by experience with the competing practices of Western schooling (and related institutions).

The families in the two communities varied in many features, including schooling, occupations, and family size, among others that make up the constellations of cultural practices of these two communities. The Mayan mothers' schooling averaged three grades completed (range 0–10). Mayan fathers' schooling averaged five grades (range 0–12). All the mothers were homemakers, and in addition, some were weavers or sold bread or handwoven clothing. Fathers' occupations included farmer, fisherman, police, merchant, and bus driver. Families averaged 3.7 children (range 2–7).

Middle-class European American participants were from Salt Lake City, a metropolitan area of about 1 million at the time of the study. Mothers averaged 16 grades of schooling (range 12–18), and fathers averaged 17 grades (range 14–19). About half of the mothers were homemakers (8); other occupations included social worker and schoolteacher. Fathers' occupations included lawyers, chefs, and real estate brokers. The families had an average of 2.8 children (range 2–7).

4. THE CONTEXT OF THE HOME VISIT

Our study made use of existing videotaped interactions from a prior study (Mosier & Rogoff, 2003) involving a friendly 2-h home visit in which a couple of researchers (a bilingual native of the United States and a local researcher fluent in the local language) asked a mother about her 1-year-old toddler's daily routine and requested her to help the toddler operate several novel objects. The novel object portion of the visit lasted about 45 min. After the mother and toddler sibling operated each object, it remained available for anyone to operate throughout the visit. We chose four of the nine novel objects for analysis (embroidery hoop, pencil box, jumping-jack puppet, and stick puppet) because the 3- to 5-year-old children as well as their toddler siblings were most interested in them.

Families had been selected on the basis of having a toddler and a 3- to 5-year old, in order for the original study to observe the toddler in the context of the presence of a slightly older sibling. The 3- to 5-year-old child's presence for the visit had been requested (at the time the visit was scheduled with the mother), but this child was not invited or instructed by the researchers to be involved (or not) with the objects and was not specifically the focus of any part of the visit. The 3- to 5-year olds were almost always clearly visible and heard in the videotapes: The taping used a wide angle to be able to include the social context of the mother–toddler interaction, and the children were quite interested in the novel objects, which contributed to their staying nearby.

The session took place in the family's usual place for receiving guests. In addition to two researchers, mother, toddler sibling, and 3- to 5-year-old child, other family members were sometimes present, especially in the Mayan setting. The setting included the usual distractions for the children and plenty of interesting objects from the home (including the children's own toys), as well as the novel objects and the video equipment. In both settings, there were a large variety of objects and people to pay attention to, including their own familiar objects.

5. CODING THE CHILD'S ATTENTION DURING OPPORTUNITIES FOR THIRD-PARTY ATTENTION

We coded the 3- to 5-year-old child's attention during *opportunities for third-party attention*, which are times in which other people (usually the mother and/or toddler sibling) were operating or explaining how to operate each of the four novel objects, and the 3- to 5-year old was not directly involved in operating the object or being directly shown how it works. Two local coders, unaware of the hypotheses, coded the 3- to 5-year-old child's predominant focus of attention in 5-s segments. Five-second segments were used, as in the prior studies of cultural differences in third-party attention, because they divided the multiparty, complex flow of interaction into chunks that were long enough to have some coherence and short enough to generally include just one predominant type of attention, based on piloting of the coding scheme. The coders classified each 5-s segment in one of four mutually exclusive categories, which were based on the coding categories of the prior studies of cultural differences in third-party attention, but adapted to the quasi-naturalistic situation[2]:

Attention to third-party object operation. The child's predominant focus of attention for the majority of the 5-s segment was third-party attention to someone else's operation or explanation of the operation of one of the four novel objects. The child was in an alert posture, energetically watching, and appeared interested in the object operation, but was not involved.

Attention to other third-party activities. The child's predominant form of attention during the 5-s segment, during which other people were

[2] To examine reliability of coding, a bilingual Tz'utujil/Spanish assistant coded the Guatemalan data and an English-speaking assistant coded the US data; both were blind to the hypotheses. In addition, the first author, who is bilingual in English and Spanish, coded 35% of the data from each community for reliability. Reliability between the blind coders and the author was good to excellent: attention to third-party object operation, Pearson $r=0.94$; attention to other third-party activities, $r=0.80$; focused on own activity, $r=0.91$; other alternatives to third-party attention, $r=0.77$; and brief glances, $r=0.81$.

operating one of the four novel objects, was alertness to other third-party events such as the activity of a sister or neighbor, a doorbell, or a street vendor calling out.

Focused on own activity. The child was not predominantly involved in third-party attention during the 5-s segment, even though other people were involved in operating one of the four novel objects at the time. The child attended to their own activity with an object other than the current novel object being operated by someone else (such as playing with one of their own toys) or attended to another activity in which they were directly involved, alone or with someone else. We distinguished whether the child's focus was one of the novel objects other than the current one being operated by someone else (*related* focus) or something other than a novel object from the study (*unrelated* focus).

Other alternatives to third-party attention. This residual category primarily included segments while other people were operating one of the four novel objects when the child's predominant focus was fussing or grabbing to get access to the objects or showing off to get attention (e.g., dancing, singing, or talking loudly and insistently). It also involved a few segments in which the child wandered off camera.

We also coded if the child appeared to be spacing out during opportunities for third-party attention (i.e., not attending to any discernible event). However, spacing out was very rare (only two segments, from one European American child).

We also coded the child's *brief glances* to the third-party object interactions. In such glances, the child looked quickly and superficially at others' operation of a target object but did not appear interested in it. Brief glances could co-occur in the same 5-s segment as attention to other third-party activities, being focused on one's own activity, or involved in other alternatives to third-party attention, but brief glances were not coded if they co-occurred in segments with attention to third-party object operation.

6. DIRECT INVOLVEMENT AND OPPORTUNITIES FOR THIRD-PARTY ATTENTION

As background, we note that the 3- to 5-year-old children from the two backgrounds seemed to be generally equally interested in the target objects. This is supported by the fact that they had a similar extent of *direct* involvement in operating or explaining how to operate the object, in about

15% of all the 5-s novel object segments that the mother and toddler operated the novel objects.

The segments in which the children were directly involved were, by definition, *not* opportunities for third-party attention. Our main interest was the children's predominant form of attention during times that they had opportunities for third-party attention.

The children from the two backgrounds had approximately equal amounts of opportunity for third-party attention. There was no significant difference across communities in the average number of time segments that children had opportunities for third-party attention (Mayan community, $M = 85$ segments; middle-class European American community, $M = 94$ segments). Because the overall number of 5-s segments in which there were opportunities for third-party attention varied among families, we analyzed the types of attention as percentages of time segments with opportunities for third-party attention (i.e., when someone was operating or explaining how to operate one of the novel objects *without* the focal child being involved).[3]

7. CULTURAL DIFFERENCES IN YOUNG CHILDREN'S THIRD-PARTY ATTENTION

7.1 Third-Party Attention

The Guatemalan Mayan 3- to 5-year-old children spent most of their time in third-party attention, either to their mother and toddler sibling operating a novel object or to third-party activities of other nearby people, in this quasi-naturalistic home situation. They did so more than twice as much

[3] Planned comparisons were used to test the predictions. (A two-tailed *t*-test was used for brief glances, as we had no prediction for this.)

A few gender differences appeared, but given the number of tests to examine gender and the small sample, gender effects should be treated as tentative: overall, girls used more *attention to third-party object operation*, $F(1) = 8.2$, $p = 0.007$, $\eta^2 = 0.2$, especially in the middle-class European American community, where girls used significantly more attention to third-party object operation than boys, in an average of 43% versus 22% of the time segments (SDs = 11.4, 9.4), $t(16) = 4.2$, $p < 0.001$. In the Mayan families, there was little difference in attention to third-party object operation between genders (58% for girls, SD = 14.5, vs. 53% for boys, SD = 18.8, ns).

For children using *other alternatives to third-party attention* (usually fussing or showing off), there was an interaction between gender and community, $F(1, 33) = 4.4$, $p < 0.05$, $\eta^2 = 0.12$. Middle-class European American boys had more segments involving other alternatives to third-party attention than girls from that community (averaging 21.4 vs. 6.0 segments, SDs = 18.6, 13.7). There was not a difference between Mayan boys and girls (*M*s = 1.7 vs. 2.3 segments, SDs = 3.1, 3.8).

as middle-class European American children (in 84% vs. 39% of the time segments).

Attention to the third-party object operation was the Mayan children's main focus of attention during opportunities for third-party attention. As expected, they spent more time attending to the third-party object operation than did the middle-class European American children, in an average of 55.6% versus 33.9% of the 5-s time segments, respectively (SDs = 16.5, 14.9); $t(35) = 4.2$, $p < 0.001$.

Mayan children also spent more time *attending to other third-party activities*, compared with the middle-class European American children. They did so about five times as much, in an average of 28.6% versus 4.6% of time segments with opportunities to attend to third-party activities with the target novel object (SDs = 16.7, 4.6); $t(35) = 5.9$, $p < 0.001$.

7.2 Other Foci of Attention

The middle-class European American children's attention during opportunities for third-party attention was focused most often *on their own activities* in which they themselves were directly involved. They focused on their own activity more than three times as much as the Mayan children, in an average of 48.4% versus 14.0% of the segments with opportunity for third-party attention (SDs = 12.7, 8.6); $t(35) = 7.8$, $p < 0.001$.

When they focused on their own activity, the middle-class European American children's activities usually were unrelated to the group's activity (such as handling one of their own toys; children from both backgrounds had plenty of unrelated objects near them). The Mayan children's own activities were almost always related to the group's activity (such as handling a previously presented novel object), averaging 94% of time segments, compared with 21% for the middle-class European American children (SDs = 10, 16); $t(35) = 16.9$, $p < 0.001$.

The middle-class European American children also more often engaged in *other alternatives to attending to third-party activities*, generally fussing or showing off, seemingly trying to garner attention to themselves. They did so in an average of 12.9% versus 2.0% of the segments (SDs = 17.5, 3.4); $t(35) = 2.7$, $p = 0.01$. Their pressure for more direct involvement may be consistent with observations that European American 9 year olds often went off-task when not directly involved in an activity, whereas Navajo 9 year olds remained attentive to the activity when not directly involved (Ellis & Gauvain, 1992).

8. CHILDREN'S BRIEF GLANCES WITHOUT SIGNS OF INTEREST IN LEARNING

During third-party attention opportunities, the middle-class European American children glanced briefly at the others operating the objects, without signs of interest in learning about operating the objects, more often than did the Mayan children. They did so in an average of 10.3% versus 4.3% of the segments (SDs = 5.8, 5.6), $t(35) = 4.2$, $p < 0.005$.

The glances seem to have served different purposes in the two communities: the middle-class European American children shot brief glances at the others who were operating the novel object most often when the children were focused on their own activity (in 67% of their glances, vs. 33% of the glances for the Mayan children). Their glances often seemed to involve checking to see if the adult was watching what they were doing. The Mayan children most often glanced at the others who were operating the object during segments in which they were attending to other third-party activities (in 67% of their glances, vs. 26% of the glances of the middle-class European American children, the remaining 7% of whose glances occurred during other alternatives to third-party attention). The Mayan children's glances seemed to be for checking to see if they could become involved in the operation of the novel object.

In the remainder of the chapter, we first examine the possibility of generalizing these cultural differences in third-party attentiveness across different circumstances and across early and middle childhood. Then, we consider possible explanations for the pattern of results—especially ways that attentiveness to surrounding events or to one's own activity may be encouraged by families and communities, how attentiveness to surrounding events might function in schools, and how encouragement of third-party attention might foster all children's learning.

9. CONSIDERING THE GENERALITY OF CULTURAL DIFFERENCES IN THIRD-PARTY ATTENTION

Our quasi-naturalistic results lend confirming evidence to the idea that young children in an Indigenous American community, where children are included in a broad range of family and community endeavors (Morelli et al., 2003), are generally more likely to attend to surrounding interactions in which they are not directly involved, compared with middle-class European American children whose families have extensive experience in Western schooling and related practices. The current study expands the contextual generality of support for this pattern beyond the instructional, scripted setting in which such differences have been studied in prior research, with older children (Correa-Chávez & Rogoff, 2009; López et al., 2010; Silva et al., 2010).

It would be valuable for future research to test whether cultural differences in attentiveness to surrounding events extend to other types of interaction. For example, do these cultural differences extend to other social interactions such as those among agemates, for example, attending to teammates while playing soccer? Do the cultural differences extend to noninteractional third-party activities such as observing another person driving, playing computer games, or working on a worksheet?

Our findings with 3- to 5-year olds combine with the previous research with 5- to 11-year olds to suggest that the cultural differences in attentiveness to third-party interactions may be general across early and middle childhood. In early childhood in our study, as in middle childhood in a study with children from traditional families in the same Indigenous Guatemalan Mayan community (Correa-Chávez & Rogoff, 2009), children showed greater attentiveness to surrounding events than did middle-class European American children. A related attentional pattern may extend even younger: 12- to 24-month-old Mayan toddlers more often skillfully attended to surrounding events while they engaged in their own activities, compared with middle-class European American toddlers, whose attention was more limited to one activity at a time (Chavajay & Rogoff, 1999; Rogoff et al., 1993).

In children's moment-by-moment, day-by-day lives, they have copious opportunities to learn and practice the ways of attending that are fostered in their communities, developing repertoires of practice (Cook, 1999; Gutiérrez & Rogoff, 2003; Rogoff et al., 2007). Their everyday experiences include efforts of their families and companions and communities to guide them to attend in one way or another. The next sections speculate on features that may explain the pattern of results, especially how attention to surrounding events or attention to one's own activity may be encouraged by families and communities.

10. WHAT MIGHT EXPLAIN THE PATTERN OF RESULTS?

We argue that important contributors to children's ways of using their attention include the socialization of attention when children are included in family and community endeavors, as in learning organized by LOPI, and when children (and their parents) have extensive experience in Western schooling. However, the socialization of attention in contributing to family and community activities and in Western schooling is accompanied by many associated cultural practices, such as the ways the children's families make a living, the presence of extended family or same-age unrelated peers, and the social density of households and neighborhoods. In turn, these are also associated with many other cultural features such as religion, languages spoken, and type of housing. Thus, inclusion in family/community endeavors and schooling should be considered as only some of the features comprising distinct constellations of cultural practices, not as free-standing "variables" that could be separated out (Rogoff & Angelillo, 2002). Nonetheless, it makes sense that common ways of socializing attention as children engage in a wide range of family/community endeavors or engage in Western schooling and preschooling and interact with parents who have extensive schooling experience are likely to be closely related to how children use their attention more generally.

As Indigenous-heritage families gain experience in Western schooling and related practices, the use of broad, keen attention to surrounding events may be reduced. Since the early 1990s when our data were collected, Mayan children now continue in school for more years than in prior generations, and thus have reduced access to a wide range of community events. Many related changes in constellations of cultural practices have occurred (Rogoff, 2011). A study done in an instructional setting, in the same town as in the present study, found that Mayan children whose families had extensive experience in Western schooling (more than 12 grades) were less attentive to surrounding events than Mayan children from more traditional families with little Western schooling (Correa-Chávez & Rogoff, 2009).

10.1 How May Attentiveness to Surrounding Events Be Encouraged by Families and Communities?

Families and communities may encourage broad attention to surrounding events as they engage in *Learning by Observing and Pitching In* (Paradise & Rogoff, 2009; Rogoff, 2014). The LOPI model points out the guiding function of community expectations, which include children being present in the activities of their families and communities and learning by observing, both during and in anticipation of making contributions. In some Indigenous Mexican communities, children's attention to ongoing events is itself seen as a contribution to the events, to attain the cultural knowledge that ensures the continuity of the culture (Corona & Pérez, 2007; Pérez Martínez, 2011). Similarly, expert South American Warao canoe makers have considered it part of their work to ensure that children are present while they make a canoe, so that the children can learn to make canoes (Wilbert, 1979; see also Chamoux, 2010; Paoli, 2003; Polak, 2012).

Children's interest in being involved and contributing, another feature of LOPI, may prompt them to take initiative to observe, rather than waiting for someone else to manage their attention (Paradise et al., 2014; see also Martínez-Pérez, 2015). In addition, parents may foster children's attentiveness by telling them to attend broadly, in general, or simply by expecting that they will attend. Pablo Chavajay reported, in the same Mayan community we studied:

> *Caregivers expect children to begin to learn through observation from birth... San Pedro caregivers always emphasize to the children to be observant in everyday activities. For example, if a child does not do a good job of work in the field, his father will usually scold him, "Haven't you seen how I showed you?"*
>
> Chavajay (1993), pp. 164–165

Such encouragement to attend broadly is quite different than the management of attention common in many middle-class families and in Western schooling, where the highly schooled adults often take charge of the timing and exact focus of children's attention, in a step-by-step manner, often with extensive explanation of what is to be noticed (Paradise et al., 2014).

10.2 How Might Attention to One's Own Activity Be Encouraged by Families and Communities?

The middle-class European American children's extent of attention to their own activities and to other alternatives to third-party attention may be fostered by long-term experience with adults closely managing children's attention as well as encouraging narrow rather than broad focus. In school settings, teachers expend considerable effort to focus children's attention on the teacher or on the children's individual work; managing children's attention is often seen as the teacher's responsibility (Paradise et al., 2014). Middle-class parents also often attempt to manage children's attention, perhaps based on their own extensive experience in Western schooling. Some researchers working in Western societies with extensive schooling have even claimed that adult structuring of children's attention is crucial for human children's learning in general (Gergely & Csibra, 2005).

Adult management of children's attention may make children somewhat reliant on being directly addressed and thus discourage children's third-party attention. Rather than paying attention to surrounding events in third-party situations, children who are used to being the focus of adult management might try to disruptively gain attention when they are not addressed directly (Correa-Chávez & Rogoff, 2009; Mosier & Rogoff, 2003; Rogoff et al., 1993; Verhoef, Morelli, & Anderson, 1997). In a secondary analysis of our videotapes, we found that 13 of the 18 middle-class European American children attempted to distract others or disrupt others' operation of the objects, and those 13 averaged 4.3 attempts to disrupt (SD = 2.5). In contrast, just 7 of the 19 Mayan children attempted to disrupt and those 7 averaged only 2.3 attempts to disrupt (SD = 1.8). Children from the two backgrounds disrupted, on average, in 3% versus 0.9% of the time segments, overall, $t(35) = 3.2$, $p < 0.005$. Disruption attempts included grabbing the target object, trying to divert attention to themselves in a loud, insistent, fussy way such as by crawling under a table and yelling and then looking to see if this is noticed, and incessantly trying to engage others in conversation about something unrelated to the objects. Instead of watching or becoming engaged in surrounding events, these middle-class European American children tried to turn attention to themselves.

10.3 How Might an Emphasis on Attending to Surrounding Events Function in Schools?

The attention patterns of children who are used to attending to surrounding events may be misunderstood when they enter schools where children are not supposed to attend to surrounding events (such as the work of their classmates). They may skillfully attend to the teacher while *also* attending to surrounding events—showing a type of alertness that might be misunderstood as distraction if the cultural pattern of attention is not understood (Chavajay & Rogoff, 1999; Correa-Chávez, Rogoff, & Mejía-Arauz, 2005; Rogoff et al., 1993). Our findings suggest that teachers should be aware that children from some Indigenous-heritage American backgrounds, including many from Mexican and Central American immigrant families, may be used to learning by keenly attending to what is going on around them, including the work of classmates (see also Mejía-Arauz, Rogoff, & Paradise, 2005; Wortham & Contreras, 2002).

Schools and teachers can support children in learning to observe and learning by observing. For example, fifth and sixth grade Mexican Indigenous (Mazahua) children progressed in understanding classroom assignments when allowed to observe. The children compared their approaches to a problem with that of their classmates and observed keenly as the teacher or classmates helped others:

> *The students… take maximum advantage of the opportunities to learn and to clarify uncertainties while the teacher passes between the lines of desks to go over and correct the exercises they are doing. When he leans over a desk and begins to look over the work, the children pile up around the desk. While he goes over the work aloud, adding corrections and short explanations, up to eight children join him with their heads squashed together, one over another above the page, to be able to observe closely each pointer that occurs*
>
> Paradise (2007), p. 34, our translation

10.4 Attentiveness to Surrounding Events May Foster Children's Learning

Children who are used to being attentive to surrounding events, *Learning by Observing and Pitching In*, may show particular skill in learning through third-party attention. Several studies suggest that Indigenous-heritage children of Mexican and Guatemalan backgrounds not only attend more keenly but also learn more from third-party opportunities than middle-class children. Guatemalan Mayan and US Mexican-heritage children from relatively traditional families were more attentive to a nearby demonstration that was not directed to them and they learned more (needing less help when unexpectedly offered the opportunity to do the activity a week later) than did European American, Mayan, and US Mexican-heritage children from families with extensive Western schooling (Correa-Chávez & Rogoff, 2009; López et al., 2010; Silva et al., 2010). Similarly, in a scripted study with 18 month olds, Yucatec Mayan children carried out more novel actions that they observed an adult showing another adult than did US (primarily European American) children (Shneidman et al., 2013). Skill in learning from observing may be quite different for children and families whose cultural experience includes an emphasis on and wide experience with learning from observing.

In conclusion, we suggest that *all* children can benefit from attentiveness to surrounding events. Attending to surrounding events is a means by which children from many backgrounds develop understanding (Hayashi & Tobin, 2011; Nielsen, Moore, & Mohamedally, 2012; Rogoff, 2003; Shimpi et al., 2013). Research indicates that European-heritage middle-class children as well as Guatemalan Mayan, Mexican, and US Indigenous-heritage children learn from observing instruction directed to another child (Correa-Chávez & Rogoff, 2009; López et al., 2010; Silva et al., 2010) and learn words, actions, and stories from attending to nearby interactions (e.g., Shneidman et al., 2009, 2013; Tsethlikai & Rogoff, 2013).

Increasing children's opportunities to learn through attention to surrounding activities could give children from all backgrounds the opportunity to learn to use their attention broadly and flexibly. Indeed, it seems to us that learning to use attention in both pointed and broad ways would be an advantage for everyone.

ACKNOWLEDGMENTS

We greatly appreciate the participation of the families and the assistance of Marta Navichoc Cotuc, Carlia Suba, and Shannon Fisherkeller. We are grateful for Christine Mosier's permission to use the videotape data for our analyses and for comments on the manuscript from Monica Tsethlikai, Debbie Siegel, Kate O'Doherty, and Maricela Correa-Chávez. This material is based on work supported by the National Science Foundation under Grant 0837898, the National Institute of Child Health and Human Development (T32HD046423), the Spencer Foundation, and the UCSC Foundation Endowed Chair in Psychology.

REFERENCES

Cardoso Jiménez, R. (2015). Learning and human dignity are built through observation and participation in work. *Advances in Child Development and Behavior, 49*, 289–301.

Chamoux, M.-N. (1992). Aprendiendo de otro modo [Learning in another way]. In M.-N. Chamoux (Ed.), *Trabajo, técnicas y aprendizaje en el México indígena* (pp. 73–93). Mexico City: Centro de Investigaciones y Estudios Superiores en Antropología Social, Ediciones de la Casa Chata.

Chamoux, M.-N. (2010). *Modalidades epistémicas y prácticas educativas*. Mexico: Centre d'études mexicaines et centraméricaines. Submitted.

Chavajay, P. (1993). Afterword: Independent analyses of cultural variations and similarities in San Pedro and Salt Lake. *Monographs of the Society for Research in Child Development, 58*(236), 162–179.

Chavajay, P., & Rogoff, B. (1999). Cultural variation in management of attention by children and their caregivers. *Developmental Psychology, 35*, 1079–1090. http://dx.doi.org/10.1037/0012-1649.35.4.1079.

Cole, M., & Means, B. (1981). *Comparative studies of how people think*. Cambridge, MA: Harvard.

Cook, H. M. (1999). Language socialization in Japanese elementary schools: Attentive listening and reaction turns. *Journal of Pragmatics, 31*, 1443–1465.

Corona, Y., & Pérez, C. (2007). The sense of belonging. In T. Wyller & U. S. Nayar (Eds.), *The given child* (pp. 125–158). Oakville, CT: Vandenhoeck & Ruprecht.

Correa-Chávez, M., & Rogoff, B. (2009). Children's attention to interactions directed to others. *Developmental Psychology, 45*, 630–641. http://dx.doi.org/10.1037/a0014144.

Correa-Chávez, M., Rogoff, B., & Mejía-Arauz, R. (2005). Cultural patterns in attending to two events at once. *Child Development, 76*, 664–678. http://dx.doi.org/10.1111/j.1467-8624.2005.00870.x.

de Haan, M. (1999). *Learning as cultural practice*. Amsterdam: Thela Thesis.

de Leon, L. (2000). The emergent participant: Interactive patterns in the socialization of Tzotzil (Mayan) infants. *Journal of Linguistic Anthropology*, *8*, 131–161. http://dx.doi.org/10.1525/jlin.1998.8.2.131.

Ellis, S., & Gauvain, M. (1992). Social and cultural influences on children's collaborative interactions. In L. T. Wineger & J. Valsiner (Eds.), *Children's development within social context: 2.* (pp. 155–180). Hillsdale, NJ: Erlbaum.

Gaskins, S., & Paradise, R. (2010). Learning through observation in daily life. In D. F. Lancy, J. Bock, & S. Gaskins (Eds.), *The anthropology of learning in childhood* (pp. 100–140). Lanham, MD: Alta Mira.

García, F. A. (2015). Respect and autonomy in children's observation and participation in adults' activities. *Advances in Child Development and Behavior*, *49*, 137–151.

Gergely, G., & Csibra, G. (2005). The social construction of the cultural mind: Imitative learning as a mechanism of human pedagogy. *Interaction Studies*, *3*, 463–481.

Gutiérrez, K., & Rogoff, B. (2003). Cultural ways of learning. *Educational Researcher*, *32*, 19–25.

Harkness, S. (1977). Aspects of social environment and first language acquisition in rural Africa. In C. Ferguson & C. Snow (Eds.), *Talking to children* (pp. 309–316). New York: Cambridge.

Hayashi, A., & Tobin, J. (2011). The Japanese preschool's pedagogy of peripheral participation. *Ethos*, *39*, 139–164.

Laosa, L. (1982). School, occupation, culture, and family. *Journal of Educational Psychology*, *74*, 791–827. http://dx.doi.org/10.1037//0022-0663.74.6.791.

López, A., Correa-Chávez, M., & Rogoff, B. (2010). Attention to instruction directed to another by U.S. Mexican-heritage children of varying cultural backgrounds. *Developmental Psychology*, *46*(3), 593–601. http://dx.doi.org/10.1037/a0018157.

Martínez-Pérez, M. (2015). Adults' orientation of children—and children's initiative to pitch in—to everyday adult activities in a Tsotsil Maya Community. *Advances in Child Development and Behavior*, *49*, 113–135.

Martini, M. (1996). "What's new?" at the dinner table. *Early Development and Parenting*, *5*, 23–34.

Matheson, H., Moore, C., & Akhtar, N. (2013). The development of social learning in interactive and observational contexts. *Journal of Experimental Child Psychology*, *114*, 161–172.

Mejía-Arauz, R., Correa-Chávez, M., Keyser Ohrt, U., & Aceves-Azuara, I. (2015). Collaborative work or individual chores: The role of family social organization in children's learning to collaborate and develop initiative. *Advances in Child Development and Behavior*, *49*, 25–51.

Mejía-Arauz, R., Rogoff, B., & Paradise, R. (2005). Cultural variation in children's observation during a demonstration. *International Journal of Behavioral Development*, *29*, 282–291.

Morelli, G. A., Rogoff, B., & Angelillo, C. (2003). Cultural variation in young children's access to work or involvement in specialised child-focused activities. *International Journal of Behavioral Development*, *27*, 264–274. http://dx.doi.org/10.1080/01650250244000335.

Mosier, C. E., & Rogoff, B. (2003). Privileged treatment of toddlers. *Developmental Psychology*, *39*, 1047–1060. http://dx.doi.org/10.1037/0012-1649.39.6.1047.

Nielsen, M., Moore, C., & Mohamedally, J. (2012). Young children imitate in third-party contexts. *Journal of Experimental Child Psychology*, *112*, 73–83.

Ochs, E., & Schieffelin, B. B. (1984). Language acquisition and socialization. In R. Schweder & R. LeVine (Eds.), *Culture and its acquisition* (pp. 276–320). Chicago: University of Chicago Press.

Paoli, A. (2003). *Educación, autonomía, y lekil kuxlejal: Aproximaciones sociolingüísticas a la sabiduría de los tseltales*. Mexico City: Universidad Autónoma Metropolitana.

Paradise, R. (2007). El conocimiento cultural en el salón de clase. In A. Candela, E. Rockwell, R. Quiroz, R. Mercado, & R. Paradise (Eds.), *La construcción social del conocimiento en el aula II*. Mexico, DF: Departamento de Investigaciones Educativas del CINVESTAV, DIE 33B.

Paradise, R., Mejía-Arauz, R., Silva, K. G., Roberts, A. L. D., & Rogoff, B. (2014). One, two, three, eyes on me! Attempting control versus guiding in support of initiative. *Human Development, 57*, 131–149.

Paradise, R., & Rogoff, B. (2009). Side by side. *Ethos, 37*, 102–138.

Pérez Martínez, E. F. (2011). Supervivencias en prácticas no verbales y verbales en comunidades de herencia cultural mesoamericana. In *Workshop on History and ICP, Austin TX*.

Philips, S. (1972). Participant structures and communicative competence. In C. B. Cazden, V. P. John, & D. Hymes (Eds.), *Functions of language in the classroom*. New York: Teachers College.

Phillips, B., Seston, R., & Kelemen, D. (2012). Learning about tool categories via eavesdropping. *Child Development, 83*, 2057–2072.

Polak, B. (2012). Peasants in the making: Bamana children at work. In G. Spittler & M. F. C. Bourdillon (Eds.), *African children at work* (pp. 87–112). Münster, Germany: LIT Verlag.

Rogoff, B. (2003). *The cultural nature of human development*. New York: Oxford University Press.

Rogoff, B. (2011). *Developing destinies: A Mayan midwife and town*. New York: Oxford.

Rogoff, B. (2014). Learning by observing and pitching in to family and community endeavors: An orientation. *Human Development, 57*, 69–81.

Rogoff, B., Alcalá, L., Coppens, A. D., López, A., Ruvalcaba, O., & Silva, K. G. (2014). (Guest Eds.), Learning by Observing and Pitching In to family and community endeavors [Special issue]. *Human Development, 57*.

Rogoff, B., & Angelillo, C. (2002). Investigating the coordinated functioning of multifaceted cultural practices in human development. *Human Development, 45*, 211–225.

Rogoff, B., Correa-Chávez, M., & Navichoc Cotuc, M. (2005). A cultural-historical view of schooling in human development. In D. Pillemer & S. H. White (Eds.), *Developmental psychology and social change* (pp. 225–263). New York: Cambridge University Press.

Rogoff, B., Mistry, J., Goncu, A., & Mosier, C. (1993). Guided participation in cultural activities by toddlers and caregivers. *Monographs of the Society for Research in Child Development, 58*(236), 1–174. http://dx.doi.org/10.2307/1166109.

Rogoff, B., Moore, L., Najafi, B., Dexter, A., Correa-Chávez, M., & Solís, J. (2007). Cultural routines and practices. In J. Grusec & P. Hastings (Eds.), *The handbook of socialization: Theory and research* (pp. 490–515). New York: Guilford.

Rogoff, B., Paradise, R., Mejía-Arauz, R., Correa-Chávez, M., & Angelillo, C. (2003). Firsthand learning through intent participation. *Annual Review of Psychology, 54*, 175–203.

Shimpi, P., Akhtar, N., & Moore, C. (2013). Toddlers' imitative learning in interactive and observational contexts. *Journal of Experimental Child Psychology, 116*, 309–323.

Shneidman, L., Sootsman-Buresh, J., Shimpi, P., Knight-Schwarz, J., & Woodward, A. (2009). Social experience, social attention and word learning in an overhearing paradigm. *Language Learning and Development, 5*, 1–16. http://dx.doi.org/10.1080/15475440903001115.

Shneidman, L., Todd, R., & Woodward, A. (2013). Cultural experience and imitative learning. In *Paper symposium at the Society for Research in Child Development, Seattle, WA*.

Shweder, R. A. (1979). Rethinking culture and personality theory, part II. *Ethos, 7*, 279–311.

Silva, K. G., Correa-Chávez, M., & Rogoff, B. (2010). Mexican-heritage children's attention and learning from interactions directed to others. *Child Development, 81*(3), 898–912.

Sostek, A. M., Vietze, P., Zaslow, M., Kreiss, L., van der Waals, F., & Rubinstein, D. (1981). Social context in caregiver-infant interaction. In T. M. Field, A. M. Sostek, P. Vietze, & P. H. Leiderman (Eds.), *Culture and early interactions*. Hillsdale, NJ: Erlbaum.

Suina, J., & Smolkin, L. B. (1994). From natal culture to school culture to dominant society culture: Supporting transitions for Pueblo Indian students. In P. Greenfield & R. Cocking (Eds.), *Cross-cultural roots of minority child development* (pp. 115–130). Hillside, NJ: Erlbaum.

Tsethlikai, M., & Rogoff, B. (2013). Involvement in traditional cultural practices and American Indian children's incidental recall of a folktale. *Developmental Psychology, 49*, 568–578.

Verhoef, H., Morelli, G., & Anderson, C. (1997, April). *Young children's attention seeking strategies in a forager and middle class US community*. Presented at meetings of the Society for Research in Child Development, Washington DC.

Wilbert, J. (1979). To become a maker of canoes. In J. Wilbert (Ed.), *Enculturation in Latin America*. Los Angeles: UCLA.

Wortham, S., & Contreras, M. (2002). Struggling toward culturally relevant pedagogy in the Latino diaspora. *Journal of Latinos and Education, 1*, 133–144.

CHAPTER TEN

Día de los Muertos: Learning About Death Through Observing and Pitching In

Isabel T. Gutiérrez*[,1], Karl S. Rosengren[†], Peggy J. Miller[‡]
*Raritan Valley Community College, Branchburg, New Jersey, USA
[†]University of Wisconsin, Madison, Wisconsin, USA
[‡]University of Illinois, Urbana-Champaign, Illinois, USA
[1]Corresponding author: e-mail address: isabel.gutierrez@raritanval.edu

Contents

Abstract

The chapter explores how young children in the state of Puebla, Mexico are socialized with respect to death by observing and pitching in during the annual celebration for *día de los muertos*. This chapter focuses on observations made of children's participation in practices related to *día de los muertos* and their experiences with death as explored through ethnographic interviews of preschool children and adults from the cities of Cholula and Puebla. We found that children were included in all aspects of *día de los muertos* and participated by hanging out, observing, pitching in, and listening. Parents (and grandparents) viewed this active participation as crucial for children to acquire the skills and traditions necessary to be responsible adults in their culture. The current research provides new perspectives regarding the study of children and death within the field of developmental psychology by focusing on how multiple modes of participation are an integral part of young children's socialization with death.

Advances in Child Development and Behavior, Volume 49
ISSN 0065-2407
http://dx.doi.org/10.1016/bs.acdb.2015.08.004

1. INTRODUCTION

In this chapter, we examine children's inclusion, participation, and "learning by observing and pitching in" (Rogoff, 2014), during *día de los muertos*, an annual celebration and remembrance of the dead, which is one of the most important national holidays in Mexico. On this occasion, typically spanning 10 days, the dead return to the realm of the living where they visit with their loved ones. While *día de los muertos* looks back to those who have died, it also looks forward to the next generation. Children are included in the festivities from earliest infancy and play a major role in sustaining the tradition. It is this feature of the ritual that sparked our interest. *Día de los muertos* teaches children about death, instills respect for the dead, and conveys that this event is an essential part of their national heritage. Children are also socialized in the specific practices with the expectation that they will provide for their deceased parents in the way their parents provided for their own departed relatives (Brandes, 2006).

This chapter is based on a study of children and adults in and around the cities of Cholula and Puebla, Mexico. The study was part of a larger program of research investigating the socialization of death in various sociocultural groups (see Rosengren et al., 2014). In this chapter, we focus on the famous *día de los muertos* celebration because it is the most elaborate death-related ritual in Mexico. One of the most striking features of *día de los muertos* is that children of every age are included. Moreover, this celebration involves weeks of preparation in which children also participate. The inclusion of children in this event is in stark contrast with mainstream American culture, in which children are often excluded from death and its associated rituals (Rosengren et al., 2014).

The results of this study are presented in two main sections. In the first and largest section, we describe the ritual of *día de los muertos* and the preparations that precede it. We present these events in chronological order. In each phase, we also describe how children are involved as observers and/or participants who "pitch in." Where relevant, we add details about the meaning of the events, as provided by parents and other adults. In the second section, we present children's perspectives, based on interviews about their experiences of *día de los muertos*.

2. DETAILS OF *DÍA DE LOS MUERTOS*

Death occupies a very special place in Mexican culture as captured in this quote by Octavio Paz (1985, pp. 57–58):

> *To the inhabitant of New York, Paris, or London, death is a word that is never uttered because it burns the lips. The Mexican, on the other hand, frequents it, mocks it, caresses it, sleeps with it, entertains it; it is one of his favorite playthings and his most enduring love.*

This quote captures the importance of death in all aspects of Mexican life. To a large extent, the annual *día de los muertos* celebration embodies the Mexican relation with death. Although *día de los muertos* takes place to varying degrees throughout Mexico, it is celebrated to a greater extent in the southern states (e.g., Hidalgo, Michoacán, Oaxaca, Puebla, Tlaxcala) where Indigenous groups are more concentrated. Even though it is a very important and solemn occasion, *día de los muertos* is not considered a time to be sad for the loss of loved ones, but a time to be happy for their return. The dead are guests at a feast that the family has prepared in their honor; they enjoy the scent of foods, incense, and flowers but cannot participate in the conversation (Haley & Fukuda, 2004). To help guide the dead home, relatives spread aromatic flowers that emit a pungent scent leading them toward the *ofrenda* (altar) where the banquet awaits them (Andrade, 1998).

The dates for *día de los muertos* are somewhat varied, occurring around the end of October and beginning of November (Greenleigh, 1991). Each day has a special significance related to how the dead relative died. In some regions, Greenleigh (1991) reports that October 27th is the day to remember spirits with no survivors to greet them and no home to visit and October 28th is set aside for those who died by accident, murder, or other violent means. In contrast, dead children are expected to come home to visit on October 31st, but to leave by November 1st to make room for the adult dead. In the afternoon of November 1st, bells toll at churches announcing the arrival of the "Faithful Dead" (adults). In the evening, complete families may go to the cemetery to offer a vigil for the souls of their loved ones. The cemeteries become busy locations with women sitting and praying, men talking and drinking, and children playing until they fall asleep from exhaustion. By midnight, cemeteries are filled with lit candles. The souls return to the world of the dead on the afternoon of November 2nd. During this entire celebration, children are active participants and observers of the cultural traditions, enjoying the festivities by helping their families set up the feast and honoring the dead, often participating in singing and dancing.

Día de los muertos instills values that foster hope; those who provide offerings trust that their own survivors will take care of them in a similar fashion after death. In this manner, an individual's immortality is assured. The multigenerational enactment of these practices ensures the future of the tradition, which plays a major role in the reproduction of national identity (Garciagodoy, 1998). One of the most important aspects of the celebration for *día de los muertos* is the significance that it has within Mexican culture. As expressed in the quote by Paz, Mexicans embrace death, as is reflected through this celebration as well as the different rituals that are practiced when someone dies. This celebration also serves to demonstrate the intensity of familial fidelity, a devotion that reaches beyond the grave. This devotion to those who have died also embraces friends and even strangers; offerings are often made to the "ánima sola" (the forgotten soul) or "el muerto desconocido" (the unknown dead).

3. *DÍA DE LOS MUERTOS* AND SURROUNDING EVENTS

The primary data for this chapter are drawn from participant observations conducted in the state of Puebla by the first author prior to and during the celebration for *día de los muertos* in October–November 2007. In the weeks leading up to the celebration, the first author went to the local market to observe how families prepared for the celebration by purchasing the elements necessary to create home *ofrendas* (altars) to honor the dead; visited the cemetery as families prepared the graves of their dead loved ones; visited many *ofrendas* in homes, schools, and places ofbusiness; and helped a family construct their *ofrenda* in memory of their two children who were miscarried. On the eve of *día de los muertos*, the first author visited Tlapanalá, Puebla and spent most of the night walking around town with families and friends who were visiting the *ofrendas* of the loved ones who had died within the last 12 months. While it is typical for families to construct an *ofrenda* in their home, generally friends and neighbors only visit *ofrendas* that honor people who have died in the last 12 months (though this practice varies by community).

On the next day, the first author went to the cemetery where families bid farewell to their loved ones who would return to the realm of the dead in the afternoon. The researcher used photographs and fieldnotes to document these various activities while also actively participating in all aspects of the celebration.

3.1 Lead-Up to *Día de los Muertos*

Preparation for *día de los muertos* is a pervasive part of everyday life during the month of October and children are involved in many different ways. During this time, children participate in activities related to *día de los muertos* in the public schools, help family members create the *ofrendas* (family altars) at home as well as clean and decorate the graves at the cemetery. Preparation generally begins with trips to the market (el mercado) to obtain the necessary elements for the *ofrenda*. Once the *ofrendas* have been set up in the homes, families visit other homes (of friends and neighbors) to pay their respect and observe the *ofrendas*. They also visit the cemetery in preparation for the main event on November 2nd when families gather to bid farewell to their dead relatives.

3.1.1 Learning About Día de los Muertos *in Public Schools*

Although much of how children learn about *día de los muertos* and specific details of the celebration occurs in the home and follows traditions that have been practiced in families for generations, children are also exposed to and participate actively in cultural practices related to *día de los muertos* in schools and the larger community. Throughout Mexico, as part of the national holiday of *día de los muertos*, public schools and teachers are obligated to teach the children about the *fiesta* and they do this by having children create an *ofrenda* at the school and decorate it with their own art (Garciagodoy, 1998). Many communities also hold official competitions for the best *ofrenda* and schools often have their students participate in these competitions. While children may see this as an amusing competition, it provides them with the opportunity to learn about their national heritage and take pride in what they are doing (Carmichael & Sayer, 1991).

3.1.2 Trips to el Mercado

In preparation for *día de los muertos*, children and their parents take trips to *el mercado* (the market) during the weeks and days before the event. During these trips, the children observe the food and other items on display, and the families purchase items that are used in the *ofrendas* and the decoration of the graves. These items include *pan de muerto* (bread of the dead), which can be found at almost any bakery during the celebration for *día de los muertos*. This bread, which is only made for this *fiesta*, will be served with hot chocolate to living guests and as an offering for the dead. *Cabecitas* (also referred to as *calavera*, small sugar skulls) are also purchased. Older children in the family (between 10 and 14 years of age) have the role of painting all the facial features of the sugar skulls (Haley & Fukuda, 2004). The *calavera* is often decorated with the individual's name. The name and *calavera* are meant to wish the individual a long and happy life. Younger children enjoy receiving the *cabecitas* with their names. Other items to be purchased include candles, whose light helps the dead find the location for the *ofrenda* and the cempaxóchitl flowers that are strewn in a trail from the front of the house to the *ofrenda*. Given their bright yellow color and pungent scent, these flowers are also expected to help guide the dead who are visiting to find the *ofrenda*.

Children are also involved in the business end of the preparation. In the town of Tamazunchale in the state of San Luis Potosí, a large percentage of the population is involved in making the special candles sold at the market that will be set on the *ofrendas* and used in the offerings. As with the specific celebration, entire families work together in this business and each member of the family will have a different task to complete. Generally, children will be given the task to cut the strings that will be used as wicks for the candles and place them on rings so the adults can dip them in boiling paraffin (Andrade, 2001).

Often children can be seen at the market just playing, running around, or having a good time. This participation through play in activity of the market brings home the everyday nature of the symbols of *día de los muertos* and the preparation for the celebration. By thinking of a market as a place to play, even one filled with symbols and objects related to death, children come to learn that ceremonies about death are normal events, not something to be feared and avoided.

3.1.3 Preparing the Family Ofrendas

A key way that children learn by observing and contributing to *día de los muertos* is in the creation of *ofrendas* that are set up in the homes and cemeteries. An *ofrenda* in the home is often placed where an altar for saints is usually located, thereby signifying a special place of honor in the home throughout the year. The location and changing of displays provides a compelling message to children about the value of religion, cultural traditions, and the importance of deceased family members.

Each *ofrenda* is typically composed of key elements including: a tablecloth, arch, pictures of the deceased, candles, water, salt, incense, flowers, food, a *petate* (reed mat), and toys (for the *angelitos*). A typical *ofrenda* found in a home is shown in Figure 1. Although there is variation in the form of *ofrendas*, the construction is considered to be a family affair, one that children are engaged in from start to finish. Usually, children pitch in by arranging the fruit on the *ofrenda* and pulling the petals from the flowers to create a floral trail to guide the dead relatives to find the *ofrenda*. Children do these activities together with siblings, parents, and grandparents. However, children's participation is not limited to merely following instructions from adults and older siblings. As children grow older, they take the initiative to perform more and more of the activities themselves, pitching in to help the entire family with the celebration. For example, older children may pitch in by becoming responsible for cooking some of the foods that will be used in the *ofrenda*.

Figure 1 A typical *ofrenda* in a home to honor an individual who died in the past 12 months. The cross at the base of the *ofrenda* which is made of bright yellow flower petals is used to guide the dead to the *ofrenda.*

As families prepare for the visit of the dead, men and women from three or four generations participate together in the purchases, preparations, and vigils. Sometimes specific tasks will be divided by age and gender, with men shopping, women cooking, and children of all ages (as early as 3 or 4 years of age) cleaning the graves, pulling the petals off the flowers to create the trail to the *ofrenda*, and running errands (Garciagodoy, 1998). The work of each family member is considered essential for the success of the celebration, as all of these different activities (e.g., shopping for the elements, creating the *ofrenda*) are important parts of the celebration. Children are expected to pitch in and participate fully in these activities.

During the visit to Puebla, the first author was invited by MP, a local artisan from the city of Puebla, to help his family which included his wife and 15-year-old son to set up their *ofrenda*. MP and his wife let their 15-year-old son decide how the *ofrenda* would be designed, something they have done for many years, since their son was a young child. The son chose to decorate the *ofrenda* with many sweets and toys. This particular *ofrenda* was created especially for two children that died as the result of miscarriages, so all the elements (e.g., sweets, toys) were added in pairs. As in other families, children are expected to pitch in to do the work involved and participate in the actual construction of the *ofrendas*. In this particular family, because there were no younger children than the 15-year-old, the first author was invited to take on roles that younger children would normally assume during the

Figure 2 A family's *ofrenda* in Puebla honoring their two children who died as a result of miscarriage. This *ofrenda* was constructed by the surviving child, his family, and the first author.

celebration. Along with the family, she visited the market to buy sweets, fruits, a new *petate* (reed mat), and candles needed for the *ofrenda*. The first author also worked alongside the family members, pulling the petals off the cempaxóchitl flowers to be used in decorations and helping to arrange the different elements that would be used for their *ofrenda* (sweets, toys, flowers, fruits, etc.). The first author also pitched in to construct the *ofrenda* (see Figure 2).

While the first author worked on the *ofrenda* along with the family, MP went on to explain that, since everyone in the family was supposed to participate, and the *ofrenda* was seen as a tribute to those who died, this provided an opportunity for young children to be taught about the celebration, especially to respect the *ofrenda* until *día de los muertos* had passed. He said,

> *That is the point because since they are little, they are participating and understanding first of all, that it is a celebration from the living to the dead. Secondly, they are taught that death is a very important aspect of our life. It's a cycle; for there to be life, there needs to be death. There can be no death without life and, vice versa, there can be no life without death. Someday, we will all go through this and it should be something natural. And as such, we should not be afraid of death. And the young ones assimilate this idea very well. That is why we, as Mexicans, do not fear death. Not so much for being fearless or machos since women also participate in this event. We could say that it is more respect. We have respect for it and, from this respect, it is another way of getting to know life.*

In interviews with the grandmother of a 6-year-old girl, she discussed her experiences growing up with this celebration as well as her own children's and grandchildren's experiences. She explained that things have really not changed at all since she was a child. The *ofrendas* have always been established in the same way, and *día de los muertos* is usually celebrated in the same traditional manner. She remembered that, when she was little, she would help her mother sell fruit at the market in preparation for *día de los muertos* and help set up the *ofrenda* at home. She talked about how she followed the same pattern with her own children and granddaughter. Together, they prepared food (*tamales*) for the *ofrenda* and took flowers to the cemetery.

She described an anecdote about one of her sons when he was about 6 years of age. Apparently, her son tried to grab something from the *ofrenda* and she told him not to do that. He responded that he would do it anyway and, by coincidence, he tripped when trying to grab it. She then told him that the *ánimas* (souls) made him trip since he was trying to grab something from the *ofrenda*, and that if he tried it again, the *ánimas* would make him trip again. According to her, this was enough of a lesson for her children to respect the *ofrenda*. Thus, the setting up and maintaining of the *ofrendas* serves to pass on traditions from generation to generation, but also can serve as a way of teaching respect for rules and traditions as well as one's ancestors. The grandmother continued to talk about how her children continue the tradition for *día de los muertos* by setting up *ofrendas* at their own homes.

As this grandmother was growing up, she recalled that her mother would describe the meaning of the elements of the *ofrenda*. For example, her mother explained that the smoke from the *copal* (incense) signified that the souls had come to eat and were already leaving. This was what she also told her own children and they in turn taught this to their children. This is clearly shown by an event she described occurring in the most recent celebration of *día de los muertos*. The grandmother talked about how her granddaughter who was 6 years old told her that the soul of a baby nephew who had died was present because of the *copal* smoke, and that she would keep him company while he ate. The granddaughter then went to the table where the *ofrenda* was placed and sat there quietly for some time accompanying the soul of the baby while he visited the home.

Children are not expected to be mere observers in the construction of the *ofrenda*, but to actively help out with the preparations and celebration. As they participate, they take on more independent roles as they learn about the meaning of unseen aspects of ritual via verbal commentary that at times is explicit. For example, as families gather to set up the *ofrendas*, adults and children have discussions about the specific things their loved ones enjoyed when they were living. These items (or symbols representing them) are then incorporated in the *ofrenda* at home. By actively participating in these conversations, children learn the value of the traditions as well as how to be adults in their culture.

3.1.4 Visiting Ofrendas *at Homes in Tlapanalá, Puebla*

On the evening of November 1st, the first author headed to the town of Tlapanalá, located about 1 h from Puebla, in the southwestern part of the state. Even though this town's population has had a large flow of immigrants to the United States (many of whom have returned), it seems that many of the traditions regarding *día de los muertos* remain robust and resilient in the face of social change. All throughout the evening and into the morning hours, friends and neighbors including the first author, walked around the town visiting the *ofrendas* that were set for those who died within the last 12 months. These particular practices vary quite a bit from town to town.

Families and friends generally only visit the *ofrendas* in homes where a family member has died within the past 12 months. These *ofrendas* are sometimes quite elaborate and the families may have spent considerable time and resources in their construction. In other homes, *ofrendas* are created to honor and welcome all the deceased family members. These *ofrendas* are not meant to be visited by extended family and friends, but are mostly prepared for the dead to visit.

When the first author arrived at the first *ofrenda* along with her companions, the family being visited was given some long candles as presents for having them at their home, a common practice that is done at every home that is visited. They then walked into a living room area with a very large *ofrenda* and chairs so everyone could sit right in front of it. Once they were all sitting, the owners of the home offered everyone some bread and sweets. While they were visiting at this home, a few other townspeople came in, including young children. It was interesting to see how some of the children were dressed in costume when coming to visit. Children wore all sorts of costumes from scary masks to pumpkins. Many of the costumes reflect the infiltration of elements of Halloween with children donning Dracula and witch costumes. Traditionally, the costumes of the children would consist of images of the dead, such as a corpse bride, or a *catrina* (female skeleton that represents death) or skeleton. During this visit, there was a little girl about 18 months of age who was sitting on her mother's lap holding a plastic jack-o-lantern for her *calavera (a gift of candy, food, or money)*. This child caught the first author's attention given that, at such a young age, she was already visiting the neighboring *ofrendas* along with other members of her family.

Figure 3 *Güisos* (i.e., all of the town's children, including adolescents) dancing in the streets of Tlapanalá, Puebla as a way of honoring those who died within the last 12 months. Most of the participants are wearing costumes or mask.

Later in the evening, around 11:00 PM, as the first author and her companions were visiting one of the *ofrendas*, the *güisos* could be seen dancing on the street. The *güisos* is a group of children (from about 3 years onward) and adolescents who go around the town visiting all the new *ofrendas* and dancing in front of these; most of them are dressed in costume and/or wearing masks (see Figure 3). The *güisos* were accompanied by a pick-up truck that had a sound system and speakers playing music. While the children danced in front of the home with the *ofrenda*, the street filled with people taking pictures; the children danced a few songs before continuing to the next home. The author and her companions encountered the *güisos* a second time as they were visiting the last *ofrenda* for the night. What is remarkable about this event is that children not only were active participants in their own families and traditions, but were welcomed into the homes of other families who lost loved ones in the past year. At the same time, this process was accompanied by dancing and music, signifying a celebration of those who have died.

3.2 The Dead Return to the Living

Dead family members are believed to visit the homes and cemeteries during the final days of *día de los muertos*. While there are family and regional differences in the timing and location of these visits, as described earlier, the day of the visit is generally determined by the age of the deceased and the means by which they died. Families may conduct vigils at the home or cemeteries to welcome the dead, and while an adult female is often the key participant in these vigils, it is not uncommon for children as young as 2 or 3 years of age to sit in vigil, waiting for the dead. This role may be taken on by children when the child was especially close to the deceased, as is the case with the death of siblings.

While working on the *ofrenda*, MP and the first author talked about some of the traditions and practices that his family had engaged in throughout the generations. MP recalled a number of anecdotes related to the celebration for *día de los muertos* involving his grandmother. He explained how, on November 2nd, his grandmother would set the table so she could receive the souls of all her dead relatives. At 12 noon, the grandmother would open the door and begin greeting all the souls. She would then tell each of the souls where to sit and would serve them the food that had been prepared as the souls are the first to enjoy the feast through the aromas. While the souls were visiting, she would sit down with them and would talk to all of them saying things like, "How are you? We have missed you. We are so glad that you came." Then, sometime later, she would put the food from the plates back in the pots since the lunch for the souls had already finished. Around 2:00 PM, she would then reheat the food and invite all the living guests to join her at the table and enjoy the feast.

The first author learned additional information about the visits from the mother of a 5-year-old girl, about how her mother set the *ofrenda* in their home. She once asked her mother when she was a young child, why if a full glass of water was placed on the *ofrenda*, the water level would go down. Her mother responded that it was because the dead had drunk it. In this particular case, she talked about how the dead's journey to return to the living was long and that they would drink a little bit of water to recover from the trip. The mother told her and her siblings that if they tried an apple or other fruit from the *ofrenda*, it would be tasteless because the dead had already taken a taste from it. Many of the parents interviewed discussed how when the loved ones visited the *ofrenda*, they consumed the essences of the food and flowers on the *ofrenda*. When the essence of the food and flowers is consumed, the flavor of the food and smells of the flowers are thought to be diminished. For this reason, once the celebration has ended, and the remaining food from the *ofrenda* is shared among the living, the food tastes very bland in comparison to how it would normally taste.

MP also told the first author a story of how his father would encourage the children to set a specific piece of *pan de muerto* for their grandmother who had died. Then, during the night, when everyone else was sleeping, he (the father) would get up and take a bite out of the *pan de muerto*. The next day, when everyone was awake, he would tell the children to go look for the *pan de muerto* to see if their grandmother had come to visit. Once the children came back telling him that the bread had been bitten, and that grandma had come to visit, he would say, "See, the souls came to visit." In addition to the *pan de muerto*, MP said that his father would also do something similar with a glass of holy water obtained from a church that was set at the *ofrenda*; he would drink part of the water and show their children how the water level had gone down as proof that their grandma had been there. When MP told these stories, he explained how grateful he is because his father played these tricks on them, since it served as a way for him to feel very close to his grandparents and become more engaged in the celebration.

In addition to the anecdotes that MP remembered from growing up, something very peculiar happened during the days the first author visited his family. Among the candy that had been set at the *ofrenda,* there were two sugar sheep that MP and the first author had bought at the market. A few days after *día de los muertos,* when the author returned to the home, MP took her to the *ofrenda* to show her what happened to the sheep. Between the time that they had set up the *ofrenda* on October 30th and the day after *día de los muertos*, November 3rd, somehow, one of the sheep lost part of its decoration. MP and his family tried to find a logical explanation as to what had happened. After giving it much thought, they concluded that it was a sign that their deceased children came to visit. While it is likely that MP and his family were playing a trick on the first author, as the first author was serving in the role of a young child during much of the celebration, this example also illustrates that adults are invested in convincing their children (and the first author) that the dead *do*, in fact, return. This belief coexists with adults' general belief that the dead are only able to enjoy the celebration through the sights and smells as only their souls are present during the visit.

3.3 Visits to the Cemetery

Another major way that children participate in *día de los muertos* is in the visits to the cemetery, the last resting place of the deceased. There are several important aspects of the visits including: decoration of the graves, family time at the cemetery, and a vigil.

3.3.1 Decoration of the Graves and Offerings

Children are generally involved in the decoration of the graves. For example, in the city of Janitzio, Michoacán children and their parents arrive at the cemetery early on the morning of November 1st carrying offerings to be placed on the graves of their loved ones. These offerings include cempaxóchitl flowers (marigolds), candy, *pan de muerto* (bread of the dead), fruit, and lit candles (Andrade, 1998).

3.3.2 Family Time at the Cemetery

The visits to the cemetery on November 2nd also involve substantial time where the families hang out, eat a meal, and listen to or create music to entertain both the living and the dead. This is also a time where families sit and informally chat and children play among the graves. An important aspect of the visits to the cemeteries is remembering the virtues and good deeds of the dead family members. Much of this occurs through informal discussion among family members, with adults playing a leading role, but all members of the family contribute to the discussion. This public remembrance informs children of values, beliefs, and traditions of their parents with the hope that they will be carried on to the generations that follow (Andrade, 1998).

In the first author's visit to the cemetery on *día de los muertos*, she could see all the townspeople who came to visit the graves; most of the people were chatting, eating, or finishing decorating the graves. Among them were numerous children who were either running around playing with siblings and friends, or simply having something to eat while spending time with their families. The overall mood at the cemetery seemed very festive, families seemed to be getting together to enjoy one another's company. There did not seem to be any feelings of sadness or grief. Personally, even though they were at a cemetery, the first author found it very comforting to see all the families together and all the graves beautifully decorated.

3.3.3 Vigil

Children also participate in vigils held at the cemeteries; however, there is regional variation in the date and timing of the visits. In some parts of Mexico, people visit the cemetery only during the day, not feeling comfortable visiting at night. In other parts, they hold vigils that last until morning. In the town of Janitzio, around midnight on November 1st, women and children of all ages begin to enter the cemetery. Together, they place the offerings on the graves of their loved ones, light candles, and prepare to spend the night praying and singing. During this vigil, men are not allowed to enter the cemetery, so they watch from outside (Andrade, 1998).

Figure 4 Children and families at the cemetery in Tlapanalá, Puebla.

Similar to Janitzio, in the town of Pacanda, Michoacán, on the dawn of November 2nd, after keeping vigil of their dead all night, the women who have been sitting motionless, and the men who have been standing outside the cemetery keeping vigil, begin to move around, engaging in conversations and sharing the food offerings that were set out the night before (Andrade, 1998). While children actively observe the differing roles of women and men in these vigils, other than helping with the decoration of the graves, the children mostly play games with each other until they become exhausted and fall asleep somewhere around the graves, close to their family (Haley & Fukuda, 2004). Figure 4 shows children and families at the cemetery in Puebla. This is another way that children in Mexico learn from the celebration of *día de los muertos* that death is not something to be feared.

While communities differ in the particular rituals performed around *día de los muertos*, children are uniformly involved and often even at the center of the ceremony. For example, in the town of Janitzio, a ceremony takes place at the cemetery during the "vigil of the little angels" (the day when the deceased children come home to visit their families). During this ceremony, which lasts about 3 h, young girls wearing fancy clothes silently remember siblings who have passed away with offerings of favorite toys, meals, and snacks. Young boys participate by carrying flowers and lighting candles. Parents generally watch the children from the sidelines.

4. CHILDREN'S PERSPECTIVES ON *DÍA DE LOS MUERTOS*

To supplement our observations of children's participation in events surrounding *día de los muertos*, we conducted ethnographic interviews with children concerning their experiences and understandings of the celebration. The sample consisted of 61 working-class *mestizo* preschoolers (3.5–6.9 years, mean age = 5.1 years) from the state of Puebla. The breakdown by age was 20 four-year-olds, 21 five-year-olds, and 20 six-year-olds.

We began the interview by presenting the interviewee with a picture of a child who was approximately the same age, gender, and ethnic background as the interviewee. Children were asked to explain what they would tell this child about *día de los muertos* if he/she were in the room. All the children were also asked if their family had celebrated *día de los muertos* the previous year; if that was the case, a series of questions was asked about that particular celebration.

Children were asked what they did with their family during *día de los muertos*. Overall, 89% of the participating children reported having celebrated *día de los muertos* with their families the previous year (95% of 4-year-olds, 86% of 5-year-olds, 85% of 6-year-olds). The majority of the children reported knowing/experiencing that the dead relative returned for *día de los muertos* (87%) and setting up an *ofrenda* for the dead relative (84%). In addition, some children reported decorating the table and/or grave (43%), going to the cemetery (28%), dressing in costume (20%), eating candy (16%), playing or attending a party (13%), and asking for *calavera* (12%). A few children mentioned praying (8%), preparing food for the celebration (5%), visiting the market (2%), and talking about the dead person (2%). The fact that some of these percentages are somewhat low for specific practices is likely due to the young age of the children.

In response to follow-up questions about the previous year's celebration, 80% of the children reported that at least one dead relative came to visit their home during *día de los muertos* (95% of 4-year-olds, 76% of 5-year-olds, 85% of 6-year-olds). Those children who responded that their dead relatives came to visit mentioned members of their immediate family (e.g., one child mentioned his dead father) and members of their extended family (e.g., uncles, aunts, cousins, grandparents).

One of the most intriguing findings from the interview study was that many children remembered having direct personal encounters with their dead relatives during *día de los muertos*. For example, more than half of the children (56%) reported having witnessed or talked to the dead. One child even went on to say that his dead grandmother told him a story about Mickey Mouse when she came to visit. Another child explained that "Because they love me very much. I saw my aunt when they came to visit."

Most of the children (80%) also said that they either saw their dead relatives eating the food provided on the *ofrenda* or found evidence (in the form of leftover food) that the dead had partaken of the feast. These are very interesting findings because most adults would say that the dead return in spiritual form and thus cannot eat or be seen. Paradoxically, however, these same adults believe that the dead enjoy the food through its aroma. Moreover, as mentioned in the preceding section, some adults remembered being told by their parents that their dead relatives consumed food or water from the *ofrenda*, and others appreciated that their parents removed food to provide "evidence" that the dead had eaten.

Some children also alluded to information that they garnered more indirectly, leading them to infer that their dead relatives returned for *día de los muertos*. For example, some children (15%) mentioned that they knew their dead relatives came to visit because one of their parents told them (e.g., "When we woke up, there was very little fruit. I didn't know and I asked mom, and she said that they came, the people who died, but now in spirit"). Others (20%) explained that they knew the dead came to visit because the necessary conditions took place: the person died, the dead knew where they had to go, the family provided food (implying that this would make the deceased relative come to visit), or, simply, it was *día de los muertos*. One 5-year-old girl offered a detailed account of how her family put smoke (incense) outside, and her dead relatives could smell the food that had been provided for them, an explanation that closely follows adult cultural beliefs about the holiday.

Children were also asked about how they felt when participating in the celebration for *día de los muertos*. About half of the children reported feeling happy or excited (51%). For example, one 5-year-old boy explained that he felt excited because "I dress as a *calavera* (skeleton) and ask for candy." A 6-year-old girl mentioned that "it makes me happy because we put flowers on the table at home." About a third of the children said that the celebration scared them (33%). One 6-year-old girl explained that *día de los muertos* "is scary because they then think that the dead ones come out of their graves. Then the dead ones are in my dreams." In addition to feeling happy or scared, 10 of the children (16%) said that they felt bad or sad when participating in *día de los muertos*. A 5-year-old boy explained, "I get sad because I miss him, the one that died. Like my uncle that already died; he was still young." Nine of the children (15%) either reported that they felt nothing when they participated in the celebration or provided no response to the question about emotions.

Overall, the percentage of children who reported feeling scared when celebrating *día de los muertos* decreased dramatically with age (i.e., 4-year-olds = 55%, 5-year-olds = 29%, 6-year-olds = 15%), whereas the percentage of children who reported feeling happy or excited increased slightly (i.e., 4-year-olds = 45%, 5-year-olds = 52%, 6-year-olds = 55%). These age trends suggest that over time children were becoming more comfortable with the celebration as they become less scared and embrace more of the celebratory aspects of the event. By being active participants in *día de los muertos*, children in Mexico were free to explore a range of emotions in the context of their family and community.

5. CONCLUSION

Previous research on the celebration for *día de los muertos* has touched on children's participation in these festivities (Andrade, 1998, 2001; Garciagodoy, 1998; Green, 1969; Haley & Fukuda, 2004). However, this is the first study to focus directly on children's socialization regarding death, including their active participation in the celebration for *día de los muertos*. This holiday and its associated preparations exemplify one common way in which adults from many cultures structure children's participation, namely, by including them in adult activities (Rogoff, 1990; Rogoff, Mistry, Goncu, & Mosier, 1993). One of the most important features of *día de los muertos,* in terms of its significance for children, is that it is an annual celebration. Since children are included in the festivities from infancy, this means that their experience of *día de los muertos* deepens over the course of their childhood and beyond. The recurring nature of the celebration and the many and sundry avenues of participation ensure that children will come to grasp the intimate relationship between life and death. As one father said, they learn that "death is a very important aspect of our life. It's a cycle; for there to be life, there needs to be death." This seems to be the most fundamental lesson of *día de los muertos*.

Our study in Puebla reveals a variety of analytically separate ways in which children participate in the rich variety of practices surrounding the celebration. Perhaps, most pervasive is the practice of simply being present. Unlike mainstream American culture, in which young children are often excluded from death (Rosengren et al., 2014), the Puebla children were included in every context in which the holiday was celebrated or prepared for: at school, in the marketplace, in the community, at home, and in the cemetery. Moreover, they were often allowed to simply "hang out," play with other children, or keep their parents company. "Hanging out" was especially common in the market and the cemetery. Although this may seem like a negligible practice, we suggest that being able to relax and play, with parents near at hand but offering minimal supervision, may have lessened children's fears of the dead and helped them feel comfortable in proximity with the dead.

Our ethnographic observations revealed that another way in which children participated in *día de los muertos* was by observing. Our study, thus, contributes to the growing body of cross-cultural evidence that children learn about an astonishing variety of domains of life through observation (Gaskins & Paradise, 2010; Lancy, 2014; Rogoff, 2003; Rogoff, Paradise, Mejía Aráuz, Correa-Chávez, & Angelillo, 2003). Again, every context in which children were included afforded this mode of participation. For example, when children accompanied their parents to the market to buy food and candles for the family *ofrenda*, children observed the displays of goods while they watched and listened as their parents made purchases. *Día de los muertos* is a visual feast; everywhere one looks, there are colorful and arresting sights: flowers, candles, sugar skulls, skeletons. This feature of the holiday draws children's attention. The smells of the cempaxóchitl flowers that guide the dead visitors as well as the incense and the intoxicating aromas of savory and sweet foods invite children's attention. These sensual elements may also enhance the memorability of *día de los muertos*.

Children participated with their feet and hands as well as their senses. In some towns, children went about in groups, dancing to music and visiting *ofrendas*. They pitched in in a wide array of specific tasks (Rogoff, 2003). Older children painted facial features on the sugar skulls and cut the strings to make wicks for the candles. Younger children pulled the petals from the cempaxóchitl flowers to create the trail to the *ofrenda*. Children also cleaned the graves, ran errands, and decorated the *ofrendas*. In one example, the older brother created a design in which his two dead siblings were represented in pairs, with matching toys and sweets.

Our interviews with parents and other adults revealed that yet another way in which children participated in *día de los muertos* was by listening to parents' and grandparents' memories and commentaries about the dead. Memories and family stories conveyed interpretations about the actions of the dead relatives, for example, that they drink water to recover from their trip from the realm of the dead. These commentaries also encouraged children to look for evidence (e.g., bites taken from the bread, sugar sheep that were broken) that the dead had visited.

Given the variety of avenues of participation, in the context of a celebration that recurs year after year, it is not at all surprising that the Puebla children become more and more adept in their participation and that they reported experiences and beliefs about death that were strikingly different from children raised in a mainstream community in the United States (Rosengren et al., 2014). Many of the Puebla children said that they witnessed or talked to the dead during *día de los muertos* and that they enjoyed the celebration. Feelings of fear associated with the dead declined dramatically across the age range from 4 to 6 years. In addition, on standard cognitive protocols, these children showed an understanding of the continuity of life beyond death (Gutiérrez, 2009).

Taken together, our observations and interviews with children and parents suggest that the experiences surrounding *día de los muertos* provide yet another example of the process of "Learning by Observing and Pitching In" (Rogoff, 2014). Much of what children come to learn about *día de los muertos* comes from observation and informal discussion. Indeed in our research, we observed many of the facets of Learning by Observing and Pitching In described by Coppens et al. (2014). Specifically, the children we interviewed and observed were incorporated into the family and community events surrounding *día de los muertos*; they eagerly contributed to the events and participated as part of a collaborative, flexible ensemble where they were free to take the initiative in certain aspects of the celebration. In addition, through observation and participation in *día de los muertos*, children learned particular skills (e.g., shopping, cooking) as well as were exposed to beliefs and values of their parents and the larger community. Much of this learning occurred in as part of an informal process that clearly fits the model of Learning by Observing and Pitching In (Coppens et al., 2014; Rogoff, 2014).

Although we have discussed the various avenues of participation separately for analytic purposes, they seem to work together seamlessly in children's experience. Future research should more explicitly address how this happens within the framework of Learning by Observing and Pitching In. Perhaps, this seamless integration helps to blur the boundaries between life and death, and between the mundane and the spiritual.

REFERENCES

Andrade, M. J. (1998). *A través de los ojos del alma, día de los muertos en México, Michoacán*. San Jose, CA: La Oferta Review Newspaper.

Andrade, M. J. (2001). *Día de los muertos en México: A través de los ojos del alma, Puebla, Tlaxcala, San Luis Potosí, Hidalgo*. San Jose, CA: La Oferta Review Newspaper.

Brandes, S. (2006). *Skulls to the living, bread to the dead: The day of the dead in Mexico and beyond.* Malden, MA: Blackwell Publishing.

Carmichael, E., & Sayer, C. (1991). *The skeleton at the feast: The day of the dead in Mexico.* Austin, TX: University of Texas Press.

Coppens, A. D., Silva, K. G., Ruvalcaba, O., Alcalá, L., López, A., & Rogoff, B. (2014). Learning by observing and pitching in: Benefits and processes of expanding repertoires. *Human Development, 57*, 150–161.

Garciagodoy, J. (1998). *Digging the days of the dead: A reading of Mexico's dias de muertos.* Boulder, CO: University Press of Colorado.

Gaskins, S., & Paradise, R. (2010). Learning through observation in daily life. In D. F. Lancy, J. Brock, & S. Gaskins (Eds.), *The anthropology of learning in childhood* (pp. 85–117). Lanham, MD: Alta Mira Press.

Green, J. S. (1969). *Laughing souls: The days of the dead in Oaxaca, Mexico.* San Diego, CA: San Diego Museum of Man.

Greenleigh, J. (1991). *The days of the dead: Mexico's festival of communion with the departed.* San Francisco, CA: Collins Publishers.

Gutiérrez, I. T. (2009). *Understanding death in cultural context: A study of Mexican children and their families.* Unpublished doctoral dissertation, Champaign, IL: University of Illinois.

Haley, S. D., & Fukuda, C. (2004). *Day of the dead: When two worlds meet in Oaxaca.* New York, NY: Berghahn Books.

Lancy, D. (2014). *Anthropology of childhood* (2nd ed.). Cambridge, UK: Cambridge University Press.

Paz, O. (1985). *The labyrinth of solitude.* L. Kemp, Y. Milos, & R. P. Belash, Trans (pp. 57–58). New York, NY: Grove Press. Original work published 1961.

Rogoff, B. (1990). *Apprenticeship in thinking: Cognitive development in social context.* New York, NY: Oxford University Press.

Rogoff, B. (2003). *The cultural nature of human development.* Oxford: Oxford University Press.

Rogoff, B. (2014). Learning by observing and pitching in to family and community endeavors: An orientation. *Human Development, 57*, 69–81.

Rogoff, B., Mistry, J., Goncu, A., & Mosier, C. (1993). Guided participation in cultural activity by toddlers and caregivers. *Monographs of the Society for Research in Child Development, 58*, 1–174 (7, Serial no. 236).

Rogoff, B., Paradise, R., Mejía Aráuz, R., Correa-Chávez, M., & Angelillo, C. (2003). First-hand learning through intent participation. *Annual Review of Psychology, 54*, 175–203.

Rosengren, K. S., Miller, P. J., Gutiérrez, I. T., Chow, P. I., Schein, S. S., & Anderson, K. N. (2014). Children's understanding of death: Toward a contextualized and integrated account. *Monographs of the Society for Research in Child Development, 79*, 1–162 (1, Serial no. 312).

SECTION II

Learning by Observing and Pitching in (LOPI) Fits with Cultural Cosmovisions

CHAPTER ELEVEN

Conceptions of Educational Practices Among the Nahuas of Mexico: Past and Present

Marie-Noëlle Chamoux[1]
Centre National de la Recherche Scientifique and CERMA-Mondes américains (UMR 8168), École des Hautes Études en Sciences Sociales, 190 Avenue de France, 75013 Paris, France
[1]Corresponding author: e-mail address: chamoux@vjf.cnrs.fr

Contents

Abstract

Historical documents and recent fieldwork indicate that, since the sixteenth century, there is robust continuity in central beliefs about learning among Nahuatl families. Nahuatl documents from nearly five centuries ago and current Nahuatl adults consider guidance and teaching to be accompaniment of the learner, more than direct action, because nobody can enter the minds and personalities of others. Learning by observing and pitching in is valued: The adults can organize good conditions of apprenticeship, they can indicate the good direction and the goal, serve as examples, and protect the learner. Across centuries, Nahuatl educational practices consist of facilitating observation by copresence, early training for attentive engagement, hiding nothing, and not preventing children from trying, as well as persuading children to be responsible, to work, and to adopt a calm attitude for paying close attention.

Advances in Child Development and Behavior, Volume 49
ISSN 0065-2407
http://dx.doi.org/10.1016/bs.acdb.2015.08.001

1. INTRODUCTION

Description of universal human development is always a challenge, for each human society in history shapes a specific environment between Nature, child, and educators.[1] The topic of human development is situated at the intersection of several disciplines. Anthropologists and psychologists have abundantly documented the variability of cultures, in which educational practices also vary: none of them is "more natural" or "more primitive" than others (Rogoff, 1990, 2003). Historiographers have put to light the role of "mentalities," collective frameworks shaping ideas and practices during time extended over centuries (the *longue durée*, Braudel, 1959). In psychology, Vygotsky, reinterpreted by Cole (1996), indicates that the human environment takes root from the prior generations, which have left material or immaterial references of their activities.

In the Mesoamerican area of México and Guatemala, scholars have reported local practices that give high educational value to learning by observation (Chamoux, 1992; Gaskins & Paradise, 2009; Nash, 1967; Paradise, 1991). Paradise and Rogoff use the specific label "Learning by Observing and Pitching In" (2009), or the acronym LOPI (Rogoff, 2014). Although a child can try spontaneously to learn by observing and pitching in, this behavior is more or less accompanied, reinforced, or blocked according to cultural contexts. In contemporary Nahuatl villages of Mexico, various practices linked to Preconquest concepts and patterns support this way of learning. For almost five centuries, the Nahuas have trusted in this method; here, I will examine some categories and linked practices that they acknowledge and use daily.

Valuable information is scattered in heterogeneous documents and observed events. For this reason, the production of data in historiographical analysis is often pragmatic. The methodology tends to pick up relevant facts and acts, symptoms and signs, and it is necessary to verify if they are certified or recurrent so they can become evidence. In this chapter, I have used linguistic data and fieldwork observations and I will give only significant examples, not all the certified occurrences.

[1] This research was supported by funds from the National Science Fundation (NSF grant #0837898) and the University of California-Santa Cruz (UCSC), CA, USA. In Mexico City, it received logistic support from the Centro de Investigación y de Estudios Avanzados del Instituto Politécnico Nacional (CINVESTAV) and from the Centre d'études mexicaines et centramericaines (CEMCA).

Nahuatl is a current language with dialectal inflections. Scholars refer to Classical Nahuatl as the dialect of Central Mexico soon after the Conquest.[2] I have taken a long time span and I have compared two sections of it: the early Colonial period (fifteenth to seventeenth centuries) and the current period (twentieth and early twenty-first centuries), which includes times when most of the villages did not have schools.

In the Colonial period, there are sufficient data for making comparisons with current observations. Various documentary sources contain very important information on Nahuatl educational ideas and practices. I have consulted ancient linguistic and historical documents and their modern compilations and comments.[3] The lexicography is very rich (Wimmer online; Bnf 362) and grammarians give many examples of uses (Launey, 1979–1980). Famous ancient alphabetic and iconographic chronicles written in Spanish and/or in classical Nahuatl (Sahagún, 1950–1982; Codex Mendoza in Berdan & Anawalt, 1997) contain descriptions of education. Modern scholars have commented about ancient formal institutions and education in the family (Berdan & Anawalt, 1997; León Portilla, 1980; López Austin, 1985), but they did not focus on "LOPI". This chapter reexamines various ancient sources, paying attention to this way of learning.

Concerning the current period, I have consulted recent glossaries, but the main source of data comes from anthropological fieldwork in Nahuatl villages of Northern Puebla (*municipios* of Huauchinango and Naupan), according to the old but ever efficient Malinowskian method: direct observations, long presence, close contact with daily and ritual life, learning of the local language, and so on. The inhabitants speak a modern variant of classical central Nahuatl, and this similarity between their language and that of the Colonial period makes it easy to compare the data.

During the first years of the investigations, most Nahuatl speaking people were monolingual. I made several visits and stays in these villages between 1969 and 2010. This study considers education out of school for children who are old enough to speak (from 3 to 12 approximately).

[2] There is no agreement about orthography. My choice for writing it is based on the modern Spanish standard, with common Colonial exceptions (X: pronounce SH; LL: pronounce L-L; apostrophe': pronounce glottal stop; U before vowel: pronounce W; UH before consonant or in final syllable: pronounce W; O: pronounce U as in Spanish). The term Nahuatl is a singular noun or adjective, and its plural is Nahua' in this language, or Nahuas in English.

[3] I have used my orthography of Nahuatl, both in citations of ancient documents and modern fieldwork. In-text citations of Sahagún give the number of the book and page referring to the English translation by Ch. E. Dibble and A. J.O. Anderson. In-text citations of Dictionnaire espagnol-nahuatl Bnf 362 (2001) are written as Bnf 362.

Despite social changes and the growth of schooling during the eighties, I observed continued existence of many ancient Mesoamerican features. The continuity of several cultural patterns over five centuries is really amazing.

In this chapter, I focus on describing various practices that promote learning by observing and pitching in. First I consider Nahuas' conceptions of knowledge and the nature of human beings that give background and coherent principles for guiding educators' behavior. Second, I relate these conceptions to local educational practices with children, in the Aztec past and in the Nahuatl present.

2. TWO SORTS OF KNOWLEDGE IN NAHUATL IDEOLOGY ABOUT LEARNING AND TEACHING

In every culture, educational approaches are shaped by a multifaceted cultural context (Rogoff & Angelillo, 2002). Categories and ideological references are important though often implicit. I will try to summarize them using linguistic and ethnographic data.

Questions about the substance and origins of knowledge was a fundamental debate in Classic Greek Philosophy. For the ancient Greeks, every human being encounters the duality of two types of knowledge: the sensible and inconstant world of things, known by individual perceptions, and the permanent world of the Ideas, known by universal Reason. Although the interrogation about various forms of knowledge would not surprise the Nahuas, their answers seem to be different. For the Nahuas, there is a duality of knowledge too, but with another criterion, which calls to mind phenomenological approaches in the twentieth century. *Nahuas point to a contrast between internal mental states, felt by individual, and the external acknowledged known, which can be accumulated and also shared.*

So the main dividing line separates two categories: (1) psychological states, abilities, and processes, which take place inside the subject and remain private and not transferable; (2) common information and accepted wisdom, accumulated in an individual or in the community, which are shareable and can be taught. Nahuatl grammar reveals these categories of knowledge, apart from semantic connotations in utterances. I will consider briefly this linguistic aspect.

A large part of Nahuatl vocabulary of knowledge has its root in the verb *mati*. Launey translates it as *to know, to feel, to have intellectual or sentimental knowledge of something* (2002). This verb is atypical within this language in an important way: it has two radicals, which are *mat-*, to know (active form), and *mach-*, to be known (passive form). This particularity increases the range of meanings. The result is a plentiful vocabulary about knowledge. The excellent Wimmer's online dictionary enumerates various uses in the Aztec past. I have found the same meanings in dictionaries of current language and in ethnological material, and I have verified my interpretations with Nahuatl speaking informants.

Nahuas' educational incitement for learning by observing and pitching in seems to aim at gaining embodied knowledge and skills (base *mat-*). Other methods, which include speech, advice, and schooling, can be used complementarily to accumulate known truths (base *mach-*), which can be taught.

2.1 Knowledge Inside the Individual (Base *mat-*)

To know is not only to gather facts, ideas, and methods. A Nahuatl assumption is that knowledge is principally a psychological phenomenon in the interiority of every individual. The base *mat-* refers to internal mental states and it indicates privacy, intimacy, and subjectivity. Knowledge is something felt and embodied in the individual mind and body, like a maternal language or how to drive a car.

Meanings that are based on *mat-* focus on individual, private, almost hidden dimensions, out of sight of other human beings. The Wimmer's online dictionary lists meanings and citations in its entry *mati*. Transitive forms are used to mean to know and to control: to feel (as internal sensation); to be conscious, to be wise, to be able to understand; to believe, to think that...; to have intellectual knowledge of... (this is almost a synonym of thinking). Some examples:

> *"he thought them [the Spaniards] gods, he took them to be gods" (Sahagun 12: 21);*
> "Se pelota, iuan nicmati se botella iuan tasas: *this [is] a ball, and I think [that these things are] a bottle and cups" (fieldwork).*

Reflexive forms allude to an internal selfquestioning into the subject: to suppose; to feel well, to feel at ease. For example, "And he who heard it thought perhaps a child wept, perhaps a baby" (Sahagun 11: 69). Linguistic incorporation develops other meanings: to recognize is *ixmati*, which incorporates *ixtli*, face or eye, and refers to a *reactivation of internal knowledge* already present in the subject (representation). For example, "*Nepaca siuatl niquixmati*," this lady, I know her (fieldwork).

Another important verb based on *mat-*, refers *to an undisclosed anticipation of action or purpose* (*i'mati*). The central meaning is that anticipation of action or aim is hidden in the secret of mind. (It presents analogy with the Classic Greek concept of *metis*.[4]) It connotes ambivalent behavior or individual

[4] The Classic Greek concept of *metis* includes wisdom and cunning (Detienne & Vernant, 1974).

attributes: to act with caution and organization or with cunning and trickery; to be skillful, careful, clever, prudent, or to be deceptive or tricky. It may incorporate nouns to specify the field of cautiousness: to be skillful, cautious with your hands (*momai'mati*, Sah10, 25–27, fieldwork); to be cautious about telling (*mocacamai'mati*, fieldwork). This concept impacts guidance and educators value positive features, like care, prudence, cleverness but suspect bad intent in other aspects, like intention to hide.

2.2 Shared or Shareable Knowledge or the Known (Base *mach-*)

Most Nahuatl terms for learning, teaching, and schooling use the passive base *mach-*, and not *mat-*. This is external and preexistent collective knowledge, acknowledged and shared by a number of more experienced persons. The Nahuatl vocabulary can express different types of "the known" and various ways for accumulating, sharing, or teaching it. The verbs *macho*, to be known (to be established), and *machia*, to be known (to be disclosed), refer to public or shareable knowledge.

Linguistic derivation produces terms for categories of the known. *Experience and science* are clearly distinguished. The noun *machistli* means "experience," as established knowledge that a single person, such as an old, experienced, or trustworthy individual, has acquired and has accumulated. The form *machilistli* means "science," as the common known information that a community can share. In Northern Puebla, we find a corresponding verb *machili*, to grasp or to perceive disclosed information (Vazquez, 1982).

Another important classification distinguishes *to inform and to teach*. To inform, to notify is transferring external information and news (*machitia*). The modern Nahuas translate it into Spanish as *dar a conocer*. But to teach, to instruct, is *machtia*: to pass down the established known.[5] The teacher is *temachtiani*, the one who instructs people. Although there is hierarchy between a teacher and an unaware student, the lexicon marks the student as active: he/she is *momachtiani*, "the one who is teaching himself/herself."

3. NAHUATL THEORIES ON THE PERSON AND EDUCATIVE ATTITUDES

There is no doubt that the Nahuas emphasize the psychological aspect of knowledge. For them, efficient skills must be internalized into each

[5] Only one vowel marks the difference between *machitia*, to inform, and *machtia*, to teach.

individual and depend on his/her capacities for training himself/herself and acquiring them: the "true" knowledge is the embodied one. This posture is consistent with well-known aspects of Mesoamerican ontology that I will summarize.

3.1 Soul, Interiority and the Powerlessness of Educators

There is a common implicit background for the various semantic classes of knowledge I have described: the theory of the soul or the spirit, which is widespread in other groups and languages throughout Mesoamerica. The Nahuas say that every human being has received a particular soul or spirit (*tonalli*) when he was born. It constitutes the deep nature of the person and nobody can change it. This soul affects personal destiny and it determines capacities and whether the person's character will be strong or weak. This deep never-changing soul can be damaged or ruined. Its presence is precarious during childhood. Of this the child is not aware. He/she is "*in ayamo quimati*," the one not yet of understanding (Sahagún 12: 57), or "*ye' conetl, a'mo quimati*," he/she [is] a child, he/she does not know (fieldwork). This soul comes slowly, and it can leave the person when he is afraid. The "loss" of *tonalli* causes illness or death. With adolescence, the soul becomes fully rooted and present. When a young person acquires complete consciousness and responsibility, adults say: "his/her soul has come." (about Mayan people: Arias, 1975; about Nahuas: Chamoux, 1992; León Pasquel, 2002).

An important aspect of *tonalli* is that it is hidden, both for the person who owns it and for the others. It is almost impossible to know the hidden nature of a person. Only gods know it in the "places of darkness," where they manage the Universe, and also those who have a special gift to see divine things can know soul: shamans, clairvoyants, or powerful leaders. Ordinary people, like teachers, parents, and other experienced adults, cannot gain this knowledge.

But another aspect of interiority is more conscious and sensitive to the person's will. Every being has an internal world of subjectivity, which is undisclosed to others (Descola, 2013, p. 116). The person can control this part of interiority. Each child is supposed to be able to use will for developing himself/herself and gaining maturity by following adults' examples.

However, educators are almost powerless to act on a child's intimacy and this causes the uncertainty or the worry that they frequently express. In classical Nahuatl, the teachers indicated their limitations clearly to the noble parents who left their child at the Aztec school: *Cuix i'tic tocalaquizque'*, *toyollo' tocontlalilizque' auh nouhyuh in ticozque', in tiquetzale'*. "Shall we perchance enclose it within him? Shall we be reassured [shall we enter inside him, shall we put here our heart]? And likewise you who have the jewel, you who have the precious feather [the child]?" (Sahagún 3: 53). In contemporary Northern Puebla, frequent conversations express the same concern: "Who knows what will spring up or emerge out of this child?"

The Nahuas consider every child to be an enigmatic black box, into which educators and parents cannot enter and where they have few opportunities to act. This conception leads logically to the Nahua idea that the keys of education are principally *inside the learner* and in his/her self-training. These ideas constitute the metaphysical background that legitimates and emphasizes methods of Learning by Observing and Pitching In, because promoting LOPI is the only tool to which educators and parents have access.

3.2 Teachers, Wise Persons, and Elders in Education

Although they cannot insert knowledge, teachers, experienced adults, parents, and elders are present near the children. Some of them have specific roles. In ancient Mexico, there were differentiated roles in schools: teacher and master (coach) (Bnf 362).[6] The teacher *temachtiani*, -term based on *mach-*, was "the one who teaches everybody the acknowledged known" by giving talks. Today this term is used for schoolteachers and professors. The master *tetlacaizcaltiani*, -term based on *izcalia*, to grow up-, was "one who grows somebody up into a man/woman" by providing training that develops skills and related behaviors. I do not know if this term is still used. Only teachers and masters were specialized in education, but nonetheless, they had limited access to children's minds.

In both the ancient and current periods, others could be wise persons, but without a special function in education. They are the soothsayers, clairvoyants, shamans, or very powerful leaders, who can see partially into the "places of darkness." They are named "possessors of knowledge" (base *mat-*: *tlamatini* in classical Nahuatl, *tlamatque'* today).[7] The contrast between the bases *mat-* and *mach-* is very clear: they are not teachers (base *mach-*: *temachtiani*). These men or women have a terrible and dangerous power inside them and see supernatural or hidden things in the World. Their knowledge

[6] "*Maestro: Temachtiani: El que lo es de educación. Tetlacaizcaltiani, el que lo es de Agüero Mexicana*" (Bnf 362).

[7] "*Letrado o Sabio Tlamatini con este nombre llaman también a sus adivinos, o agüero*" (Bnf 362).

cannot be taught. The Nahuas frequently say that the knowledge of shamans is not "like school knowledge" but is "something of another class."

In classical and current Nahuatl, an experienced and respected person is called *machise'*, "the one who has much acquired knowledge" (see *machistli*, experience) and was distinguished from teachers or soothsayers. They are trustworthy and could have an advisor's role outside of school. Their knowledge did not include seeing the supernatural world.

Apart from these persons, there are all other adults, and particularly parents, grandparents, godfathers, etc. who are in charge of children and are the main educators out of school. Young unmarried men and women, older brothers, sisters, and other teenagers can fulfill an important, but slightly different, role, as we will see.

3.3 Principal Aspects of Educative Guidance

There are common norms in educational guidance, but also some variants, according to the status of elders who are there (fieldwork). Common norms refer to Nahuatl conceptions of "true" embodied knowledge. A persistent feature is that each person normally should remain almost silent in ongoing work activity in order to be cautious and efficient. As knowledge is an internal process, educators expect self-building of it and so they avoid disturbing the child's concentration when the child is pitching in. They use neither advance verbal description of the task nor work breakdown in gesture. They give only few verbal instructions when some problem happens in a child's ongoing work, because they consider it is dangerous and ineffective to frighten children when they pitch in. Consequently the Nahuatl right way to speak to them is using few words in a quiet voice, with few and discreet reprimands. But instructors can comment on the child's work after it is done, and they can advise the learner in idle moments of family life.

Variants take place according to elders' social status and age: young unmarried persons and teenage siblings may reprimand children more curtly. Maybe this attitude refers to the idea that an older but immature person is less frightening and dangerous than a complete adult. So young persons have a great role for emphasizing social norms of conduct.

For example, in a cheap restaurant in the market place, I observed a Nahuatl mother with a baby, and her girls about 7 and 15. As they came in and sat down, the little girl knocked the table through awkwardness. The teenage girl immediately reprimanded her young sister in a low voice. The mother did not pay attention and remained silent (fieldwork).

In this way, adults' and young peoples' modes of guidance are complementary.

Although educators feel powerless to influence the subjective process of attaining knowledge, they have developed means to guide children and to incite them to Learn by Observing and Pitching In.

4. PROMOTING LEARNING BY OBSERVING AND PITCHING IN

There are three aspects to the parent's educative tasks. First, they organize conditions to facilitate the child's development and the definitive integration of the child's spirit, protecting the child from "loss of soul." Secondly, they show models of correct adult behaviors and goals. Thirdly, they must show the importance of the endeavor and of the will to acquire awareness and responsibility.

Conditions for learning by observation have been reported across the whole world in various contexts, since Fortes in Taleland (1938). But different cultural backgrounds shape educators' daily practices. Copresence, a notion that Goffman proposed in 1963, impacts education. But copresence is not only staying together in the same space and time, which have natural physical characteristics all over the world. Each situation of copresence carries variable cultural and social norms that predefine a child's place, the right way to speak to him, what is permitted, reproved, or forbidden, and what is good or not for development. Norms can be explicit or implicit, and many of them are taken for granted by parents or other adults.

4.1 Facilitating Copresence

In Nahuatl current local communities, copresence takes place in daily life, in most family activities, in many places: at home and the neighborhood, local community, market place and shops, as well as when traveling, at churches and at ritual sites, in fields and woods, etc. In educational practices, it is central to avoid any obstacles that could prevent observation by a child. There really are few limitations to children' presence.

It would be wrong to think that adults have an excessive teaching attitude or a complete lack of it during these moments. The Nahuas do not fill their time of copresence speaking, questioning, or explaining: most often they appear almost silent. We could believe they are focusing their attention on their activity and not on the children who are there. But it is quite the opposite: they can work and, at the same time, look after the children;

they do not leave them without discreet supervision. Like I observed in Nahuatl villages, scholars have reported that Mayan people can employ simultaneous attention to multiple events (Chavajay & Rogoff, 1999; Correa-Chávez & Rogoff, 2009; Correa-Chávez, Rogoff, & Mejía Arauz, 2005). As in Nahuatl communities, these scholars have observed a lot of verbal and nonverbal subtle interactions between adults and children in copresence, which are subtle and understated if we compare them with occidental practices (León Pasquel, 2002).

Norms of physical distance, or proxemics (Hall, 1966), vary according to a child's age. Nahuas let toddlers cling to them and never reprimand them. Between 3 and 6, children may come close to observe somebody's activity, without being told off. If a toddler comes dangerously too near or disturbs a person who is working, Nahuas just laugh softly in warning to divert his/her attention or they take him/her away gently. Over 6 to 10, there is some change. Adults let the child come near but briefly and quietly prevent access if there is any danger. But young persons do not allow the close presence of children over 7: they tell the child off with discreet but harsh verbal remarks: "*chulo* !, run away !," or with nonverbal messages, such as an angry look.

The adults and elders supervise where the children move about. Every nuclear or compound family is traditionally settled in a house with a yard and a garden. Within this domestic space, there is no strict segregation according to age or gender. There are no private rooms for boys or girls, for adults or kids. Every child may go everywhere and no place is forbidden. During the ceremonies and feasts that take place in the domestic space, adults tend to group together by gender, but the children may go everywhere (fieldwork). Therefore there is always vigilance. One or more adults or adolescents have the implicit or explicit responsibility for looking after the small children. Ancient texts report this vigilance: *in tetlamacaya' in quimittaya' pipiltzitzintin*: "And those who served look to the small children." (Sahagún 2: 97). In the contemporary villages, it is common to hear: "*Xquitta in conetl*: keep an eye on the child" (fieldwork), concerning children under about 4.

Outside the domestic space, there are some slight limitations according to age and gender for reasons of training. Boys over 4 may go to play alone in the very near street, but girls stay within the domestic place to play. These practices correspond to well-known ancient Aztec rituals, which consisted of burying the boy's umbilical cord outdoors in a battlefield, and the girl's one near the fireplace in the kitchen, to attract children to the places of their future gender role and keep them there. Among contemporary Indians who are undocumented immigrants in the North, there is another sort of "battlefield" and another sort of "home" for burying the umbilical cord: the ground of the United States of America. So parents hope their children will remain forever in that country. In the Nahua villages of Mexico, the authorized space is extended to the neighborhood for girls around 7–10, but only to fulfill some task (to go to the well, to the mill, etc.), not to play. Concerning adolescents about 10, copresence varies according to gender: boys may go out in the neighborhood, but parents do not allow a girl to go out in the street alone, for reasons of morality and security (fieldwork).

In larger spaces, children are never alone and are accompanied by a responsible adult. In the work place, it is common to see parents with kids from 2 or 3 or a mother carrying her baby in her shawl. When a woman goes out to forage in the woods and uncultivated lands, she takes her very young boys and girls. When a man goes to work in his *milpa* or field, he takes his boys over 7, and he generally takes his girls only at harvest time, but this is not a strict rule. It is also common to see young boys watching working men fulfilling communal tasks (*tequio*).

In the public spaces of Ancient Mexico, such as the market place, gender affected copresence: fathers took their boys over 5 to the market but left the girls at home. The presence of a noble girl in the market place was incongruous (Sahagún 6: 98). In contemporary Puebla, boys and girls may go to the market place with their parents. The adults' main intention is to train the child, and they also receive a little help from the child's participation (Rogoff, Paradise, Arauz, Correa-Chávez, & Angelillo, 2003).

4.2 Making "the Known" Available to Children

4.2.1 No Secrets for Daily Activities, Skills, and Tools

As a corollary of copresence, daily acts, skills and tools are not hidden within the family sphere. In the same way, Nahuas do not forbid children to touch tools. In daily contexts, secrets are disapproved of.

However, supernatural mystery involves secrets out of the power and understanding of ordinary human beings: such mystery constitutes a divine fact, which must be endured. The nature of the deep personal soul inside the individual is one of these uncontrollable mysteries. But education can impact another sort of secret: the private will of each human being, controllable by that person. Nahuas suspect this second form of secret can be used to hide something from others with bad intentions, and they disapprove of this use.

In ancient documents, hiding acts and things often was considered suspect and linked to spiteful persons, thieves, bad workers, or deceitful merchants. In the villages of Northern Puebla, I have observed the same distrust when a person was found hiding something. People suspected him of wrongdoing, theft, or witchcraft. The distrust about secrets in daily and productive activities go hand in hand with the high value attributed to learning by observing and pitching in.

4.2.2 Making Acts and Their Results Apparent

In modern schooling, traditions of "assembly-line instruction" are prevalent: places for teaching are separated from productive activities; teachers directly control learners' attention and behavior (Rogoff, 2003). Like an actor, the teacher speaks and shows the material to be learned and the students listen and watch, like spectators. Among the Nahuas, educators have slightly different pedagogic attitudes. They do not exactly "show" the material to be learned from top to bottom, but they try "to make it apparent" so that the learner can grasp it.

The Dictionnaire espagnol-nahuatl Bnf 362 gives various didactic verbs for "to manifest" and I have tried to translate them literally[8]: *texipantlaliya*, to put in front of people' eyes; *teiximachtiya*, to teach people in front of eyes; *machixtiya*, to endeavor to use his eyes for knowing; *tenextiliya*, to make [something] apparent to people. This last term is based on *nesi* (or *nezi*), to appear, which is used for dawning both in classical and current Nahuatl. At the school, it means to show: "*San ma yec nicmati secpa otechnexti in maestra.* It's just that I know the right [answer]; the teacher has made it manifest to us at another time." (fieldwork).

4.3 Training Attention Through Fulfilling Specific Tasks

Generally, who fulfills some task is determined by social organization, with named division of labor into well-known categories: division of labor by age, gender, social class, caste, boss, and subordinate, etc. But another aspect of doing a task is psychological personal engagement and responsibility: mostly it is linked to the need for close attention. Interpretations of historical documents on Ancient Mexico have pointed to educational scripts describing required tasks according to age and gender, in the same way the old chronicles did. This approach emphasizes the social organization of education and the scripts that adults followed. But reconsidering the sources with the concept of LOPI, deeper information comes to light.

Many years ago, I noted very early training in carrying some load on the back, both in ancient and contemporary Mexico (Chamoux, 1992,

[8] "*Manifestar. Texipantlalía teiximachtía machixtía tenextilía*" (Bnf 362).

pp. 80–81). Training in mental skills is underlying and less visible. In ancient texts, children's tasks seem meaningful. Apart from some obvious physical techniques, these tasks show evidence of *training to develop the skill of paying attention*. Gathering spilt corn, the basic and sacred food, is an example: "They trained [boys around 6] and engaged them in some personal services providing help to their parents; for example, in the market place, [children] gathered grains of corn they had spilt on the ground, or beans or other little things that traders had dropped: this was the children's function." (Codex Mendoza, in López Austin, 1985, p. 99).[9]

In current market places, children around 8 or 9 are engaged in tasks requiring attentiveness, for example looking after their parents' bags, packages, or stall, and going to exchange a peso bill to get small change, etc. Many of these services require the child to pay close attention to fairly valuable things (food, goods, money, etc.). Keen attention is also required when parents entrust a toddler or small child to an older son, daughter, or nephew for a moment: attention is a strategic component of care and it is trained through such involvements.

4.4 Preparing Responsibility Step by Step

Close attention involves responsibility and trust. During the first 10 years, increasing participation in the family's activities provides a social and affective frame for the child, and the parents promote attention and responsibility step by step. For the parents, the "help" which results is limited. But for the child, it is an active way to become mature and to feel pride. Over 10, a child's participation is more effective, more intense, and educational practices are more directive.

Ancient documents contain descriptions of guidance for parents on how to promote learning by observing and pitching in. The famous Codex Mendoza shows a model (López Austin, 1985, pp. 99–109) that mixes verbal and nonverbal pedagogical acts according to the age of the child. This document presents especially interesting data on children' education from 3 to 7. Before 8, punishments are not mentioned and verbal incitation to observe the parental model is prevalent.

---

[9] [A los seis años] "*los ejercitaban y ocupaban en servicios personales de que en algo aprovechasen a sus padres, así como en los tiangues, lugares de mercado, para que cogiesen del suelo los granos de maíz que por él estuviesen derramados, y frijoles y otras miserias y cosas que los tratantes dejaban derramadas: esto a los muchachos.*" (López Austin, 1985, p. 99).

At about 3, the Codex indicates that the child is not given responsibility. The document shows a boy near his father and a girl near her mother, in order that each child can see his/her parent as a gender model. The parents are giving verbal advice to their children. In contemporary Nahuatl communities, parents fulfill daily tasks and leave the child to play near them, without expecting any help. Sometimes a mother tells the child about some danger in a joking way. This first early step implies verbal and nonverbal interaction, without asking the child to do anything.

At about 4, parents are speaking about gendered activities and related things: the father is giving little orders to his son; the mother is showing spinning tools and speaking to her daughter. In the same way, I have observed today that this step is mainly dedicated to letting the child observe and listen. Parents may give gendered toys to a child who wants to play at imitating adults. But they consider that playing is not an efficient way to gain knowledge, because there is no responsibility.

At about 5, some responsibility and more keen observation are introduced. The boy is receiving verbal orders and carrying firewood, ritual packages and a broom (to sweep was part of ritual). The girl is looking at technical processes that require more attention. There is no indication that mother is talking when spinning. In contemporary villages, every person fulfilling a task normally remains almost silent. Children see this working behavior, take it for granted and reproduce it.

At about 6, the Codex shows that the children begin pitching in and have a little responsibility. The boy is going to the market place with his father and has to gather little things. The girl is beginning to spin with her mother's instructions. In contemporary villages, both boys and girls can help their parents by doing little tasks sporadically, for example going to pick useful plants, or going to the market place with their parents.

At about 7, responsibility really begins. Children are doing productive tasks: boys fishing and girls spinning.[10] In modern Nahuatl villages, parents require children to do various easy tasks and to take responsibility: carrying something, sweeping, shucking corn, going to the mill or shop, babysitting, helping to harvest and looking after any livestock. Before the extinction of textile crafts, girls were sometimes spinning. Parents expect responsibility in these tasks.

Between 8 and 12, parents put the emphasis on willingness to learn, responsibility, and efficient participation in family activities. They do not

[10] "*los aplicaban en darles* [*a los muchachos*] *sus redes con que pescaban, y las madres ejercitaban a sus hijas en hilar y en darles buenos consejos*" (López Austin, 1985, p. 99).

use rewards, only brief congratulations and approval. Punishments are allowed. In ancient times, they could threaten children over 8 and physically punish them over 9. In contemporary families, they occasionally use shame and punishments seem infrequent. On a few occasions I have seen parents reproaching their child for lack of care, attention, or responsibility, and I have seen children over 8 with tears in their eyes or sad faces.

4.5 Encouraging Keen Attention Through Advice

Documents about ancient Mexico report moral advice that parents gave to their children. These talks did not take place during work, but at other moments within the family. Much of the advice concerned encouraging observation and keen attention by the child to things and processes that occur in copresence. The rich vocabulary refers not only to sight and hearing, but also to willingness, initiative, and active engagement in learning. Observing is to see, to be watchful (*itta*); to look at something, to watch (*tlachia*); to try hard to see, to engage his/her eyes (*ixtiya*). Hearing (*caquí*) is not only to hear the sounds made by things or tools and to listen to experts, but also to understand with intelligence and to follow advice.

The chronicles provide many examples of the sentences that Aztec parents addressed to noble girls to pay attention:

> Xitlachiya, xitlacaqui, auh xitlamati, iuhcan i, in tlalticpac: *"See, hear, and know how it is on earth." (Sahagún 6: 94);*
> Uel xquitta in atl, in tlaqualli, in quenin yecaui, in quenin mochiua, in quenin yectiya: *"Look well to the drink, to the food; how it is prepared, how it is made, how it is improved." (Sahagún 6: 95);*
> uel xonmixti, uel xonmixtzaiana, uel xonmopacho, in quenin chiualo: *"look with diligence, open well thine eyes, apply thyself well to how it is done." (Sahagún 6: 96).*

In a contemporary village, I asked: "How do you say 'Observe!' in Nahuatl?." A young woman answered: *Xiquitta quen quichiuh'tica uan iuhcon ticchiuas*, which means exactly: "Watch how they do it and you will do it the same way" (fieldwork). It is her way of saying: "Learn by observing and pitching in." In fact, Mesoamerican children spontaneously observe educators' actions with keen attention for learning (Correa-Chávez & Rogoff, 2009; lópez et al., 2010; Silva, Correa-Chávez, & Rogoff, 2010).

4.6 Valuing Calm, Care, and Patience

Contrasting attitudes can be observed among Mexican middle-class families and Nahuas. In middle-class families, we can see children who are frequently turbulent, restless, noisy, impatient, pestering or demanding attention, and it seems that parents consider these behaviors as "natural" and "normal." In contrast, Nahuatl children are quiet; they do not speak much and look at people and things with discreet but keen attention. Only toddlers demand attention and they are immediately satisfied. Similar contrasting behaviors have been reported in other settings (Ochs & Izquierdo, 2009; Rogoff, Mistry, Göncü, & Mosier, 1993).

Nahuatl parents and educators value calm in speech and in movement, which is an appropriate and polite attitude, both in ancient and present times (Sahagún 6:100, fieldwork). But a calm attitude and knowledge are also linked: the verb *i'mati* means to be clever, calm and cautious. Sources clearly express this: the good craftsman is fully grown [*moscaliani*], discreet (*mi'mati*), prudent (*moyolnonotzani*: conversing with his heart), having a good memory (*tlalnamiquini*). He is "a willing worker, patient, calm." (Sahagún 10: 25).

Contemporary data includes modes of guidance for children to be quiet. On the one hand, adults and parents have peaceful attitudes: serving as examples through their own quiet behavior and quiet voices; not disturbing the child's concentration by excessive verbal instructions; using only brief and discreet remarks during work. So they show the right way: calmness, caution, and moderation in speech.

On the other hand, young people and siblings are more directive and harsh. I report an observation that shows how children's excessive movements are calmed, according to cultural Nahuatl norms and the role of young persons. At a bus station, a mother in Nahuatl clothing, her son about 16, and her daughter about 8 were waiting for the bus. The young girl was not quiet. She was going back and forth in the bus station, touching candy and toys in the shop. Her mother was not paying attention to her and remained silent. Her brother called the girl with very quiet voice, but she did not obey. Then the boy gave her an angry look and made a short unarticulated sound: and the girl immediately calmed down.

Although learning by observing and pitching in is not specific to Mesoamerica (see Lave, 2011), it is a pattern reinforced in all this area, as illustrated in this volume. Ancient and modern Nahuas consider that "true" knowledge is a private thing, embodied within the subject, and that observing and pitching in are the most efficient ways to learn. They think that children's growth happens without anyone's aid, as with plants, and the parents' role is to accompany children, providing protection, care, and good conditions. Linked educative practices imply free observation and legitimate participation in the family and local community life, insofar as possible

(Lave & Wenger, 1990). They involve guidance toward quiet and measured behaviors, which promote keen attention. They encourage responsibility in domestic life, according to the child's maturation.

Today Nahuatl people have entered modernity. Daily life must be reorganized in the family. Schooling as well as adults' wage working and trading outside the home and the local community limit the opportunities for copresence and observation. Parental models have rivals in school, on television, and in videogames and these new models attract young people's attention. Yet the main purpose of education, rooted in language and practices, has not changed: to aid the building of private knowledge and social norms of behaviors, which allow the continuity of the community.

REFERENCES

Arias, J. (1975). *El mundo numinoso de los mayas. Estructura y cambio contemporaneo.* Mexico: Sep-Setentas.

Berdan, F. F., & Anawalt, P. R. (1997). *The essential Codex Mendoza.* Berkeley, CA: University of California Press.

Braudel, F. (1959). *Histoire des Civilisations: le passé explique le présent, L'encyclopédie française, tome XX: Le monde en devenir (histoire, évolution, prospective).* Paris: Société nouvelle de l'Encyclopédie française.

Chamoux, M.-N. (1992). *Trabajo, técnicas y aprendizaje en el México indígena.* México: Cemca-Ciesas.

Chavajay, P., & Rogoff, B. (1999). Cultural variation in management of attention by children and their caregivers. *Developmental Psychology, 35,* 1079–1091.

Cole, M. (1996). *Cultural psychology: A once and future discipline.* Cambridge, MA: Harvard University Press.

Correa-Chávez, M., & Rogoff, B. (2009). Children's attention to interactions directed to others: Guatemalan Mayan and European American patterns. *Developmental Psychology, 45,* 630–641.

Correa-Chávez, M., Rogoff, B., & Mejía Arauz, R. (2005). Cultural patterns in attending to two events at once. *Child Development, 76,* 664–678.

Descola, P. (2013). *Beyond nature and culture.* Chicago, IL: University of Chicago Press.

Detienne, M., & Vernant, J.-P. (1974). *Les Ruses de l'intelligence, la Mètis des Grecs.* Paris: Flammarion.

Dictionnaire espagnol-nahuatl. Bnf 362 (2001 [XVIIth century?]). Paris: Bibliothèque nationale de France, manuscript. Paleography: S. de Pury Toumi, on line. http://celia.cnrs.fr/Fr/Pub_Doc.htm.

Fortes, M. (1970 [1938]). Social and psychological aspects of education in Taleland. In J. Middleton (Ed.), *From child to adult* (pp. 14–74). Garden City, NY: Natural History Press.

Gaskins, S., & Paradise, R. (2009). Learning through observation in daily life. In D. F. Lancy, J. Bock, & S. Gaskins (Eds.), *The anthropology of learning in childhood* (pp. 85–117). Lanhman, MD: Alta Mira Press.

Goffman, E. (1963). *Behavior in public places.* New York, NY: The Free Press.

Hall, E. T. (1966). *The hidden dimension.* Garden City, NY: Doubleday.

Launey, M. (1979–1980). *Introduction à la langue et à la littérature aztèque, t. I-II.* Paris: L'Harmattan.

Launey, M. (2002). On some causative doublets in Classical Nahuatl. *Language, 48*, 301–318.

Lave, J. (2011). *Apprenticeship in critical ethnographic practice*. Chicago, IL: University of Chicago Press.

Lave, J., & Wenger, E. (1990). *Situated learning: Legitimate peripheral participation*. New York, NY: Cambridge University Press.

León Pasquel, M. d. L. d. (2002). El miedo y el espacio en la socialización infantil zinacanteca. In A. Breton, A. M. Becquelin, & M. H. Ruz (Eds.), *Los espacios mayas: Usos, representaciones, creencias* (pp. 505–539). México: UNAM (Centro de Estudios Mayas)—CEMCA.

León Portilla, M. (1980). *Toltecayotl. Aspectos de la cultura náhuatl*. México: FCE.

López Austin, A. (1985). *La educación de los antiguos nahuas, tomo 1*. México: SEP.

López, A., Correa-Chávez, M., Rogoff, B., & Gutierrez, K. (2010). Attention to instruction directed to another by U.S. Mexican-heritage children of varying cultural backgrounds. *Developmental Psychology, 46*, 593–601.

Nash, M. (1967). *Machine Age Maya, the industrialization of a Guatemalan community*. Chicago, IL: The University of Chicago Press.

Ochs, E., & Izquierdo, C. (2009). Responsibility in childhood: Three developmental trajectories. *Ethos, 37*(4), 391–413.

Paradise, R. (1991). El conocimiento cultural en el aula. niños indígenas y su orientación hacia la observación. *Infancia y Aprendizaje, 55*, 73–86.

Paradise, R., & Rogoff, B. (2009). Side by side: Learning by observing and pitching in. *Ethos, 37*(1), 102–138.

Rogoff, B. (1990). *Apprenticeship in thinking: Cognitive development in social context*. New York, NY: Oxford University Press.

Rogoff, B. (2003). *The cultural nature of human development*. New York, NY: Oxford University Press.

Rogoff, B. (2014). Learning by observing and pitching in to family and community endeavors: An orientation. *Human Development, 57*, 69–81.

Rogoff, B., & Angelillo, C. (2002). Investigating the coordinated functioning of multifaceted cultural practices in human development. *Human Development, 45*, 211–225.

Rogoff, B., Mistry, J., Göncü, A., & Mosier, C. (1993). Guided participation in cultural activity by toddlers and caregivers. *Monographs of the Society for Research in Child Development, 58*(Serial No. 236).

Rogoff, B., Paradise, R., Arauz, R. M., Correa-Chávez, M., & Angelillo, C. (2003). Firsthand learning through Intent participation. *Annual Review of Psychology, 54*(1), 175–203.

Sahagún, F. B. d. (1950–1982). *The Florentine codex. General history of the things of New Spain*. (translated by A. J. O. Anderson & C. E. Dibble, 12 vol. (1st/2d edition): Santa Fe/sail Lake City: The School of American Research and the University of Utah.).

Silva, K., Correa-Chávez, M., & Rogoff, B. (2010). Mexican heritage children's attention and learning from interactions directed to others. *Child Development, 81*, 898–912.

Vazquez, F. N. (1982). *Tla'topamitl nauatl Kojchinankokayotl uan kaxtilantla'toli*. Pátzcuaro: Programa de etnolinguística, SEP-CIESAS-INI.

Wimmer, A. (s.d). Dictionnaire de la langue nahuatl classique. On line: http://nahuatl.ifrance.com/ or http://sites.estvideo.net/malinal/.

CHAPTER TWELVE

Learning to Inhabit the Forest: Autonomy and Interdependence of Lives from a Mbya-Guarani Perspective

Carolina Remorini[1]
Consejo Nacional de Investigaciones Científicas y Técnicas, Universidad Nacional de La Plata, La Plata, Argentina
[1]Corresponding author: e-mail address: carolina.remorini@gmail.com

Contents

Abstract

This chapter examines the ideas of reciprocity, respect, autonomy, and interdependence of lives and the impact of these on children's learning. Using an ecological perspective that recognizes humans' relationship with other living beings that inhabit the forest, this chapter is based on ethnographic research conducted in two Mbya-Guarani communities (Argentina). Respect and reciprocity are key for children to develop as part of the community and the forest and they are related to children's well-being and health. I describe Mbya perspectives on children's growth and development, emphasizing the balance between interdependence and autonomy as complementary goals and values, providing examples of environmentally relevant skills to grow up in the forest. These skills are associated with particular ways of *inhabiting* the forest, including learning how to *walk* in it and developing *entendimiento* (understanding). These make possible children's integration in community life through their participation and collaboration in daily activities. I attempt to articulate these ideas with the theoretical framework of *Learning by Observing and Pitching In*, especially concerning ways of organizing and supporting children's learning processes in the context of their engagement with multiaged and more experienced group of people.

Advances in Child Development and Behavior, Volume 49
ISSN 0065-2407
http://dx.doi.org/10.1016/bs.acdb.2015.09.003

1. INTRODUCTION

Although some cultural analyses still use simplistic dualisms such as collectivism versus individualism, a balance between individual and collective goals and values is noticeable in many Indigenous communities in which individuals from different generations share daily activities and children are encouraged to interact in multiaged groups (Rogoff, 2003). In this chapter, I argue that an analysis of individuals' interdependence and autonomy in those communities needs to occur in the context of understanding local cosmologies that define appropriate relationships among humans and between humans and other living beings.

Through these pages I examine the importance of concepts of reciprocity, respect, autonomy, and interdependence of lives in children's learning in a community that views child development as an ecological process, the Mbya Guarani people in Argentina. The chapter expands and discusses some facets of what Rogoff and colleagues defined as Learning by Observing and Pitching In (LOPI, 2003, 2007, 2009, 2014), which they suggest is a common approach to fostering child development in many Indigenous communities of the Americas.

Most of the research on LOPI to date has been done in North and Central America; my ethnographic work among the Mbya extends LOPI research to an Indigenous people in Argentina and focuses attention on the deep interrelations among children, families, communities, and the forest environment. This work is based on the results of my ethnographic observations of children's participation in daily activities in two Mbya-Guarani communities as well as interviews regarding local knowledge, beliefs, and values around children's behavior and development, developmental milestones, and their relation with childrearing practices (Remorini, 2009).

Mbya perspectives and practices regarding children's learning and development emphasizing reciprocity, respect, autonomy, and interdependence must be understood within the framework of ecological relationships between people and their environment. Mbya-Guarani are one of the

Indigenous peoples living in the Argentinian Northeast[1] in the southern extension of the Paranaense Rainforest. As a result of multiple factors, the Mbya have moved through the Paranaense Rainforest since pre-Hispanic times. Ethnographic and historical studies about Mbya people have emphasized their constant spatial mobility as they make use of these rainforest resources and search for areas having favorable conditions for *Mbya reko*, that is, the Mbya way of life ("Sistema" or "Costumbre" Mbya; Remorini, 2009). In spite of the current reduction in extent of the Paranaense Rainforest, Mbya subsistence is still based on the combination of hunting–gathering and horticulture activities within the forest, although dedication to these activities varies according to communities' location and the impact of government policies.

Mbya people are acknowledged for their deep relationship with the forest ("monte" or *ka'aguy*). They do not just *live in* the forest, in the way that Western people usually understand the verb "to live." They consider themselves—together with other living beings—*part* of this environment, which is essential from their point of view for the continuity of the *Mbya reko* (Mbya way of life). The expression *Mbya reko* refers to cultural practices learned and performed throughout generations, including the appropriate ways of *dwelling* (Ingold, 2000) in the forest and relating with the forest's inhabitants.

I investigated daily childrearing practices and their relation to caregivers' knowledge and values about child development from an ecological perspective. According to an ecological perspective, development is a result of people's participation and engagement with their environments; as a result, people are both shaped by and actively shape their environments (Bronfenbrenner, 1987; Rogoff, 2003; Weisner, 1984). The ecology of

[1] The Mbya presence in Misiones Province dates back to the end of the nineteenth or beginning of the twentieth century, when they moved from the southeast the current territory of Paraguay, to Argentina and Brazil, significantly expanding its territory (Garlet, 1997; Remorini, 2001). According to most recent estimates, the Guarani total over 6500 people in Argentina, with high and sustained growth rates (Grumberg and Melià, 2008). However, according to official sources, there are 3975 people in Argentina who identify themselves as belonging to the Mbya-Guarani people (Instituto Nacional de Estadística et al., 2004–2005). Their language belongs to the Tupí-Guaraní linguistic family. The Mbya communities that I worked in are located between Cainguas and Libertador General San Martín Departments (Misiones Province).

human development relates patterns and pathways of development to the enduring and changing environments in which people live. In that framework, it is assumed that learning processes are sensitive to changes in people's environment.

Contrary to conventional approaches to child development, based on the idea that environment *influences* the child, for the ecology of human development, the unit of analysis is the *child-in-its-environment* as a whole, not as separate entities. Children are engaged in their environment through their participation in routine activities which requires the learning and practice of different skills (Ingold, 2000, 2006; Rogoff, 2003). At a methodological level, this approach focuses on everyday activities as a locus for studying children's development, taking up and revalidating ideas about human action proposed by Malinowski (1964) and Dewey (1916, 1938) and derived from philosophical pragmatism (Crivos & Remorini, 2007).

This approach fits with a central idea underlying LOPI (Rogoff, 2003, 2014)—the coherence between children's learning processes in different community settings and its connections with relevant everyday experiences. In Benedict's terms (1964), there is *continuity* between children's experiences across cultural domains and practices. Cultural practices such as those involved in LOPI are connected with many other features of children's and families' lives as aspects of coherent constellations of cultural practices that transform across generations. The idea of constellations contrasts with treating cultural practices as variables that operate independently (Rogoff, 2014).

Building off these ideas, this chapter is divided into three parts. In the first part, I examine Mbya understanding of their relationship with other living beings that inhabit the forest, emphasizing the ideas of reciprocity, respect, and interdependence of lives and their impact on children's learning. In the second part, I discuss Mbya perspectives on children's growth and development in a framework of balance between interdependence and autonomy as complementary childrearing goals and values. In that framework, I provide some examples of environmentally relevant skills to learn to inhabit the forest. In the third, I consider the conceptual differences between an integrated, ecological cosmology that emphasizes children's learning through participation and the division into individual versus collective, which is common in many conventional approaches in social sciences. I attempt to articulate these ideas with some facets of LOPI, concerning ways of organizing and supporting children's learning processes in the context of their engagement in activities that involve interaction with other people.

2. ENVIRONMENT, LEARNING, AND INTERDEPENDENCE OF LIVES

Understanding how people perceive and experience their environments is key for anthropologists and psychologists interested in the particular ways in which physical, cognitive, emotional, and social skills develop across the life span. Theoretical and empirical studies based on the ecology of human development highlight that human skills are developed through children's active engagement in their specific environments. As Ingold stated,

> *Human capacities are not genetically specified but emerge within processes of ontogenetic development. Moreover the circumstances of development are continually shaped through human activity... There is no way of describing what human beings are independently of the manifold historical and environmental circumstances in which they become - in which they grow up and live out their lives.*
>
> ***(2006: 259, 273)***

In accord with these ideas, we need a relational and historical approach, going beyond traditional dichotomies such as organism/environment, nature/culture, innate/acquired, individual/society, autonomy/interdependence, and material/symbolic.

Similar to Rogoff's (2003) criticism against "boxes and arrows" as a way of explaining how culture/environment "*influences*" development, Ingold defends the necessity to move beyond the dualistic idea "individual *plus* environment":

> *The 'plus' signifies a simple addition of one thing to another, both of which have their own integrity, quite independently of their mutual relations... The environment is specified as a set of physical constraints, in advance of the organisms that arrive to fill it.... [This approach] in fact is profoundly antiecological.... A properly ecological approach, to the contrary, is one that would take, as its point of departure, the whole-organism-in-its-environment*
>
> ***Ingold (2000: 20, 21)***

It is thus necessary to understand what it means to *dwell in* or to *inhabit* an environment, which is different than merely to live in it. If we accept this perspective, we must consider development as an *emergent* of these interactions between children and the environments in which they participate. Based on such ideas, Mbya-Guarani perspectives of *inhabiting* the *monte* (forest) serve as an ethnographic example for understanding children's learning in those communities.

In this regard, I argue that it is necessary to situate interactions between children and the environments in which they participate within the framework of local cosmologies. This is because the cosmologies define ontologies and the appropriate relationships between humans and other living beings (Descola, 2001) and provide arguments to explain, justify, and control human behavior. In that sense, the diversity of cultural understandings about expectable ways of interaction between children and others (humans or not) is a central aspect to take into consideration when analyzing human development because these local understandings are the basis of cultural models about the life course and development, having an impact in children's daily experiences.

Mbya people do not separate the natural from the social environment; the Western dichotomy nature/culture makes no sense for these Indigenous peoples. According to Mbya cosmology, in the forest "*todo tiene espíritu*" (everything has spirit), which means that "natural" entities (species) have will, desire, and intention. All of these beings—not just people—have power and agency. The relationship between all these is modeled on the relationship between human beings, as it is thought that all these entities can contain something like the human community (Descola, 2001; Ingold, 2000). In that sense, the distinction between *environment* and *nature* corresponds to the difference between seeing people as part of the environment or as a separate entity. Following from this distinction, it is interesting to note that the Western idea of nature requires an "external observer" (like a scientist). However, for Mbya people, humans, plants, animals, and also *dueños* ("guardians") and other spiritual beings are part of each other's environment.

The interactions between all of these entities are affected by specific rules that regulate daily behavior and have moral implications having to do with *reciprocity* and *respect*. As described in several studies (Cadogan, 1997; Pissolatto, 2007; Remorini, 2009, 2010, 2012), from Mbya perspective, humans' health and well-being depend on appropriate interactions between them and their environment, including respect of taboos and proscriptions regarding entities considered harmful. Our ethnographic research (op. cit.) showed that a wide range of children's illness affecting their development and their integration in community life are explained and justified based on lack of *respect* and *reciprocity* with other forest inhabitants. In that sense, we notice a strong interdependence of lives, as they depend on each other for living, growing, and/or being healthy.

Mbya children are taught early that they are part of the "*monte*" and of the "*teko'a*" (community-kin group)[2] and they learn rules to interact with other inhabitants by observing and taking part in others' behaviors and attitudes from a very early age. The actual experiences children have with their environment during their participation in collective activities, such as hunting or gathering, are an important source of learning these rules. As they accompany others in hunting and gathering expeditions, they take part in the actions that are deemed necessary in order to be respectful to the spirits of other species and to the ancestors. In this regard, the following quote coming from Bolin's (2006) ethnographic study of Chillihuani people from Peru could be applied to Mbya childrearing:

> *As soon as the children become conscious of their environment, they are introduced to a culture of respect. Respect is not only given to other people and deities, but is conveyed also to all forms of life.*
>
> ***Bolin (2006: 33)***

To understand how *reciprocity* and *respect* contribute to learning processes, we can consider hunting as an example of activity to which boys are introduced. Most boys will first accompany their male relatives in hunting when they are between 7 and 8 years old based on the adults' assessment of a child's maturity and responsibility. As with many other hunting people around the world, Mbya men explain success in hunting by combining personal technical abilities with the idea of a necessary *collaboration* or *cooperation* between the prey and the hunter (Descola, 2001; Ingold, 2000; Rival, 2001). For this *collaboration* to be possible, people must follow some scripts, such as to ask for permission to the prey's owners in order to be *respectful* with them. *Dueños* (guardians, or *ija* in Mbya) are spirits that care for some animals, plants, and specific places (e.g., rivers and streams) and regulate their human use for subsistence purposes.

Reciprocity and *respect* are promoted daily in order to allow children to be aware of interdependence of all forms of life in the forest, including among people. One way of promoting this idea is to share food. In every household I visited, there was always food prepared and available (e.g., in a pot on the patio) for people to eat as they wish, and visitors were invited to share *mate* and the local type of bread (*chipa*). If someone has no food, his/her relatives

[2] *Teko* is a term with multiple meanings which refers to human life, the way of living and the conditions to make possible this way of living. *Teko'a* is usually translated as "village" or "community" or "patrilineal kin group." However, a more appropriate translation, according to Mbya understanding, could be "the place in which *teko* is performed." For a more detailed analysis see Remorini (2009).

are supposed to bring it to him/her, expecting reciprocity in the future. If a child or an adult has access to certain kinds of food, for instance, the meat of certain animals such as peccaries (*kochi*, considered a sacred animal), they must bring it to the *teko'a* to be cooked and shared with relatives and neighbors. When someone breaks this rule, for example, by not sharing the product of hunting and eating it alone in the forest, the peccary's *dueño* (guardian) may be offended. As a result, the hunter could suffer serious illness. In some extreme cases, hunters may be reached by an evil spirit and, as a result, be transformed into a jaguar, losing the human condition (via *djepota*: metamorphosis). Symptoms of this are visible changes in his appearance, including changes in his teeth (Pissolatto, 2007; Remorini, 2009).

Because the process of becoming a *Mbya*—becoming *human* and part of the *teko'a*—is gradual and full of risks, the whole community is responsible for protecting children. Adults' or other relatives' lack of *respect* and *reciprocity* for other living beings may have serious consequences for children's well-being and health. For instance, infants are considered vulnerable and they can fail to achieve the human condition if they are harmed by spirits. This can happen when their parents or siblings do not behave in an appropriate way, such as described earlier. As a consequence, infants may become "angry," "aggressive," or "weepy"—behaviors considered to be symptoms of an illness which puts children at risk of losing their human condition. In those cases, the intervention of the religious leader (*Opyguã*) is required to cure the child (Remorini, 2009, 2012).

These explanations could be seen as irrelevant or even irrational for many people, including many natural and social scientists. However, for Mbya people, these explanations play a major role to learn how to *inhabit* the forest, which, in turn, are connected to their perspectives on children's learning and development. In what follows, I describe some examples of daily activities in which children are involved, in order to articulate the ideas about interdependence of lives, autonomy, and learning of environmentally relevant skills.

3. GROWING UP THROUGH LEARNING ENVIRONMENTALLY RELEVANT SKILLS

The process of becoming a *Mbya* requires adult guidance and support. Childrearing practices ("*mitã ñemongakuaa*," literally, "to make the child grow") are oriented to promote physical growth, health, and the development of socially recognized skills—"*oguata*" (walking) and *kakuaa* (understanding) being the most important. In Mbya language, *kakuaa* means "to grow" but also "to know, to understand." In this sense, a mature child is one who has achieved understanding. This process of *growing* is recognizable by *transformations* in children's physical, cognitive, and social skills, which justify changes in the way they are named in the community. For example, a child that is breastfed is called "*mitã okambu*," whereas a child who is able to eat is "*mitã ikaru*." Similar distinctions are made for the child who crawls ("*mitã opoñĩ*") versus the child who is able to walk ("*mitã oguata*"), and the child who is able to talk "*mitã ijavu*" (Remorini, 2009, 2010).

From the Mbya perspective, *walking* is a crucial skill to be considered a human being (Cadogan, 1997). The transition from crawling to standing up and walking upright is one of the most important developmental milestones and is promoted by several daily practices, such as daily massages, use of several amulets, and motor training using specific objects like a special cane frame installed in the courtyard to support the child in practicing standing and walking (*mitã amba*) (Remorini, 2009, 2010).

However, walking is not merely a physical or motor skill. Walking is a way to *experience* the world, as *Ñamandu Ru Ete* (Our Father, the main deity) created the *Yvy tenonde* (The First Earth) through walking on it (Cadogan, 1997; Remorini, 2009). For Mbya people, walking means to create and transform the forest, through everyday subsistence activities (Crivos et al., 2007; Remorini, 2010). Learning to walk in the forest implies putting into play a variety of sensory and cognitive skills such as keen observation and active listening, but also the ability to recognize differences in smell and taste. Learning to walk through the forest is a crucial skill for both girls and boys to grow up as a Mbya.

Learning to walk is especially important because girls and boys participate from a very early age in gathering and horticulture, accompanying adults and doing some "simple" tasks such as helping to clean or to put the seeds in the holes made by adults with the digging stick. In accompanying adults in gathering, children develop sensory and perceptual skills such as taste and smell involved in the recognition and collection of medicinal plants. Hunting is probably the activity that requires the most complex abilities; it involves different tools, such as traps, bows, and arrows (less frequent today), and firearms (more recently). Each technological choice implies a deep knowledge about the habits of prey, their vulnerabilities, and the environments they frequent (Cebolla Badie, 2000; MacDonald, 2007; Remorini, in press; Rival, 2001). Consequently, hunting is an activity in which boys are involved later in childhood. Children's gradual involvement in activities with different levels of complexity allows them to develop environmentally relevant skills over time, ranging from recognition of animal's footprints to building a trap (Cebolla Badie, 2000; Gaskins, 2000; Hawkes, O'connell, & Blurton, 1995; Lancy, 2012; Mignot, 1996; Padawer & Enriz, 2009; Paradise & De Haan, 2009; Rogoff, 2003; Rogoff et al., 2007).

As the child develops *kakuaa* (understanding), parents show greater concern to educate children in the self-control of extreme emotions like anger, temper, or senseless crying, as these limit the child's ability to participate in community life. The development of understanding together with self-control allows children to collaborate with others and to perform different activities in the forest. This kind of education promoting self-control and awareness of other's interests and needs starts after the name-giving ceremony (near the age of one year), when children are formally recognized as members of the *teko'a* (Remorini, 2009, 2012).

Kakuaa allows children to collaborate in activities that require *reciprocity* and *responsibility* such as care of other people. One example of this is the respectful treatment of relatives, especially elders, who are considered "grandmothers" or "grandfathers" of every child of the *teko'a*. Children should visit elders every day and be attentive to their needs, bring them food, or just keep them company. Some parents "give" some of their children to elders so they will not have to live alone and to collaborate with and take care of them. Similarly, children could be responsible for the care of their siblings, making a valuable contribution to household activities.

Observations of daily life and people's narratives show that interdependence between children and their environment is a central aspect of childrearing and education. However, balance between interdependence and autonomy is acknowledged. Parents consider children's autonomy to be crucial for their participation in the community life. Children's engagement in household routines and their responsibilities regarding relatives and elders are combined with a strong respect for self-determination and autonomy. Parents' narratives about goals and values of childrearing fit with practices that I observed that demonstrate respect for children's interests, initiative, and preferences.

Respect for children's autonomy is seen from a very early age with one particularly notable example of this demonstrated in mothers' attitudes toward breastfeeding. In Mbya communities, infants are breastfed on demand. Mothers are usually seated on low seats while doing handwork. As mothers work, toddlers go back and forth to the women and when the toddlers are hungry they lower the neckline of the mother's blouse, holding her breast with both hands, and breastfeed themselves standing beside her. They repeat this action as many times as they need. The "availability" of their mother's body facilitates the child's autonomy in feeding.

As children get older we see other examples in the allotment of household chores to children based on their preferences (whether they prefer to take care of siblings, cook, or participate in hunting or gathering) and the respect for children's initiative in collaborating. Parents and other relatives carefully observe children's individual preferences and promote the learning of specific skills (to be a skillful hunter or to know about medicinal plants). Another example is seen in the interest adults show in listening every morning to the children's dreams during family breakfast. In Mbya culture dreams are part of "real life" and talking about dreams help to organize daily activities and to prevent illnesses or accidents.

4. AN INTEGRATED ECOLOGICAL COSMOLOGY EMPHASIZING LEARNING BY PARTICIPATION RATHER THAN DIVIDING INDIVIDUAL VERSUS COLLECTIVE

Since its beginning, anthropology has been interested in the diversity of cultural practices associated with "transmission" and "acquisition" of skills during infancy and childhood. These concepts are under criticism, due to current ecological perspectives that claim that we can better understand the dynamics of human development—and also of cultural change—if we consider them as a result of practice and training during participation in specific settings or environments. In this regard, children's learning processes do not occur in the way defended by classical approaches derived from Durkheim's dualistic ideas about "*collectivité*" versus individuals.

The framework of LOPI helps to understand children's learning in ecological contexts in which learning is not generally managed by adults' direct instruction, as in Mbya communities. On the contrary, learning processes occur through children's integration and active participation in the ongoing endeavors of their families and communities (Rogoff, 2014). In those contexts, adults facilitate and support children's learning, by recognizing children's initiative, interests, and possibilities, rather than controlling or constraining their behavior and attention. It could be said that in that kind of learning situation, more experienced individuals *orient* or *educate* children's attention toward some relevant features.

LOPI emphasizes respect for children's initiative and autonomy (Rogoff, 2014) in relation to interdependence between people and their environment broadly defined, in settings where *collaboration* and *reciprocity* are central aspects of community organization. As ethnographers have described for many Latin American Indigenous societies and is the case in Mbya communities, children have been observed to participate

> *in almost all community events, learning by observing keenly and pitching in to shared endeavors with initiative because the activities mattered for family and community success and wellbeing; the children's responsible help and learning were supported by family and community arrangements*
>
> ***Rogoff (2014: 75)***

In this framework, collaboration and exchange with others become crucial. Instead of cultural ideas/representations "transmitted" and imposed upon the individual's experience—following Durkheim and British social anthropologists' legacy—the individual's experience in specific settings is the *locus* of analysis (Crivos & Remorini, 2007).

This distinction holds importance for understanding the emergence of new ideas. In the conventional, dualistic vision dividing individual versus *collectivité*, people's perception and understanding of the environment would derive from cultural constructions transmitted through generations as a homogeneous and invariable corpus, relatively impervious to the actual constraints and features of specific activity settings, and in other words, impervious to time and history. However, other ways to understand learning, such as that presented in the LOPI model and other ecological approaches, are more sensitive to the ways of thinking of people like the Mbya and numerous other Indigenous communities.

From an ecological approach, learning can be seen as a creative process derived from the recognition of problems emerging during active participation in specific activity settings/environments. Learning requires applying, testing, or discarding previous knowledge and/or "discovering" new knowledge in order to achieve the best fit with the current situation. This process of learning and training begins in childhood but is continuously actualized through practice in changing environmental conditions. Mbya children's and adults' direct experience with the forest and its inhabitants is the basis of new learning, and because of the forest's changing conditions, this kind of learning is fundamentally different than learning based on a model of transmission of information.

Even when Mbya adults actively intervene by setting up the features or conditions in the environment aimed at facilitating children's growth and development, not all of them result from an intentional decision-making process on the adult's part. Most of these developmental conditions *emerge* in the framework of interaction between the child and its environment. Contrary to mechanic perspectives on socialization, adults' practices provide environmental conditions for promoting children's learning and development but do not determine the process and the results (Ingold, 2000). Otherwise, children's ability to innovate as well as to make autonomous decisions in learning would be limited. Indeed, it would deny children's agency in their own development process.

The interaction between adults and children allows the adult to see what is needed on the part of the child, and thus the interaction itself facilitates the adult intervention. Adults facilitate and support children, considering they are part of the activity and make contributions to it, an idea that contrasts with classical socialization approaches. This also contrasts with intentional decisions—outside of interaction—about what children should learn, often seen in schools. In that sense, unlike conventional approaches to learning and socialization, LOPI highlights that relevant skills develop as children participate with others in specific settings, not as "recipients" of adults' instruction and "transmission of knowledge." Further, the LOPI model emphasizes that evaluation occurs in the process of interaction, to facilitate children's contributions.

An image coming from Mbya understanding of *inhabiting* their environment provides a useful way of looking at the mutuality involved in children's learning. The "wild" and "domesticated" are not considered opposites, as many spaces within the forest such as paths, houses, patios, and gardens are always full of human "signatures" (Crivos et al., 2007). From a Mbya perspective, the notion of forest, *ka'aguy ete*, does not translate into the idea of a "pristine" forest. Mbya consider the forest as to be a result of their present activity and those of their ancestors. As with the Huaorani, Achuar, and Chillihuani people from South America (Bolin, 2006; Descola, 2001; Rival, 1998, 2001), Mbya are engaged in their environment, transforming it and being transformed by it through their participation in routine activities and by dwelling in it. Their understanding of "nature" is not based on the distinction between wild and domesticated.

In the same way, Mbya do not consider children to be "wild" or "raw" material that needs to be *domesticated* by rational and intentional procedures, an idea that underlies some conventional approaches to children's learning. Rather, they see child development as a process of *transformation* by participation in routine activity settings (also appearing as one of the key features of

LOPI), which requires adult guidance and support. This participation involves not only the child's observation and keen attention to others' activities and behaviors but also interaction and collaboration with others who inhabit the *teko'a* and the forest. In this regard, Mbya education and rearing practices are not based in instruction, but in allowing children to be part of the community endeavors, and learning through this to develop valuable skills that are considered crucial to growing up in the forest. In this framework, adults and children contribute to the process of learning by transforming themselves and transforming their environment.

ACKNOWLEDGMENTS

This research was supported by National University of La Plata and National Council of Scientific and Technological Research (CONICET). I want to thank to Mbya-Guarani people for their cooperation and warm hospitality during my fieldworks and for sharing their knowledge and daily life with me. Finally, I want to thank this volume editors (Barbara, Maricela, and Rebecca) for their comments and valuable contributions to the final version of this chapter.

REFERENCES

Benedict, R. (1964). *Continuidad y discontinuidad del condicionamiento cultural. Historia y elementos de la sociología del conocimiento*. Buenos Aires: EUDEBA.

Bolin, I. (2006). *Growing up in a culture of respect. Child rearing in highland Peru*. Austin, TX: The University of Texas Press.

Bronfenbrenner, U. (1987). *La ecología del desarrollo humano: Experimentos en entornos naturales y diseñados*. Barcelona: Paidós.

Cadogan, L. (1997). *Ayvu Rapyta. Textos míticos de los Mbyá-Guaraní del Guairá*. Fundación León Cadogan.

Cebolla Badie, M. (2000). El conocimiento Mbya-guarani de las aves. Nomenclatura y clasificación. *Suplemento Antropológico*, *XXXV*(2), 9–188.

Crivos, M., Martínez, M. R., Pochettino, M. L., Remorini, C., Sy, A., & Teves, L. (2007). Pathways as "signatures in landscape": Towards an ethnography of mobility among the Mbya-Guarani (Northeastern Argentina). *Journal of Ethnobiology and Ethnomedicine*, *3*, 2. http://dx.doi.org/10.1186/1746-4269-3-2. http://www.ethnobiomed.com/content/3/1/2.

Crivos, M., & Remorini, C. (2007). Entre el individualismo y el colectivismo. El contexto de la acción en la etnografía funcionalista y en la filosofía pragmatista. In J. Ahumada, M. Pantalone, & V. Rodríguez (Eds.), *Epistemología e historia de la ciencia (Selección de trabajos de las XVI Jornadas)*. Córdoba: Universidad Nacional de Córdoba.

Descola, P. (2001). Construyendo naturalezas. Ecología simbólica y práctica social. In P. Descola, & G. Pálsson. (Coord), Naturaleza y sociedad. Perspectivas antropológicas. Mexico: Siglo XXI.

Dewey, J. (1943 [1938]]). *Experiencia y educación*. Buenos Aires: Losada.

Dewey, J. (1946 [1916]]). *Democracia y educación. Una introducción a la filosofía de la educación*. Buenos Aires: Losada.

Garlet, I. (1997). *Mobilidade Mbya: Historia e significacao*. Dissertation, Porto Alegre: Pontificia Universidade Católica do Rio Grande do Sul.

Gaskins, S. (2000). Children's daily activities in a Mayan village: A culturally grounded description. *Cross-Cultural Research, 34*, 375–389.

Grumberg, G., & Melià, B. (2008). *Guarani Retã 2008: Povos Guarani na Fronteira Argentina.* Brasil e Paraguai: CTI.

Hawkes, K., O'connell, J. F., & Blurton, J. N. (1995). Hazda Children's foraging: Juvenile dependency, social arrangements and mobility among hunter-gatherers. *Current Anthropology, 36*(4), 688–700.

Ingold, T. (2000). *The Perception of the Environment: Essays on livelihood, dwelling and skill.* London and New York: Routledge. http://dx.doi.org/10.4324/9780203466025.

Ingold, T. (2006). Against human nature. In D. Aerts, N. Gontier, & J. P. Van Bendegem (Eds.), *Evolutionary epistemology, language and culture.* The Netherlands: Springer.

Instituto Nacional de Estadística y Censos, Argentina, Provincia de Misiones (n.d.). Encuesta complementaria de pueblos indígenas (ECPI) 2004–2005. http://www.indec.gov.ar.

Lancy, D. (2012). The chore curriculum. In G. Spittler & M. Bourdillion (Eds.), *Working and learning among Africa's children.* Berlin: Lit Verlag.

MacDonald, K. (2007). Cross-cultural comparison of learning in human hunting: Implications for life history evolution. *Human Nature, 18*, 386–402. http://dx.doi.org/10.1007/s12110-007-9019-8.

Malinowski, B. (1964). El problema del significado en las lenguas primitivas. In C. K. Richards & L. A. Ogden (Eds.), Buenos Aires: Paidos básica.

Mignot, J. M. (1996). Exemples de techniques d'acquisition de produits alimentaires mises en oeuvre par les enfants Massa Bugudum. In I. de Garine, A. Froment, C. Binam Bikoi, & J.-F. Loung (Eds.), *Bien manger et bien vivre. Anthropologie alimentaire et dévéloppement in Afrique intertropicale: du biologique au social* (pp. 425–432). Paris: L'Harmattan.

Padawer, A., & Enriz, N. (2009). Experiencias formativas en la infancia rural mbyá-guaraní. *Avá: Revista de Antropología, 15*, 315–330. http://www.scielo.org.ar/pdf/ava/n15/n15a17.pdf.

Paradise, R., & De Haan, M. (2009). Responsibility and reciprocity: Social organization of Mazahua learning practices. *Anthropology and Education Quarterly, 40*(2), 187–204.

Paradise, R., & Rogoff, B. (2009). Side by side: Learning by observing and pitching in. *Ethos, 37*, 102–113.

Pissolatto, E. (2007). *A duração da persona. Mobilidade, parentesco e xamanismo mbya (guarani).* Sao Paulo: Ed. UNESP. Instituto Socioambiental.

Remorini, C. (2001). Caminar a través del monte. Una aproximación a la movilidad Mbya en el pasado y en el presente. *Actas de las II Jornadas sobre Poblamiento, Colonización e Inmigración en Misiones* (pp. 309–326). Posadas (Argentina): Ediciones Montoya.

Remorini, C. (2009). Aporte a la Caracterización Etnográfica de los Procesos de Salud-Enfermedad en las Primeras Etapas del Ciclo Vital, en Comunidades Mbya-Guaraní de Misiones, República Argentina. *Dissertation.* La Plata: Universidad Nacional de La Plata /Edulp. http://sedici.unlp.edu.ar/bitstream/handle/10915/4293/Documento_completo__.pdf?sequence=5.

Remorini, C. (2010). Crecer en movimiento: Abordaje etnográfico de la crianza y el desarrollo infantil en comunidades Mbya (Argentina). *Revista Latinoamericana de Ciencias Sociales sobre Ninez y Juventud, 8*(2), 961–980.

Remorini, C. (2012). Childrearing and the shaping of children's emotional experiences and expressions in two Argentinian communities. *Global Studies of Childhood, 2*(2), 144–157. http://www.wwwords.co.uk/GSCH.

Remorini, C. (in press). El papel de los niños en la obtención, elaboración, circulación y consumo de alimentos en comunidades Mbya (Argentina). Anthropology of food.

Rival, L. (1998). Domestication as a historical and symbolic process. In W. Balée (Ed.), *Advances in historical ecology.* New York: Columbia University Press.

Rival, L. (2001). Cerbatanas y lanzas. La significación social de las elecciones tecnológicas de los Huaorani. (Coord). In P. Descola & G. Pálsson (Eds.), *Naturaleza y sociedad. Perspectivas antropológicas*. Mexico: Siglo XXI.

Rogoff, B. (2003). *The cultural nature of human development*. Canada: Oxford University Press.

Rogoff, B. (2014). Learning by observing and pitching in to family and community endeavors: An orientation. *Human Development*, *57*, 69–81.

Rogoff, B., Moore, L., Behnosh, N., Dexter, A., Correa-Chavez, M., & Solís, J. (2007). Children´s development of cultural repertoires through participation in everyday routines and practices. In J. E. Grusec & P. D. Hastings (Eds.), *Handbook of socialization* (pp. 490–515). New York: Guilford.

Weisner, T. (1984). Ecocultural niches of middle childhood. A cross-cultural perspective (Org.). In A. Collins (Ed.), *Development during middle childhood*. Washington, DC: National Academy Press.

CHAPTER THIRTEEN

Learning and Human Dignity Are Built Through Observation and Participation in Work

Rafael Cardoso Jiménez[1]
[1]Corresponding author: e-mail address: tun_kojpk@yahoo.com.mx

Contents

Abstract

This chapter focuses on how children learn through work in ongoing family and community endeavors in an Indigenous Mexican (Mixe) community, where cultural values emphasize that human dignity is derived from work and from collaboration with the work of other people, animals, and the natural world. The chapter highlights the central role that work plays in children's learning, and how attentive and more casual observation and accomplishment of endeavors are important tools that children employ in learning.

1. INTRODUCTION

In this chapter, I address the notion of dignity and the central importance of contributions to life through the work done by people, and the work carried out by the elements and phenomena of Earth-Nature, in the framework of the life of the Mixe people. In the Mixe conception,

Advances in Child Development and Behavior, Volume 49
ISSN 0065-2407
http://dx.doi.org/10.1016/bs.acdb.2015.09.004

particularly of the Indigenous community of Tlahuitoltepec, Mexico, work is closely linked to learning.

Based on this, I describe the ways in which work gives a dignified place for children, adolescents, and adults within family and community, and I also address the ways in which the people give special recognition to animals and to the elements and phenomena of Earth-Nature for the work they perform. I establish, from the voices of the people and my interpretations as a native of this community, that humans (*Jää'y*) have the possibility of life only as long as they are in interaction with natural entities, and appreciate their contributed work.

Work itself has a distinct conceptualization in Mixe: *tunk-pëjkk*. *Tunk* means "work," and *pëjkk* is "to acquire something." In this case, *tunk pëjkk* is having, incorporating, acquiring the experiences generated in the performance of work. Work is not seen as only the implementation of actions in a mechanical way, but there are processes of reflection, life lessons, and experiences that are incorporated in the person. In this way, work transforms the person in the process of doing it, and bestows dignity.

People learning through *tunk-pëjkk* (work and the appropriation of the effects of the performance of work, Cardoso, 2008) can be described as *Learning by Observing and Pitching In* (LOPI, Rogoff, 2014), given that children and adolescents learn in the activities that they perform in family and community settings. The theoretical framework of LOPI emphasizes the central role of observation in performing family and community activities. Much like Rogoff (2014), who speaks of "wide, keen attention," and Gaskins and Paradise (2010), who talk about "open attention," I stress the role of observation in the process of carrying out work.

In this chapter, I distinguish between two forms of observation: observation as synonymous with seeing or looking, and keen observation. I give examples of learning through keen observation where people are not studying the surrounding work, but rather observing casually, but perceiving the process by which work and actions develop. Further, I document that the activities that are observed and learned are not copied nor simply moved from one place to another, but instead people make appropriations, leading to their own styles of carrying out an activity; every generation modifies the practices of the previous generation, adapting themselves to the changing conditions of life (see Rogoff, Najafi, & Mejía-Arauz, 2014).

In the first part of this chapter, I explain the ways in which work dignifies people, I give observations that show that humans/people are a socio-natural entity, and I discuss the importance of collaboration between people and with nature. Later, I move on to consider that observation and participation are the basis of learning and creativity of individuals as they form their repertoires of practice.

2. THE PERFORMANCE OF *TUNK-PËJKK* (WORK) DIGNIFIES PEOPLE

People's important learning takes place in the performance of work. For the Mixe population, work is known as *tunk-pëjkk*, which refers to the ability of people to put themselves into their efforts, putting their hands, feet, and body in motion for the performance of actions in life and for life. People work together in order to obtain food and to recreate their mind and spirit. If there is no dignified work, collaborative work, there is no dignified life. Humans/people live and recreate life by working.

Work is of vital importance given that "it is precisely the element creating a people, the capacity of a people to transform nature for their benefit, but also to recreate nature itself" (Floriberto Díaz in Robles & Cardoso, 2007: 328). For that reason elders, with many life experiences, insist that accomplishing work makes life possible. Señora Salustia recalls the following invitation and encouragement from the elders to the children and adolescents of Tlahuitoltepec:

Kootsyë mëny'ë pëtë''ëktë,	Get up at dawn,
tuntë-pëktë,	work and make the work your own
pawenmaytyë sutsooj mjujky'ättët,	think about how and from what you will live.
tiij mtajuky'ättëp.	
Në'wejtë-në'kajtë,	Sprout, get up,
ku jyäjtä'äkt	everything should be in place by sunrise.
tum exaaj jëtë''n tukkii'jyë	

(Floriberto Díaz in Robles & Cardoso, 2007: Interview)

Historically among the Mixe people, work has played an active role in the transmission of knowledge and ways of life. In pre-Columbian times, a noble Aztec urges his daughter to observe well in order to learn to work and embrace the contribution expected of women (with similar urgings to boys to learn the work of men):

Here is your charge; what you will have to do:
[...] Wake up, get up in the middle of the night [...].
Speak, beg the Lord, our Lord, the one who is the night and the wind [...].
And this done, when you are ready, what will you do? How will you fulfill your womanly duties? Well, do not water and metate *(grinding stone) exist? No spindle or loom? Look well at the water and food, how they are, how they are made, how they are improved, in what form the water and meals are good [...].*
Pay attention, open your eyes, lean forward to see how this is done. This is how you will spend your life; this is how you will protect yourself. This is how you will be valuable [...]
Like this, look closely, embrace it, that which is woman's work: the spindle and the loom [...].
Open your eyes well to see what Tolteca art is like, what the art of feathers is like, how they embroider with colors, how they count the threads, how they dye them, the women, those who are like you, our ladies, the noble ladies. How they place the heddle threads, how they arrange the warp threads, how they measure.
Look well, lean forward...

(Flortentine Codex cited in Chamoux, 1992: 13)

Work is so necessary that it does not even end with death (*o'ojkën-tëkëë'yën* means to become earth again). The Mixes believe that the deceased continue working during the transformational journey and in the hereafter, in the other world, since, as documented by Reyes (2001), in *Ja tuk it* (in the other place, in the other world) there is a place very similar to this one: it has its land, its water, its air, its fire, its sky, its sun, its moon, and its stars. That there, just as here: one works, eats and drinks, dresses and wears shoes. For the Mixe people, there is a widespread practice that when someone dies, he or she is provided water, food, sandals, and other objects such as clothing that were used in this life in order to quench his or her thirst and hunger, to not be injured along the way, and so as to have everything necessary for the work that is required during this transformational journey.

The notion of work after physical death is not exclusive to the Mixe people. Juan Núñez del Prado (cited in Bolin, 2006) documents that the place of the dead, according to Andean ideology, is a beautiful place of cultivation where everyone works, including children; the land is fertile and there is abundant harvest without losses or calamities.

3. A HUMAN/PERSON (*JÄÄ'Y*) IS A SOCIO-NATURAL ENTITY

For the Mixe and other people of Indigenous American origin, the person, the human being is not an entity separate from the other beings of creation. The person/human is but another thread with which the living beings weave their lives.

Life is like a spider's web where everything is interconnected, in which what one does has either a positive or negative repercussion on everyone else. The human being is neither inferior nor superior in regards to the other living beings of creation, but is brother or sister of plants and animals. The person/human lives peacefully and with dignity when respecting Nature. Floriberto Díaz (Mixe anthropologist from the Tlahuitoltepec community) says, "it is neither madness nor a superstitious occurrence for our fathers and mothers to have taught us that we must talk to the land in order to work it" (in Robles & Cardoso, 2007: 53). Human existence is inconceivable without the work of the plants, of the animals, of the water, of cold, of heat, of stones, of earth as a whole.

4. RECIPROCITY BETWEEN THE WORK OF THE PEOPLE, OF THE DOMESTIC ANIMALS, AND OF THE ELEMENTS AND PHENOMENA OF THE EARTH-NATURE

As mentioned, plants, animals, and the elements and phenomena of Earth-Nature work to enable the existence of all; for that reason, they have a place and recognition of dignity from people. Cattle work (*tuntëp*) in preparing the soil for planting the cornfield; sheep provide wool for the making of overcoats; dogs protect the house and help in hunting wild animals. Because of the work carried out by domestic animals, they have a worthy place in the home of the people. People take care of and protect animals. When one falls ill, families perform specific rituals in which they ask the Creator and the Giver of Life for its recovery, its reproduction and abundance; there are even families who make pilgrimages to temples and sacred places of other communities and cities, for the purpose of requesting the health of their animals, which contribute to the work and economy of the family.

On the twentieth day after a calf is born, a ritual is held in which relatives gather and present wishes for its healthy growth and for it to work as the adult animals do. Those who engage in hunting wild animals hold rituals where they offer food and drink to Earth-Nature and ask for the well-being of the dogs who collaborate in the hunt, so that they do not get tired from running and so that serpents do not bite them.

People do not have any way of getting by without the work of the elements and phenomena of Earth-Nature, "the mother-child relationship between the land and we the people is not a metaphysical, spiritual, or imaginary matter; it is a material, real, existing relationship... but it is not only material, but transcends to the depth of the matter." (Floriberto Díaz in Robles & Cardoso, 2007: 52). Life on Earth and in all of Nature is a great weaving together that is both concrete and mystical. This concept can be understood and explained with the principle of the "multifaceted universe" (Cardoso, 2009: 53) in which the whole is composed of many faces and voices.

In order to understand the depth of the importance of the work of the elements and phenomena of Earth-Nature in the worldview (cosmovision) of the Mixe, I will now present some examples of the work of the natural world.

Ja tsuuj ja poj (the wind and the night) are living entities that are characterized by their capacity to shift and mold; they reach places where no other beings have access. The wind works in the respiration of people, animals, and plants; it keeps people alive. The wind works in people's dreams. In dreams, one has the ability to see or interpret what may happen to one or one's relatives. The wind and the night receive the food and beverages that people offer to Earth-Nature. It is the wind that is in charge of finding and returning the spirit of a person when it has detached itself and is lonely somewhere.

Ja nëëj ja mejy, ja mejy ja anaaw (the water as sea, thunder, rain, river, or stream) is freshness and vital liquid. The water is what works so that seeds sprout, so that plants grow green again, bloom, and bear fruit. The water is what gives animals and people something to drink. The water awakens the people, cleans the people, and cures the people. Water as rain, natural spring, river, lagoon, or sea is the space and food of the birds, the butterflies, the lizards, the serpents, the fish. All the animals come to put their mouths in it to quench their thirst and to continue with life. The water accompanies people who embark on the path of transformation toward the land which receives them into itself.

Ja usjts ja ääy (the plants and the greenery) work to provide freshness, joy, and respiration. Plants are the primary food for people, the people's drink and medicine. *Ja moojk ja xëjk* (the corn, the cornfield) work to give face and word to the people. Corn has been the principle food of the peoples of pre-Hispanic origin for thousands of years. It is the quintessential ritual food that the people offer up to Earth-Nature and the Creator and Giver of Life.

Ja et ja nääjx (The Earth) is the mother of all living beings. The Earth works by nursing the plants and the animals. The earth carries *(tsyëm'ijtypy)* all the plants that have rooted into her body; the earth carries the rivers and the sea. On the surface of the earth live the deer, the rabbit, the fox, the birds, the insects. "The earth is what gives us the security of our return to her; as Indigenous people, that is our reward, that is our heaven. And because it is certain that we will return to her, although we would disappear or the rivers take us" (Floriberto in Robles & Cardoso, 2007: 53).

The place and recognition bestowed by the people to the thunder, to the sea, to the cloud, to the air for the work that they do is very special. During the sowing of corn, the people offer the Earth-Nature special food made of corn, tepache (a ritual drink made of water, pulque, and raw cane sugar), and poultry. For the work of *Konk Mejy, Konk Anaaw* (the water, the guardian of water, the thunder), food made of corn is prepared in the shape of lightning, which is placed in the bosom of the earth, in the sowing of corn; this is done as a request for rain (*menpë këtäkpë*), since water is an indispensible entity in the lives of the people. For any important event, people resort to the mountain, to the wind, to the night, to the rocks, to the sun. It is to them that the people turn when there are illnesses or misfortunes; and it is to them that the people thank deeply when there is success, when there is happiness.

However, although everyone and everything in this world must work, according to the Mixe conception, work has not been traditionally seen as an onerous obligation, as I mentioned. And as it is something in which everyone participates as part of a dignified existence, it is fundamentally collaborative as well. In the following section, I address the topic of the importance of collaboration in work. And I give an example of how work creates social bonds between people.

5. WORK AND COLLABORATION

Although in many cases work is difficult and heavy, people create pleasant social environments in order to carry it out. In the paving of a house, hauling the mortar (a mixture of sand, gravel, and cement) is heavy, but with conversations, jokes, laughter, and guffaws, this activity becomes enjoyable. Though pulling weeds from the cornfield is tiring, the socialization about events within the community makes the job appealing and enjoyable. It appears that generating an agreeable atmosphere in process of heavy work is also present in other native cultures. Bolin (2006) documents that in the highlands of Peru, the shared work done by the *Chillihuani* community are spaces of coexistence and truly parties; in other words, collective works become opportunities for social harmony and learning.

At the family level, if all members fulfill the part of the work that is theirs to do, a pleasant atmosphere is generated and lived. For example, if the members of the family participated and fulfilled the sowing of the corn, the carrying of firewood, the preparing of the food, everyone is content; if on the contrary, some member did not work but makes use of everyone else's completed work, that person is considered lazy and his or her attitude generates discord.

In the community context, the person who excels at work is recognized by being named to a community *cargo* (post), which is unpaid. If in this position, he or she does well, in other words, if the person works and organizes the work well, this person is appointed into a position with more responsibilities in order to fulfill the role of father and mother of the community. After fulfilling the posts, he or she becomes part of the council of elders whose function (unpaid) is to guide the community leaders, in their turn.

Collaborative work is developed with a base in reciprocity and contribution to the well-being of the family and community. In collaborative work, the participants are aware of its purpose; for example, in a family dedicated to the preparation of tamales, both the mother and daughters who are involved know that selling 300 or 400 tamales at the market is done in order to obtain economic resources or other food products through bartering.

When larger quantities of tamales are requested from these women, they know that they will not be able to accomplish the task by themselves, so they turn to other women to collaborate with them. The other women accept to collaborate because they know that to make 2000 tamales requires several people, because they know that they will be paid a certain amount of money, and because they have ties of reciprocity. If these women help in making the tamales this time, they know that at some point in the future they will need help in planting their cornfield. Thus between them are bonds of cooperation through work.

The distribution of work and collaboration can be seen in the following case. Two adolescents wash the totomoxtle (dried corn husks) and the corn leaves; the woman of the house cooks the nixtamal (boiled maize) and prepares the amarillo (thick stew for the meat) for the tamales; the other women clean, wash, and place the cleaned chickens on the embers. In the early morning, when the preparation of tamales begins, work is distributed in the following way. One woman calculates the dough needed for one tamal; the eldest daughter flattens each one with a manual tortilla press to make them into small tortillas; a woman puts the thick soup, or amarillo, inside of the small tortillas in order to make them into tamales; another woman wraps the raw tamales with a corn leaf or some totomoxtle; and another sets the tamales on the table. Once this part of the activity is finished, they all take the raw tamales to where they will be cooked. The older women are the ones who take the tamales out of the pot as they have more experience in the care and management of the steam. The woman of the house says that they distribute the activities according to who does what best without implying that anyone is unable to do the entire process of making tamales.

All of these examples underline the importance of work in Mixe life. In fact, in the Mixe language, and in the local version of the community of Tlahuitoltepec, there is no word that exclusively describes learning that is not associated with the notion of *tunk-pëjkk* (activity, work). On the contrary, learning is embodied in gaining mastery of the abilities and skills acquired through fulfilling the activities of the home, of the field, and of other contexts. The next section describes the processes of learning in the Mixe community, focusing especially on the processes of observation.

6. LEARNING TO WORK BY MEANS OF OBSERVATION AND PARTICIPATION

To contribute to the discussion of LOPI (Rogoff et al., 2014), I report on some of the activities that Tlahuitoltepec Mixe girls, boys, adolescents, and adults carry out in the family and in the community, assuming that it is within the undertaking of the activities that learning comes to life.

Before addressing learning through observation, it is worth clarifying that one can speak of observation in two ways: as synonymous to seeing, where there is no explicit intention of learning although one does learn, and keen observation where there is clear intention to learn something.

Observation constitutes part of carrying out work; effective participation is the consummation of work. That is, one learns to make tamales not only because one observes others doing this work but also because one carries out the activity. One learns to cook the corn, grind the nixtamal, and wrap the tamales by being present and participating in the activity.

Based on personal experience, many activities are done without the intention of learning although learning is achieved; instead these activities are done to satisfy needs. For example, we learned to cut firewood because we needed to bring firewood home, not to learn to cut firewood. Similarly, there are a variety of activities we learned without the explicit intention of learning, such as washing clothes, picking peaches, and washing potatoes.

In other cases, attentive observation is required. For example, learning to make clay pots requires time and patience because one must repeatedly handle and mold the clay, and until the skills are acquired one must observe what is being done step by step. Learning to weave an overcoat requires concentration in addition to attentive observation in order to warp the threads, affix the warp beams, tighten the cloth with the batten sword.

Henceforth, I shall refer to the practice of attentive observation in which there is clear intention of learning the activity.

7. OBSERVATION AND CREATIVITY

Learning by means of observation and contribution (LOPI) "is not simple imitation or uninventive reproduction of existing forms and practices" (Paradise & Rogoff, 2009: 113). On the contrary, it represents educational practices that are believed to be a cultural tradition of humanity although especially prevalent in some societies (Paradise & Rogoff, 2009). These forms of learning are known as informal learning that, from my point of view, I call nonclassroom education, education within life and for the sake of life.

In Tlahuitoltepec, Señor Etilberto (a craftsman) says that when he learned to do the work he currently does, he did not spend much time fixedly watching the sequence of actions performed by the person or people, but soon noticed how the activity was carried out. The phrase that he used was "ya lo vi" ("I saw it right away"), meaning that with rapid, keen, and even unnoticed observation, he was ready to do the observed activity, and not as a copy, but rather in his own way, in his own style, in which he brings into play his creativity to produce something new, something distinct. One can say that he makes an appropriation between what he observes and what he does after the observation. He is satisfied when he does the unexpected, not the normal, not the everyday. For example, he carves images into wood, which he inserts into doors. The carved motifs vary, but generally allude to Mixe life. In this way, Señor Etilberto learned masonry, carpentry, blacksmithing, tile gluing, wood carving, electrical installation, drawing, pedal weaving, agronomy, and plumbing, among others.

I illustrate the use of attentive observation and creativity of four women who learned to make tortillas and tamales by participating and observing.

Señoras Canciana and Inocencia (who were born in 1925 and 1949, respectively), learned to make tortillas at the age of nine by briefly and unobtrusively, but attentively, observing the adults. During their era it was not common to ask for instructions, there were only general indications; any specific issues were left to them to figure out. They observed while working; not by sitting down or staying still in one place.

Although Señora Inocencia learned from Señora Canciana to make tortillas, she acquired a distinct style, her own style. Señora Canciana had developed an extraordinary ability in making tortillas- she only needed to pat the dough between her hands in order to make the tortillas. Although Señora Inocencia learned from Señora Canciana, she uses a plastic bag cut into a circular shape to measure and she puts the corn dough on the *metate* (grinding stone) to be able to pat it into shape with only one hand. The process of appropriating without making an exact copy or repeating the activity is clearly shown.

Nidia and Xóchitl (born in 1971 and 1999, respectively) also learned to make tortillas by observing and doing the task. They say that they cannot conceive of learning without doing the activity, but that indeed it is in carrying out the work that they notice many things that allow them to reorient their actions. It is in the doing of the activities where they bud, awaken, and break loose—the Mixe notion of education.

8. REPERTOIRES OF PRACTICE AND VARIABILITY

There are many differences in ways of learning between people and communities which are an expression of the richness of diversity. Learning by the means of the kind of observation described here is not an exclusive practice of the Mixe people; many other peoples develop this tradition. Further, not all members of a community learn in the same way, generally there are differences in the ways and styles of learning. Some people require more time to attentively observe the sequence of actions, and others require little time to learn. For example, Señora Salustia relates that when she wove overcoats in the early 1960s, her sister-in-law observed the work for long periods of time and asked a lot of questions, however, it took her a long time to learn. In contrast, her brother-in-law observed the work a few times and without asking questions, and he learned how to weave overcoat fabric quickly and very well.

Given that life changes and so do the resources of work for learning and constructing knowledge, the idea of repertoires of practices presented by

Rogoff, Najafi, Dexter, Correa-Chávez, and Solís (2007) could be applied here, in the sense that people may carry out activities in different ways or implement them in a way that suits the particular ways of a community. For example, due to different repertoires of practice, a woman may grind the nixtamal with the *metate* (grinding stone) in a place where there is no electricity, or she can make use of an electric mill in a place where electricity is available. It can be said that people have the possibilities of performing activities according to the context and necessities of their lives.

The motivation to make tortillas and tamales has changed across the century and with individual and social circumstances. Señora Canciana, born in 1925, learned to make tortillas and cook food because she had to feed her father in the absence of her mother, who had died when Canciana was a child. Señora Inocencia, born in 1949, because of being the eldest sister and her parents' requests, used to cook for the family while the rest of the members did other activities, also for the benefit of the family. At the age of nine, Señora Nidia, born in 1971, helped her mother make and sell tortillas, given that her father did not defray the expenses for her and her brother to attend school. Selling tortillas represented a source of income to buy some clothing, shoes, and school supplies. Xochitl, born in 1999, cooks tortillas and tamales to help her mother; she is motivated because she gets thirty or fifty pesos from each sale. She saves this money to buy herself clothes and shoes of her choice, as well as part of the materials required in school. Although all of these women use observation to learn, they use it in different manners and for different reasons.

Nowadays—for whatever reasons—work is considered by the youth as something onerous. This phenomenon is visible not only in this community, but it is present in other parts of the world. Jessica Martinez reported the following words of a community elder, from her fieldwork in the native Rubina community on the Huasaga river in 1994:

> *I am thinking with my heart, feeling that schools are leaving my grandchildren empty. I see my grandson growing and growing in vain, without doing what I used to do at his age. If he does not learn anymore, he will not be able to say: My grandfather taught me this way, my grandfather was a hunter. And his children will not be able to say: This is the way we, the Achuar, are.*
>
> **(Martinez, Jessica in Bertely, Jorge Gasché, and Rossana Podestá, 2008: 275)**

Nevertheless, and in spite of everything, work is irreplaceable as long as people want to continue with life or intend to reorient their actions in a way that allows them to navigate a dignified life.

REFERENCES

Bolin, Inge. (2006). *Growing in a culture of respect: Child rearing in Highland Peru*. USA: University of Texas Press.

Cardoso, Rafael. (2008). *Wejën Kajën (brotar, despertar): Noción mixe de educación*. Tesis de maestría, México: Departamento de Investigaciones Educativas (DIE) del Centro de Investigaciones y de Estudios Avanzados (Cinvestav) del Instituto Politécnico Nacional (INP).

Cardoso, Rafael. (2009). Educación escolar y educación no escolar. In *Revista Aquí estamos* (pp. 44–54). México: CIESAS y Programa Internacional de Becas de Posgrado de la Fundación Ford (IFP) (Año 6, núm.10, enero–junio 2009).

Chamoux, Marie-Noëlle. (1992). *Trabajo, técnicas y aprendizaje en el México indígena*. Mexico: Ciesas-Cemca (Centro de Estudios Mexicanos y Centroamericanos). Traducción de Paloma Bonfil.

Gaskins, S., & Paradise, R. (2010). Learning through observation in daily life. In D. F. Lancy, J. Bock, & S. Gaskins (Eds.), *The anthropology of learning in childhood* (pp. 85–117). Lanham, MD: Alta Mira Press.

Martínez, Jessica. (2008). "La actividad mediada y los elementos del aprendizaje intercultural a partir de una experiencia educative con maestros indígenas de la Amazonía Peruana" en Bertely, María; Jorge Gasché y Rossana Podestá (Comps) (2008) Educando en la diversidad. Investigaciones y experiencias educaticas interculturales y bilingues, Ediciones Abya-Yala, Quito, Ecuador.

Paradise, Ruth, & Rogoff, Barbara. (2009). Side by side: Learning by observing and pitching. *ETHOS*, *37*(1), 102–138. http://dx.doi.org/10.1111/j.1548-1352.2009.01033.x. ISSN 0091–2131 online ISSN 1548–1352. © 2009 by the American Anthropological Association. All rights reserved.

Reyes, Juan Carlos. (2001). Tuk it ets ja tuk it (este mundo y el otro mundo). La concepción de la relación muerte-vida en la cultura ayuujk. In *Conferencia dicha en el Evento cultural "Sobre la muerte", organizado por la comunidad normalista de la Escuela Normal Bilingüe e Intercultural de Oaxaca, en su sede San Jerónimo Tlacochahuaya, Tlacolula, Oaxaca; México.*

Robles, Sofía y Rafael, Cardoso (Comps.) (2007). FLORIBERTO DÍAZ, ESCRITO. Comunalidad, energía viva del pensamiento mixe, Ayuktsënää'yën-ayukwenmää'ny-ayujkmëjk'äjtën, Programa Universitario Nación Multicultural (PUNM-UNAM), México.

Rogoff, B. (2014). Learning by observing and pitching in to family and community endeavors: An orientation. *Human Development*, *57*, 69–81.

Rogoff, B., Najafi, L., Dexter, B., Correa-Chávez, A., & Solís, M. (2007). Children's development of cultural repertoires through participation in everyday life routines and practices. In J. E. Grusec & P. D. Hastings (Eds.), *Handbook of socialization: Theory and research* (pp. 490–515). New York, NY: The Guilford Press.

Rogoff, B., Najafi, B., & Mejía-Arauz, R. (2014). Constellations of cultural practices across generations: Indigenous American heritage and learning by observing and pitching in. *Human Development*, *57*, 82–95.

CHAPTER FOURTEEN

Learning by Observing, Pitching in, and Being in Relations in the Natural World

Megan Bang*[,1], Ananda Marin[†], Douglas Medin[†], Karen Washinawatok[‡]

*University of Washington, Seattle, Washington, USA
[†]Department of Psychology, Northwestern University, Evanston, Illinois, USA
[‡]Menominee Nation, Menominee, Wisconsin, USA
[1]Corresponding author: e-mail address: mbang3@uw.edu

Contents

Abstract

This chapter describes a central tenet of Indigenous American social interaction, which emphasizes mutuality in collaboration and caring in Indigenous communities. This includes interactions with an agentive natural world, in which more-than-human beings act as participants in the lives of humans and vice versa. We argue that research on children's learning should take a broader view of interactional partners to include the natural world.

1. INTRODUCTION

In this chapter, we argue that specific attention to the diversity of places and agentic actors constituting family and community life could expand the power of the model of *Learning by Observing and Pitching In* (LOPI; Rogoff, 2014) and more broadly our understanding of human learning. LOPI has made visible the impacts of western formal education on observing and pitching in practices. For example, research taking up LOPI

Advances in Child Development and Behavior, Volume 49
ISSN 0065-2407
http://dx.doi.org/10.1016/bs.acdb.2015.10.004

has demonstrated how western industrial forms of education have segregated children and adults in a variety of forms whereas some Indigenous heritage communities continue to enact communal relationships across generations both deeply shaping learning and contributing to the work of family and community life (e.g., Alcala, Rogoff, Mejia-Arauz, Coppens, & Dexter, 2014; Coppens, Silva, et al., 2014; Coppens, Alcalá, Mejia-Arauz, & Rogoff, 2014; López et al., 2014; Paradise, Mejia-Arauz, Silva, Dexter, & Rogoff, 2014; Rogoff, Najafi, & Mejia-Arauz, 2014). However, studies taking up LOPI (likewise in the broader field) have tended to focus on human–human interactions, often with human-produced mediating artifacts, in largely human-centric contexts. Indeed, this has become the quintessential model of formal education and largely the organizing context in studies of informal learning.

In our work, we have studied the ways in which forms of human–nature relations shaping cultural practices impact knowledge, reasoning, and learning about, in, and with the natural world in cultural ecologies (e.g., Bang, 2015; Medin & Bang, 2014; see also: Lee, 2008; Rogoff, Paradise, Arauz, Correa-Chávez, & Angelillo, 2003). We have broadly referred to this orientation as relational epistemologies and sought to characterize the ways in which activity and learning unfold, especially in the context of outdoor practices. Building with LOPI, we suggest that observing and creating human–nature relations (e.g., relations with land, water, and more-than-human (MTH) life) is a routine, though deeply underexplored, part of human learning, and activity that impacts both what is learned and how learning happens.

In this chapter, we use a range of studies we, with colleagues, have conducted with three communities (rural Indigenous, urban Indigenous, and suburban European-American), focused on social practices that occur outdoors, like fishing, hunting, gardening, and walking, to explore observing practices and the ways in which human–nature relations shape Observing and Pitching In, in cultural ecologies. To make this argument, first we think about why to engage with the framework of cultural ecologies and the implications such engagement has for the study of learning. Then we suggest and explore how cultural ecologies are constituted with MTH actors. We use several studies that focus on specific cultural practices to demonstrate the ways in which cultural ecologies relate to people's conceptions of interrelations among people and the natural world. Finally, we present two examples in which being in relations with the natural world shapes how observing and pitching in occurs.

2. WHY CULTURAL ECOLOGIES?

Scholars engaged from socio-cultural perspectives argue that advancing foundational knowledge about human learning requires expanded focus on the constellations, or ecologies, of processes of interaction that people participate in, particularly in everyday contexts, and the forms of social life that emerge in these contexts and across development (e.g., Goodwin, 2013; Gutiérrez & Rogoff, 2003; Lee, 2008; Nasir, Rosebery, Warren, & Lee, 2006; Rogoff, 2003; Vossoughi & Gutiérrez, 2014). In many settings, observing and contributing to everyday events is an important local ecology for the apprenticeship process (Rogoff, 2014). Goodwin (2013) argues that a central aim of cultures and distinctive ways of knowing is apprenticing new participants to become competent and consequential actors in dynamic cultural ecologies.

Conceptualizing culture as dynamic, contested, and variably distributed within and across various human communities, analytically shifts researchers' focus to reciprocal relationships between individuals and their environment (Hirschfeld, 2002; Nasir et al., 2006). We have taken an "ecosystems approach" to culture (Medin, Ojalehto, Marin, & Bang, 2014; Ojalehto & Medin, 2015) focusing attention to the multiplicities of interactions and systems level dynamics rather than focusing on components in isolation. Building from these views, we argue that "socialization," or the education of attending and observing (LOPI facet 5; Ingold, 2011), may depend on a wide range of agents and relationships as well as an individual's interpretation of and reaction to their environment. Thus as we have suggested, one way in which cultural communities may differ from each other is with respect to what or who constitutes community, especially with respect to human–nature relationships.

3. MORE-THAN-HUMAN (MTH) CONCEPTIONS OF COMMUNITIES

The multiplicity of relations between humans and MTH life that children may engage depends largely on the kinds of relations their own community entertains with the MTH world (Ojalehto, Waxman, & Medin, 2013). A significant amount of work implicitly or explicitly imposes western frameworks on ways of knowing and thus limits the ways in which we can understand the range of human activity (Henrich, Heine, & Norenzayan, 2010; Lave, 2011; Lee, 2008). In our work, we have been particularly concerned with this with respect to Indigenous meanings and constructions of, with, and in the natural world. Increasingly, we have been interested in assumptions about MTH life, more specifically the ascriptions of agency, intentionality, and personhood—or their negation—in Indigenous ways of knowing (Cajete, 2000; Cardoso Jiménez, 2015; Kawagley, 1995; Remorini, 2015) and more broadly cultural ecologies.

Recently, Bang and Marin (2015) explored how the idea that humans are the only agentic actors in the natural world, a view commonsensically held in western perspectives of the natural world (see Latour, 2012), is itself a kind of anthropocentrism and a learned cultural model, as opposed to a universal truth (Bang, 2015). Our intent in this study was not to debate the truth claims of a particular knowledge systems or constructions of agentic actors. We aimed to characterize cross-cultural differences in sense making during activity on its own terms rather than in comparison to what is considered accurate in a western normative model. We found that multiple ontological assumptions of MTH agency emerged in shared observational endeavors and joint activity and had significant impacts on the nature of the activity.

In our work in the design of learning environments in which community members are the decision makers, the construction of MTHs as central actors has been a central design focus. For example, at the American Indian Center of Chicago our work with youth involving a medicinal garden was framed in terms of (re)-making relatives. At various times elders have emphasized the importance of acknowledging, demonstrating respect, and maintaining relations with MTH life as well as to what western folks call "non-living natural kinds" meaning water, rocks, wind, etc. In short, from the community design team's perspectives, "agents and relationships" are not restricted to humans. When children in Indigenous communities are taught that plants are our relatives, they are being apprenticed into conceptualizing plants as part of a cultural community and not simply an object in the domain of biology. This perspective is clearly distinct from the more typical western model where the concept of community is confined to human beings and usually does not centrally include plants, animals, and natural kinds. We suggest that this perspective has implications for learning by observing, particularly in the context of learning about, with and in the natural world.

Cultural differences in orientation toward community and its ties to conceptions of human–nature relations appeared in a study we did with

Native-American (Menominee) and European-American hunters in rural Wisconsin. We asked hunters to name the most important plants and animals in the forest and to tell us how important each kind is to themselves (see Ross, Medin, & Cox, 2007) as well as to the forest—a way of asking about their perception of relationships. Game animals were rated as equally important across communities, but Menominee hunters rated nongame animals to be more important both for themselves and for the forest than did European-American hunters. This supports the hypothesis that, in contrast to European-American hunters, Menominee hunters attend to MTH life in broader ways and have multiple perspectives in defining relations, hunting being one of them. Menominee hunters also reported various kinds of plants to be more important to the forest as well as to themselves, compared with European-American hunters. In their justifications for these assignments of value, more than half of Menominee participants explicitly stated that every plant has a role or part to play and hence is important to the forest. Further, several Menominee hunters mentioned that if something is important to the forest, then it is important to them. No European-American hunter provided these kinds of justifications. They were more likely to report either that a plant had little use to the forest or that they could not think of any.

The perspectives of community discussed above may shift who is considered to be a learner and "what" individuals see themselves contributing to throughout the learning process (LOPI facet 1). In addition, the idea that everything has a role to play may cultivate a wider and keener scope of observation and motivate a deeper analysis of how MTH and humans might build a sense of belonging or contribute to the forest (LOPI facet 2; see also Cardoso Jiménez, 2015; Remorini, 2015). For example, in response to whether porcupines help or harm the forest, a common response among almost all majority-culture hunters was to note that porcupines are destructive because of their habit of girdling and killing trees. Menominees know about this effect too, yet some gave positive ratings and justified them by explaining that this action opens up light into the forest, which in turn allows smaller plants to grow, which in turn provides ground cover that helps maintain soil moisture. Thus, Menominee's wider scope of observations and understanding of causal links with porcupines' behaviors enabled them to see porcupines as making contributions to the forest when European-Americans did not. Further this lead Menominee participants to differently value porcupines as members of the forest community. There are many aspects of Indigenous practices that have deep logic and awareness about complex relations and impacts (Deloria, 1979) that may not be readily detected by non-particpants.

Menominee hunters tended to think of the forest as a community in general and in particular, as a community where cultural practices central to their identity could be enacted. One hunter told us that when he goes into the forest he thinks about the fact that his ancestors many hundreds, if not thousands, of years ago may have been standing exactly where he is standing and engaged in the same activity engaged with plant and animals. It mattered that he was in a particular forest and not just any forest that might have game in it. In short, his cultural community included the forest and its parts.

If cultural ecologies value these forms of wide keen observations and relation making with MTH in similar ways, then we are suggesting that the possible forms of learner's motivation and interest in belonging and contributing may reflect these sorts of patterns and ultimately expand the scope of learners' opportunities to make valued contributions. Thus, those outside of similar perspectives may not readily see the relevance or importance of a learners' motivation or the expanded scope of opportunities to contribute.

We do not think that it is too much of an exaggeration to suggest that despite their extensive knowledge of the forest, European-American hunters tended to think of the forest as a "container" that housed the game animals that they were targeting. A further analogy may help: if you have misplaced your car keys and are hunting for them in your house, you are key-focused. You may look at places where they usually are left but your focus is pretty much on the keys. Of course you know a great deal about your house, what is in it, and what functions are supported by its structure and contents but this knowledge is largely irrelevant to the task at hand.

In another study, we hypothesized that people who reflected conceptions of agency that applied to MTH entities in the natural world would be more likely to engage in practices that foregrounded nature (e.g., berry picking and forest walks) and have MTHs as central actors in activity. Conversely, we predicted that people who did not hold this view of agency would engage in practices that background nature (e.g., snowmobiling and playing sports) and be less likely to have MTHs as central actors in activities (see Bang, 2009; Bang, Medin, & Atran, 2007). Rural and urban Native-American (specifically Menominee) parents and children reported engaging significantly more frequently in outdoor practices that foregrounded nature and some form of MTH life (e.g., fish, deer, etc.) was a primary contributor in the practice, while European-Americans engaged significantly more in practices that backgrounded nature and MTHs had no or very few primary interactive roles in the practice.

These results suggest to us that the scope of LOPI is magnified when cultural ecologies include MTH relatives. Inclusion of MTH relatives expands the ground within which multiple facets of LOPI are enacted. One way to interpret the above examples is to suggest that the Menominee hunters' view that a broader range of kinds are important is because they were seeing them not from their own perspective. More specifically, if the goals of learning include consideration and responsibility (facet 4 of LOPI), the Menominee hunters in this example are reflecting an assumption that this goal applies to learning to be considerate of and responsible to MTHs important roles in the community. The Menominee hunters' justifications reflected a wider scope and expectation of contribution, as reflected in the above porcupine example. We suggest that the assumption that everything has a role to play cultivates a sense of mutual reciprocity that shapes interaction and may increase a sense of responsibility and belonging beyond humans. If cultural ecologies include MTH life, there are significantly increased relations and opportunities and responsibilities to pitch in too.

4. THE ROLE OF ATTENTION TO MTH AGENCY IN ADULT–CHILD INTERACTIONS

We have found that with children that were between the ages of 4 and 8, the idea of agency of MTHs shaped adult–child interactions during Native families' walks in a forest (Bang & Marin, 2015; Marin, 2013, submitted). The families displayed distinct modes of what consideration, responsibility, and contributions meant (LOPI facet 4). For example, when one family used plantain to help sooth a scrap they made sure to offer thanks to the plant. We also found shifts in the nature of guidance (LOPI facet 5) and assessment in the form of question asking (LOPI facet 7). Parents often used questions to guide observations and assess knowledge. Likewise, children used questions to point kinds out and gather information. In addition, older children often adopted their parents form of question asking with younger siblings. Each of these facets impacted the eagerness of children and adults to continue along on their walk and contribute to the activity at hand—identifying and naming kinds, making sense of natural phenomena (e.g., river flow, erosion, etc.) and building relationships with place (LOPI facet 2). We will illustrate these with specific sections of transcript from family interactions.

The following excerpt is from a father (Seth) and his 4-year-old son, Keith, who began their forest walk with the father immediately setting a goal for them to observe or watch for turtles:

Seth (father): We got to watch for some turtles now, enit?
Keith: Mm-hmm
Seth: Hmm, What do you think? Huh. Why hmm? So they don't bite you? (pause) Come on, they won't bite you, son.
Keith: We have to watch for some turtles.
Seth: Yep. We have to get them off the road, enit? Why do we take them off the road?
Keith: Yep.
Seth: Hum? Why do we take them off the road?
Keith: Because - so cars don't run them over
Seth: Yep, so they get safely to the other side, enit?
Keith: Yep.

In setting this goal for the forest walk, the father was reinforcing a previously learned activity (moving turtles). This is an example of a way in which relational construals with MTHs can impact notions of pitching in by developing a wider scope of what and whom one should attend to, observe, and be responsible to—in this case turtles. Indeed the father extends and guides Keith's explanation from being focused on the cars' impact to the turtles' well-being and of getting to the other side. This is, a kind of perspective shift, not unlike Menominee hunters in previous studies reasoning from MTH perspectives.

Conceptions of MTH agency, specifically around communicative capacities, shifted the nature of learning, and observation in the following excerpt, involving a mom, Jackie, and her two sons, Jeremy (6.5 years old) and Samuel (4 years old). Immediately before this excerpt the family had found a dead tree and Samuel was enamored with it. He began to step toward the tree and Jeremy warned him against it because he saw "glowing eyes." Nonetheless, after several further exchanges the boys decided to investigate the dead tree.

Jeremy: We should first check with the stick. Something came out, maybe. Don't get too, that close
Samuel: Hello? Hello?
Jackie (mother): When you say that, do you think something's going to answer you? ((laughter))
Jeremy: Nothing's in there, guess I was wrong. Maybe, it just a illusion, that I was seeing.
Jackie: Some people say that like animals, they a, they'll understand, like um, if you speak in Anishinabe, so maybe you should be saying "boozhoo" [hello]
Jeremy: Boozhoo?
Jackie: Mm hm

The mother's initial reaction, a kind of guidance and assessment (LOPI facets 5 and 7), seems to reject Samuel's assumption that he could communicate with the animal in the tree, by asking whether he thought the animal could respond to him. This assessment from Jackie instantly reshaped Jeremy's motive to engage with the life form in the tree and Jeremy produced a narrative of himself that was negative in connotation marked by a decline in eagerness and even resignation that there was nothing in the tree. We see this as a narrowing of the possible forms of contributions and possible relations with MTHs but it also seems to momentarily undermine Jeremy's confidence in his own contributions. This was followed by Jackie's rapid reorientation to Samuel's assumption of MTH agency in her second utterance. This time she provided guidance to Jeremy's attempt to communicate across species. Jeremy immediately reengaged in efforts to communicate, nonverbally demonstrating a kind of "oh guess I could be right." This interaction was dynamically shaped by the orientations of human and MTH relations which may not have emerged had we not conducted this study in the context of a forest walk, evidencing the need for increased study of learning and observing across a range of places and with expanded notions of what and who constitutes community.

Increased efforts to understand dynamics of human–nature relations in all of their multiplicities and their impacts on the ways in which human learning and development unfolds may prove to be critical to developing socially and ecologically just and sustainable communities in the twenty-first century. In this chapter, we have argued that the scope and power of LOPI would increase by including focus on the forms of relations, possible agencies, and the places of practices. Both to expand LOPI and in the broader field we need to better understand practices that are not saturated in human–human interactions and indeed include the broader community.

ACKNOWLEDGMENTS

We have been involved in research partnerships with the American Indian community of Chicago and the Menominee Nation for more than 15 years. This chapter is intended to reflect what we have collectively learned and continue to work toward.

REFERENCES

Alcala, L., Rogoff, B., Mejia-Arauz, R., Coppens, A. D., & Dexter, A. L. (2014). Children's initiative in contributions to family work in indigenous-heritage and cosmopolitan communities in Mexico. *Human Development*, *57*(2–3), 96–115.

Bang, M. (2009). *Understanding students' epistemologies: Examining practice and meaning in community contexts*. Unpublished doctoral dissertation, Evanston, IL: Northwestern University.

Bang, M. (2015). Culture, learning, and development and the natural world: The influences of situative perspectives. *Educational Psychologist*, *50*(3), 220–233.

Bang, M., & Marin, A. (2015). Nature–culture constructs in science learning: Human/non-human agency and intentionality. *Journal of Research in Science Teaching, 52*(4), 530–544.
Bang, M., Medin, D., & Atran, S. (2007). Cultural mosaics and mental models of nature. *Proceedings of the National Academy of Sciences of the United States of America, 104*, 13868–13874.
Cajete, G. (2000). Indigenous knowledge: The Pueblo metaphor of Indigenous education. In M. Battiste (Ed.), *Reclaiming indigenous voice and vision* (pp. 181–191). Vancouver, BC: UBC Press.
Cardoso Jiménez, R. (2015). Learning and human dignity are built through observation and participation in work. *Advances in Child Development and Behavior, 49*, 289–301.
Coppens, A. D., Alcalá, L., Mejia-Arauz, R., & Rogoff, B. (2014). Children's initiative in family household work in Mexico. *Human Development, 57*(2–3), 116–130.
Coppens, A. D., Silva, K. G., Ruvalcaba, O., Alcalá, L., López, A., & Rogoff, B. (2014). Learning by observing and pitching in: Benefits and processes of expanding repertoires. *Human Development, 57*(2–3), 150–161.
Deloria, V. (1979). *The metaphysics of modern existence.* Harper San Francisco, Vol. 11.
Goodwin, C. (2013). The co-operative, transformative organization of human action and knowledge. *Journal of Pragmatics, 46*(1), 8–23.
Gutiérrez, K. D., & Rogoff, B. (2003). Cultural ways of learning: Individual traits or repertoires of practice. *Educational Researcher, 32*(5), 19–25.
Henrich, J., Heine, S. J., & Norenzayan, A. (2010). The weirdest people in the world? *Behavioral and Brain Sciences, 33*(2–3), 61–83.
Hirschfeld, L. A. (2002). Why don't anthropologists like children? *American Anthropologist, 104*(2), 611–627.
Ingold, T. (2011). *Being alive: Essays on movement, knowledge and description.* UK: Taylor & Francis.
Kawagley, A. O. (1995). *A Yupiaq worldview: A pathway to ecology and spirit.* Prospect Heights, IL: Waveland Press.
Latour, B. (2012). *We have never been modern.* Cambridge, MA: Harvard University Press.
Lave, J. (2011). *Apprenticeship in critical ethnographic practice.* University of Chicago Press.
Lee, C. D. (2008). The centrality of culture to the scientific study of learning and development: How an ecological framework in education research facilitates civic responsibility. *Educational Researcher, 37*(5), 267.
López, A., Ruvalcaba, O., & Rogoff, B. (2014). Attentive helping as a cultural practice of Mexican-heritage families. In *Mexican American children and families: Multidisciplinary perspectives* (p. 76). UK: Taylor & Francis.
Marin, A. (submitted). Ambulatory Turns: Ecologies of Attention, Mobility, Land, and Learning. Mind, Culture, and Activity.
Marin, A. M. (2013). *Learning to attend and observe: Parent-child meaning making in the natural world.* Doctoral dissertation, Northwestern University.
Medin, D. L., & Bang, M. (2014). *Who's asking?: Native science, western science, and science education.* Cambridge: MIT Press.
Medin, D. L., Ojalehto, B., Marin, A., & Bang, M. (2014). Culture and epistemologies: Putting culture back into the ecosystem. *Advances in Culture and Psychology, 4*, 177–217.
Nasir, N., Rosebery, A. S., Warren, B., & Lee, C. D. (2006). Learning as a cultural process: Achieving equity through diversity. In K. Sawyer (Ed.), *The Cambridge handbook of the learning sciences* (pp. 489–504). Cambridge, UK: Cambridge University Press.
Ojalehto, B., & Medin, D. (2015). An ecological perspective on culture and concepts. *Annual Review of Psychology, 66*(1), 249–275.
Ojalehto, B., Waxman, S. R., & Medin, D. L. (2013). Teleological reasoning about nature: Intentional design or relational perspectives? *Trends in Cognitive Sciences, 17*, 166–171.
Paradise, R., Mejia-Arauz, R., Silva, K. G., Dexter, A. L., & Rogoff, B. (2014). One, two, three, eyes on me! adults attempting control versus guiding in support of initiative. *Human Development, 57*(2–3), 131–149.

Remorini, C. (2015). Learning to inhabit the forest: Autonomy and interdependence of lives from a Mbya-Guarani perspective. *Advances in Child Development and Behavior, 49*, 273–288.

Rogoff, B. (2003). *The cultural nature of human development*. Oxford University Press.

Rogoff, B. (2014). Learning by observing and pitching in to family and community endeavors: An orientation. *Human Development, 57*(2–3), 69–81.

Rogoff, B., Paradise, R., Arauz, R. M., Correa-Chávez, M., & Angelillo, C. (2003). First-hand learning through intent participation. *Annual review of psychology, 54*(1), 175–203.

Rogoff, B., Najafi, B., & Mejia-Arauz, R. (2014). Constellations of cultural practices across generations: Indigenous American heritage and learning by observing and pitching in. *Human Development, 57*(2–3), 82–95.

Ross, N., Medin, D., & Cox, D. (2007). Epistemological models and culture conflict: Menominee and euro-american hunters in wisconsin. *Ethos, 35*(4), 478–515.

Vossoughi, S., & Gutiérrez, K. (2014). Toward a multi-sited ethnographic sensibility. In J. Vadeboncoeur (Ed.), *NSEE yearbook*. New York: Teachers College Press.

CHAPTER FIFTEEN

Using History to Analyze the *Learning by Observing and Pitching In* Practices of Contemporary Mesoamerican Societies

Rubén Flores*[,1], Luis Urrieta Jr.[†], Marie-Noëlle Chamoux[‡], David Lorente Fernández[§], Angélica López[¶]

*Department of American Studies, The University of Kansas, Lawrence, Kansas
[†]Department of Curriculum & Instruction, Cultural Studies in Education Program, University of Texas at Austin, Austin, Texas, USA
[‡]Centre National de la Recherche Scientifique and CERMA-Mondes américains (UMR 8168), École des Hautes Études en Sciences Sociales, 190 Avenue de France, 75013 Paris, France
[§]National Institute of Anthropology and History of Mexico
[¶]Psychology Department, University of California, Santa Cruz and Marymount California University
[1]Corresponding author: e-mail address: flores@ku.edu

Contents

Abstract

The analysis of Indigenous learning practices in Mexico and the United States typically relies on ethnography, oral history, and participant observation as the methodology for understanding the socialization processes of Mesoamerican societies. In this chapter, we consider the importance of using historical analysis as an added methodology for understanding the Indigenous learning practices by considering three case studies of Indigenous communities in Mexico, where a consideration of historical patterns have proven fruitful for understanding the contemporary Learning by Observing and Pitching In (LOPI) practices. These communities include the Nahua people of the state of Puebla, the P'urhépecha communities of the state of Michoacán, and the Nahua people of the Texcoco area to the southeast of Mexico City. We conclude that a consideration of the

Advances in Child Development and Behavior, Volume 49
ISSN 0065-2407
http://dx.doi.org/10.1016/bs.acdb.2015.09.005

cultural patterns that have developed in Mesoamerican societies across time would benefit contemporary researchers as one component of their LOPI research.

1. INTRODUCTION

Contemporary conceptual interpretations that shape our understanding of Indigenous learning practices in the United States and Mexico can be vitally informed by historical knowledge. Indeed, historical analysis complements our understanding of cultures as historically produced repertoires of practices that endure and/or change for communities over time, as Gutiérrez and Rogoff (2003) have written. And if Indigenous-heritage cultures are dynamic mixtures of enduring, changing, and/or innovative repertoires of practices that emerge out of specific social–historical contexts for participating in family and community life, then the turn to history can help us to understand the participatory characteristics of Indigenous cultural practices and the connection of those practices to particular places of origin (Rockwell & Gomes, 2009). History can help us to understand how Indigenous people and cultures, simultaneously ancient and modern, preserve ways of knowing, while negotiating and creatively adapting to changing social and material conditions (Bonfil Batalla, 1987).

This chapter uses findings based in historical analysis to think about the "historicity of the present" (Rockwell, 1999) in the relationship of Indigenous learning practices over time to contemporary learning practices in Latin American cultural communities, whether those are found in the United States or Mexico. This collaborative work emerged from a workshop organized in Austin, Texas in February 2011 that was designed to examine the historical basis of practices from the Indigenous communities of preconquest Mexico and Central America, hereafter referred to as Mesoamerica, that have to do with learning in the manner of *Learning by Observing and Pitching In* (LOPI).[1] Such practices included collective collaboration, inclusion, and contributions of children in family and community activities, the role of work in giving a person dignity and being "gente" (persons), the importance of reciprocity, the role of individual autonomy, the use of keen attention, nonverbal communication, silence, being calm, *respeto* (respect), being *acomedida/o* (helpful without being asked for help) and sensitivity to what is expected and needed, and the role of narrative and distinct rhythms of communication.

[1] In addition to the authors, the workshop participants included Barbara Rogoff of the University of California, Santa Cruz and Édgar Martínez Pérez of Universidad Autónoma de Chiapas.

This chapter focuses on understanding the past as an integral component of contemporaneous social practices: To what extent are we confident that the historical record supports the idea that these cultural practices have been characteristic of Indigenous communities over extended periods of time? What is the evidence for this? Is there evidence of the unique use of these cultural practices in Indigenous communities, or does the evidence indicate blending with practices of other cultural communities over time? How so? Do Indigenous practices identified as *LOPI* continue to be vibrant, have they been adapted, or have they been forgotten across multiple generations in the history of Mesoamerica? The aim is to bring the historicity of these LOPI practices to the attention of an audience that is generally unfamiliar with the history of Indigenous Mexico and Central America.

The resort to history as a means of understanding social practices in contemporary communities poses inherent risks, including a misreading of unique cultural structures, a mismatch between the ethical priorities of the community and those of the researchers, and an analytical lens that is narrower than the more complex social fabric of the communities in question. But three reasons persuaded us to move in the direction of recognizing the possible distinctive contributions that the extended past has made to contemporary Indigenous-descent learning practices in the United States and Mexico. First, the distinctive patterns of labor and education practice reflected in Mexico-descended communities in both the United States and Mexico have been increasingly noted by scholars in various disciplines. As such, researchers must be open to the full range of possibilities, both spatial and chronological, from which these practices may have originated.

Second, to the extent that distinctive social practices are considered organic by the distinct communities themselves, understanding the full complexity of such practices may aid educators and psychologists to adapt normative school practices to social practices that are considered integral in such communities. Such a concern would be less important if school performance for Latino youth was not a pressing concern for educators in the contemporary United States. But given differential rates of school performance, social scientists must ask broad new questions about the origins of social practices within social communities whose presence will continue to pose major challenges for school systems that were designed for European-heritage populations more than a century ago. Finally, we also believe that recognizing the possible distinct contributions of Indigenous societies to contemporary learning practices helps us in one of the central goals of modern educational practice: the challenge of intercultural dialog. Sensitive educational practice demands that we be porous to the distinctive contributions, historical and contemporary, made by the variety of social groups around which contemporary modern society in Mexico and the United States is organized.

Our analysis is organized in four parts. We first examine the theoretical dimensions of *LOPI*, seeking to articulate its particular presence in the Indigenous social structures of Mexico and Central America. Next we present three case studies from our converging work on LOPI practices, one each from the Mexican states of Michoacán and Puebla, and one from Mexico City. Third, we synthesize the common features of our cases in order to suggest the importance of using history to understand the continuing relevance of LOPI practices to scholars today. Last, we close by observing that earlier generations of social scientists were attuned to LOPI practices in Mesoamerican societies and created a rich body of work that can be profitably used by contemporary researchers.

2. INDIGENOUS KNOWLEDGE SYSTEMS AND *LOPI*

The role of past experience in shaping those social practices related to processes of *LOPI* can be better understood by developing a narrative about their historical continuity across generations in Indigenous Knowledge Systems. Rogoff, Paradise, Arauz, Correa-Chávez, and Angelillo (2003), Rogoff et al. (2007), Rogoff, Alcalá, et al. (2014), Rogoff, Najafi, and Mejía-Arauz (2014), and López, Najafi, Rogoff, and Mejía-Arauz (2012) define *LOPI* (formerly known as *intent community participation*) as a form of learning that takes place with initiative and access to abundant community activities alongside more experienced and supportive peers and adults. Such a learning tradition appears to be especially common in Indigenous-heritage and Mexican-heritage communities where formal schooling has not been historically prevalent. *LOPI* activities tend not to be a collection of separate, step-by-step behaviors, as in more formalized schooling instruction models (Rogoff, Alcalá, et al., 2014; Rogoff, Najafi, et al., 2014; Rogoff et al., 2003), but organic, coordinated practices, including assessments, that encourage children's contributions during mutual endeavors while maintaining a high degree of acceptance of children's efforts. Through these collective practices, "... children participate in the same activities of the everyday life of the community as do adults, contributing in real ways as they learn about their shared economic and social reality" (Paradise & Rogoff, 2009, p. 106). LOPI represents a constellation of social features in which specific practices relate to each other and cannot be isolated without destroying the coherence of culture (Rogoff, Najafi, & Mejía-Arauz, 2012). Without adhering to romantic perceptions of cultures as coherent wholes (Rosaldo, 1988), we do maintain that cultural processes "hang together" in patterned constellations that endure, change and are innovated across history (Rogoff, Pérez González, Chavajay Quiacaín, & Chavajay Quiacaín, 2011).

Indigenous knowledge includes a broad array of knowings that are often particular to local communities and rooted in history yet which encompass a wide range of specific practices, relationships, and cognitive understandings. Such knowledge(s) can be as broad and abstract as learning what it means to be a member of a community through the notion of respect or by participating in *el trueque* (bartering) alongside neighboring communities, or as specific as learning how to count, seriate, or to predict the weather. Knowings within Indigenous knowledge also encompass larger and broader understandings about the world and how to survive in it (Barnhardt & Kawagley, 2005). Battiste (2002) defines Indigenous knowledge as "... an adaptable, dynamic system, based on skills, abilities, and problem-solving techniques that change over time depending on environmental conditions ... (p. 11)." Battiste's definition of Indigenous knowledge not only includes an abundance of skill sets, but also a larger, organic breadth of "competency" (Barnhardt & Kawagley, 2005) that includes both ways of knowing and ways of being in the world, such as being *acomedida/o*, a concept studied by Angélica López and colleagues, and defined as:

> *... attentive helping without being asked. This cultural value system may encourage children's voluntary, spontaneous assistance to others in family and community work [that appears to be widespread in Indigenous communities of the Americas]...*
>
> **López, Ruvalcaba, and Rogoff (2015, p. 76).**

Indigenous contemporary practices, like being *acomedida/o*, as described above, are acquired as life-long processes and as a responsibility that model competent and respectful behavior in community life (Battiste, 2002).

Within these knowledge structures of Indigenous-heritage communities, learning (*aprender* in Spanish) literally means "to apprehend" or "to catch" and is an active form of comprehension. Indigenous contemporary community practices like the *trueque*, the *cargo*, or the *tequio* (all forms of community-wide collaborations), respectful behavior, and being *acomedida/*o are acquired through participation, often with minimal intervention and direct instruction. They are, in other words, a type of learning that takes place by "seeing and doing" (Battiste, 2002).

LOPI, or "side-by-side" learning (Paradise & Rogoff, 2009), seems to be more prevalent in societies in which children are integrated in the range of everyday adult community life (Peele-Eady, 2011; Rogoff, Alcalá, et al., 2014; Rogoff et al., 2007, 2003; Rogoff, Najafi, et al., 2014). While aspects of LOPI have been observed in various contexts (Rogoff et al., 2003, 2007), especially in Indigenous communities around the world (Paradise & Rogoff, 2009), these should be recognized as "indicative and not definitive" of the way Indigenous-heritage people organize learning (Barnhardt & Kawagley, 2005, p. 10). Indigenous-heritage communities can organize learning in multiple ways. For example, Chavajay (2006) found that Maya mothers in Guatemala with more years of formal schooling used more school-like ways of interacting with their children, such as asking children more recall questions and offering more verbal explanations of activities being carried out. Such school-like practices can also coexist with LOPI in the same community.

However, the research also shows that observation, listening-in, and participation with initiative are important in first-hand learning through LOPI (Rogoff et al., 2003). Children's observations of adult activities have often been characterized as keen, long, and often involving intense concentration, qualities that are thought to include active cognition, social, and emotional participation (López, Correa-Chávez, Rogoff, & Gutiérrez, 2010). Children are usually not segregated into children's activities or children's spaces and are expected to take initiative and responsibility in their participation in community life (Bolin, 2006; Rogoff et al., 2003).

LOPI has been observed to be common in a number of contemporary American Indigenous communities, especially in families with limited years of formal schooling (Bolin, 2006; Chavajay, 2006; Chavajay & Rogoff, 2002; Correa-Chávez & Rogoff, 2009; Gaskins, 2000; Paradise & de Haan, 2013; Urrieta, 2013). Although some learning through LOPI exists in everyday life in all societies, acquired and expected knowings in Indigenous communities form part of the common funds of knowledge (Moll et al., 1992) and cultural wealth (Yosso, 2005) that Latina/o Indigenous children bring to the context of the U.S. schools. Lamentably, the organization of teaching and learning in schools generally does not acknowledge such Indigenous *saberes* (knowings), nor does it recognize the teaching and learning practices that are most familiar to Indigenous students, their families, and communities (Brayboy & Maughan, 2009).

Paradise (1994) with Mazahua children in Mexico illustrates important aspects of the learning practices of Indigenous family and community-based learning. Paradise and de Haan (2009) found that in the Mazahua adult–child and child–child interactions they observed at a local market in Mexico City, "… adults do not explicitly organize learning activities or attempt to teach their children in the Western sense; it is generally assumed that children are capable of taking initiative and of gradually learning by themselves to take on adult roles" (p. 197). Although keen observation and pitching in as forms of participation might be interpreted as an unorganized and *laissez-faire* way of learning from a formal schooling perspective, to the Mazahua mothers observed, it was a valuable form of tacit collaboration in which learning occurred through daily interaction (Paradise, 1994). Nonverbal behavior and judicious use of speech were also observed while teaching and learning activities occurred in other Indigenous communities (Lancy, 2008). Similar approaches to teaching and learning have been observed in other Indigenous communities of the Americas, including those located in the Andes of Peru (Bolin, 2006) and in the Western United States (Brayboy & Maughan, 2009). Martínez Pérez (unpublished manuscript, 2011) has suggested based on ongoing work in Chiapas, for example, that children contribute to their community by participating, listening, and observing. Their contribution is made merely by being there and learning the necessary cultural signs that assure the survival of the community.

LOPI and Indigenous learning pedagogies are a broad base for organizing learning. According to Battiste (2002), "Indigenous pedagogy values a person's ability to learn independently by observing, listening, participating with a minimum of intervention and instruction" (p. 11). Indigenous pedagogy and the basic form of LOPI are dynamic and experiential, and view Indigenous knowledges and competencies as living processes to be absorbed and understood by community members (Battiste, 2002; Brayboy & Maughan, 2009). In contrast to behaviorist learning models, these teaching and learning pedagogies are broader in scope, since the general flexibility of these approaches allow every child to explore his/her own unique capacities, learning styles, pace of learning, and knowledge bases (Battiste, 2002) in the process of acquiring family and community knowing(s). By contrast, in Western-style schooling age gradation has become connected to curricula often thought to be developmentally appropriate according to age and grade levels. Students are often restricted in their access to more advanced curricula, or older peers, unless they can show competency in the different gradations. Emphasis is often placed on the steps of the process rather than on the comprehensive outcomes of the process.

But where did the emphasis on *collective collaboration* come from? Below, we have addressed the role of *cuatequitl* in Aztec community shared work, the history of the *cofradía* system in Mesoamerica, and the emphasis on reciprocity in the *compadrazco* system. Our analysis is intended to be a sketch for nonhistorians, based on what we know of the history of Mexico's regions. We are guided by sensitivity to interdisciplinary and intercultural subjectivity, recognizing that openness in our approach had to be a fundamental axiom of our inquiry. We feel it important to identify the institutional structures in which people operated, whether those were rural or urban, metropolitan or provincial, and informal rather than formal. And our temporal focus includes all epochs, including recent years and distant moments in the past.

3. HISTORICAL CONTINUITY AND *LOPI*

Recent work on LOPI has reaffirmed long-standing observations in Mesoamerican scholarship of evidence for the historical continuity of communal norms that may reach as far back as the sixteenth century (Lorente Fernández, 2012; Paradise & de Haan, 2009). Our chapter provides analysis based on our own converging research projects. Some instructive examples of *collective collaboration* include: first, the concept of communal work among the Nahua people of the mountains of Puebla, 80 miles to the northeast of Mexico City. A second is the *trueque* system of communal exchange among the P'urhépecha-descended communities who live in the central Mexican state of Michoacán. A third example includes the notions of *respeto* (mutual respect) among the Nahua people of the Texcoco region to the east of Mexico City that exist parallel to competing norms conventionally taught in the public school.

In each of these cases, socialization practices that emphasize communal collaboration take place outside of the institutional structures generally associated with the public school (Lorente Fernández, 2012). These practices manifest community values that stand in stark contrast to pedagogical practices associated with a majority of non-Indigenous groups in contemporary Mexican society. In each of these cases, furthermore, the evidence is strong that communal practices may date from before the Spanish Conquest.

3.1 Communal Labor

Among the Nahua people of Puebla, Marie-Noelle Chamoux has noted the importance of concepts of work to the formation of ideas of civic participation in the community that are of long-standing duration. Commonly understood through the terms *cargo* and *tequio*, these norms revolve around the relationship of communal labor to civic and theological balance in the social structure and reside outside of contemporary notions of civic participation cultivated by the local public schools. Among the Nahua, communal labor represents a particular contribution to the general cosmological conception of the proper functioning of the universe. Such labor is divided into a differential series of contributions in which each person or entity—human beings, natural beings, and gods—fulfills his or her obligations according to skill, gender, rank, or class (Chamoux, 1986).

The *cargo* system is a basic supporting mechanism of the government structure of local community that can be conceptualized as an administrative unit that operates with great autonomy. It circumscribes both civil and religious hierarchies and it involves shared communal work among community members and their related community associations, including the *cofradías* and *danzas* (Chamoux, 1986). While the actual *cargo* system is of Spanish heritage, it presents a distinctive "style" in Mesoamerican societies. Therefore, the *cargo* system manifests characteristics that reflect features whose ideological origins can be attributed to prehispanic society.

For example, religious beliefs, ceremonies, and rituals that date to precolonial Mexico are still invoked when the communal authorities perform public works projects. When a local mayor recently succeeded in persuading community members to accept a new tax in order to establish public water service to his community, he used his authority by underscoring his reputation for having a special pact with the Aztec gods of water.

In general, these prehispanic ideologies that are manifested in contemporary social practices link community welfare, prosperity, and health to religious and spiritual rituals and not merely to temporal political decisions by the community authorities. Often, burdensome organization of *fiestas*, offerings and ceremonies, sacrifices, ritual meals, and receptions accompany the responsibilities manifested in the *cargo* system. The Nahuas of Puebla call these costs *tequitl* and consider them to be a sort of tax. Despite these burdens, however, Nahuas believe that authorities who do not achieve their *tequitl* are guilty of a lack of "respect" (*mahuitzotl*). The failure to achieve the *tequitl* could result in plagues whose effects would harm the citizens of the entire community, as punishment for the failure to fulfill one's tribute to the community and to the proper functioning of the world.

A *cargo* generally concerns male members of the community but its sacred dimensions involve all members of their households and remain easily within view of the children. Familiarization with the *cargo* system occurs when fathers are asked to fulfill a required responsibility. (In general, single men accomplish *cargos* only of very low office within the community.) Mothers are active, as well, generally as participants in the many rituals and ceremonies related with the office and as coordinators of guest receptions that may include preparing food and beverages, buying flowers and incense, and serving guests. Such service may vary according to the feasts and regions. In general, all adults and adolescents of the household are tasked with assisting in such preparations. Children, meanwhile, watch the ritual aspects of those *cargo* responsibilities that take place within the home. Thus, while the importance of the *cargo* system as a way of serving the local community is clear, future participation by younger generations is achieved through the implicit messages conveyed by observation and participation, representing local forms of *LOPI* (Chamoux, 1986). Such participation is considered natural to the child and even underscored with an injunction frequently presented to them by their parents: "Así es el mundo" (*This is how the world is*).

The concept of shared community work manifested in the form of a labor tribute is related to the concept of the *cargo* but functions in a different way. Known through use of the terms *tequio* and *cuatequitl*—two terms that derive from the word *tequitl* and are often equivalent in day-to-day practice—the labor tribute is considered a strong duty required of all men in the community. *Tequio*, also known with the more mainstream term "faena," often involve service or work for community projects such as constructing roads, public service projects, or the introduction of new services such as formal education, potable water, and clinics (Warman, 2003). The labor tribute is not an exclusively Mesoamerican institution, but it does have a particular history that is unique to the communities in question.

In the distant past, the labor tribute served two functions. First, it was used as a vertical labor tribute by the Nahua peoples that benefited the supra-local entities or ruling classes of the society. These included the state, temples, priests, and Indian or Spanish lords. Second, it was a horizontal labor tribute that benefited the local community in general. In the Aztec and colonial periods, for example, it functioned in the service of public works. In contemporary Nahua communities, meanwhile, the labor tribute can occasionally still function vertically in the service of supra-local political bodies, but more generally it is confined horizontally to achieve social benefits for the immediate community. It is a testament to the staying power of the labor tribute in the Nahua communities that the Mexican central state used shared communal work throughout the twentieth century to build roads and schools and to develop electrification, and that community members who migrate to the United States for work send back contributions in the form of money to support public works projects.

Both the *tequio* and the *cuatequitl* labor tributes are obligatory, enforceable by coercion or sanctions that include fines or imprisonment. Only children, seniors, the sick, those males who are serving in communal office (whether high or low), and ritual specialists who perform communal ceremonies are exempt. At times, a male may be authorized to substitute another to take his place, usually by sending a family member or an unrelated paid laborer. Worktime is usually without pay, but community officials frequently offer drinks to those who are performing the labor tribute, usually after the work has been terminated at the end of the day. On other occasions, officials sometimes offer partial payment that originates from public subsidies.

In the context of Latin America, the labor tribute has often been idealized as a consensual institution with roots in "primitive" collectivism or celebrated as a surviving characteristic of "authentic" Indian communities. In reality, however, the labor draft is not always consensual. Coercion that results in a forced labor tribute may result from internal political decisions within the community, by dictate of external authority, or when the community balks that the benefit is not truly public. Abuses of the labor tribute are also not uncommon. Historical and contemporary archives are filled with reports denouncing excessive demands for the *tequio* or *cuatequitl*, "unjust" uses of the labor draft, and locations for the performance of work that are outside of authorized sites.

The result of the complicated place of the labor tribute in Nahua society is the socialization of community youth into a communal system of work that is expected in support of the public welfare. At the same time, the youth are quick to notice the inherent tensions generated by a system of community labor. Familiarity with the kinds of conflicts that may arise from the community labor tribute is, in fact, part of the process of becoming a citizen of the community.

3.2 Trueque, a Community System of Reciprocal Exchange

A second example of contemporary *LOPI* processes that emphasizes communal collaboration and has historical roots in the past involve the *trueque* of the P'urhépecha-descended peoples who live in the central Mexican state of Michoacán. Therefore, the cultural ethnographer Luis Urrieta has documented a community system of exchange that socializes individual members into P'urhépecha ethnic affiliations by virtue of the obligations that it confers on members of the extended community (Urrieta, 2011).

The *trueque* is a practice that has been documented as being uniquely Indigenous throughout all of the Americas (Humphry, 1985). It is practiced across distinctive local communities that reside within a given geographic area rather than exclusively, within any one community. By definition, it involves the interchange of products that are of similar value without the intermediary use of money. According to Hugh-Jones (2005)

> *... the trueque takes place between parties of relative equal standing, in which each side enjoys an equal part of the exchange ...*

At the same time, a certain form of respect exists in the *trueque* between the participating communities that is based on the equality that they mutually recognize with one another. This mutual equality is conducive to a level of confidence among the participants that they will not be exploited or robbed by others during the exchange, since participants trade among others considered as equals.

In general, each community brings to the *trueque* the unique products that it produces and that thus distinguishes it from other communities around it. In the region known as the Lacustre P'urhépecha, these specialized products predate the arrival of the Spanish, although their use was partially redefined by the *pueblos-hospitales* (subsequently known as the *repúblicas de indios*) that were organized by the Franciscans according to the utopian vision of Don Vasco de Quiroga. The community of San Miguel Nocutzepo is known for its cultivation of maize, beans, squash, wheat, lentils, and firewood, while the community of Jarácuaro is known for its production of hats and brooms. The community of Arócutin, meanwhile, is known for its production of reed mats and hand fans, both of which are made of tule and *chuspata*, while the community of San Pedro Pareo and Huecorio are known for growing vegetables-like *jitomate*, onion, cilantro, and cabbage. Santa Fe de la Laguna produces pottery goods and Cuanajo produces wooden utensils and small furniture. Once reunited in a single location, participants in the *trueque* from these communities exchange their goods for others from neighboring communities. They negotiate the terms of a fair and oftentimes generous exchange, even as the reunion itself functions to reaffirm the shared community identities of the communities in question. In this manner, the "ethnic boundaries that one or more of the parties claims by virtue of the goods it produces" (Hugh-Jones, 2005) are simultaneously reaffirmed within the *trueque*.

It is in view of the *pueblo*-affirming function of the exchange that the *trueque* becomes an interethnic space, even as it functions as an activity of exchange, reciprocity, and shared understanding. In the *trueque*, communities celebrate their commonalities as P'urhépecha people while simultaneously marking out the pseudoethnic identifications that they maintain across their respective *pueblos*. In an interview by Luis Urrieta that took place in the community of San Miguel Nocutzepo (March, 2010), the organizer of the *trueque*, Don Chente (pseudonym), commented as follows:

> *This (the trueque) is an ancient practice. Since before the Spaniards, this has been the manner in which our communities have sustained themselves, without the use of money, solely based on the concept of exchange. This latest version of the trueque that you see here began anew some 16 years ago. It now moves from community to community, so that each place gets the things that it needs and so that each community can distribute the goods that it produces. When the trueque arrives at a particular community, it is a great favor to the people there who cannot leave their homes. It is also an opportunity to enjoy one another's company. It is a celebration.*

Just as Don Chente indicated, the *trueque* serves a variety of social and cultural functions, not merely an economic one. A social encounter takes place among the communities that are each distinctive in their own ways and sometimes distant from one another, yet in a manner that allows them to recognize their similarities and relation to one another. Although Nocutzepo is a community where P'urhépecha is no longer spoken and has not been spoken as a primary language for more than 150 years, P'urhépecha has regained importance in the community through the creation of a bilingual P'urhépecha/Spanish elementary school in 2005. Most people in Nocutzepo do not identify themselves as P'urhépechas, in large part because they do not speak the P'urhépecha language. Don Chente commented also on this matter:

> *I believe this [Nocutzepo] is a community where many cultural practices have been lost. This [trueque] is a way to renew those practices once again. Like I told you, it is an ancestral practice, what we have done here, and more than anything it is the shared celebrations of community that have been reestablished.*

Here, Don Chente, who identifies himself as a Cuanajo P'urhépecha, and who speaks the language, underscores his view that Nocutzepo has not ceased to be a P'urhépecha pueblo, even if it may have "lost," in his view, many of its former cultural practices. If we follow Don Chente's logic—and by extension, pay attention to the function of the *trueque* that took place that day (March 21, 2010) in Nocutzepo—the space of exchange was also an Indigenous space, by virtue of the fact that it fostered the re/creation of things P'urhépecha within the community.

3.3 Respeto and Reciprocity

A third example of LOPI practices of communal collaboration rooted in the remote past comes from the Nahua communities of the Lake Texcoco region to the east of Mexico City that have been the subject of work by anthropologist David Lorente Fernández. Lorente Fernández has argued that the meaning of *respeto* (respect) has a deep relationship to notions of reciprocity within the cultural structure of the Nahua peoples of central Mexico (Lorente Fernández, 2012).

In the communities of the Sierra de Texcoco, a Spanish-descended or mestizo concept of respect operates as a hegemonic value that is transmitted within the institution of the public school. This form of respect is rooted in hierarchical differences in day-to-day relations and is principally based on the obedience and deference due to gender and age. At the same time, however, there appears within the domestic space of these communities an alternative form of respect that is completely different from the mestizo concept alluded to above. This different practice may be said to reside in the willingness of the individual to establish social interchange and to perform actions that can be returned reciprocally by others.

Inhabitants of this area occasionally refer to this alternative form of respect through the náhuatl term *ica tla'sotla*, which is defined as the intent to establish harmonious relations with others, whether they can be represented by individual human beings, the family, the community, the gods, or other supernatural entities. In this alternative value system, *respeto* implies that the individual intends to establish relationships and perform actions that others can in turn reciprocate, in order to foster a process of relationship formation that lasts over time. To be "respectful," in this sense, is for the individual to orient himself in relation to those around him in a manner that allows him to form a series of increasingly larger concentric social units around him that are inclusive rather than exclusive. To be "respectful," furthermore, implies that the individual has been converted into a person—into a fully mature human being who has earned the status of community member. *Respeto* permits the formation of larger social units comprised of other individuals, who, as persons themselves, allow the individual to establish lasting relationships of interdependence (Lorente Fernández, 2012).

Many organizing features of Nahua community social life revolve around this principle of *respeto*. These include the family structure, the structure of communal affiliation (through such institutions as the *fiestas* and *mayordomías*), and regional affiliations that are cemented reciprocally when local communities interact during ceremonies honoring the religious saints.

Ultimately, the end goal of this structure of relationships is to convert the individual into a Nahua "person" representing a fundamental moral value into which the community socializes its children. For this reason, *respeto* among the Nahuas is considered to be a moral value onto itself that can be transmitted to others, but also a manner of measuring the extent to which other important lessons have been successfully learned by children in the community.

Children are taught to be respectful by participating in collective activities and through the repetition of stories that manifest the desired moral values. In collective activities, close relatives show children that it is important to share their activities with the larger group and to willingly offer their assistance with household work regardless of whether they are directly asked to contribute. Such work can be minor help with household maintenance, for example, or other child-guided activities that require the assistance of their parents or other adults in the household. A child who willingly helps and participates alongside the group is understood to be creating reciprocal relationships with others around him. For this reason, the child is understood to be "respectful." *Respeto*, then, is inculcated through the performance of labor within the context of family and community activities that take place in the conduct of daily social life (Lorente Fernández, 2012). A gender division of activity does exist, with girls being socialized to help with upkeep of the home and other domestic duties while boys are socialized into agricultural labor, work in the community arbors and forests, and care of domestic animals. Because children are expected to participate in both family activities by helping parents and relatives with work around the home and in community activities by participating in social activities outside of the immediate family, these Nahua children are socialized into an idea of *respeto* that reflects our understanding of LOPI practices.

Respeto is also inculcated through the repetition of stories within the context of the home environment, at moments of intimate adult–child interaction (with parents, grandparents, uncles, neighbors) during the day. For example, stories about domestic life or supernatural beings (the *ahuaques* who are the guardians of water and who are said to reside in the natural springs surrounding the community, for example) often include a moral tale about the importance of *respeto*. These stories are designed to show that the transgression of community norms or imbalance in the normal order of things should be corrected to the normal order through repair for the damage that may have ensued. This is usually done through ceremonial offerings. The idea of restitution, and of avoiding punishment or supernatural sanction by returning the order of things to an original position, implicitly carries the Nahua notion of *respeto* with it. And although stories may speak primarily about the *ahuaques* or other supernatural entities, children logically infer that the cultural logic of *respeto* extends to other ordinary dimensions of social life. In this manner, *respeto* becomes a value that is considered fundamental to the proper order of the cosmos (Lorente Fernández, 2006, 2012).

The concept of *respeto* also plays a fundamental role in the development of the child into a citizen of the community. *Respeto* is central for socializing the child into family and community events upon which the circulation of family possessions and gifts depends. In such a system, to have a large measure of *respeto* implies that one has the requisite measure of humanity required to live in community. By contrast, the absence of *respeto* suggests closer affiliation to the world of the animals rather than to the world of people.

This idea of *respeto* in Mesoamerica takes place only in the context of concrete relationships and social activities, and as immediate reminders that serve as guides to the proper completion of the activity taking place. It constitutes a central component in the cultural identity and social life of Indigenous-heritage communities. And as Marie-Noelle Chamoux notes below, its reflection in historical sources, such as the Nahua codices, indicates that it has maintained noteworthy historical continuity over an extended period of time, from the pre-Columbian era to the present day.

4. HISTORY AS A TOOL IN THE ANALYSIS OF INDIGENOUS-HERITAGE COMMUNITIES

The evidence is strong for the deep historical roots of the *LOPI* processes described above, and, as a consequence, for the contributions that an analysis of the distant past can make to our understanding of contemporary cultural practices in specific Mexico-descended communities in Mexico and the United States.

In the case of Chamoux's study of Puebla, for example, it is important to note the deep historical roots of those labor structures among the Nahua that she has described for the *cargo* and *tequitl* systems. The terms *tequitl* and *coatequitl*, for example, were already in use as early as the sixteenth century, the former denoting "tribute" or "the object produced by work," the latter denoting a "public work or one that otherwise belongs to the community" (Molina, 1970). The Spanish term *tequio* is a derivative form of the original náhuatl term *tequiyotl*, which was defined to be a "contribution" or "tax contribution." These signifiers exist in all of Mesoamerica, whether in the form of Nahuatl terminology or other Indigenous languages.

The work of Parodi similarly has underscored the *cuatequitl* as a prevailing feature of the Aztec social structure in the sixteenth century:

> *(F)rom the second half of the sixteenth century until the first third of the seventeenth century ... Indigenous workers were expected to participate periodically in the cuatéquitl, for limited periods of time, receiving in turn for their work some form of remuneration that had been previously established by public authority. All Indigenous men, with the exception of nobles, seniors, the sick, and children, were obligated to lend their labor to the cuatéquitl system. The precursors of the forced labor tribute are to be found, meanwhile, in the precolonial period. During the government of Nezahualcóyotl, the maceguales were obligated to cultivate the lands of the community, and to repair and to erect the buildings of the community, although each calpulli performed his own particular specialty.*
>
> ***Parodi (1978, p. 57).***

We should like to point out Chamoux's observation that religious beliefs and rituals that date to precolonial society are still invoked today by community authorities on the occasion of public works projects. Chamoux presents the specific case of a recent mayor who was presumed to have made a special pact with the gods of water, the result of which was the conveyance of water to his community. As Chamoux argues, such an example manifests characteristics reflective of features whose origins can be attributed to prehispanic society now more than 500 years distant. Moreover, the practice continues to reinforce the social ethic of serving the community rather than simply oneself, by asking all adults and adolescents to assist even as children learn by observing the ritual aspects of the *cargo* system.

Urrieta's work, meanwhile, presents us the case of processes in community participation that had declined in use over the last century, but then were reestablished in 1994 as a response to NAFTA, as contemporary Indigenous practices among the P'urhépecha-descended communities of Michoacán. In the process of conducting ethnographic fieldwork on the idea of the *trueque*, Urrieta documented the authority of Don Chente, the contemporary organizer of the bimonthly exchange system known as *trueque P'urhépecha* in the region. Don Chente lamented the erosion of cultural practices in the Lacustre P'urhépecha that once had been common among the P'urhépecha peoples of the Lake Pátzcuaro region, arguing that Nocutzepo "is a community where many cultural practices have been lost." Notwithstanding the loss of cultural practices in Nocutzepo, however, Don Chente affirmed the return of the *trueque P'urhépecha* as a return to an ancient practice that had once been more common within the communities in question.

That cultural forms once practiced in the region of Urrieta's work remain ingrained not merely in local memory but in actual local practice are underscored by the effective practice of the *trueque* today among women in the city of Pátzcuaro. There, an exchange system referred to as *el cambio* (the exchange) takes place each Tuesday and Friday morning in a small hidden plaza located near one of the city's downtown churches (often called templos) that draws in women from many surrounding *pueblos*. No money is exchanged, just local goods and products, as in the *trueque P'urhépecha* observed in Nocutzepo. While many of the women of Nocutzepo claimed to no longer know the original protocols of the *trueque P'urhépecha* system, which rotates from *pueblo* to *pueblo* every 2 weeks, the Pátzcuaro *cambio* remains a way of exchange that many of the women of Nocutzepo participate in every week.

This example shows us that although the *trueque P'urhépecha* is often interpreted today as an activity that only Indigenous people participate in, it does not follow that others in *mestizo* or neighboring communities are distant in their practices from processes whose historical roots lie within Indigenous communities (recall that most people in Nocutzepo do not identify as P'urhépecha). Although Indigeneity is often contested because of issues related to linguistic and community authenticity, some practices remain despite cultural transformation over time, even if they are labeled differently.

In the case of the Nahua community of the Texcoco area near Mexico City, Lorente Fernández argues that the strong integration of the Nahua sense of *respeto* among community members indicates that the practice is of long duration rather than short. That the Nahua notion of *respeto* penetrates many distinctive realms of Nahua social life suggests that it is a core characteristic of Nahua culture of long precedence and not one of recent adoption into the culture (Lorente Fernández, 2012). The idea that *respeto* is intrinsic to many dimensions of group life and one's relationship to the supernatural—intrinsic, in other words, to the various dimensions of Nahua culture—leads us to believe that it is a social value with deep historical roots.

Respeto is a central axis upon which Nahua cultural life has historically turned across many centuries. Evidence exists for the practice of this form of *respeto* in precolonial records and colonial-era chronicles, both of which describe how social values were transmitted to children via the elaboration of parental advice to their children. For example, the Florentine Codex (Lorente Fernández, 2012) depicts a father instructing his son, "Son, remember that all things are interconnected." In the case of the Texcoco area near Mexico City, contemporary Nahua communities conserve a classification system based on the náhuatl language through which they delineate the socially defined age cohorts of their children—a system that has been in place since the pre-Columbian era—based on an association between the distinctive age ranges and the specific types of labor and household work their children engage in. Such a system is deeply tied to the communal concept of *respeto*, as well as daily social life, family collaboration, and social interdependence within the cultural community (see "Children's everyday learning by assuming responsibility for others: Indigenous practices as a cultural heritage across generations" by Lorente Fernández, this volume).

The long history of the community practices charted by Chamoux, Urrieta, and Lorente Fernández within particular Indigenous communities in Mexico and Central America allow us to form some conclusions about the need for the use of historical analysis as a tool of ongoing research in the context of both Mexico and the United States. In the first place, the historical method can be profitably used as part of the collective effort to map the distinctiveness of particular community social practices with more precision. We know that cultural practices are distinctive and related to other features of the cultural structure. But as in the work of Chamoux, Urrieta, and Lorente Fernández, the work of translating particular analytical observations into precise and systemic descriptions of community practices can be broadened by extending our inquiries chronologically in the effort to better understand the function and ongoing presence of such practices within specific societies. The questions raised through the use of history cannot always be answered neatly or succinctly. But asking them does suggest a way to make our understanding of Indigenous practice more precise as it has evolved over time and into the present. We can better theorize how particular forms of *respeto* or collective labor became central across time to the self-understandings that have guided communities as they have shaped their learning processes. We can better understand how changes in social locations have shaped community practices. We can better understand whether such practices remained substantially intact across generations or have been modified in substantial ways.

A second conclusion about the importance of a historical view is that the use of history as a tool of analysis can provide an additional source of ethnographic observation for ongoing work that is centered on present-day communities. Turning to the extended historical past allows researchers to make use of the many community studies completed since 1930 as additional starting points for ethnographic clues about particular learning practices and what previous scholars have theorized about them. These studies included work produced by individual scholars in the United States and Mexico, university projects in both the United States and Mexico, and the work of the various units of the Mexican state after the Mexican Revolution. Urrieta's observations show, meanwhile, that present-day ethnographic accounts of community practices are equally valuable contributions to ongoing work by contemporary researchers and may, as Don Chente affirms in his discussion of the *trueque P'urhépecha* system, orient us to ask new questions about historical processes that may antedate later, twentieth-century transformations. A longer historical frame has also allowed Chamoux and Lorente Fernández to consider the importance of sixteenth-century social structure to forms of community practice among the Nahua peoples of Mexico that are still vibrant today according to the ethnographic analysis.

The third conclusion regarding the importance of historical analysis as a tool of investigation is that it broadens our ethical consideration of non-European-heritage communities by revealing the extent to which community practices within Mexican and Mexican-American societies are based on the cultural patterns of long-standing duration in Mexico and Central America that have been carried forward to contemporary generations of immigrants in the United States. Angélica López and colleagues have recently argued based on the interviews conducted in Guadalajara, Mexico, and California, for example, that the value of being *acomedida/o* has been commonplace for Mexican and Mexican-American children for centuries and may be rooted in the Indigenous-heritage practices of Mexico. To be *acomedida/o* can be defined as helping or contributing not because a person has been asked to participate, but because one acts on the opportunity to pitch in and be helpful. Being *acomdedida/o* implies having human quality, *respeto*, and *educación*, similar to the definition within the Nahua community of Mexico that a good child is "a child that helps out." As one respondent commented, "*Es como una parte que te inculcan, como parte de tu comportamiento para que tu imagen sea agradable ante los demás*" (It is something that they inculcate in you, like a part of your behavior so that your image is seen as pleasant to others.). In a broader sense, being *acomedida/o* may stem from an "Indigenous emphasis on collaboration, collective action, and horizontal social relations where everyone is expected to help out" from a young age (López et al., 2012, p. 876). The cultural value of being *acomedida/o* may be, in fact, an important link that helps to explain the continuing presence of collaboration and helping in Mexican-heritage and Indigneous-heritage children.

Understanding the historical links between Mexico and Central America, on the one hand, and the United States, on the other hand, are important to our understanding of family and community-based LOPI practices in the context of the rapidly Latina/o immigrant Indigenous and Indigenous-heritage communities of the United States. Sometimes referred to as diasporic communities (Bhatia and Ram, 2001; Urrieta and Martínez, 2011), such communities attempt to maintain connections and commitments to their pueblos of origin and see themselves in collective ways, where children's contributions and responsibility to community life begin early and remain important throughout the life cycle. Orellana (2001) and Reynolds and Orellana (2009) have indicated that Latina/o children's responsibilities to their households and communities represent an often-ignored component of their out-of-school learning practices in the U.S. society.

Understanding how learning is organized in family and community contexts, and in Indigenous homeland community practices, including those observed in Puebla by Chamoux, Nocutzepo by Urrieta, and Texcoco by Lorente Fernández, can help the U.S. educators to understand how larger social and cultural practices-like *ser acomedida/o*, studied by López, remain valuable to Indigenous-heritage peoples even as they go unaddressed in the context of the U.S. school. Indeed, Indigenous practices persist as people of Indigenous-heritage pueblos increasingly migrate to the United States, and as they maintain and recreate aspects of their *pueblo's* social and cultural life in which their children widely participate (Kearney, 2004; Leco Tomás, 2009).

Changes have clearly occurred to Indigenous and settler communities over time, including those wrought by the evangelical movements and the imperatives of the postrevolutionary Mexican government. And it is critical to remain mindful of the danger of assigning identity by ascription, or essentializing, especially given that there is no agreement on what constitutes "Indigenous" identity (Bonfil Batalla, 1987; Villoro, 1950). Some claims of Indigenous identity stress actions and attitudes that predate the colonial encounter. Some accept the categories created by the Mexican state. Others have suggested that Indigenous language use alone cannot be an absolute measure, since ideas and syntax within local forms of Spanish may originate from non-European communities despite the contemporary use of the Spanish language.

Yet while we must be circumspect enough to acknowledge that contemporary social practices may have been imposed or borrowed from colonizer communities or may have resulted from settler and Indigenous interaction in

Mexico, our attempt to understand the function and place of socialization and learning practices in Mexico means that we must be sensitive to the broad range of originating factors from which they may have emerged. The history of social practices necessarily requires a consideration of the identity of groups in relation to one another, and thus requires that we remain open to the possibility that contemporary social practices may have originated within Indigenous communities at moments in the recent or remote past.

5. CONCLUSION: HISTORICAL OBSERVATIONS OF LOPI PRACTICES

We close by noting that analyzing the long history of social practices in contemporary Indigenous communities is not unique to contemporary researchers, but it is instead further validated by the work of former generations of scholars who sought to explain socialization practices in Mesoamerican communities during earlier moments in social science research (Beals, 1943). Scholars in the United States, Europe, and Mexico are today embarked on the attempt to understand the socialization processes in contemporary Mexico, but attempts to understand the history of socialization practices among Mexico's Indigenous communities has long been a characteristic of the scholarly literature.

For example, two Americans trained in psychology in the 1920s and 1930s traveled to Mexico and studied the relationship of the school to organic learning processes in Mexico's Indigenous communities as part of attempts to better understand the function of the school in the modern industrial age (Flores, 2014). Both traveled to Indigenous communities in the vicinity of Mexico City, including visits to the states of Querétaro and Hidalgo. There, they saw practices in community life that impressed them favorably.

One was American philosopher John Dewey, who enshrined his thoughts about community labor in Mexico in now-famous articles that were published in the United States in 1926. Until he encountered Indigenous communities in Mexico who were contributing their communal labor to the building of new schools, he wrote, he had despaired of finding learning practices and the moral systems they reflected that were capable of responding to the destructive capacities of industrial society. But in Mexico, Dewey noted the fresh vitality of Mexico's Indigenous-heritage communities and celebrated the congruence of their learning practices with those of

Mexico's new public schools. "I am willing to go further and say that there is no spirit of intimate union of school activities with those of the community than is found in this Mexican development," he said (Dewey, 1926).

American psychologist Loyd Tireman was just as impressed by attempts to harness organic learning practices in Indigenous communities of Mexico as a tool in understanding how to reformulate narrow learning practices in the United States. In the wake of the educational reform movements that followed the end of the Mexican Revolution, Mexico's Indigenous population reflected cultural practices that Tireman believed were central to the spirit of communal advancement that he sensed in Mexico. "It is almost impossible to portray adequately the attitude of the Mexican people toward education. Everywhere, I saw them building or repairing school buildings, making a home for the teacher and helping in other ways" (Tireman, 1931, p. 122). The men and women that Tireman met suffered from a poor economic situation, but he was struck by their communal sense of effort as they helped to build new rural schools that could complement the social practices of their social communities.

As Marie-Noelle Chamoux has noted above in her discussion of the Nahua people of Puebla, the communal practices of Mexico's Indigenous peoples have often been idealized as "socialist" institutions with roots in "primitive" collectivism, or as evidence of an "authentic" subjectivity that has been rendered in orientalist language. The labor tribute system of the Nahua, for example, has been celebrated as a surviving vestige that authenticates Nahua identity as an exemplar of Mesoamerican indigeneity.

Yet the observations of Dewey and Tireman were more than romantic interpretations of communal practices within Mexico's rural communities. These Americans had been trained in psychology and educational learning practices at major research institutions, and as such, were intent on documenting cultural practices outside of formalized schooling models in the interest of using new practices for the purpose of reengineering schools in the United States.

In our own judgment, Dewey and Tireman witnessed practices in collective collaboration that were unfamiliar to them in the 1920s and 1930s, in the context of the dominant norms in U.S. education practice whose destructiveness they were trying to transform. Something in the way that Indigenous communities in Mexico were organized seemed profoundly different to them, even though they never managed to state that difference in a fully convincing way, and even though they never fully escaped their colonialist assumptions about the communities they were watching, including, for example, their belief that all Indigenous communities shared a beneficent view of the Mexican state. Ultimately, it would require much further work to establish precisely what they witnessed in Mexico. But they seem to have witnessed the results of the same kinds of community socialization practices that we are intent on better understanding today. If it is true that Mexico's Indigenous communities remain vibrant via their socialization practices in the present day, it seemed to have been true from the perspective of other researchers nearly 100 years ago, as well.

We need not be naïve in our consideration of these earlier studies as part of our present-day research efforts to better understand the LOPI practices in Mesoamerican societies. To study the labors of Dewey and Tireman, for example, does not mean that we should be uncritical of their moral and methodological presumptions, just as we should not be uncritical of our own. Instead, we should be open to the idea that researchers in the past have been as impressed with the social features and unique characteristics of the Indigenous societies of Mexico and Central America. Such openness can only enhance the sources that we used to understand the LOPI practices in contemporary U.S. and Mexican societies as we continue to better understand the deep and complex societies of the peoples of the Americas.

Indeed, that researchers in the past have been as impressed with the unique features of Mesoamerican societies as we are today only underscores our view that LOPI has been a characteristic of Indigenous learning practices of long-standing duration whose place in contemporary Mesoamerican societies is integral to Mesoamerican cultures. In the face of political, economic, and social changes in Indigenous cultures wrought by the Spanish conquest and the subsequent centuries of colonial rule, major features of Indigenous societies remained vibrant to a profound degree. These central features of social practice and identity are not isolated vestiges of past cultural structures, but inherent cultural logics of long-standing duration that continue to manifest themselves today in the social lives of the numerous Indigenous societies of Mesoamerica. The use of historical inquiry alongside present-day ethnographic work shows us that LOPI practices, including collective collaboration, the role of work in giving a person dignity and being "gente" (persons), the importance of reciprocity, the role of individual autonomy, and *respeto* (respect), are Indigenous practices that in some instances are five centuries old. As such, they are part of the Mesoamerican *longue durée* that continues to extend into contemporary Mexico and the United States today.

REFERENCES

Barnhardt, R., & Kawagley, A. O. (2005). Indigenous knowledge systems and Alaska Native ways of knowing. *Anthropology and Education Quarterly, 36*(1), 8–23.

Battiste, M. (2002). *Indigenous knowledge and pedagogy in First Nations education: A literature review with recommendations*. Ottowa: Indian and Northern Affairs Canada.

Beals, R. (1943). *The aboriginal culture of the Cahita Indians*. Berkeley, CA: University of California Press.

Bolin, I. (2006). *Growing up in a culture of respect: Child rearing in Highland Peru*. Austin, TX: University of Texas Press.

Bonfil Batalla, G. (1987). *México profundo: Una civilización negada*. Mexico: Editorial Grijalba.

Brayboy, B. M. J., & Maughan, E. (2009). Indigenous knowledges and the story of the bean. *Harvard Educational Review, 79*(1), 1–21.

Chamoux, M.-N. (1986). The conception of work and labor in contemporary Nahuatl-speaking communities in the Sierra de Puebla. In *Paper presented at the American Anthropological Association 85th Annual Meeting, Philadelphia (3–7 December 1986)*. Available from, https://halshs.archives-ouvertes.fr/halshs-00408768/document.

Chavajay, P. (2006). How Mayan mothers with different amounts of schooling organize a problem-solving discussion with children. *International Journal of Behavioral Development, 30*(4), 371–382.

Correa-Chávez, M., & Rogoff, B. (2009). Children's attention to interactions directed to others: Guatemalan Mayan and European American patterns. *Developmental Psychology, 45*(3), 630–641.

Dewey, J. (1926). Mexico's educational renaissance. *The New Republic, 48*, 116–118.

Flores, R. (2014). *Backroads pragmatists: Mexico's melting pot and civil rights in the United States*. Philadelphia, PA: University of Pennsylvania Press.

Gaskins, S. (2000). Children's daily activities in a Mayan village. *Cross-Cultural Research, 34*, 375–389.

Gutiérrez, K., & Rogoff, B. (2003). Cultural ways of learning: Individual traits or repertoires of practice. *Educational Researcher, 32*(5), 19–25.

Kearney, M. (2004). *Changing fields of anthropology: From local to global*. Lanham, MD: Rowman & Littlefield.

Lancy, D. F. (2008). *The anthropology of childhood: Cherubs, chattel, and changelings*. Cambridge: Cambridge University Press.

Leco Tomás, C. (2009). *Migración indígena a Estados Unidos: P'urhépechas en Burnsville, Norte Carolina*. Morelia: Universidad Michoacana de San Nicolás de Hidalgo.

López, A., Correa-Chávez, M., Rogoff, B., & Gutiérrez, K. (2010). Attention to instruction directed to another by U.S. Mexican-heritage children of varying cultural backgrounds. *Developmental Psychology, 46*, 593–601.

López, A., Najafi, B., Rogoff, B., & Mejía-Arauz, R. (2012). Collaboration and helpfulness as cultural practices. In J. Valsiner (Ed.), *The Oxford handbook of culture and psychology* (pp. 869–884). New York, NY: Oxford University Press.

López, A., Ruvalcaba, O., & Rogoff, B. (2015). Attentive helping as a cultural practice of Mexican-heritage families. In Y. M. Caldera & E. W. Lindsey (Eds.), *Mexican American children and families* (pp. 76–91). New York, NY: Routledge.

Lorente Fernández, D. (2006). Infancia nahua y transmisón de la cosmovisión: Los *ahuaques* o espíritus pluvialves en la Sierra de Texcoco, México [Nahua Childhood and the Transmission of Worldview: The *Ahuaques* or Rain Spirits in the Sierra of Texcoco, México]. *Boletín de Antropologa Universidad de Antioquia, 20*, 152–168.

Lorente Fernández, D. (2012). Ser respetuoso es ser "persona": El niño en la pedagogía moral de los nahuas del Centro de México [To be Respectful is to be "A Person": Children and

Moral Teaching among the Nahuas of Central Mexico]. *Revista de Dialectología y Tradiciones Populares*, *67*, 431–452.

Martínez Pérez, E. F. (2011). *Supervivencias en prácticas no verbales y verbales en comunidades de herencia cultural mesoamericana*. Workshop on history and ICP, Austin, TX.

Orellana, M. F. (2001). The work kids do: Mexican and Central American immigrants children's contributions to households and schools in California. *Harvard Educational Review*, *71*(3), 366–390.

Paradise, R. (1994). Interactional style and nonverbal meaning: Mazahua children learning how to be separate-but-together. *Anthropology and Education Quarterly*, *25*(2), 156–172.

Paradise, R., & de Haan, M. (2009). Responsibility and reciprocity: Social organization of Mazahua learning practices. *Anthropology and Education Quarterly*, *40*(2), 187–204.

Paradise, R., & Rogoff, B. (2009). Side by side: Learning by observing and pitching in. *Ethos*, *37*(1), 102–138.

Peele-Eady, T. B. (2011). Constructing membership identity through language and social interaction: The case of African American children at faith missionary Baptist church. *Anthropology and Education Quarterly*, *42*(1), 54–75.

Reynolds, J. F., & Orellana, M. F. (2009). New immigrant youth interpreting in white public space. *American Anthropologist*, *111*(2), 211–223.

Rockwell, E. (1999). Recovering history in the study of schooling: From the Longue Duree to everyday co-construction. *Human Development*, *42*, 113–128.

Rockwell, E., & Gomes, M. A. R. (2009). Introduction to the special issue: Rethinking Indigenous education from a Latin American perspective. *Anthropology & Education Quarterly*, *40*(2), 97–109.

Rogoff, B., Alcalá, L., Coppens, A., López, A., Ruvalcaba, O., & Silva, K. (2014). Children learning by observing and pitching in their families and communities. *Human Development*, *57*(2–3), 65–171 (special issue).

Rogoff, B., Moore, L., Najafi, B., Dexter, A., Correa-Chávez, M., & Solís, J. (2007). Children's development of cultural repertoires through participation in everyday routines and practices. In J. E. Grusec & P. D. Hastings (Eds.), *Handbook of socialization: Theory and research* (pp. 490–515). New York, NY: Guilford Press.

Rogoff, B., Najafi, B., & Mejía-Arauz, R. (2014). Constellations of cultural practices across generations: Indigenous American-heritage and learning by observing and pitching in. *Human Development*, *57*(2–3), 82–95.

Rogoff, B., Paradise, R. M., Arauz, R., Correa-Chávez, M., & Angelillo, C. (2003). Firsthand learning through intent participation. *Annual Review of Psychology*, *54*, 175–203.

Rogoff, B., Pérez González, C., Chavajay Quiacaín, C., & Chavajay Quiacaín, J. (2011). *Developing destinies: A Mayan midwife and town*. New York, NY: Oxford University Press.

Tireman, L. (1931). *The rural schools of Mexico*. Albuquerque: University of New Mexico Press.

Urrieta, L., Jr. (2011). *Prácticas Indígenas: El Trueque*. Austin, TX: Taller Sobre Prácticas Indígenas.

Villoro, L. (1950). *Los grandes momentos del indigenismo en México*. Mexico City, Mexico: El Colegio de México.

CHAPTER SIXTEEN

"My Teacher Is Going to Think They're Crazy": Responses to LOPI Practices in U.S. First-Grade Classrooms

Jennifer Keys Adair[1]
The University of Texas at Austin, Austin, Texas, USA
[1]Corresponding author: e-mail address: jenniferadair@utexas.edu

Contents

Abstract

This chapter explores how children and adults have been responding when they watch first graders in the United States using their agency in classrooms that value and permit children to Learn by Observing and Pitching In (LOPI). First, I explore how video-cued ethnography helped to capture on film practices in classrooms that support LOPI through the Agency and Young Children Project. Then, I detail what happened when I showed these films to first-grade (age 6–8) children of Latina/o immigrants, elementary school administrators, teachers, and parents as a means to elicit ideas, perspectives, and concerns about the early education of young Latina/o children of immigrants. Findings from the initial analysis indicate that deficit views of immigrant families in the United States may prevent teachers and administrators from supporting LOPI.

Advances in Child Development and Behavior, Volume 49
ISSN 0065-2407
http://dx.doi.org/10.1016/bs.acdb.2015.09.001

1. INTRODUCTION

In this chapter, I report on how children and adults have been responding when they watch first graders using their agency in classrooms that value and permit children to Learn by Observing and Pitching In (LOPI; Rogoff, 2014). I begin by explaining the Agency and Young Children project and highlighting the research method: video-cued, multivocal ethnography. It was this research process that prompted our team to notice all of the LOPI practices in the classrooms we studied. It turned out in our study that when children had a lot of agency in their learning—to influence how and what they learned—they used elements of LOPI on a regular basis. After sharing some stories from the classroom, I describe how participants in the study responded to seeing filmed examples of a classroom with many Latina/o children of immigrants using elements of LOPI. I try to make sense of why their responses to LOPI practices were so different and sometimes harsh. It turns out that deficit ideas about Latina/o children of immigrants impacted the participants' responses to children using their agency at school and in particular, how they viewed the viability of LOPI as a part of classrooms serving Latina/o children of immigrants.

My work typically involves filming in classrooms with many Latina/o children of immigrants and then showing those films to parents, teachers, administrators, and the children themselves. I show them films so that they can share their expertise with me about what the practices in the films mean to them, how valuable they are, and the types of learning experiences and practices that get closer to what immigrant communities would like for their children beginning school. This methodology is referred to as video-cued ethnography and was developed in the 1980s by Joseph Tobin and colleagues (see Tobin, Hsueh, & Karasawa, 2009 for an explanation of the method).

In my latest study, I have focused on how increased amounts of agency in young children's learning affects their social and academic development from the perspectives of children, teachers, and parents. The project focuses on young children of Latina/o immigrants in Texas schools. As part of the project, my research team and I have been making films of first-grade classrooms where Latina/o children of immigrants have more-than-typical access to using their own agency. Our work defines agency in the context of learning as the "being able to influence and make decisions about what and how something is learned in order to expand capabilities." This conceptualization of agency is taken from humanistic economics, specifically the work of ul Haq (1996) and Sen (1999, 2003) who have written extensively that agency is a requirement for people and nations to expand their capabilities or, in other words, to have freedom. Eventually, we spent one school year in Ms. Bailey's classroom and also made a film highlighting the practices there. (For in-depth descriptions of Ms. Bailey's classroom and our conceptualization of agency in learning, see Adair, 2014.)

2. FIRST GRADERS IN THE UNITED STATES USING LOPI

We noticed early on in our project that when the young children in our study had agency in their classrooms, they often did things right out of the LOPI framework (Paradise & Rogoff, 2009; Rogoff, 2014). In Ms. Bailey's classroom, children used their agency to get out of their seats to help one another, initiate projects, ask lots of questions to one another or the teacher, collaborate in order to complete tasks, observe one another to get ideas, spend time walking from group to group, and talk a lot without the teachers' permission.

Although our study had not begun as a study of LOPI practices, we soon realized that given the opportunity to use their agency and choose how they learned, the students in Ms. Bailey's classroom were choosing LOPI practices. There were larger indications of LOPI as well. In Ms. Bailey's classroom, there was a sense of community. Children demonstrated an eagerness to contribute their growing set of knowledge and skills to the classroom community. The children used their agency to belong to multiple learning experiences and to work with and by one another, rather than on their own. Anyone was able to initiate a project or contribute to an idea. For example, 1 day Jose noticed a rainbow on the floor and exclaimed to no one in particular that there was a rainbow on the floor. Interested children came over and took on a variety of participatory roles in the emerging scene. Some came and stood right behind Jose, peering at the rainbow, as if trying to see it from the exact perspective. Another child looked up from across the room and watched intently by looking from where the rainbow was on the floor to the children watching it. Two more children came over while yelling "Where? Where?" When they arrived next to Jose, they demanded that Jose show them and then they started stepping carefully all around the rainbow trying to see it from all the angles they could. They eventually figured out that the rainbow was coming from light that was going through the fish tank.

2.1 Everyday Routines of Observing and Pitching In

Other elements of LOPI that happened everyday included children's ways of observing and pitching in around a common endeavor as opposed to an individual task or achievement-oriented goal (Rogoff, 2014). Also an element of LOPI, children seemed to be paying attention to multiple learning scenes at one time and when help was needed and they could contribute, they seemed to show up. For example, in the mornings, children arrived, chatted with one another, and eventually settled into their chairs at tables to write in their journals. This usually meant writing some numbers such as the date as well as more "free writing" where they wrote or drew about something interesting that happened to them.

One morning when we were filming, Mary was working on writing down the date. She had already looked back through her journal to figure out that yesterday had been the 20th and that particular day was the 21st. "Where's the 21? How do you write the 21?" she yelled out while pointing around. Oscar, a boy at a table next to hers, looked up at her and then looked where she was pointing. He walked over and pointed at the number board, saying "It's over there!" Oscar motions for her to come with him to the board and look at the number board together. He points to the number 11 and begins counting from there. "11, 12, 13, 14 ..." until he arrives at 20. He then starts to say 21 but before he can finish, Mary exclaims, "OH!!" and runs back to her seat and writes the number. She keeps looking up to check her number and then finishes. Oscar goes back to his own work.

Through a series of steps and without directly telling her the answer, Oscar helped Mary figure out the number 21 and how to write it on her own. Oscar could have told Mary the answer. It would have been simpler, easier, and faster. And yet like the class in general, Oscar's priority was to engage Mary in a learning experience rather than give her the answer.

Jose's interest in the rainbow and Mary's inquiry about the number 21 demonstrate the overall inclusion of LOPI practices. In both cases, learning could have been isolated or quickly stopped. I can imagine and have seen in my many years of working in preK-1st grade classrooms that Jose's question would have been dismissed in order to begin the morning's activities or Mary's question quickly answered by a teacher, assistant, or another child. Instead, both inquiries prompted social engagement or in LOPI language, a shared endeavor (see also Adair & Colegrove, 2014). The inquiry was shared and the ways in which children could participate were many. The level of sophisticated collaboration and initiative used by the children in Ms. Bailey's class seemed to stem from a general eagerness to contribute and belong to the whole group. The children made many decisions during the day to keep interactions and contributions going, rather than end them quickly with an answer. Children held wide, keen attention to their own work along with emerging scenes around them. They looked for opportunities to help out. Typically, children were eager to have others contribute to their learning, even being quite patient when classmates wanted to teach them skills they already knew. These aspects of LOPI were routine.

3. USING FILM TO COMPARE RESPONSES TO MS. BAILEY'S CLASSROOM

I thought that if I made a film showing young Latina/o children of immigrants using their agency in sophisticated, routine ways then those watching would not be able to argue that it was impossible for young children to learn this way. One of my main hopes for the study was to show administrators, teachers, and policymakers who serve public elementary schools serving Latina/o immigrant communities some alternative ways of learning that can increase children's ability to use their agency instead of diminishing it. I wanted a robust set of examples of children using their agency to learn important sets of knowledge and skills.

This project came out of working within many immigrant communities over the past 10 years. In many school settings, I have seen young children of Latina/o parents yelled at, punished, diminished, and ignored at school. They walk in strict lines and are often told to be quiet; that learning is quiet and still. At the same time, I see wealthier schools with mostly Anglo children walking, skipping, or spinning their way to class. I hear their ideas validated at school and their "disobedience" being described as creative or energetic. I thought that if I could just film the learning that happens when children of Latina/o immigrants use THEIR agency at school, I could begin to address the educational disparity in so many elementary schools across the country. I also thought I could validate the feelings of many teachers serving within immigrant communities that children are capable of much more than standards, assessments, and administrative pressures allow them to be. Perhaps, this was naïve or overly ambitious. Regardless, it did not go the way I had imagined.

We did make a short 18-min film that showcased some of the daily routines. Much of the film captured elements of LOPI that were part of daily classroom life, including the scene of Oscar helping Mary figure out how to write the number 21. When we took the film around to different schools and districts in Texas, we specifically chose those with the same demographics as the classroom in the film: Schools with majority Latina/o children of immigrants in financially struggling communities within urban, rural, and border town settings.

Our process was to show the film to groups of superintendents, principals, preK-3rd grade teachers, first-grade students, and their parents. Most of the superintendents and principals in our study were of Hispanic heritage. Those who were not were of European heritage. In our group of teachers, about one-third identified as Latina/o. The remaining two-thirds of the teachers were of European heritage.

Ms. Bailey, the teacher in the film, was herself West African and her classroom was almost all in English. Because she speaks Spanish as one of her five languages, sometimes children speak in Spanish to her. One scene in the film depicts a boy answering an English-spoken question in Spanish. The teacher translates his answer into English and praises the boy.

Most of the parents we interviewed were recent immigrants to the United States from Mexico, Guatemala, or El Salvador and spoke Spanish at home. We also interviewed a handful of parents who were born in Japan, Argentina, Brazil, and Morocco. About 10% of the parents were of European heritage and were in our interviews because their children attended bilingual or dual language classrooms. In all cases, the English-heritage parents themselves did not speak Spanish. Children were predominantly bilingual, Spanish speakers and had at least one immigrant parent. Exceptions were the small percentage (~5%) of European-heritage children participating in dual language programs.

4. THAT WILL NOT WORK FOR THE CHILDREN AT OUR SCHOOL

When we showed the films to different stakeholders, we started to notice a troubling pattern that continued throughout the data collection process. When we showed the film to principals and superintendents, they all spoke positively (regardless of their background) about the amounts of agency the children had in their learning. Yet, they were quite sure that what worked for the children in the film would not work for their own students. These administrators generally admired what the teacher was able to do with the students in her class. They used words like independence, self-reliance, and self-regulation as positive outcomes of the practices they saw in the film.

(The communal nature of the classroom that had attracted our research team to film it was rarely part of the response from U.S. elementary and district administrators.) Then, they explained why these practices were impossible to implement in their own schools.

Principals and most of the superintendents lamented that the practices children used for their learning simply would not work in their schools, with "their children." They said things like, "Well its too bad that will not work at our school" or "it seems like the children in the film have a lot of vocabulary but our children don't" or "Our children don't come to school speaking English so they have a lot of catching up to do."

In the first few interviews with administrators, I along with my researchers were a little shocked. We always explained before showing the film that we chose their school to interview because their community was so similar to the communities of the children in the film. The children in the film were mostly children of Mexican immigrants, lived in Spanish-speaking households and were experiencing economic hardships. We only conducted focus group interviews with schools and districts that had between 70% and 90% of families qualifying for free and reduced lunch, just like the school in the film. We only went to schools and districts that had the same or close percentage of immigrant families from the same countries, mainly from Mexico and Central America. We explained all of this before showing the film. But then when the film ended, the administrators told us that the practices in the film would not work in their schools because their children were so different from the ones in the film.

Many administrators in our study seemed to forget or be unable to accept, after watching the sophisticated learning portrayed in the film, what I had explained right before the film—that the children in the film were from the same (or at least more similar than different) demographic sample. I am not insisting or even suggesting that communities within a variety of situations and contexts should respond the same way to the film or even that similar demographics should yield similar responses. It is only that the reasons the administrators gave as to why the practices would not work were rooted in the children's backgrounds that were believed to be or must be different enough from those in the school to excuse the administrators' schools from offering them.

After the first few interviews with administrators, out of a mix of curiosity and admittedly some frustration, I started to push back against their rationales for why the practices would not work with the children at their school. I reminded the participants that actually the majority of the children in the film had arrived at school speaking Spanish with little English. Almost all of the children in the film had Spanish-speaking immigrant parents from Mexico, Guatemala, or El Salvador. I reminded them about the basic demographics and connected those to their own school. To this, the administrators responded that the children in the film must have a lot of support at home and have parents who can work with them at home. One principal explained, "You can just tell with their vocabulary that they get a lot more support at home."

As a researcher, I felt pretty stupid by this point. I had thought that if I showed children of Latina/o immigrants learning with a range of sophisticated learning practices including elements of LOPI that no one could really say it was impossible. The films would prove it was possible. And yet, when administrators watched the films of children using LOPI, they forgot or could not accept that the children at their own schools were from similar backgrounds and circumstances as the children in the film. So the practices and the environment that allowed LOPI to be a possibility was not going to happen at their schools.

Ironically, the practices they and all the other participants watched did match many in the LOPI framework, a set of practices directly observed in families and communities throughout Mexico and Latin America as well as within Latina/o immigrant families living in the United States (Rogoff et al., 2014).

5. TEACHERS' RESPONSES TO THE FILM

The preK-3rd grade teachers in our study responded in more or less the same way as the administrators. In almost all the focus groups—with an exception I will explain shortly—the teachers seemed proud of the ways in which their classrooms were similar to the filmed classroom but also proud and confident about the ways in which it was not. They explained that like the teacher in the film, they tried to help their students be independent and responsible for their own learning. Sometimes teachers thought the practices were too chaotic but admitted that some noise and children initiated activities were important. They emphasized that such opportunities to have freedom should be earned, in a kind of contractual approach such as seen in many European households (see Alcalá, Rogoff, Mejía-Arauz, Coppens, & Dexter, 2014) as children are taught about and practice proper behavior and basic reading and writing skills.

The teachers typically explained differences between their classrooms and the filmed classroom as being a natural result of one of three things. First, teachers said sometimes they could not do the practices in the film because they would not effectively prepare children for testing grades, which in the United States begins officially in grade 3. They explained that the early grades were preparation for the higher grades where children would have to be independent and prepared for tests, with higher content and longer amounts of time concentrating and working. They wanted their kids to like school but also be ready for the next grade.

Second, some teachers cited their own personality as a reason to have a more rigid and command-oriented, adult-controlled classroom. They simply could not handle the noise or the potential for noise. They noted that the teacher in the classroom seemed "comfortable" with the noise. They thought that if they tried the same thing in their own classrooms, it would be chaos.

Cited much more often than testing pressures or personality, however, was that children's circumstances or family backgrounds would prevent such learning experiences from being effective. "Children did not arrive speaking English at all." "Our kids do not get a lot of support at home." "Parents don't understand." "We have a hard time getting parents to be involved or even care about what's going on." The teachers, in fact, followed the same pattern of rationale as used by administrators for why such practices were impossible at times for their own classrooms. Some teachers cited migrant families as being a reason. Others cited lots of families who did not have much education themselves. Almost all of the teachers cited a lack of vocabulary in their own children and noted the expanded vocabulary of the children in the film. They did not consider the possibility that the expanded vocabulary might be a result of letting children use their agency to talk, share ideas, and collaborate for the majority of the day.

5.1 Exception to the Teachers' Responses

The exception to this pattern was a focus group conducted with two Latino, bilingual first-grade teachers in an urban school. Both male, one was an immigrant himself from Mexico and the other was the son of immigrants from Mexico. When they watched the films, they were sad, even angry. The tone of the interview following the film was rather quiet. At first, I thought their quiet meant disinterest or annoyance so I was trying to be more entertaining as an interviewer. After a few minutes, I could see that my energetic tone was inappropriate and that I simply needed to ask them what was wrong.

They said that they wished they could do what the teacher in the film did. They wanted to hear their children's stories. They wanted their students to be able to work with one another, initiate projects, and work collaboratively on topics the children thought would be good for the group. They wanted the children's use of practices to be connected to real life. But they could not.

I asked them why and they told me that they have a 15-min schedule to their day. They were supposed to be within 15 min of the other first-grade teachers and always on the subject or activity listed. And then, they showed me the schedule posted next to their door. This left them little time to allow children to determine how they learned or what they learned or to take the time that observing and pitching in requires in classroom settings. There was little time to include children in the creation of curriculum or using children's stories as prompts for lessons and projects or as Turkanis (2001) wrote about her own teaching "to make use of children's interests and experience as a key impetus" (2001, p. 91).

There are many aspects of these teachers' situation that is of interest to a study like mine but for our discussion; here, it is important to note that their rationale for not being able to have practices like in the film had nothing to do with the children. This is one of only three instances in our research project where children or their families were not blamed for why teachers could not give the children agency in their learning or why elements of LOPI would not work in classrooms at a school like theirs, with children and families like theirs.

Another exception was a superintendent (who identified as the son of Mexican immigrants) on the United States/Mexico border. He blamed himself and society for not working hard enough to give young children from his community opportunities to use their agency at school. He thought more agency would help children develop what he called "twenty-first century" skills. Without naming LOPI specifically, he explained the importance of many elements of LOPI including learning a new skill through research and watching others, working in groups for learning rather than achievement, collaboration, and paying attention to many ideas and processes at a time.

The last exception was a principal who came to the United States as a young child from Mexico. She blamed policymakers for making the tests so powerful in the educational lives of young children. She told us that the constant district surveillance of her and her teachers made their practices removed from what they would want to do with the children. They were terrified of being seen as underperforming by the state. To help all students do well on tests, they had to spend most of their time on knowledge and skill sets directly linked to the test. The rest of the adult participants in our study blamed the children and families.

6. PARENTS' RESPONSES TO THE FILM

The immigrant parents in our study were also mixed in their responses to the film. This part of the data is complicated and requires much more explanation than is possible here. Yet, it is safe to say that the parents had a much wider variety of responses than the teachers, administrators, or children.

Some of the parents said the classroom was noisy, chaotic, and disorganized. Some parents liked the practices but worried about children speaking over one another. They questioned whether the teacher could really know what all of the children were up to if she was working with one small group, while the others worked on their own. Most parents liked how children helped one another, most often citing the scene in the film in which Oscar helps Mary with the number 21. This makes sense as a culturally valued practice connected to LOPI. The parents all appreciated the teachers' warmth and care for the children.

There was disagreement among parents about how the teacher handled conflict. For example, in the film, there is a scene that plays out over a few minutes of two boys—Jorge and Matthew—getting into an argument. The teacher sends them to the side of the room to work it out among themselves; the teacher is not involved in their conversation. Jorge and Matthew go and start talking. They take turns explaining why they are mad. At first, they do not accept each other's rationale and continue talking about it. Then, Jorge explains that Matthew stepped right on his toes and then did not even say sorry. Matthew says that he tried to say sorry but that Jorge did not even look up. This creates a pause in the conversation. Matthew says he is really sorry. Soon, they return to the teacher and announce that they fixed it. Soon, they walk out to recess, arms around each other.

When parents responded to this scene, they had mixed responses. Some parents loved this approach, wishing they could do the same at home. Others were skeptical, worried that this approach might benefit bullies and not the more vulnerable children who because of personality, language, or gender might not stand up for themselves. However, the elements of LOPI that came out in the scene including Jorge and Matthew participating and responding to one another in a shared endeavor as well as helping one another out as a way of participating and belonging to their friendship and the larger class elicited positive responses from parents. They appreciated children participating in solving the problem. They valued children learning to be part of the group through real experiences rather than just being told to behave.

7. FIRST-GRADERS' RESPONSES TO THE FILM

When we showed the film to the first graders, typically 5–7-year-old children, kids had immediate and strong responses to the scenes in the film. Unlike with other participants, we did not show the entire 18-min film to the first graders. Instead, we chose four scenes and showed them one at a time. We stopped after each one to have a discussion that usually lasted somewhere between 3 and 5 min. The scene we showed first in each focus group was with Mary, Oscar, and the number 21.

We asked them, "What do you think about the boy helping the girl with numbers?" As researchers, we thought this might be kind of a leading question because of the word helping. Surely, the kids would automatically respond that the helping was good. But to our surprise, the kids universally thought the helping was bad; that the boy was going to get in trouble with the teacher. Some kids even called him a bad kid.

The children we interviewed almost universally thought the students in the film were behaving badly. While watching the scenes (before we stopped the film to ask questions), they often commented out loud to one another, "They are so loud!" "They are not following the rules," or "Oh no, they are not raising their hands." The children sometimes pointed out materials they had in their own classrooms such as the number board. "Hey we have one of those in our classroom." And yet when we asked them in the discussions if there was anything the same between their class and the film, they often said "No" or "Nothing." One girl explained, "It looks different. Because we are so much quieter."

When we specifically asked the first graders about Oscar helping Mary, they said it was not ok. Again, like many times in this research, I became surprised and then frustrated. So even with the children I started pushing back. I started asking "really? You think what they are doing is bad?" (Obviously not a good research question.) To this, they nodded up and down emphatically. They did not even really consult with one another, like they did with so many other questions we asked. The kids explained that teachers want you to raise your hand, not just get out of your seat. Inappropriately incredulous, I asked a particularly talkative and confident group about whether their teachers would really think the kids in the film were bad. One student put me in my place, probably annoyed at how many times I was asking the same question. Our exchange went like this.

JA: They [your teachers] won't think that this classroom is good?

S: They're going to think they're crazy.

It seems clear from the data emerging as part of the study that the responses by administrators, teachers, and especially parents to agentic, culturally situated practices are mixed. For young children of immigrants, they are not. The initiative, cooperation, pitching-in practices used by the children in the film, all elements of LOPI, are not ok at their school. There is no place for them and they are considered bad behavior at school. And the first graders disagreed, in theory, with their teachers who had told us that their classrooms were somewhat similar to the one portrayed in the film.

8. STRONG MESSAGES ABOUT LEARNING AND BEHAVIOR

The message received by Latina/o children of immigrants in our study seems to be that they should not use these kinds of practices for their own learning in school. Even when the first graders were in districts or schools with administrators who valued children belonging and contributing to a classroom community as a core aspect of early schooling or who desired children to have access to aspects of LOPI in the classroom (even though they did not call them LOPI by name), the children were operating under the assumption that such practices were not right at school.

We usually asked children "Is there anything you saw in the movie that you wish you could do at school?" It was hard for children to tell us what they wished they could do at school. They usually looked at one another for a while before shrugging. When we were patient, some children would hesitantly answer. In every case, they sheepishly said that they would like to help their friends like they saw a boy help a girl in the movie.

9. DEFICIT IDEAS AND LEARNING PRACTICES

The rationales given by teachers and administrators for withholding LOPI and other sophisticated, communal learning approaches included children's lack of vocabulary, nonsupportive parents, Spanish-speaking homes, migrant working situations, and poverty. While testing pressures were a consistent part of discussions, they were not the main rationale. Rather than biological (age-driven) or even political (institutional) reasons for whether children at school can handle learning experiences that include LOPI, participants explained that the situations of children and families prevented such practices from working. This implies that these educators think that it is because of the children and families' lives, situations, backgrounds, cultural values, circumstances that they cannot handle learning experiences that include authentic uses of their agency. Thinking that some children can handle LOPI elements, as part of school, and others cannot situates those who cannot as having a deficit. These deficit views got in the way. The teachers and administrators' views that the children in their schools from Latina/o immigrant communities would not be successful with LOPI kinds of learning were so strong that the educators struggled to see the practices and experiences as being possible even when there were examples of them being possible on film.

As the pendulum of U.S. education swings away from standardized testing, as it is starting to, and there is more talk about teacher autonomy and about agency for teachers and students in classrooms, it is important to be honest about the reasons why children of Latina/o immigrants and other marginalized communities attending schools in the United States are denied many sophisticated learning experiences even in the beginning years of school. It is not only because of testing pressures, although this was definitely a factor in our data.

Our study suggests that taking away testing pressures alone will not allow wider sets of learning experiences that emerge from children's use of agency and their own LOPI-related culturally informed practices and ideas about learning, to be a routine part of children's learning. While easing testing pressures will surely give teachers time and space to teach in many different kinds of ways, those ways will still be limited if they think the children in their classrooms cannot handle LOPI-related learning experiences. Teachers and administrators need to better understand how their expectations for young children are connected to the levels of respect, connection, and admiration they have for their families and communities.

Increased autonomy may help give teachers courage and permission to try giving young children more agency, which would then allow children and families to share more stories, talents, and funds of knowledge with teachers. This pattern of trusting children to use their agency and then watching the stories, experiences, and learning that results, in my experience, helps spiral away from deficit ideas that push teachers to prevent children from using approaches like LOPI.

As for my work, I have not given up on using filmed examples to document aspects of LOPI and to gather feedback and ideas about agency and learning. I hope that the conversation continues with honest attention to the role of agency as a deserved, critical, and equitable part of the early learning experiences of children from Latina/o communities.

ACKNOWLEDGMENTS

My deep appreciation to Dr. Kiyomi Sanchez-Suzuki Colegrove and Molly McManus for their careful data analysis as part of the Agency and Young Children project team. Also to Barbara Rogoff, Maricela Correa-Chávez, and Rebeca Mejía-Arauz for their generous and supportive feedback. Finally, thanks to the Foundation for Child Development who has generously funded the AYC project as part of the Young Scholars Initiative.

REFERENCES

Adair, J. K. (2014). Agency and expanding capabilities in early grade classrooms: What it could mean for young children. *Harvard Educational Review, 84*(2), 217–241.

Adair, J. K., & Colegrove, K. S. (2014). Communal agency and social development: Examples from first grade classrooms serving children of immigrants. *Asia-Pacific Journal of Research in Early Childhood Education, 8*(2), 69–91.

Alcalá, L., Rogoff, B., Mejía-Arauz, R., Coppens, A. D., & Dexter, A. L. (2014). Children's initiative in contributions to family work in indigenous-heritage and cosmopolitan communities in Mexico. *Human Development, 2–3*, 96–115.

Paradise, R., & Rogoff, B. (2009). Side by side: Learning by observing and pitching in. *Ethos, 37*(1), 102–138.

Rogoff, B. (2014). Learning by observing and pitching-in to family and community endeavors. *Human Development, 57*(2–3), 69–81.

Rogoff, B., Alcalá, L., Coppens, A. D., López, A., Ruvalcaba, O., & Silva, K. G. (2014). Learning by observing and pitching in to family and community endeavors. *Human Development, 57*(Special Issue), 165–171.

Sen, A. (1999). *Development as freedom*. New York: Alfred Knopf.

Sen, A. (2003). Development as capability expansion. In S. Fukuda-Parr, et al. (Eds.), *Readings in human development*. New Delhi and New York: Oxford University Press.

Tobin, J., Hsueh, Y., & Karasawa, Mayumi. (2009). *Preschool in three cultures revisited*. Chicago: University of Chicago Press.

Turkanis, C. G. (2001). Creating curriculum with children. In B. Rogoff, C. G. Turkanis, & L. Bartlett (Eds.), *Learning together: Children and adults in a school community*. Oxford: Oxford University Press.
ul Haq, M. (1996). *Reflections on human development*. London: Oxford University Press.

CHAPTER SEVENTEEN

Learning by Observing and Pitching In and the Connections to Native and Indigenous Knowledge Systems

Luis Urrieta Jr.[1]
Department of Curriculum & Instruction, Cultural Studies in Education Program, University of Texas at Austin, Austin, Texas, USA
[1]Corresponding author: e-mail address: Urrieta@austin.utexas.edu

Contents

Abstract

This chapter opens a broader dialogue of Learning by Observing and Pitching-In (LOPI) with Native and Indigenous Studies, and Native and Indigenous Education, drawing particular attention to how LOPI can provide a model for better understanding Indigenous pedagogy in Indigenous Knowledge Systems (IKS). As Battiste (2002) pointed out, "Indigenous pedagogy values a person's ability to learn independently by observing, listening, participating with a minimum of intervention and instruction." Like LOPI, IKS include *ways of knowing* and *ways of being* in the world, with life-long processes and responsibilities that model competent and respectful behavior. The chapter explores similarities and differences between IKS and LOPI by analyzing each perspective's scope, defining features, and foundational origins, as well as what each contributes to our understanding of Native and Indigenous communities, especially in terms of learning and incorporation into adulthood and family and community life.

Advances in Child Development and Behavior, Volume 49
ISSN 0065-2407
http://dx.doi.org/10.1016/bs.acdb.2015.08.003

1. INTRODUCTION

This chapter explores the relation of Learning by Observing and Pitching-In (LOPI) with Indigenous Knowledge Systems (IKS), drawing particular attention to how LOPI can provide a framework for understanding Indigenous pedagogy in IKS. Battiste's summary (2002, p. 11), from an IKS perspective, fits well with the efforts of LOPI to describe how Indigenous American communities organize children's learning: "Indigenous pedagogy values a person's ability to learn independently by observing, listening, participating with a minimum of intervention and instruction."

Indigenous pedagogy is part of larger and millennial systems of Indigenous knowledge that are particular, yet share similarities across various Native and Indigenous[1] communities in America.[2] Battiste defines IKS as "...an adaptable, dynamic system, based on skills, abilities and problem-solving techniques that change over time depending on environmental conditions..." (Battiste, 2002, p. 11). IKS include skill sets, but also encompass broader landscapes of competencies including ways of knowing and being in the world in relation to self and others, that are acquired as life-long processes and responsibilities that model competent, respectful behavior (Barnhardt & Kawagley, 2005; Cajete, 1994).

LOPI is a framework based on long-term ethnographic and experimental empirical studies of learning and development in Indigenous and Indigenous-heritage community contexts (Rogoff, 2011, 2014). LOPI has been defined as a form of family and community-based learning that occurs primarily by "observing and pitching-in," with children's initiative and access to abundant community activities alongside more experienced and supportive peers and adults (Rogoff, Paradise, Mejía Arauz, Correa-Chávez, & Angelillo, 2003). LOPI is observed to be especially prevalent in Indigenous American families and communities with limited exposure to formal schooling (Paradise & Rogoff, 2009; Rogoff, 2014).

While LOPI as a model (in progress) was developed based on observed Indigenous knowing(s), LOPI and IKS are both simultaneously similar and different. LOPI, the written and articulated model, is in part the product of Euro-Western academia and serves at present primarily research, scholarly, and educative purposes. IKS, on the other hand, are millennial generally

[1] In this chapter, I use the terms Native and Indigenous together and interchangeably to denote the Native peoples of America.

[2] The term "America" in this chapter includes Native and Indigenous people from Alaska to the Patagonia as opposed to the Euro-American, United States-centric name for itself as America.

unwritten empirical (tested over time through experiences) and normative (socialization processes) *ways of knowing* and *ways of being* in the world and serve the purpose of guiding everyday relational life between living and non-living things (Battiste, 2002, p. 19; Morales Velásquez & Lepe Lira, 2013). Classical Western thought typically organizes and categorizes hierarchies of knowledge by comparing and contrasting similarities and differences, often creating boundaries between epistemological classifications. In this chapter, I compare LOPI and IKS with the purpose of disrupting the often perceived binary between IKS and Western knowledge in order to highlight the ways in which the LOPI model has gained important insight from IKS over prolonged engagement with Indigenous communities and with significant conceptual contributions from Indigenous scholars. Importantly, I highlight how LOPI can also inform researchers, educators, and schooling by bridging the knowledge systems of Indigenous communities and Western-style schooling. In this regard, LOPI can be understood as a hybrid model that can inform Western knowledge and schooling of the knowledge systems and learning pedagogies of Indigenous communities.

This chapter will thus analyze each perspective's scope, defining features, as well as their foundational origins, and what each contributes to our understanding of Native and Indigenous communities, especially in terms of children's learning and incorporation into adulthood. In order to explore the relation between LOPI and IKS, it is important to situate Native and Indigenous peoples' *ways of knowing* and *ways of being* (IKS) and Euro-western knowledge within the context of Indigenous Studies and Native Education. Native and Indigenous peoples in the Americas have indeed endured repeated attempts at physical, cultural, and epistemological genocide through European settler colonialism(s), nationalist projects, and Euro-Western knowledge systems, often instituted through schooling (Stannard, 1992; Wolfe, 2006).

2. VIOLENCE, ERASURE, AND NATIVE PEOPLES

Native and Indigenous people in this chapter include the original inhabitants of America (North and South), who have continuously occupied this land for millennia prior to European invasion. It is not my intention to essentialize a line of "pure" Indigenous descent. Given migratory trends, geographic and Euro-colonial dislocation, and intermarriage, it would be nearly impossible to claim a pure line of descent. However, it is important, for the purposes of this chapter, to address the commonalities observed across Indigenous cultures in order to address IKS and LOPI, while not essentializing, homogenizing, or romanticizing the experiences and knowledge(s) of

Native and Indigenous peoples, and by extension of Indigenous-heritage[3] peoples. Although the concept of culture[4] has been used in problematic ways, a more nuanced and complex understanding of it can also be useful in drawing parallels across Native community contexts without relegating Indigenous peoples to the relics of history, or to one-dimensional, and static perspectives.

Various forms of colonialism(s), including enduring forms of the coloniality of power, have brought on different forms of Native dispossession, erasure, and enslavement (Grosfoguel, Maldonado-Torres, & Saldivar, 2005). Settler colonialism, a form of colonialism based on invasion of and possession of the Indigenous land and its resources, and in which the dehumanization and elimination of Native peoples is the organizing structure for invasion (Wolfe, 2006, p. 388), has been widely theorized and studied by Northern (U.S. & Canadian) Native scholars (Dennison, 2014; Smith, 2012). Colonialist economic and political systems throughout America objectified and exploited Indigenous peoples through forced labor, removal, erasure, and/or extermination policies, which continue to this day through blood quantum, Native language fluency, and other forms of reified colonialist policies of Indigenous surveillance and authenticity (Garoutte, 2003; Lee, 2009; Sturm, 2002).

Through a process of infantilization, Native and Indigenous communities were often placed under the "tutelage" of Europeans, Euro-descendants, and later the nation-state. These processes physically removed, dispersed, and/or contained entire Indigenous communities for the purposes of land dispossession. Native peoples were displaced and relocated to distant lands for forced labor such as mining and agriculture. In Abya Yala[5] (Latin America) where Indigenous peoples were not necessarily physically removed into demarcated reservations and reserves through policies of containment, as in Canada and the USA, they were historically exploited and contained as pseudo-slave labor through the *repartimiento*, *encomienda*, and later *hacienda*, *latifundio*, and *finca* systems and many took refuge in very remote and isolated areas to survive.

3 Drawing on anthropologist Bonfil-Batalla (1987), I define Indigenous heritage communities as those who may or may no longer collectively self-identify as indigenous, but in which ways of knowing and being (*usos y costumbres*) continue to endure (Urrieta, 2013).

4 The concept of "Culture" has been abundantly critiqued as a product of Western colonialist anthropology especially because it is often used to essentialize and to police Indigenous authenticity (Tuhiwai Smith, 1999).

5 Abya Yala is the name used for the American continent by the Kuna since before Columbus's arrival. Abya Yala means "land in its full maturity" or "land of vital blood" in Kuna. Aymara leader Takir Mamani from Bolivia advocates for the use of the name Abya Yala in support for indigenous rights.

In the nation-building period throughout the continent, especially in contexts with larger Indigenous populations such as Mexico, Guatemala, Peru, Ecuador, and Bolivia, Native peoples became iconic and romanticized as symbols and images of a noble and glorious past, but a despised, deplorable, and degenerate present (Urrieta, 2003). Archeologists, ethnologists, anthropologists, and social scientists borne out of colonialist enterprises (Tuhiwai Smith, 1999) played a crucial role in these countries' efforts to document a type of fossilized grandeur of Native societies in monumental national ethnology and anthropology museums. Early twentieth-century social scientists also played a crucial role in sustaining ideologies of living Native and Indigenous people as a "problem," or obstacle to national modernist progress because of their perceived racial physical, genetic, and/or cognitive deficiencies (Dennison, 2014).

Anti-Indian campaigns occurred in many contexts throughout America, including through land allotment in the USA by way of the Dawes Act in 1887, which privatized communal land holdings into individual plots and thus opened up and invited white settler encroachment into Indian Country. Mexico's northern siege against the Apache, Comanche, Seri, Pima, and Yoemem, and the *Casta* Wars in the south in the Yucatan (Sheridan, 1999) are also examples of national "frontier" consolidation efforts by the Mexican government at the expense of Native communities. Argentina's genocide of Natives in Patagonia in the 1870s to expand its agricultural and ranching economies, and El Salvador's military massacre of Pipil Natives in 1932 in order to encroach upon and privatize Indigenous *ejido* communal land holdings are but a few examples of the annihilation/extermination economic approach to Native peoples as "problem" by nation states throughout America. Most often these genocidal acts, often perpetrated by the state's military forces, as was the case with the U.S. Cavalry at Wounded Knee and Sand Creek, of El Salvador in 1932 and of Guatemala in the 1980s, are erased from the national consciousness through the glorification of settler colonial modernist histories, and patriotic nationalisms usually taught in schools (Wolfe, 2006).

3. NATIVE AND INDIGENOUS EDUCATION

The architecture of early nation-building projects looked to education and schooling as a way to assimilate Native and Indigenous peoples into Euro-dominant cultural, social, and economic practices. Many missionary as well as nationalist efforts to impose schooling on Native children by force were implemented from Canada to Argentina, often in the form of boarding schools that literally physically removed Native and Indigenous children from their home communities, sometimes through abductions. Native children were then isolated and indoctrinated in Western ways and often endured many hardships including physical, emotional, and sometimes sexual abuse (Lomwaima, 1995). Ideological indoctrination in schools included explicit and implicit curricula on individualism, private property rights, competition, and national official histories lauding the civilizing efforts of the (Euro-white and *Mestizo/Ladino*) national ideologies, almost always at the cost of Native/Indigenous/First Peoples' his/her stories, knowledge(s), and cosmological worldviews (Wolfe, 2006).

These early schooling campaigns usually functioned in a reductionist, binary rationale, framed as either/or propositions such as of assimilation or annihilation, success or failure, English or Native language(s), Indigenous Knowledge(s) or Western knowledge, in which Native cultures, identities, and knowledge(s) were framed as "savage," inferior, or infantile, and pitted against the official Euro-centered "civilizing" propaganda of the various nation-building projects. To remain Indian often meant to remain "primitive," while to assimilate, especially through schooling was often propagandized as a way to "save" or "rescue" the humanity of the Native. The enduring dark legacy of forced Native schooling indeed was in this missionary racist, patriarchal, and often violent approach to "kill the Indian, save the man" (Churchill, 2004). The "Indian problem" in several national contexts throughout America, such as Canada, the USA, Mexico, Guatemala, Bolivia, Peru, and Ecuador, was thus often framed as a binary or dichotomy because in Euro-Western views, either Native peoples assimilated by ridding themselves of their culture, language, and "ways," or they would remain "backward," "unwanted," and a "hindrance" to national stability and especially would be considered a fiscal burden to Euro-Whites/*Mestizos*/*Ladinos*' economic development (Champagne, 2005).

Various early schooling efforts in Indigenous communities throughout the continent focused on teaching Native children the official European language of each nation-state, which ranged from English and French, to Spanish and Portuguese. Native languages were often not referred to as languages, but as *dialectos* (dialects) at the benign end of the spectrum, and were considered grunts and gibberish at the other extreme. Such negative and racist views of Native languages and cultures rendered them useless for the "modern" state and were often considered inappropriate and unfit for formal schooling, unless they facilitated the acquisition of the national European language or religion. To this day, bilingual intercultural education in Native languages is still limited to primary grades, and the goals remain to learn national languages and curricula, and are generally not meant to preserve Indigenous knowledge(s) or languages (Dietz, 1999).

Throughout America, school curricula continue to promote nationalisms, patriotisms, and loyalty to the nation-state through assimilation. Patriotic, and sometimes very militaristic rituals in schools, force on Native and Indigenous students a type of body discipline intended to penetrate the deepest corners of their being, especially because the very organization of learning is so foreign to the ways in which Native communities organize learning. State-led citizenship programs and disciplinary techniques on and through children's bodies focus on a type of often passive, rote, repetitive, civic socialization for assimilation (Lazar, 2010). The coercive pull of assimilation through private and state-sponsored schooling still continues to largely perpetuate the binary that pits indigenous cultures, knowledge(s), and languages against mainstream and standardized notions of success, modernity, and economic integration.

4. NATIVE RESISTANCE(S) AND AGENCY IN EDUCATION

Native and Indigenous people have, however, always resisted and struggled for cultural and linguistic recognition, autonomy, and sovereignty throughout the continent (Champagne, 2005), by responding in various ways to compulsory schooling. Some communities refused schooling until it was imposed through legal enforcement. For example, Tuck and Yang (2014, p. 414) document through an iconographic image of Hopi prisoners in Alcatraz Island that "In 1895, nineteen Hopi men were incarcerated in the prison facility..." because, as reported by a San Francisco newspaper, "they would not let their children go to school." Tuck and Yang further add that the U.S. Government imposed policies across Hopi lands demanding the removal of Hopi children to attend distant boarding schools. In Guatemala, Rogoff's long-term Tz'utujil Maya informant "Chona," now in her 80s, also reported that when she was a child, the *alguaciles* (bailiffs) went door-to-door to force parents to send their children to school (Rogoff, 2011). Besides communities refusing schooling, common acts of resistance included absenting children from school, resisting schooling through desertion and attrition, and not succumbing to the cultural erasure of subtractive schooling processes (Urrieta & Martínez, 2011; Valenzuela, 1999).

More integrative Native and Indigenous educational community struggles usually demanded that schooling meet their community's needs through culturally competent and culturally relevant teaching and that curricula be adjusted to their own local cultural, social, and economic realities, which many times meant a strong call for education in Native languages in addition to official European languages (Hornberger, 2008; Manuelito, 2005). During the twentieth century, several nations in America passed legislation to implement Native and Indigenous education programs, often however with the normalized imposition that "Western knowledge" would be the basis of the curriculum and under the assumption that this was the only knowledge leading to viable economic opportunities.

This inadvertently re/centers codified Western knowledge as the standard and as the fiduciary by which all other knowledge(s) are measured and deemed valid or acceptable (Doxtater, 2004; Urrieta & Machado-Casas, 2013). Bilingual, Bi/Multi/Inter/Pluricultural education programs in Native and Indigenous languages are thus often seen as deficient, "remedial," and as roadblocks to community development, modernization, and economic growth, and a manifestation of Indigenous peoples' resistance to national integration, national stability, and international economic development. This view is also sometimes shared by Native and Indigenous communities due to internalized oppression, but also because Native and Indigenous communities often want access to Euro-Western curricula, skills, and competencies of Euro-Western schooling in order to access higher education and external economic opportunities as perceived through a modernist development ideology.

It is noteworthy also that many Native and Indigenous students have done well in schools and some have acquired high levels of education, including in some of the most prestigious universities (Brayboy, 2004). Some Indigenous students have become skilled in navigating between cultures, knowledge(s), and languages, and subsequently some devote their acquired credentials and skills to work for the benefit of their communities. (Many more, however, work outside of or leave their communities in order to pursue professional careers and also because of lack of economic opportunities in reservations, and rural and marginalized areas, throughout the continent (De la Piedra, 2009).) Native and Indigenous scholars have been instrumental in documenting the knowledge(s) of their communities in many fields and disciplines, but primarily in Native and Indigenous Studies (Deloria, 1991; Forbes, 2008; Smith, 2012) and in Native and Indigenous education (Cajete, 1994; Grande, 2004; Kawagley, 1995; Lee, 2009; Okakok, 1989; Tippeconnic, 1999).

5. NEOLIBERAL BI/MULTI/INTER/PLURICULTURAL EDUCATION

In the late twentieth and early twenty-first centuries, neoliberal economic reforms have supported globalization efforts through various trade agreements throughout the continent between nation states. These international development plans have also driven educational reforms that impact Native and Indigenous communities. These efforts have been propelled by organizations such as the World Trade Organization, the World Bank, the International Monetary Fund, Inter-American Development Bank, Organization for Economic Cooperation and Development, and U.S.-based organizations like USAID and the National Endowment for Democracy (Gustafson, 2009).

In some instances, these neoliberal impositions are often framed within a broader global human rights discourse often said to be in response to the needs of Indigenous communities (Speed, 2002). These reforms specifically target Native and Indigenous communities and are framed within a nationalist pluriculturalist, multiculturalist, or interculturalist discourse, generally of Indigenous inclusion and of cultural rights recognition, especially in Abya Yala, but with neoliberal impulse that assures that the recognition is minimal while the impetus for the global capitalist order continues. Such cultural rights projects with neoliberal economic ends have been referred to as "neoliberal multiculturalism" (Hale, 2005). Many current Indigenous education initiatives by nation states such as bilingual education and multi/inter/pluricultural education for Indigenous communities often function under neoliberal reform processes, where Native and Indigenous people are culturally minimally recognized, in exchange for the further encroachment of late capitalism.

The further expansion of Western-style schooling, even in the multi/inter/pluricultural forms mentioned, often justified by nation states and international interests as a form of economic development in terms of human resources, especially in "underdeveloped" nations, is a way to further encroach into marginal minority and Native and Indigenous communities with external global economic systems (Gustafson, 2009). Neoliberal educational reforms, through strategies of marketization emphasizing competition, individualism, choice, and enforced through data-driven accountability systems and standardized "best practices," urge nations to compete and promote national and international educational standards in order to improve "human capital, social equity (never equality), and poverty reduction" (Gustafson, 2009, p. 165).

Standardized high-stakes testing at the national and international level has become widespread and supported by national and international entities guided by cost–benefit, and cost-effective austerity formulas that are heavily invested in market-driven education practices. Such globalized market-driven practices rely on universalized assessments, such as the Programme for International Student Assessment (PISA), to compare student achievement used to rate and rank nations' development indices. These educational standards and assessments, based on political, usually elite normative strategies relying on "claims of universal (i.e., economic) knowledge" (Gustafson, 2009, p. 162), continue to marginalize Native and Indigenous people by devaluing IKS, including within bilingual inter/multi/pluricultural education programs, even when such programs are often aimed at remedying past injustices, at least rhetorically, by addressing (minimally) Native and Indigenous cultural and linguistic rights.

Conversations on the fiscal and social burdens of inadequate education for minorities and Indigenous peoples, in the long-run, often pique the interest of economists and analysts. Such is the case for Guatemala, after the Guatemalan peace accords in 1995. The Guatemalan government invested (reluctantly) in Indigenous education, including passing a National Languages Law (in 2003) recognizing 21 Mayan languages, Xinka, and Garífuna and also implemented bilingual bicultural education programs throughout the nation. Although this symbolized a great triumph and possibility for Maya communities, who are the majority population in Guatemala, the reproductive model of public schools, or what Rogoff et al. (2003) refer to as "assembly-line instruction," was not geared toward biliteracy in Mayan languages and Spanish, but ultimately toward Spanish literacy. Recent studies have found that there is a correlation between increasing (Spanish) literacy rates and increased Mayan bilingualism, but also increasing Mayan language loss especially in children (England, 2003). Throughout America Indigenous women generally tend to have the least access to education, the highest Spanish illiteracy rates, and represent the highest percentage of Native language speakers (Hornberger & Coronel-Molina, 2004).

Rogoff et al. (2003) and Chavajay (2006) also found that the more years of schooling Mayan mothers had, the less they tended to organize their children's learning in Native ways, by "seeing & doing," and instead used more verbal, step-by-step explanations and recall questions to teach their children specific tasks, as is often used in assembly-line instruction. It is important to highlight that organizations like USAID finance curriculum writing for early childhood education programs as well as UNICEF's funding of schools, especially in conjunction with locally established, but foreign run NGOs. International development interests are clearly at play in these emerging national Indigenous education trends that tend to be guided by external forces rather than by Indigenous communities themselves.

This analysis of past and current Native and Indigenous education raises important questions about the overall social, cultural, and economic trade-offs of schooling for Native and Indigenous peoples. It is important to note how unequal the outcomes of schooling are for Native peoples generally, and even for members of the same communities regarding gender and class differences, especially when there are high attrition rates, low levels of achievement, and the criminalization of Native youth in schools. For example, work with Diné youth shows that Native youth, like other minorities of Color, tend to be criminalized through harsh school discipline policies that create school-to-prison pipelines often leading to juvenile detention and adult incarceration (Manuelito, 2005).

This analysis also highlights that settler colonialist practices, or what Native scholar Jean Dennison (2014) refers to as "whitewashing," persist through schooling in the Euro-Western-oriented institutions Native and Indigenous children attend, even when these schools and educational programs are said to be bilingual and bi/multi/inter/pluricultural. Meanwhile an ongoing struggle continues between settler, corporate interests that persist in displacing and dispossessing Native/Indigenous/First Nations peoples from their ancestral homes through the continued encroachment on Native lands for resource extraction, mining, hydroelectric power, hydrocarbon extraction, agribusiness, pharmaceutical exploration especially of Native botanical knowing(s), lumbering, and cattle grazing. Despite this continuous onslaught, Native and Indigenous peoples continue persisting and surviving, finding guidance in tried and exploratory *ways of knowing* and *ways of being* in the world (which are fundamental parts of IKS).

6. INDIGENOUS KNOWLEDGE SYSTEMS AND LEARNING BY OBSERVING AND PITCHING IN

The overview of the historical and current contexts of Native and Indigenous knowledge and schooling presented above indicate that LOPI does not emerge from the same socio-historical-political location as IKS.

LOPI addresses a small part of what IKS encompass by providing a Western-scientific heuristic model for the schematic organization and understanding of IKS. LOPI also provides a blueprint for understanding how Native and Indigenous communities generally organize learning and explores the different aspects, or facets, of what that learning encompasses.

LOPI also provides an important disruption and alternative to the ways in which Native and Indigenous communities' knowledge systems (IKS) have been understood (or misunderstood) and devalued as deficient or deviant (Grande, 2004; Lee, 2009). LOPI approaches Indigenous ways of organizing learning from an asset-based perspective that can potentially help reorient the ways Euro-Western knowledge, research, and educators have traditionally constructed Indigenous knowledge(s) and Indigenous ways of organizing learning. And while LOPI is subject to the general critiques[6] charged against research conducted in Indigenous communities for Western academic purposes, LOPI does provide Western scholars and educators with new insights on, and new ways to think about IKS and about Indigenous learning pedagogies in more complex and more favorable ways.

Indigenous cultural practices are inherently participatory, relational, and connected to particular places of origin, people, and their natural surroundings (Cajete, 1994; Rockwell & Gomes, 2009). Indigenous peoples and cultures engage in complex dynamic assemblages of repertoires of practices (Gutierrez & Rogoff, 2003) that are simultaneously ancient and newly innovative, preserving millennial ways of knowing, while negotiating and creatively adapting to the changing social and material conditions of their survival (Bonfil-Batalla, 1987).

It is these simultaneously millennial and new ways of knowing and being that are commonly referred to as Indigenous Knowledge Systems (IKS). IKS do not refer to knowledge or epistemology in the Western sense, but, in accord with IKS, encompass a wide range of "knowledge(s)" including, but not limited to, epistemic, ontological, and axiological knowing(s) that are not engaged distinctively, but rather in interrelation with each other (Brayboy & Maughan, 2009).

In IKS, knowledge(s) are always co-constructive and co-constructed processes, which means that these are not individual internal processes, but always collaborative, relational, and generative (Bolin, 2006). Such

[6] The general critiques charged against research conducted on Indigenous communities for Western academic purposes usually indict research as a colonialist, invasive, voyeuristic practice that dehumanizes Native peoples by objectifying them, and making them vulnerable to epistemological appropriation (Tuhiwai Smith, 1999).

relational knowing(s) can be as broad and abstract as learning what it means to be a person (*gente*) and a *member* of a community, and/or as specific as learning dexterity by counting and seriating through weaving. According to Native scholars (Barnhardt & Kawagley, 2005; Cajete, 1994), IKS encompass larger and broader cosmological knowing(s) about the world and how to survive in it, rather than the often narrow and disconnected focus of book learning taught in schools. Because these are simultaneously millennial and new knowing(s), their origin stems from the long-term empirical knowledge (tested through generations and generations of peoples over centuries), who creatively survived and thrived in relation to each other, their natural surroundings, and their spiritual situatedness, encountering old and new situations and socializing children and youth into community life (Bolin, 2006).

IKS therefore include skill sets, but also encompass broader breadths of cultural, social, economic, and spiritual competencies (Barnhardt & Kawagley, 2005). Indigenous knowing(s) are acquired as life-long processes and responsibilities that model competent and respectful behavior toward others and the natural world (Cajete, 1994) and form part of families' and communities' funds of knowledge (González, Moll, & Amanti, 2005) and community cultural wealth (Yosso, 2005). IKS are learned through participation in ongoing family and community activities, with minimal intervention or direct instruction, a learning by "seeing and doing" (Battiste, 2002) that the LOPI model attempts to describe, building in part on the observations of scholars of IKS. Minimal intervention is a principle of IKS because the motivation to participate must be intrinsic, optimizing participation and motivation for learning. Given the wide breadth of what IKS encompass, what are the connections between IKS and LOPI? What does the LOPI model contribute to our understandings of IKS?

7. LOPI'S CONTRIBUTIONS FOR UNDERSTANDING IKS AND INDIGENOUS LEARNING PEDAGOGY

LOPI is a heuristic model for IKS and for understanding how Indigenous communities organize learning. Although it is the product of Western rationalist and empiricist thought, it is also the result of over four decades of individual and collaborative ethnographic and experimental studies of learning in Native and Indigenous communities (Rogoff, 2014). Many of these studies are based on prolonged and relational engagement with communities where the researcher was either a member of that community or established long-term and sometimes life-long commitments and kin-like relations with community members (Rogoff, 2011). In that sense, the development of the LOPI model is also based on relational commitments, conceived in part as the result of trusting relationships between researchers and communities. Psychologist Barbara Rogoff has primarily coordinated and guided LOPI's development in collaboration with numerous colleagues, including Indigenous and Indigenous-heritage colleagues, in psychology, anthropology, sociology, history, education, and other fields who conduct research in Indigenous communities of Abya Yala, the USA, and Canada, myself included.

In its early development, LOPI was formerly known as learning through *intent community participation*, which seemed much more limiting, but the general goal of understanding the organization of learning was the same. LOPI is conceptually broadly defined as an active, participatory form of organizing learning that occurs through collaborative, coordinated cultural activities (Rogoff et al., 2003). LOPI is described as a form of learning that occurs by "observing and pitching-in," with initiative and access to abundant community activities alongside more experienced and supportive peers and adults (Rogoff et al., 2007). While aspects of learning through LOPI have been observed mostly in Indigenous communities and with Indigenous children (Rogoff et al., 2007, 2003), LOPI practices occur in other contexts. LOPI is consistent with IKS, in that the observed learning practices are generally recognized as "indicative and not definitive" of the ways Indigenous people organize learning (Barnhardt & Kawagley, 2005, p. 10).

While Rogoff and colleagues (Lopez, Najafi, Rogoff, & Mejía-Arauz, 2012) often refer to these recognized practices as cultural differences at the micro level, and constellations of practices over time, their approach should not be conflated with previous ethnographic studies based on cultural difference theories of learning that were often misused to generalize particular "traits" to individuals and collectives based on racial or ethnic groupings (Au, 1980; Erickson & Mohatt, 1982). Rogoff and colleagues are careful to distinguish their use of cultural difference from the "learning styles" tradition in education, which often was misused by shortsighted scholars to generalize the cultural practices of learning in different ethnic groups in the USA. These generalized assumptions, although sometimes well intended, often fell into deficit thinking about groups of people, especially when appropriated as taxonomies, inventories, or profiles of groups of learners by education practitioners (Valencia, 1997). Gutiérrez and Rogoff (2003) complicate these "trait approaches" by highlighting peoples' developed proclivities as a result of certain historical engagements with specific cultural activities over time, and not necessarily with inherent affinities outside of historical and cultural activities.

LOPI has also generally been used to compare and contrast the organization of LOPI to the ways Western schooling has traditionally organized learning. The organization of learning in Western schooling is primarily from a functionalist tradition influenced by Taylorism, Keynesianism, and Fordist ideas that led to standard regimentation, efficiency models, mass production, and the step-by-step processes of schooling in the first half of the twentieth century. Behaviorism, which guided learning through direct instruction teaching, with an active and directive teacher controlling the pace, sequence, and content of learning, also had a major influence on schooling (Palincsar, 1998).

Rogoff and colleagues have referred to this organization of learning, common in traditional Western schooling, as assembly-line instruction. Rogoff (2014) states that the contrasts made between LOPI and assembly-line instruction are purposeful, yet not necessarily oppositional because these are not necessarily opposing pedagogies. While this comparison can reify binaries and dichotomies between what we think of as Western and non-Western, Indigenous and non-Indigenous ways of knowing and being, the comparison serves the purpose of better understanding these two, *of many*, approaches to organizing learning. The comparison between LOPI and assembly-line instruction also serves the important purpose of providing Western academics and educators with a heuristic model for gaining some insight on IKS and Indigenous learning pedagogy. The contrast between these two ways of organizing learning can better help Western school educators to see school practices as cultural practices that are not neutral, normal, and natural, but as practices that have been standardized to particular values and that privilege particular ways of knowing and being, while devaluing many other ways of organizing learning and Other(ed) knowledge systems. LOPI can help educators and researchers to see beyond the conventional knowledge of their disciplines and fields as they tap into a broader and more nuanced view of Native and Indigenous, and Other(ed), knowledge systems, and pedagogies of learning.

What does LOPI teach us about the organization of learning in Indigenous communities? What have we learned about learning through LOPI? Learning activities in LOPI are not generally organized as separate, step-by-step progressive behaviors as in assembly-line instruction but as authentic, coordinated practices, themselves assessments, encouraging children's contributions during participation in endeavors with a high degree of acceptance of children's efforts (Rogoff et al., 2007). Through collective practices, "...children participate in the same activities of the everyday life of the community as do adults, contributing in real ways as they learn about their shared economic and social reality" (Paradise & Rogoff, 2009, p. 106). Learning through observing and pitching-in, or "side-by-side" learning (Paradise & Rogoff, 2009), is more prevalent in societies in which children are integrated in the range of everyday adult community life (Lancy, 2008; Peele-Eady, 2011). This would be in contrast to families and communities that over time have developed a segregation of children from adult community life by creating especially designed and planned children's spaces, whether for bureaucratic efficiency, for pushing children out of the labor force, or for sheltering children from adult socio-political and economic realities.

In an ethnographic study I conducted in San Miguel Nocutzepo in Central Mexico (Urrieta, 2013), I observed that children and youths' learning in family and community life was not artificially created (segregated), but flowed with the everyday aspects of life, especially through household and economic practices. Nocutzepo ways of organizing learning, unlike the suburban child who sells lemonade in the summertime to learn a lesson on capitalist entrepreneurship, were real, purposeful, and encompassed a totality of shared, lived experience. For example, boys often worked along with their fathers in construction, the most common work activity performed by men for cash after, and usually in compliment of, subsistence agriculture.

Boys helped their fathers by preparing cement mixes, bringing certain tools or needed material like sand and gravel, or simply by observing quietly. José, a 9-year old boy I observed in 2010, worked along with his father Martín for 3 weeks, putting in a small cement roof and plastering the brick walls of a small room. José joined Martín after school during the first week of observation in late June. Instead of going home, José would change into work clothes and join his father. When summer vacation began in July, José worked 9-h days along with Martín for the remaining 2 weeks observed. Both usually worked in silence with only an occasional indication by Martín of what needed to be done, including hand and facial gestures. José usually mixed cement or handed Martín certain tools. Martín sometimes only pointed to a section of the wall and José would remove the excess cement right away when plastering. During the 3 weeks, Martín was only rarely observed explicitly telling José how to do something, yet José was always observant of his father and ready to contribute.

When interviewed, Martin explained that José knew that they were poor and that life was hard, and that his best inheritance for José would be to teach him *how to work*. Clearly, Martín is not only referring to skills for laying bricks but to teaching José about "how to live well" (*sesi'irekua*), not in terms of a comfortable life from a economic perspective, but to live well in his personal, familiar, and social relations (Morales Velásquez & Lepe Lira, 2013). Similar "work practices" were observed throughout the community.

This representative example supports that observation, listening-in, and participation with initiative are important in LOPI (Rogoff et al., 2003), including third-party attention (López et al., 2012). José was always attentive and ready to contribute to the work without being asked to. Children's observations of adult activities, like José's, in LOPI have often been characterized as keen, long, and with intense concentration, an indication of active cognition, social, and emotional participation (López, Correa-Chávez, Rogoff, & Gutiérrez, 2010). Children in indigenous communities, like José, have been observed to be expected to take initiative and responsibility for participating in community life (Ames, 2013; Bolin, 2006). Learning through observing and pitching-in in indigenous families and communities has been observed especially in families with less years of formal schooling (Chavajay, 2006; Gaskins, 2000; López et al., 2012), which was the case with Martin and José.

Lamentably and not surprisingly, assembly-line instruction generally does not acknowledge IKS or the learning practices most familiar to Native and Indigenous students, families, and communities. This includes institutional programs that are supposed to be especially designed for Native students. Brayboy and Maughan (2009) offer an interesting example in which a group of Native students in a university teacher education program designed to prepare Native preservice teachers to work with Native students completely overlooked the IKS and the relational ways of knowing of the Native students in the program. This "formal" instruction resulted in a disconnection between the Native preservice teachers and the non-Native teacher educators who insisted on growing beans in empty milk cartons, an "artificial" science learning activity, while overlooking Native cosmological knowing(s) on the relational multipurpose of growing seeds in Native environments.

Ethnographic research on Mazahua children in Mexico also illustrates important aspects of the learning practices of indigenous families and community-based learning (Paradise, 1994). Paradise and de Haan (2009) found that Mazahua mothers and other adults "...do not explicitly organize learning activities or attempt to teach their children; it is generally assumed that children are capable of taking initiative and of gradually learning by themselves to take on adult roles" (p. 197).

Although keen observation and pitching-in as forms of participation might be interpreted as unorganized and laissez faire ways of learning from a formal schooling perspective, for Martín in Nocutzepo and the observed Mazahua mothers in Mexico City, it was a valuable form of tacit collaboration in which learning occurred through interaction (Paradise, 1994). Nonverbal communication and judicious use of speech were also observed in other Indigenous communities' learning activities and reflected complex systems of communication and social competence (Lancy, 2008; Manuelito, 2005).

Learning in IKS and as interpreted in the LOPI framework is a broad base for organizing learning that leads to high degrees of learner originality as well as specialization. It is not restrictive. José would eventually develop his own style of building, adding his own texture, trying his own creative designs, while also simultaneously specializing within the architectural conventions of building. According to Battiste (2002, p. 11), "Indigenous pedagogy values a person's ability to learn independently by observing, listening, participating with a minimum of intervention and instruction." LOPI helps to highlight the dynamic and experiential ways of Indigenous pedagogies, and views Indigenous knowing(s) as living processes to be absorbed and understood by community members throughout the life span (Battiste, 2002; Brayboy & Maughan, 2009). Indigenous ways of organizing learning, unlike the rigid, homogenizing, and increasingly standardized testing culture of schools, allow *every* child to explore his/her own unique capacities, learning ways, pace of learning, and to develop their own expertise in the processes of acquiring their family's and community's knowing(s) (Battiste, 2002; Urrieta, 2013).

For example, women in Nocutzepo claimed to have their "own" individual tortilla style, and claimed to be able to identify who made the tortillas by looking at their shape, size, and girth, which they learned to develop from an early age. This degree of originality and specialization in tortilla-making reflects a general philosophical orientation in the community toward learning that is not based on unorganized, careless ways to teach, but rather on broad very supportive approaches for organizing learning that resulted in highly specialized, meaningful lessons by seeing and doing. Most women learned how to make tortillas, but the pace and "way" of that learning was based on their individual needs and interests as girls. Guiding behaviors and noncontrolling attitudes, such as Martin's toward José, and the mothers toward their daughters' tortilla-making, encouraged children to continue taking initiative in adult activities as they improved their practice and with the understanding that each child would eventually figure out how to accomplish tasks "their way." Not learning was not an option; Martin needed and expected José to learn "how to live well" by teaching him "how to work," like the mothers needed their daughters to learn how to make tortillas, but the pace and "way" of that learning was based on José's and every child's needs and interests.

8. CONCLUSION

Native and Indigenous communities have long and rich histories of survivance and relational knowledge systems embedded within millennial cosmological systems of knowing. Researchers, scholars, and educators working with Native and Indigenous children, families, and communities can use the LOPI model as a heuristic to begin to understand the bases for the knowledge(s) and learning in these communities. Educators working with Indigenous and Native students should value the richness of the educational experience in everyday family and community life, including students' strengths and capacities as mature persons capable of taking initiative in their own learning.

Recognition of the history of genocide and discrimination targeted against Indigenous people, especially of Native and Indigenous children in schools, is vital (Barillas-Chon, 2010; Lee, 2009; Lomwaima, 1995). Intra- and inter-cultural understanding is central to, and for, creating inclusive culturally relevant models of learning communities; LOPI offers an asset-based model for communities where learning is based on a "seeing and doing" orientation. Most importantly, researchers, scholars, and educators need to understand that the ways of organizing learning highlighted as assets through LOPI are not careless and unorganized ways of organizing learning, but broad approaches for organizing learning embedded in IKS that result in highly specialized yet creative, meaningful lessons that meet each child's, family's, and community needs.

Native and Indigenous ways of organizing learning can thus provide educators with philosophical, theoretical, and practical pedagogical alternatives to the increasingly homogenizing, rigid, and data-driven neoliberal ways of schooling. Schooling can incorporate aspects of LOPI as alternative, inclusive, and more noninterventionist approaches to organizing teaching and learning that result in meaningful, contextual, and specialized learning for all students. This can be accomplished in part by embedding skills instruction within meaningful and purposeful community contexts and collaborative, communal activities that involve students and families in authentic, rather than aesthetic ways in schools and classrooms.

This chapter shows that the *ways of knowing* and *ways of being* acquired by children and youth in Native and Indigenous family and community life are important for learning skills, and also for acquiring conceptual socially relevant and relational understandings and behaviors related to family and community cohesiveness and well-being.

Implications for research include a challenge to Western scholars not to be assuming that learning *only* occurs within the accepted conventions of Cognitive and Developmental Psychology, the Learning Sciences, and within the walls of a school building. Instead, IKS and LOPI can help to broaden our definitions of how children learn, how adults help them do so, and how anyone can tell if they have done so.

Understanding how Indigenous and Native communities organize learning, and the philosophical, theoretical, and pedagogical foundations in IKS behind learning processes, can especially help expand teaching and learning theories, as well as expand the learning possibilities that Indigenous learning practices can offer educators and students. Millennial Indigenous empirical knowledge(s) can inform Western knowledge and the organizational aspects of meaningful school learning, not just for Indigenous and Native students, but for all students. The challenge, however, is on researchers, scholars, educators, and educational policy makers to take a personal and professional stance on pursuing trans/formative change.

ACKNOWLEDGMENTS

This chapter was written with the support of a University of Texas, College of Education Dean's Fellowship. Special thanks to Barbara Rogoff, Rebeca Mejía Arauz, and Maricela Correa-Chávez, and to all of the "Tallerines" for many years of generous knowledge sharing.

REFERENCES

Ames, P. (2013). Niños y Niñas Andinas en el Perú: Crecer en un Mundo de Relaciones y Responsabilidades. *Bulletin de L'Institut Français d'Études Andines, 42*(3), 389–409.

Au, K. H. P. (1980). Participation structures in a reading lesson with Hawaiian children: Analysis of a culturally appropriate instructional event. *Anthropology & Education Quarterly, 11*(2), 91–115.

Barillas-Chon, D. W. (2010). Oaxaqueño/a students' (un)welcoming high school experiences. *Journal of Latinos and Education, 9*(4), 303–320.

Barnhardt, R., & Kawagley, A. O. (2005). Indigenous knowledge systems and Alaska native ways of knowing. *Anthropology and Education Quarterly, 36*(1), 8–23.

Bonfil Batalla, G. (1987). *México profundo: Una civilización negada*. Mexico: Editorial, Grijalba.
Battiste, M. (2002). *Indigenous knowledge and pedagogy in first nations education: A literature review with recommendations*. Ottawa: Indian and Northern Affairs Canada.
Bolin, I. (2006). *Growing up in a culture of respect: Child rearing in highland Peru*. Austin: University of Texas Press.
Brayboy, B. M. J. (2004). Hiding in the ivy: American Indian students and visibility in elite educational settings. *Harvard Educational Review*, *74*(2), 125–152.
Brayboy, B. M. J., & Maughan, E. (2009). Indigenous knowledges and the story of the bean. *Harvard Educational Review*, *79*(1), 1–21.
Cajete, G. (1994). *Look to the mountain: An ecology of Indian education*. Durango, CO: Kivaki Press.
Champagne, D. (2005). Rethinking native relations with contemporary nation states. In D. Chapagne, K. Torjesen, & S. Steiner (Eds.), *Indigenous peoples and the modern state* (pp. 1–23). New York: Alta Mira Press.
Chavajay, P. (2006). How Mayan mothers with different amounts of schooling organize a problem-solving discussion with children. *International Journal of Behavioral Development*, *30*(4), 371–382.
Churchill, W. (2004). *Kill the Indian, save the man: The genocidal impact of the American Indian residential schools*. San Francisco: City Lights Books.
De la Piedra, M. T. (2009). Hybrid literacies: The case of a Quechua community in the Andes. *Anthropology and Education Quarterly*, *40*(2), 110–128.
Deloria, V., Jr. (1991). *Indian education in America*. Boulder, CO: American Indian Science and Engineering Society.
Dennison, J. (2014). Whitewashing indigenous Oklahoma and Chicano Arizona: 21st century legal mechanisms of settlement. *PoLAR: Political and Legal Anthropology Review*, *37*(1), 162–180.
Dietz, G. (1999). Indigenismo y EducAcción Diferencial en México: Balance de Medio Siglo de Politícas Educativas en la Región Purhépecha. *Revista Interamericana de Educación de Adultos*, *21*(1–3), 35–66.
Doxtater, M. G. (2004). Indigenous knowledge in the decolonial era. *American Indian Quarterly*, *28*(3/4), 618–633.
England, N. (2003). Mayan language revival and revitalization politics: Linguists and linguistic ideologies. *American Anthropologist*, *105*(4), 733–743.
Erickson, F., & Mohatt, G. (1982). Cultural organization of participant structures in two classrooms of Indian students. In G. Spindler (Ed.), *Doing the ethnography of schooling: Educational ethnography in action* (pp. 132–174). New York: Holt, Reinhart and Winston.
Forbes, J. (2008). *Columbus and other cannibals*. New York: Seven Stories Press.
Garoutte, E. M. (2003). *Real Indians: Identity and the survival of Native America*. Berkeley & Los Angeles: University of California Press.
Gaskins, S. (2000). Children's daily activities in a Mayan village. *Cross-Cultural Research*, *34*, 375–389.
González, N., Moll, L., & Amanti, C. (2005). *Funds of knowledge: Theorizing practices in households, communities, and classrooms*. Mahwah, NJ: Lawrence Erlbaum and Associates.
Grande, S. (2004). *Red pedagogy: Native American social and political thought*. Maryland: Rowman & Littlefield.
Grosfoguel, R., Maldonado-Torres, N., & Saldivar, J. D. (2005). Latin@s and the Euro American Menace: The decolonization of the US Empire in the 21st century. In R. Grosfoguel, N. Maldonado-Torres, & J. D. Saldivar (Eds.), *Latin@s in the World-System: Decolonization struggles in the 21st century U.S. empire* (pp. 3–27). Boulder, CO: Paradigm Publishers.
Gustafson, B. (2009). *New languages of the state: Indigenous resurgence and the politics of knowledge in Bolivia*. Durham: Duke University Press.

Gutierrez, K., & Rogoff, B. (2003). Cultural ways of learning: Individual traits or repertoires of practice. *Educational Researcher, 32*(5), 19–25.

Hale, C. (2005). Neoliberal multiculturalism: The remaking of cultural rights and racial dominance in Central America. *PoLAR: Political and Legal Anthropology Review, 28*(1), 10–28.

Hornberger, N. (2008). *Can schools save indigenous languages? Policy and practice on four continents*. New York: Palgrave Macmillan.

Hornberger, N., & Coronel-Molina, S. (2004). Quechua language shift, maintenance, and revitalization in the Andes: The case for language planning. *International Journal of the Sociology of Language, 167*(2004), 9–68.

Kawagley, A. O. (1995). *The Yupiaq worldview: A pathway to ecology and spirit*. Prospects Heights, IL: Waveland Press.

Lancy, D. F. (2008). *The anthropology of childhood: Cherubs, chattel, and changelings*. Cambridge: Cambridge University Press.

Lazar, S. (2010). Schooling and critical citizenship: Pedagogies of political agency in El Alto, Bolivia. *Anthropology and Education Quarterly, 41*(2), 181–205.

Lee, T. (2009). Language, identity, and power: Navajo and Pueblo young adults' perspectives and experiences with competing language ideologies. *Journal of Language, Identity and Education, 8*(5), 307–320.

Lomwaima, K. T. (1995). *They called it prairie light: The story of Chilocco Indian school*. Lincoln, NE: University of Nebraska Press.

López, A., Correa-Chávez, M., Rogoff, B., & Gutiérrez, K. (2010). Attention to instruction directed to another by U.S. Mexican-heritage children of varying cultural backgrounds. *Developmental Psychology, 46*, 593–601.

Lopez, A., Najafi, B., Rogoff, B., & Mejía-Arauz, R. (2012). Collaboration and helping as cultural practices. In J. Valsiner (Ed.), *The Oxford handbook of culture and psychology* (pp. 869–884). New York: Oxford University Press.

Manuelito, K. (2005). The role of education in American Indian self-determination: Lessons from the Ramah Navajo community school. *Anthropology and Education Quarterly, 36*(1), 73–87.

Morales Velásquez, J. J., & Lepe Lira, L. M. (2013). Parankuecha, diálogos y aprendizajes: Las fogatas de Cherán como praxis educative comunitaria. *International Journal of Multicultural Education, 15*(3), 61–75.

Okakok, L. (1989). Seeing the purpose of education. *Harvard Educational Review, 59*(4), 405–422.

Palincsar, A. S. (1998). Social constructivist perspectives on teaching and learning. *Annual Review of Psychology, 49*, 345–375.

Paradise, R. (1994). Interactional style and nonverbal meaning: Mazahua children learning how to be separate-but-together. *Anthropology and Education Quarterly, 25*(2), 156–172.

Paradise, R., & de Haan, M. (2009). Responsibility and reciprocity: Social organization of Mazahua learning practices. *Anthropology and Education Quarterly, 40*(2), 187–204.

Paradise, R., & Rogoff, B. (2009). Side by side: Learning by observing and pitching in. *Ethos, 37*(1), 102–138.

Peele-Eady, T. B. (2011). Constructing membership identity through language and social interaction: The case of African American children at faith missionary baptist church. *Anthropology and Education Quarterly, 42*(1), 54–75.

Rockwell, E., & Gomes, M. A. R. (2009). Introduction to the special issue: Rethinking indigenous education from a Latin American perspective. *Anthropology & Education Quarterly, 40*(2), 97–109.

Rogoff, B. (2011). *Developing destinies: A Mayan midwife and town*. Oxford: Oxford University Press.

Rogoff, B. (2014). Learning by observing and pitching in to family and community endeavors: An orientation. *Human Development, 57*, 69–81.

Rogoff, B., Moore, L., Najafi, B., Dexter, A., Correa-Chávez, M., & Solís, J. (2007). *Children's development of cultural repertoires through participation in everyday routines and practices. Handbook of socialization: Theory and research.* New York: Guilford Press, pp. 490–515.

Rogoff, B., Paradise, R., Mejía Arauz, R., Correa-Chávez, M., & Angelillo, C. (2003). Firsthand learning through intent participation. *Annual Review of Psychology, 54*, 175–203.

Sheridan, T. E. (Ed.), (1999). *Empire of sand: The Seri Indians and the struggle for Spanish Sonora, 1645–1803.* Tucson: University of Arizona Press.

Smith, A. (2012). Indigeneity, settler colonialism, white supremacy. In HoSang, D. M, O. LaBennett, & L. Pulido (Eds.), *Racial formation in the twenty-first century* (pp. 66–90). Berkeley: University of California Press.

Speed, S. (2002). Global discourses on the local terrain: Human rights and indigenous identity in Chiapas. *Cultural Dynamics, 14*(2), 205–228.

Stannard, D. E. (1992). *American holocaust: The conquest of the new world.* Oxford: Oxford University Press.

Sturm, C. (2002). *Blood politics: Race, culture, and identity in the Cherokee Nation of Oklahoma.* Los Angeles: University of California Press.

Tippeconnic, J. W., III (1999). Tribal control of American Indian education: Observations since the 1960s with implications for the future. In K. G. Swisher & J. W. Tippeconnic, III (Eds.), *Next steps: Research and practice to advance Indian education* (pp. 33–52). Charleston, WV: ERIC Clearinghouse on Rural Education and Small Schools.

Tuck, E., & Yang, W. K. (2014). Time exposure. *Educational Studies, 50*(4), 414–415.

Tuhiwai Smith, L. (1999). *Decolonizing methodologies: Research and indigenous people.* London: Zed Books.

Urrieta, L., Jr. (2003). Las identidades también lloran/Identities also cry: Exploring the human side of Latina/o indigenous identities. *Educational Studies, 34*(2), 147–168.

Urrieta, L., Jr. (2013). Familia and Comunidad-based Saberes: Learning in an indigenous heritage community. *Anthropology and Education Quarterly, 44*(3), 320–335.

Urrieta, L., Jr., & Machado-Casas, M. (2013). Book banning, censorship, and ethnic studies in urban schools: An introduction to the special issue. *The Urban Review, 45*(1), 1–6.

Urrieta, L., Jr., & Martínez, S. (2011). Diasporic community knowledge and school absenteeism: Mexican immigrant pueblo parents' and grandparents' postcolonial ways of educating. *Interventions: International Journal of Postcolonial Studies, 13*(2), 256–277.

Valencia, R. (1997). *Genetic pathology model of deficit thinking (chapter 3). The evolution of deficit thinking.* Washington, DC: The Falmer Press.

Valenzuela, A. (1999). *Subtractive schooling: U.S.-Mexican youth and the politics of caring.* Albany: State University of New Cork Press.

Wolfe, P. (2006). Settler colonialism and the elimination of the native. *Journal of Genocidal Research, 8*(4), 387–409.

Yosso, T. (2005). Whose culture has capital? A critical race theory discussion of community cultural wealth. *Race, Ethnicity, and Education, 8*(1), 69–91.

CHAPTER EIGHTEEN

Children's Participation in Ceremonial Life in Bali: Extending LOPI to Other Parts of the World

Yolanda Corona*,[1], Dewa Ayu Eka Putri†, Graciela Quinteros*
*Autonomous Metropolitan University, Mexico City, Mexico
†Udayana University, Denpasar, Bali, Indonesia
[1]Corresponding author: e-mail address: druktso30@gmail.com

Contents

Abstract

This chapter extends a model of how children in Indigenous communities of the Americas Learn by Observing and Pitching In (LOPI; Rogoff, 2014) to another region of the world, by examining which aspects of the model can be applied to the ways in which Balinese children learn with their peers and adults. We describe clear parallels in the role of observation and communication, the social organization of endeavors, and children's motivation to participate as they learn the music of gamelan (the traditional orchestra) that is used in religious ceremonies.

Advances in Child Development and Behavior, Volume 49
ISSN 0065-2407
http://dx.doi.org/10.1016/bs.acdb.2015.08.002

1. INTRODUCTION

The present article examines the generality of a model of children's learning, called "Learning by Observing and Pitching In" (LOPI) through children's intent participation in their families' and communities' endeavors (Rogoff, 2014). Research leading to this model has shown that children in Indigenous communities of North and Central America are incorporated into virtually all community activities, where they find countless opportunities to observe and participate in meaningful cultural practices (Coppens, et al. 2014; Morelli, Rogoff, & Angelillo, 2003, Paradise & Rogoff, 2009).

In this model, development can be characterized as broadening arenas of participation, with transformation of specific forms of participation across the lifespan (Rogoff, 1996; White & Siegel, 1984). The repertoire of practices involved in LOPI seems to apply (and to develop) across the whole lifespan. In this sense, cultural practices involved in LOPI "are connected with many other aspects of children's and families' lives as aspects of coherent constellations of cultural practices" (Rogoff, 2014, p. 77).

We examine the relevance of this model for children's learning in Bali, building on research in Mexico carried out over the last decades by two of the present authors (Corona, 2011a, 2011b; Corona & Pérez, 2002; Corona, Quinteros, & Padilla, 2005). One of the important findings from the research in Mexico has been the understanding of the critical role played by ceremonial life and religious festivals as social scenarios that provide new generations with a wide range of learning opportunities, allowing children to participate at their own pace in a social context where adults have a very open and tolerant attitude. In particular, we have seen many aspects of LOPI in the different ceremonial practices for the local God in Tepoztlán, México, where children have an important role: "In this situation, we could see a transference of responsibilities where the younger members of the group acquire increasing abilities enabling them to participate more suitably in the festivity" (Corona & Pérez, 2007). This form of participation is based on Learning by Observing and Pitching In, through an intense collaboration in the ceremonial practices. That is why we had pointed out that children "always seem to be interested in capturing all the details of that particular activity in order to adjust their action to collaborate with responsibility" (Corona & Pérez, 2007, p. 136).

Since 2011, we have had the opportunity to do research on the society of the island of Bali, characterized by a culture in which ceremonial life is one of the main axes of daily life. In this small island belonging to Indonesia, a predominantly Muslim country, people practice Balinese Hinduism, a religious tradition in which both their ancient animistic beliefs and certain aspects of Buddhism are embedded. The daily life of the island includes an infinite variety of offerings that include music, dance, various artistic performances, and a variety of ceremonial objects that are offered in temples to please the gods and as expressions of gratitude to God for having created the universe and all forms of life on earth. Children are an integral part of these activities, in which they gradually take more active roles through keen observation, imitation, and engagement, along with their peers and also under the joyful guidance of adults.

This chapter presents ethnographic data about the socialization of children in Bali, providing information regarding certain learning situations in the family and the community. Specifically we discuss the participation children have in the musical gamelan cultural practice, widely used in ceremonial life. We do this from an anthropological perspective that dialogs with the LOPI model, which has been represented by a prism that has seven interrelated facets that we reproduce below.

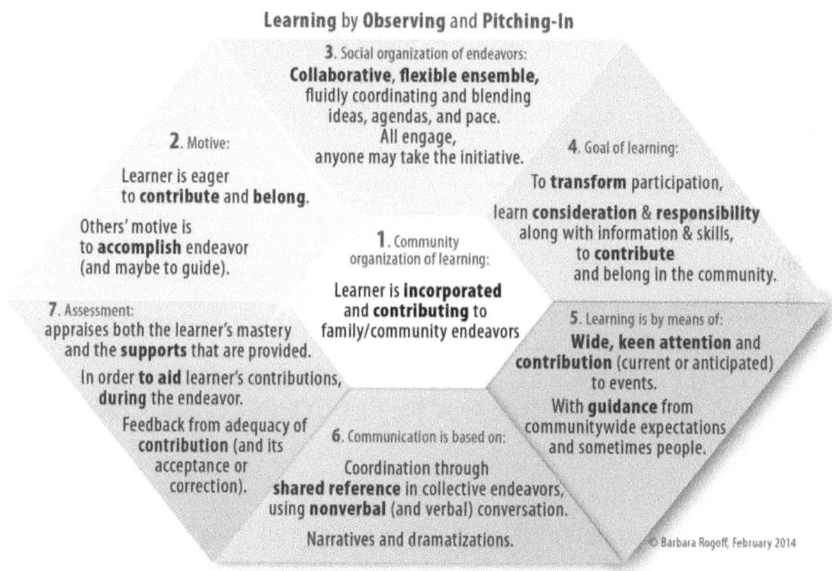

The prism structure makes reference to manifold activities, which in fact can be considered as interconnected practices that are prevalent, according to the author, in many indigenous-heritage communities of the United States, Mexico, and Central America.

From our perspective, this model also has significance in Bali's context. What is important for us to highlight is that in Balinese society, this constellation of practices is closely intermingled with the Cosmovision and the axis of Balinese spirituality. These two aspects are a basis of profound signification that permeates the logic of all cultural practices, the norms of social interaction and because of that, the way of learning. That is why even when we talk about learning in this article, we are referring to children's appropriation of a "Balinese way of being" through participating in a set of cultural practices.

2. METHODOLOGICAL CONSIDERATIONS

The information for this article comes from field work carried out in Bali during the years 2012–2014, and also from the personal experience of the Balinese author, who is an anthropology student, a dancer, and a member of a gamelan ensemble. Most of our field work was carried out in central Bali. Most of the observations of gamelan rehearsals were carried out in Ubud, dubbed "the cultural city," in the Sanggar Seni Cudamani, a private music and dance studio. We attended rehearsals and performances by girls, boys, young people, and adults. Also we did different kinds of interviews: with informants of the Sanggar Seni Cudamani, and of another Sanggar (studio) in Ubud; with two gamelan orchestra conductors; and with three informants from Negara, in West Bali. Eight families that have two or three children and live with their extended family (virilocally) were also interviewed.

3. CHILDREN'S PARTICIPATION IN COMMUNITY ACTIVITIES IN BALI: A FORM TO BELONG AND CONTRIBUTE

In general, to observe Balinese life is to look at a life cycle with deep interrelations and connections. Bali is well known all over the world for having a noble traditional culture that has withstood time. This is attributed to the idea that tradition, culture, and religion breathe as one and constitute the soul of the Balinese people.

One can observe that Balinese people in this area have a lot of cultural practices to integrate the new generations into their traditions and to teach them the value of their spiritual and ethical imperatives from the moment they are born. The belief in reincarnation makes children dearly appreciated, as they are thought to hold the spirit of an ancestor. This also results in their being treated respectfully, as well as in their being invited to become part of the community in order that they may develop a sense of belonging and a liking for participating in collective actions.

In these activities, children are introduced to a philosophy oriented to keep a harmonious relation between people and God, people and nature, and people to each other, and thus to comprehend that the actions performed by everyone in collective contexts are an offering for others, and therefore must be made from the heart and with joy. The most deeply spiritual connection is related to happiness, because it has to do with the heart. That is why a very important ethical value for children is to learn "to be happy," which means to be connected with the soul.

"We believe about atman," said Dewa Ayu, when she explained this to the other two authors of the present chapter. For the Balinese people, *atman* is perceived to be the eternal entity within the body. After death, when all the five elements of the body are dissolved, *atman* remains.

> *We believe in macrocosmos and microcosmos, so we humans are the reflection of the universe. All things in the world are manifestation of God, and when atman becomes one with your body there is a very strong connection and a deep feeling of happiness. Since we are born humans, also we have "awidia": desire, jealousy, madness; the enemies of human beings that contaminate the atman itself. We believe that arts, bhakti yoga and positive things can purify the heart and produce a harmony of the atman in your body. When you are connected with that you are happy.*
>
> ***Dewa Ayu***

In our research, in Mexico, we found that the people of Tepoztlán considered the inclusion of children in the ceremonial spaces and the arts to be a central aspect of their socialization and for developing a sense of belonging (Corona & Pérez, 2007). We found the same in Bali, but with a subtle difference related to their view of spirituality: For Balinese people, these activities are considered a direct way to unify the soul with the body, to connect with the heart, and to feel happy. That is why Balinese ceremonial practices permeate the daily life of families and are one of the activities in which children engage from a very early age: little babies attend the ceremonies in the arms of their mothers, and when they start to walk and can stand by themselves they happily make attempts to dance or to explore musical instruments.

4. THE COMMUNITY SPIRIT: TO BELONG AS A SENSE OF COLLECTIVENESS

The three main community spaces where children learn and participate on this island are: home, the collective space in each neighborhood (or *Bale banjar*), and the temple. In these spaces, there is a strong emphasis on cooperation and mutual assistance for many of the everyday activities, mainly those related with grand ceremonies. This is one of the main ethical imperatives promoted in very young children and constitutes a core value in their socialization. Thus, children are always incorporated in the activities of mutual cooperation, together with young people, and women and men who work in large groups in order to complete all the work required, especially in community practices such as the religious ceremonies and festivities. This community spirit is so important that they have many expressions for naming the organizational systems based on reciprocity, such as *rukun*, "mutual adjustment"; *gotong royong*, "joint bearing of burdens," *tolong-menolong*, "reciprocal assistance" (Geertz, 1983, Kaler & Sang, 2008), and *ngayah*, "doing work together selflessly and with sincerity." These words show the different kind of reciprocity that are established in social relations.

Young children continuously accompany their relatives in almost every activity they do and they pitch in from the first years of their life. Parents are very open and look favorably upon boys or girls who want to participate, showing appreciation with a smile or some gentle words for the small contributions that the children want to offer: to sweep, to carry the plates at lunch time, to do the offerings with the mother, and so on. We can say that children learn through the home system first; they also participate in the activities of the community space, and in those of the temple.

In this sense, the community organization for learning always implies contribution and the possibility to fully integrate in collective activities because of a sense of belonging. Therefore, the first and second facet of LOPI model can be considered pertinent in Balinese society.

We saw, for example, how the children want to contribute and belong one day when we visited a family and could see the grandmother weaving small baskets used for religious offerings while her two young granddaughters were playing around her in the garden. Then the younger girl—almost 5 years old—went to grandma and started to help her and to chat with her. Their talk was very lively and full of laughter, and when the child did not know how to continue her weaving, the grandmother—who had been looking sideways at the child's work—showed her how to continue it, without interrupting the conversation with her. Soon the elder sister, who was 7 years old, joined them and started making baskets on her own. From that moment on, she was the one who helped her younger sister to finish the small baskets. She—like the grandmother—showed her sister with her hands how to do it properly, almost without any verbal instruction. Later, the mother asked her child to go with her, to help place the offerings in different parts of their home, as we can see in Figure 1. Thus the grandmother, sister, and mother encourage the youngest child's involvement and sense of belonging.

The model of Learning by Observing and Pitching In proposes that the emphasis in communication is nonverbal (as well as verbal) conversation with shared reference in mutual endeavors; we can see in the previous example that grandma used a strategy of demonstration—not verbal instructions—in order to support her younger granddaughter how to weave the small baskets for the offering. The fact that the elder sister also does the same when she joined them can indicate that this nonverbal form of communication is part of a natural form of learning in everyday life. We also see that a social function of adults or other members with more experience is, as LOPI proposes, to support or guide learners' contributions, during the endeavor, because learning purposes always are related with social activity purposes. In other words, social purposes of any activity and learning purposes are totally coordinated.

Figure 1 Mother and her older child placing the offerings in different parts of the house.

In the previous description, we could see a small sample of the interaction between three generations in a daily task related to ceremonial life. As we can observe, the girls feel free to spend their time playing and sharing leisure activities, as well as to join in and help their grandmother with initiative and in a very comfortable form. Usually, in this area it is the grandmothers' task to weave the little offering baskets, and they do not expect any help from their daughters or granddaughters, so there is not an explicit demand for assistance but a pleasant acceptance of the contribution that the girls want to make.

This same type of collaboration is also evident at the level of the community where, for example, a grand ceremony is performed in one of the temples, and each village family goes to the community space in order to prepare the offerings required for the ceremony. Participation can be in the form of work, of bringing materials for the offerings—e.g., rice or bananas, weaving the baskets, sweeping the temple, dancing and playing music, or merely witnessing the dances for the ceremony. Children perform many small tasks with their friends, such as helping their parents to sweep the temple or helping to prepare the offerings; also, the ceremonial leader usually incorporates their help in distributing holy water to the people. We can see, as Rogoff mentioned, that "Learners are eager to contribute and belong as valued members of their families and communities." That is why they can naturally integrate in the activity "with initiative," and to "fulfill valued roles" (Rogoff, 2014, p. 74).

Another important aspect of the familiar learning setting, which we mentioned before, is that the grandma naturally creates a pleasurable environment around a shared domestic job, rather than turning it into a moment of intentional teaching or linking it to what the girls "must" do. We will see in the next section the important role that joy plays in the formal traditional way of learning the gamelan.

5. SOCIAL ORGANIZATION OF LEARNING SETTINGS FOR CHILDREN TO PARTICIPATE IN THE GAMELAN ORCHESTRA

Religious ceremonies in Bali are characterized by a richness of diverse artistic expressions. Dance, gamelan music, and other performances are always present in the religious festivities because they are considered as offerings highly valued by the gods. In the next section, we will see how the community motivates their young children to learn the arts and provides many opportunities for them to familiarize themselves with these activities. Parents and adults in general consider the arts as equally important—or maybe more—than school learning.

We first mention briefly the importance of the gamelan music in Bali and then we analyze the informal ways family and community have for immersing the children in this cultural practice. The particular contexts of formal learning settings that the community offers to children who are interested in joining the orchestra are discussed later.

6. THE IMPORTANCE OF GAMELAN MUSIC IN BALI

Gamelan is the traditional orchestra in Bali, consisting of various percussion instruments, such as metallophones, gongs, and xylophones, as well as flutes and drums. The number of instruments may range between 5 and 60, and some of the ensembles are portable and easy to carry, like the belengajur and the gamelan angklung, used mainly in processions and in ceremonies outside the temple.

The presence of gamelan in Bali has a long history, and its appearance is associated with the time of the kings in the fourteenth century. Gamelans were then very luxurious and expensive and could be found only at the royal palace, where they were played during dance and music performances and in religious events in the presence of the king as a symbol of god. Today, there are gamelans virtually in every village, in the temples or in the community art academies known as *sanggar* or *sekeha*. They are played not only in religious ceremonies but also in numerous cultural and social events. Before the 1970s, they were played exclusively by men in music performances; however, women's groups first arose in the 1980s, followed by children's gamelans. The Bali Arts Festival—one of the most famous in the island, bringing together a huge local and international audience—has played a major role in the dissemination of this music, holding men's gamelan competitions since 1970. In 1985, the governor of Bali witnessed a women's gamelan performance, after which he decided that women's groups should also be included in the Festival; this in turn favored the propagation of children's gamelans, which today have a strong presence in most of the communities, and therefore, in this yearly event.

One important aspect to consider is that in gamelan, togetherness is crucial because this music can only be played along with another player or in a group; it cannot be played individually. This refers to both the musical aspect and to philosophical and religious notions. The concept of *rwabhinneda*, which has been discussed by Eiseman (1990), refers to complementarity, to the manner in which two different parts make up a whole. In Bali, this not only is a philosophical concept but regulates social relationships and is applied to both the arts and everyday life. The simplest examples of *rwabinneda* are the black/white, day/night, male/female dualities. In gamelan music, this permeates the entire execution, because most instruments come in pairs: there is a female drum and a male drum; the female has a deeper sound. The metallophone section (*gangsa*), a row of knobbed pot gongs played by four musicians (*reong*), and the melody-carrying instruments are also paired. The off-tuning system (*ngumbang-ngisep*), where one member of the pair is tuned slightly higher than the other, creates the beats and the resulting sound waves when the instruments are played simultaneously. In this case, the principle of *rwabhinneda* produces the shimmering of Balinese gamelan.

Angelo (2012) and Small (1987) in their research about Bali agree that music must be not a noun but a verb. "Music is not properly regarded as a thing in gamelan practice (i.e., a composition, an instrument, a composer) even though it is that too" (Angelo, 2012, p. 207). "Musicking" expresses the act of taking part in a musical performance. As Small said "Musicking creates the public image of our most inwardly desired relations, not just *showing them to us* as they might be but actually *bringing them into existence* for the duration of the performance" (Small 1987, pp. 69–70, cited by Angelo, 2012, p. 208). The gamelan master Tjokorda Raka said that what is more important is that Balinese people believe in the power of gamelan, as a ritual ceremony and as a practice that "does something to people in an environment" because "it is inhabited by a Greater Being that is deeply collective" (Angelo, 2012, p. 207).

We will examine now two ways in which the teachers and the community at large integrate children who want to learn to play traditional gamelan music: the first way is informal and is addressed to all the kids, as a way of motivating them to learn music. The second way is formal and is addressed only to children that want to play in the gamelan orchestra. Here, they learn in the sanngar or community academies (not related with the school), where the learning process is guided by a traditional Balinese educational approach.

7. INFORMAL SETTINGS FOR LEARNING MUSIC: THE FAMILY AND COMMUNITY

Children in Bali first develop an interest in the arts by watching and listening to rehearsals in their family and in their community. Balinese children are not usually cared for by strangers but by members of their family, with whom they continuously attend religious ceremonies. During music performances, babies hear the melody while their relatives hold them in arms and rock them joyfully to the beat of the music, allowing them to immerse themselves in the powerful cadence of this type of musical harmonies. If they like this artistic expression, they begin to show their interest by approaching and exploring the instruments (Figure 2), as well as attending the rehearsals to listen to the music and watch how it is played. As Rogoff, Paradise, Arauz, Correa-Chavez, Angelillo (2003) has found, intent participation is a common way of fostering learning in many indigenous American communities, because adults in general recognize the importance of children being allowed to observe, listen, and participate in the main events of the community.

In the village of Pengosekan, for instance, the children can sit by their parents during a gamelan rehearsal. Likewise, the audience of music performances at the temples always includes village children who watch, surrounded by their families and acquaintances. During these events, the children move freely between listening to the music and playing with their friends, and these occasions are excellent for developing a love for the arts, as what they see and hear is pleasurable, beautiful, and very attractive for them. This aspect can be observed in Figures 3 and 4.

These cultural experiences are very powerful for children. They imply a comfortable "acculturation" process that provides them with abundant

Figure 2 Baby boy exploring the kendang or drum. As he is learning to walk, his uncle is taking care of the boy and the instruments.

Figure 3 Girls observing the rehearsal.

Figure 4 Girls playing on their own motivated by the rehearsal.

information and experience that will enhance formal learning once they attain the age of 5 or 6 years, at which point they generally begin a more formal practice in preparation for public performances at the temple.

It is therefore an initiation into music in which children are surrounded by an atmosphere of cultural messages about how to interact in various ceremonial and collective settings where the needs and interest of children are respected. What is important for children to learn in these contexts is not just related to musical skills, but to a "way of being and living in society." That is, what's key is to become a Balinese person through feeling the music, enjoying this ceremonial practice and loving the arts.

There is a belief that certain skills for the arts run in the family or in the blood line. In the case of author Dewa Ayu Eka, she was taught by her mother—who also plays the drum. Her uncle said "She got the rhythm before she was born, because she could feel the music in the womb of her mother." Her mother too received teachings and support from an uncle, indicating an intergenerational transmission of the musical arts.

As we can see, children are an integral part of most of the rituals and ceremonies. They often play a very important role in the celebration of the festivity, and therefore they are allowed and encouraged to play various instruments. A good example is the participation of children in the festivity of Galungan, one of the most important religious feasts in Bali, where boys play the balengajur ensemble and dance with the *barong*, a mythical creature that protects the community from evil (Figure 5).

In keeping with the LOPI model of understanding learning processes, it is essential to understand the community social organization of these settings, especially the idea that children are eager to participate by observing, listening, and pitching in as a form to belong and to feel themselves "part of a collective." Similarly adults recognize the importance of children being allowed to participate in the musical and ceremonial practices, as a way for them to become familiar with these highly valued cultural activities.

As we shall see in the next section, these experiences, built through a long process, are very useful for the children interested in the formal learning

Figure 5 Children playing the gamelan balengajur with the barong.

of gamelan. Their interactions with different musical instruments allow them to learn different melodies and rhythms, and also to know which instrument they like most.

8. FORMAL SETTINGS FOR LEARNING GAMELAN MUSIC: REHEARSALS IN THE COMMUNITY ACADEMY OF ARTS

Sanggar Cudamani—a community art academy which opened in 1997 and began offering teachings for children in 1999—is a good illustration of what takes place in community learning environments. The idea was proposed by I Dewa Putu Berata, a famous local musician and composer. During an interview, he spoke to us about important aspects to be considered when teaching children:

> *What I want to create is a place where children can enjoy playing music. I ask them to come early so they can have some recreational time: they come, spend some time together, chat and play before they start rehearsing. I don't want them to feel that playing gamelan is a duty, it is not: it is a pleasure because it is performed from the heart. That is what I want to transmit. It was my childhood experience of life—full of joy derived from the atmosphere of art—, which made me very eager to become an artist.*

This way to experience the art is also transmitted to the children during the rehearsals. The teacher always emphasizes that they can only play the gamelan if they enjoy and feel happiness in their hearts and that the main goal of being part of the orchestra is doing an offering with pure heart and not "to be the best player."

The testimony of Dewa Ayu when she started this formal education shows us the perspective of the student: "when I first performed, I felt shame and nervousness, but then every time we practiced, every single day the teacher told us to enjoy ourselves. The message he always tried to transmit was: 'Enjoy yourselves! Feel happy, This is the thing you like to do! This performance is an offering to God and for everyone!' He kept telling us not to be nervous but to feel good. His purpose and the result was to build positive thinking in the children also. It made us feel like it would be a beautiful experience."

In addition, the time reserved for recreation and for socializing before the children rehearse is also a good experience for the teachers, allowing them to observe and gain a deeper understanding of the children's world as well as of their individual interests and skills.

When the children begin to learn, they already have a basic understanding of the melodies because they have frequently observed and listened to the rehearsals and performances from a very early age. Some have certain preferences as to the instruments they want to play, but they are also aware that they need to be flexible, as we can see in the testimony of Dewa Ayu:

> *I remember that when the children arrive, they go and choose the place they want, and some like to play the same instrument; if a child is good at playing an instrument, the leader moves him or her to another position. Children learn simple songs, and after they finish learning a song, the teacher also can ask them to move to another instrument. So when we become teenagers, we know which our favorite instrument is, we each know what we really want. And it does not really matter which instrument we choose to play because every instrument is important.*

Since there is no written score for gamelan music, the teacher goes to the child, sits in front of him or her, and plays simultaneously on the same instrument, but in reverse, so that the child can follow him by mirroring. Other children learn by ear, and it is quite usual to hear them sing their part as a way of memorizing the melody. The teacher creates a flexible learning environment in which at times the children play their own part or practice those fragments that they have forgotten, with the aid of a friend, who, like the teacher, sits facing them and shows them the proper way to strike the little hammer they use for playing.

In this formal traditional context, the teacher demonstrates the sequences of hand movements and the learners or students repeat and repeat, because the essential emphasis on the learning process has to do, not with instruction, but with practice.

This aspect has a great deal to do with the philosophy behind the pedagogy of Gamelan music in traditional education:

> *The method of the teacher is strange. He says nothing, does not even look at the children. Dreamily he plays through the first movement. He plays it again. He then plays the first phrase alone, with more emphasis. He now indicates that the children are to commence. Two or three make a tentative attempt, following him, and watching every movement. The phrase is repeated, and they try again. Another joins in…bit by bit the children who are learning the melody go from phrase to phrase, forgetting, remembering, gaining assurance. The teacher remains silent, unless to point out a repeated mistake; generally he is gazing off into space. At the end of an hour, however, several children can play through the whole melody.*
>
> ***McPhee (1938, pp. 7–8), cited by Merriam (1964).***

The level of synchronization between instruments and players is very complex. For that reason, the children need good concentration and at the same time an open awareness of the performance of the ensemble as a whole. This can only be achieved if children practice again and again in order to surrender to the melody. Children learn that playing is not just about the audience or themselves, it is about feeling happiness in their hearts, and sharing joy. In this way, each person present is part of the community.

As the teacher Tjokorda Raka said, "repetition is related not only to technique but also to the feelings, and mainly to the heart and soul." Only thus is it possible to build a "living entity," an expression with a deep sense of communion involving a big responsibility that the children share joyfully with their peers. "The sense is related to the mood, although it is not the same as the mood. Rather, this sense has to do with being in pure contact with the heart." (Angelo, 2012, p. 202).

The way teachers transmit these ideas to children is by using simple words and examples. They do not try to explain concepts. Instead, they invite recollection of how the children feel when they do their offerings at temple. "It is the same when you put flowers in your hand, when you are giving offerings: you feel happy." In this way, when the children are playing, the teacher observes how they play, how they feel, and then demonstrates the intended feeling for them. He repeats it again and again, in order that they can understand what this means. It requires a long process for the children to understand this.

Therefore, another of the skills that the children must develop, which relates to the way of learning and communicating in LOPI, is a keen collective sensitivity and nonverbal communication that helps them to interpret the subtle signs made by others, allowing them to meet the demand of flexibility and fluidity that the gamelan presents. In this way, children learn not only information or skills but also responsibility and consideration for others (facet 4 of LOPI).

Actually this form of learning can confuse Western people, because teachers do not like to theorize or talk much about the method; also, rehearsals include some moments of entire freedom, where children can come from the back row and ask a friend to show them how to play their part. If one of the members of a duet of instruments hears that the other is not playing properly, he shows him the rhythm and how to handle the little hammer on the instrument. Thus, several couples or small groups of the whole ensemble may often be rehearsing different fragments of the melody at the same time.

A student who came to Bali from the United States to learn Gamelan told us:

> *Sometimes I tried to understand some aspects of the music and I asked the teacher, but he told me 'it is best not to talk'—everything is demonstration: the teacher repeats or sings the notes and the rhythm. Members with more experience show their peers how to move the hands and how to play the xylophones with the mallet. This style is difficult for me, because I feel it is a little chaotic; the method is very different from the way I learn music in the USA: each rehearses his part, sometimes two are trying to understand theirs and repeat and repeat between them, and sometimes someone comes from the other side and tries to show them how to do it.*

Thus, the teaching/learning relationship is structured within a flexible organization in which children feel free to offer or request help from their peers and in which an atmosphere of collaboration is prevalent and allows finding together the rhythm. The teacher guides the learning and organizes it in such a way that the more advanced children may take the initiative of teaching their classmates. This connects with facet 3 of LOPI related with the social organization of endeavors: Here, there is a flexible atmosphere of collaboration, where all engage and all can lead in a very open way. The interlocking of numerous instruments, where each plays a different part while being complementary to and incomplete without the other, is another clear example of the importance of complementary action and existence, which children learn through their immersion in this kind of music.

However, when children learn music in Bali, there are several differences with the LOPI model in the central role that joy has in the learning process. Another aspect to be taken into account is that lessons include a previous time for socialization and play, which enables the children to begin the learning session with a joyful attitude.

9. GAMELAN MUSIC AS A WAY TO BUILD CHARACTER AND DEVOTION TO THE SOCIAL ENVIRONMENT

Gamelan music involves many profound philosophical aspects, but the most usual way for the teachers to explain these to the children is through the understanding of togetherness and belonging. In practical terms, this translates not only as cultivating a sense of responsibility and awareness of others but also patience and self-control, as everyone involved focuses on a common goal. The children relate in a respectful manner to one another and to their instruments in order to regulate and time their playing with that of their partners. This coordination with awareness of how their actions impact other's ability to participate relates to the cultural value of *respeto* "a form of consideration valued in Mexico, in which people pay attention to the direction of the group, use subtle forms of communication, and avoid interrupting others' activities" (Ruvalcaba, Rogoff, López, Correa-Chávez, & Gutiérrez, 2013).

This consideration has deep meaning to the Balinese people. Pak Dewa Berata, the director of the Cudamani academy, told one of us that gamelan music is a way "to create or build character and devotion to the social environment." Associating the word devotion with social environment is not a common idea for the western mind, but in Bali it is directly related to one of the main principles in their religious beliefs. This principle, called Tri Hita Karana, has to do with the need for keeping balance in three areas: harmony with God, harmony with the environment, and harmony between humans. This last aspect entails not only behaving in good ways, but also thinking good thoughts and speaking good words in order to protect the sense of community as well as relationships between neighbors.

This idea underlies the collective effort and the relationships of joy and support that are established within the children's gamelan group, to create a profound collective sense and a deep mutual understanding. This is reinforced by the family and by the community, e.g., when the children are to give a public performance, the teenagers and adults help them prepare what they need and provide them full support. There is an expectation that the children will perform as professionals, but even more important is that they should enjoy playing the music. The performance at the temple is very joyful because the children play together with their friends and are appreciated by their families and by the villagers at large. On this occasion, the teacher does not mention their mistakes but acknowledges and appreciates their great effort in performing. The children naturally try to do their best when they know that they are rehearsing for a public performance or for a friendly competition between children of different communities within the context of a festival. In these public situations, the children feel extremely proud of belonging to and representing their village.

This is related to the motive and the goal of learning shown in the prism of LOPI, since the children are aware that, in belonging, as they do, to a community, the collective is the basis and the core of their expression. Through these means, they are also learning to be good persons, to reinforce their values in order to have a good life.

10. FINAL REFLECTIONS

The model proposed by Barbara Rogoff about Learning by Observation and Pitching In, has been a useful tool for us to examine in a detailed way the various facets that are involved in the learning processes of Balinese children. Our study points at very similar aspects: a pattern of children's extensive contribution in ongoing community activities, a keen interest in observing others' efforts, and a very flexible social organization of endeavors. Additionally, we found that there is a social emotional respect toward others, and an emphasis on demonstration and nonverbal communication in learning settings.

The main difference that we found has to do with the inseparability of spiritual, religious, and cultural life in Bali, which is reflected in the everyday behavior of Balinese families. In this area, respect and love for girls and boys is linked to parents' ethnotheories regarding children's development. Parents believe that they must respect the freedom required by the children to integrate themselves into community activities at their own pace, emphasizing that they should find pleasure in the tasks in which they participate.

Joy and pleasure are cultivated in Bali in the relationships not only with children but with everyone else as well; this special quality, particular to this culture, permeates especially the settings for learning of gamelan. Joy has to do with a very profound spiritual dimension, for according to this culture, God dwells in the heart, and we must "put our heart" into every activity that we perform. The special importance that they attach to joy is related also with the capacity of children to be in touch with the divine, and to the possibility that they can relate with the potential source of an expression that is connected to the best qualities of human beings.

The contribution of this study is to show that in an Indigenous culture where the sacred and the profane are not divided, the world view and spiritual values are a substrate of deep meaning that is the basis of everyday life and are so all-encompassing as to guide and give shape to the social organization of learning. Balinese music is like Balinese life: it reflects devotion to the community, harmony, cooperation, and balance. Through learning gamelan music, children learn in a beautiful way, not only how to play music, but how to be a Balinese person.

REFERENCES

Angelo, E. (2012). The duty of gamelan. A gamelan pedagogue's philosophy of work. *Nordic Research in Music Education, 14*, 195–216.

Coppens, A. D., Silva, K. G., Ruvalcaba, O., Alcalá, L., López, A., & Rogoff, B. (2014). Learning by Observing and Pitching In: Benefits and processes of expanding repertoires. *Human Development, 57*, 150–161. Karger AG Basel.

Corona, Y. (2011a). Early childhood and cultural diversity. An ethnographic narrative from Mexico and Bali. In *Problemy Wczesnej Edukacji: Rok VIII. Childhood in cultures and with cultures (issues in early education)*. Poland: Polskie Towarzystwo Pedagogiczne. No. 3 (18).

Corona, Y. (2011b). Ser niño en Tepoztlán: cuatro generaciones. In *Anuario de investigación 2011* (pp. 193–215). México City: UAM.

Corona, Y., & Pérez, C. (2002). Childhood and cultural resistance: The participation of children in community resistance movements. In N. Del Río (Ed.), *The vulnerability of Mexican children in a globalized world*. México City: UNICEF, UAM.

Corona, Y., & Pérez, C. (2007). The enrichment of community relations through children participation in ceremonial life. In T. Wyller & U. Nayar (Eds.), *The given child*. Germany: Vandenhoeck & Ruprecht.

Corona, Y., Quinteros, G., & Padilla, M. (2005). Relación epistolar entre niños de dos pueblos. In *Anuario de investigación* (pp. 614–635). México City: UAM-X.

Eiseman, F., Jr. (1990). *BALI, Sekala & Niskala: Essays on religion, ritual, and art*. Jakarta, Indonesia: PT Java Books.

Geertz, C. (1983). *Local knowledge: Further essays in interpretive anthropology*. New York, NY: Basic Books.

Kaler, S., & Sang, P. (2008). Structure and process in facilitating community action in Bali. *Learning Communities: International Journal of Learning in Social Contexts, 2*, 55–66. Indonesia and Australia: Number 2.

Merriam, A. (1964). *The anthropology of music*. Evanston, IL: Northwestern University Press.

Morelli, G., Rogoff, B., & Angelillo, C. (2003). Cultural variation in young children's access to work or involvement in specialized child-focused activities. *International Journal of Behavioral Development, 27*(3), 264–274.

Paradise, R., & Rogoff, B. (2009). Side by side: Learning by Observing and Pitching In. *Ethos, 37*, 102–138.

Rogoff, B. (1996). Developmental transitions in children's participation in sociocultural activities. In A. J. Sameroff & M. M. Haith (Eds.), *The five to seen year shift: The age of reason an responsibility*. Chicago: University of Chicago Press.

Rogoff, B. (2014). Learning by Observing and Pitching In to family and community endeavors: An orientation. *Human Development, 57*, 69–81. Karger AG Basel.

Rogoff, B., Paradise, R., Arauz, R. M., Correa-Chavez, M., & Angelillo, C. (2003). First-hand learning through intent participation. *Annual Review of Psychology, 54*.

Ruvalcaba, O., Rogoff, B., López, A., Correa-Chávez, M., & Gutiérrez, K. (2013). Children's Consideration of others: Nonverbal respeto in request for help by Mexican-heritage and European-heritage children. In *Culture in pshychology: Variation within and across national borders international association for cross-cultural psychology, conference*. Los Angeles.

Small, Ch. (1987). *Music of the common tongue*. London: Calder.

White, S. H., & Siegel, A. W. (1984). Cognitive development in time and space. In B. Rogoff & J. Lave (Eds.), *Everyday cognition. Its development in social context*. Cambridge, MA: Harvard University Press.

AUTHOR INDEX

D

E

F

G

M

U

V

W

Y

Z

SUBJECT INDEX

Note: Page numbers followed by "*f*" indicate figures and "*t*" indicate tables.

B

C

J

K

L

S

T

U

CONTENTS OF PREVIOUS VOLUMES

VOLUME 5

VOLUME 6

VOLUME 7

VOLUME 8

VOLUME 9

VOLUME 10

VOLUME 11

VOLUME 12

VOLUME 13

VOLUME 14

VOLUME 15

VOLUME 16

VOLUME 17

VOLUME 18

VOLUME 19

VOLUME 20

VOLUME 21

VOLUME 22

VOLUME 23

VOLUME 24

VOLUME 25

VOLUME 26

VOLUME 27

VOLUME 28

VOLUME 29

VOLUME 30

VOLUME 31

VOLUME 32

VOLUME 33

VOLUME 34

VOLUME 35

VOLUME 36

VOLUME 37

VOLUME 38

VOLUME 39

VOLUME 40

VOLUME 41

VOLUME 42

VOLUME 43

VOLUME 44

VOLUME 45

VOLUME 46

VOLUME 47

VOLUME 48